SPECTRUM SERIES

PHONICS

TABLE OF CONTENTS

PHONICS

STRUCTURAL ANALYSIS

VOCABULARY

DICTIONARY SKILLS

INSTRUCTIONAL CONSULTANT
Mary Lou Maples, Ed.D.
Chairman of Department of Education
Huntingdon College
Montgomery, Alabama

EDITORIAL AND PRODUCTION STAFF
Series Editor: Joyce R. Rhymer; *Project Editor:* Mary Lou Griffith;
Production Editor: Carole R. Hill; *Senior Designer:* Patrick J. McCarthy;
Associate Designer: Terry D. Anderson; *Project Artist:* Gilda Braxton Edwards;
Artist: Shirley J. Beltz; *Illustrators:* Lisy Boren, Joel Snyder; *Cover Illustrator:* Sally Vitsky

Send all inquires to:
McGraw-Hill Children's Publishing
8787 Orion Place
Columbus, Ohio 43240-4027

ISBN 1-57768-122-3 6 7 8 9 10 POH 05 04 03 02 01 00

Organized for successful learning!

The SPECTRUM PHONICS SERIES builds the right skills for reading.

The program combines four important skill strands — phonics, structural analysis, vocabulary, and dictionary skills — so your students build the skills they need to become better readers.

Four types of lesson pages offer thorough, clearly focused, systematic skills practice. That means you can focus on just the skills that need work — for the whole class, a small group, or for individualized instruction.

R Blends

Name

In some words, the letter **r** follows another consonant. To say these words, blend the sound of the first consonant with the sound of **r.**

frog	**dress**
brown	**pretty**
green	**tree**
cry	

Read the words and look at the pictures. Draw a line from each word to the picture it tells about.

trap crayon	drum grin
truck dress	frame prize
grass tray	crow bridge
prince crab	bride frog

INSTRUCTION PAGE . . . The skill being covered is noted at the bottom of each student page for easy reference.

The SPECTRUM PHONICS SERIES is easy for students to use independently.

Although phonics may be an important part of a reading program, sometimes there just isn't enough time to do it all. That's why PHONICS offers uncomplicated lessons your children can succeed with on their own.

Colorful borders capture interest, highlight essential information, and help organize lesson structure. And your children get off to a good start with concise explanations and clear directions . . . followed by sample answers that show them exactly what to do.

In addition, vocabulary has been carefully controlled so your children work with familiar words. Key pictures and key words are used consistently throughout the series to represent specific sounds. And a sound-symbol chart at the back of the text helps your students quickly recall sound-symbol relationships.

R Blends

Name

Read each sentence and the words beside it. Write the word that makes sense in each sentence.

1. Fran took a trip on the train.	train drain brain
2. My friend got first ________ for a painting.	press dress prize
3. We took a ________ to the park.	trip drip grip
4. Did the baby ________ in his crib?	cry try dry
5. Is ________ the color you like best?	tray pray gray
6. I broke my ________ pencil.	crown drown brown
7. I saw a green ________ jump over a log.	frog trot from
8. Juan likes ________ jam and bread.	price grape bride
	drive broke

REINFORCEMENT PAGE . . . Comprehension exercises that use context as well as phonics skills to help build the connection from decoding to comprehension.

Turn page for more information.

Easy to manage

REVIEW PAGES . . . Frequent reviews emphasize skills application.

ASSESSMENT PAGES . . . Assessment pages give you helpful feedback on how your students are doing.

PROGRESS CHECK

Silent Consonants

Name

Read the words in the list below. Then read the clues that follow. Write a word from the list to match each clue.

snack	clock	knee	night	knife	wrong
kneel	rock	duck	write	eight	light

1. a bird that likes to swim
duck
2. the time when it is dark
7. a thing that tells the time
8. a tool used to cut meat

knees

95

REVIEW

Silent Consonants

Name

Read the words and look at the pictures. Circle the word that tells about each picture.

check (chick) click clock	knob knot knock know	wrist wrote write wrong
light tight night sight	rack rock sock stuck	locket rocket jacket pocket
rock sock lock dock	knit knob knee kneel	wrist wrote wrong wrap
knock knob knit knee	wrong wrap wrist write	knife knight bright fright

94 Review of symbol-sound association of words containing silent consonants: *kn, wr, ck, gh*

Teaching Suggestion 7, Page T-14 Extending Activity 27, Page T-21

Prefixes

Words to use: unpack, refill, redo, unlock, undress, unwrap, replay, unhappy, reuse

Name

Read each sentence and the word beside it. Add **re-** or **un-** to the word to complete each sentence. The word you form must make sense in the sentence.

1. I must reread this book. — read
2. Was Pablo unkind to you? — kind
3. I will retell this story. — tell
4. Can you redraw the picture? — draw
5. Jimmy must rewrite his work. — write
6. The new rule of the game is unfair. — fair
7. Did Ramona repaint her house? — paint
8. It is unwise to throw away your paper. — wise
9. Driving too fast is unsafe. — safe

ANSWER KEY . . . Gives you the help you need when you need it — including student pages with answers for quick, easy reference.

Beginning Sounds

Name

Name the pictures. Write the letter that stands for the beginning sound of each picture name.

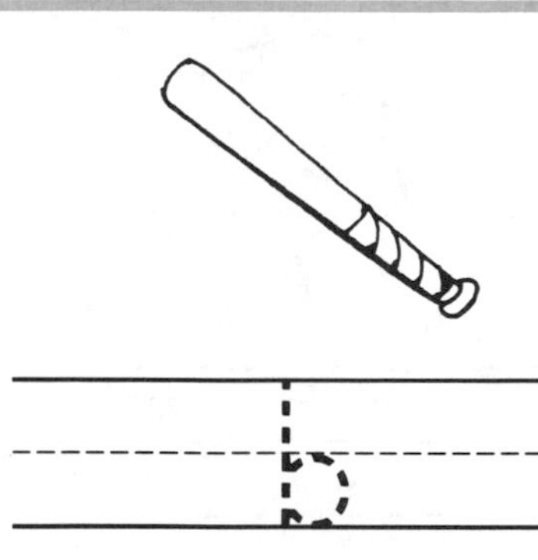

b

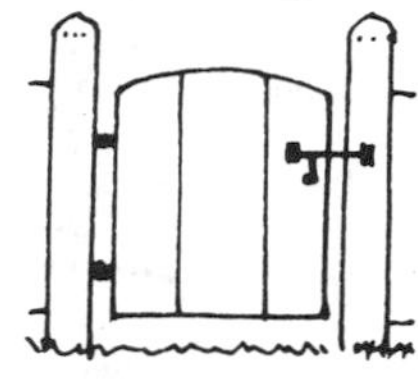

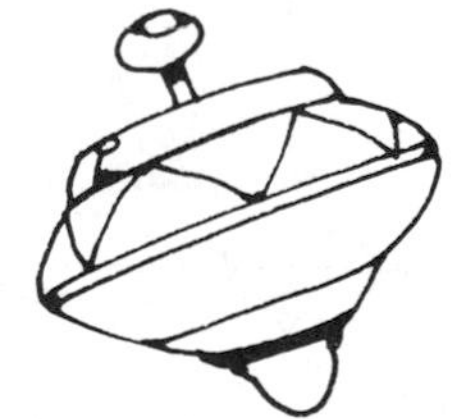

Beginning Sounds

Name ______________________

Name the pictures. Write the letter that stands for the beginning sound of each picture name.

n

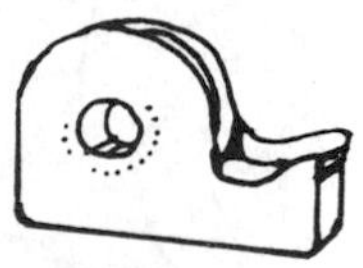

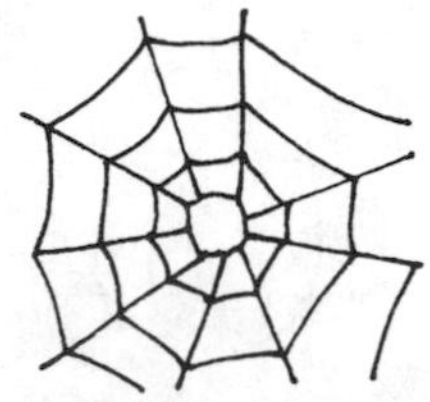

Ending Sounds

Name

Name the pictures. Write the letter that stands for the ending sound of each picture name.

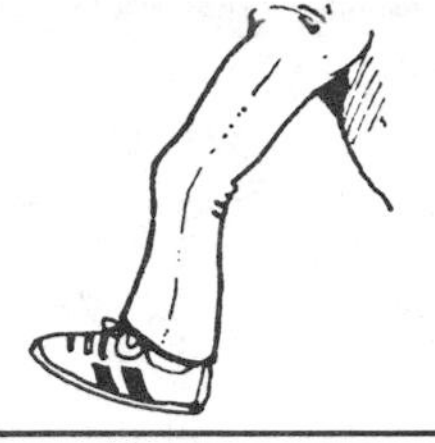
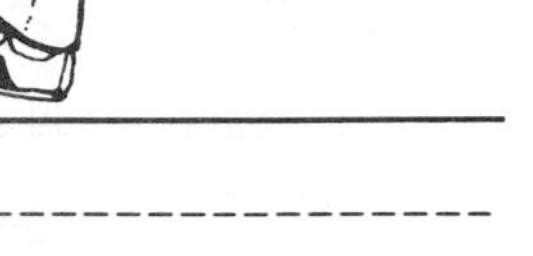

Ending Sounds

Name ______________________

Name the pictures. Write the letter that stands for the ending sound of each picture name.

g

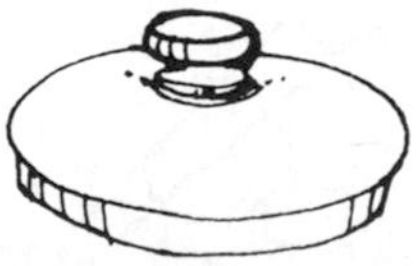

Beginning and Ending Sounds

Name ______________________

Name the pictures. Write the letters that stand for the beginning and ending sounds of each picture name.

dog	i	o
e	a	u
o	a	e
u	a	i

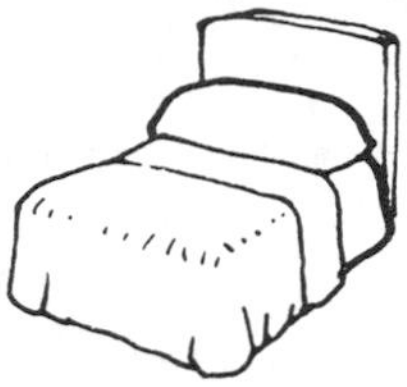

Assessment of sound-symbol association of initial and final consonants

Short *A*

Name

Fan has the short-**a** sound. This sound is usually spelled by the letter **a.**

f**a**n 

Name the pictures. Write **a** below each picture whose name has the short-**a** sound.

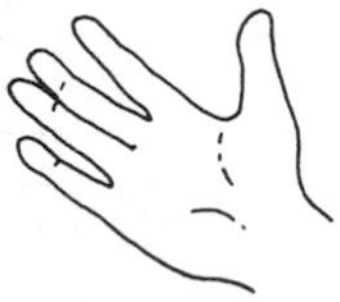

a

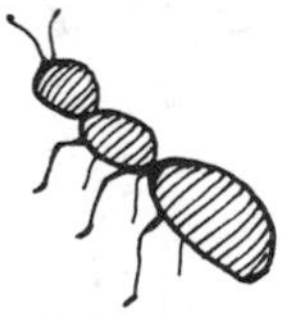

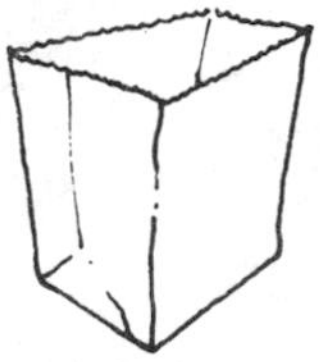

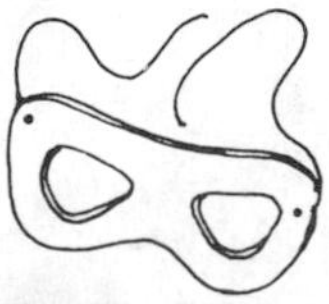

Short *A*

Name ________________

Read the words and name the pictures. Draw a line from each word to the picture it names.

f**a**n

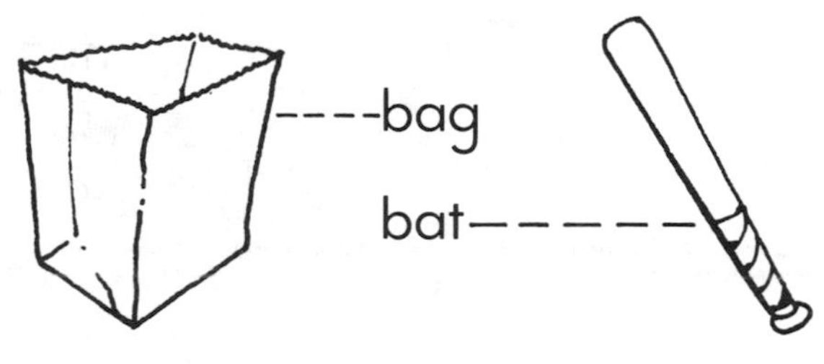

bag

bat

can

cat

man

map

hat

ham

1+1=2

add

ax

cap

cab

pan

van

tag

rag

Short *A*

Name ______________________

Read each sentence and the words beside it. Write the word that makes sense in each sentence.

f**a**n

1.	My cat ___ran___ from a car.	rat ran rag
2.	Dan put ham in the ______________.	tan pat pan
3.	Ann will ask for a new ______________.	hat has had
4.	Pat gave her ______________ to Jan.	sat at cat
5.	The ______________ sat in the cab.	mad man had
6.	Please hand me that ______________.	as ax at
7.	Pam took a nap on the ______________.	map mat bat
8.	Anna hit the ball with a ______________.	bad had bat
9.	Jimmy will ______________ his mother.	ask ant at

Short *I*

Name

Bib has the short-**i** sound. This sound is usually spelled by the letter **i.**

bib

Name the pictures. Write **i** below each picture whose name has the short-**i** sound.

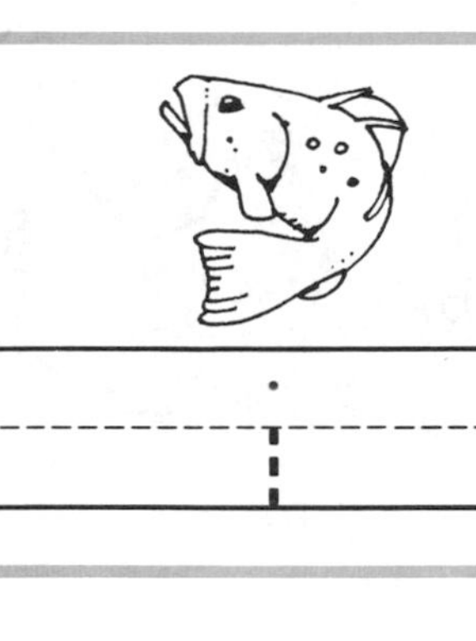

i

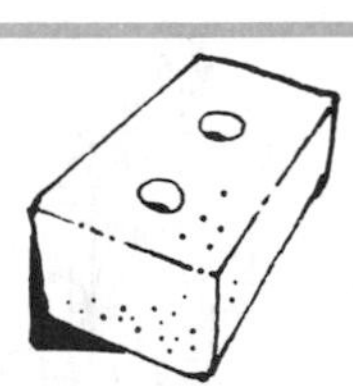

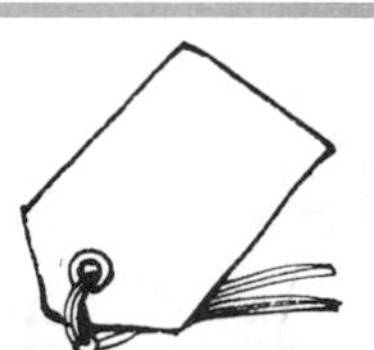

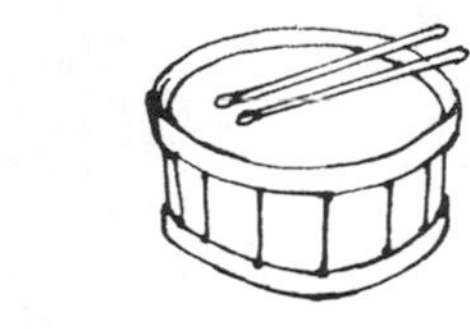

Short *I*

Name ______________________

Read the words and look at the pictures. Draw a line from each word to the picture it tells about.

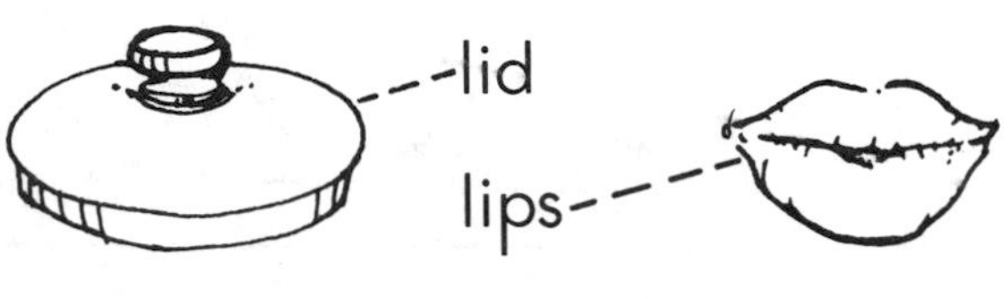

bib

crib

spill

grill

mitt

milk

hill

hit

sip

ship

drip

dig

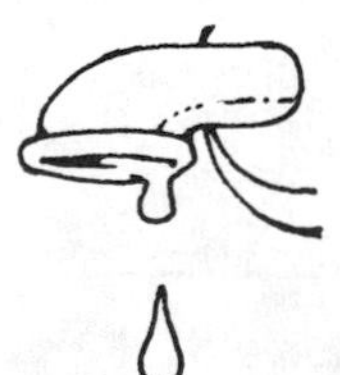

six

sit

Symbol-sound association of short-*i* words

Short *I*

Name ______________________

Read each sentence and the words beside it. Write the word that makes sense in each sentence.

1.	Jim will ___sit___ with us.	sit rim six
2.	Did she hit or ______ the ball?	dig miss rid
3.	The ______ cats hid from him.	mitt mix six
4.	They live on a ______.	hill him hit
5.	Kim can ______ the crib.	fin fix mix
6.	This pan has a tin ______.	lit pit lid
7.	Lin had a ______ of milk.	sip sit six
8.	Mother can ______ the rip.	pit pin pig
9.	Is your dog ______ or little?	bit bib big

Short O

Name

Top has the short-**o** sound. This sound is usually spelled by the letter **o.**

t**o**p

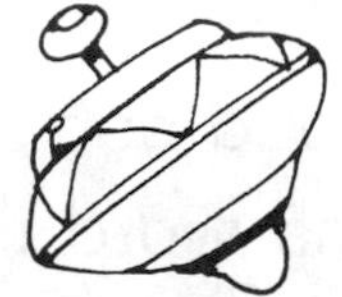

Name the pictures. Write **o** below each picture whose name has the short-**o** sound.

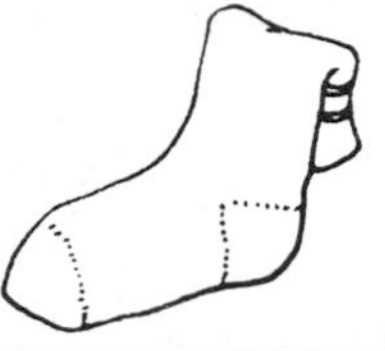

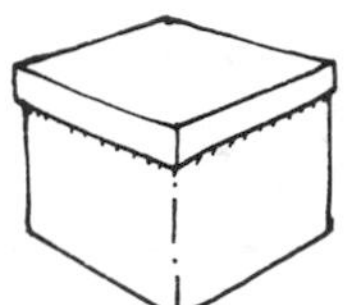

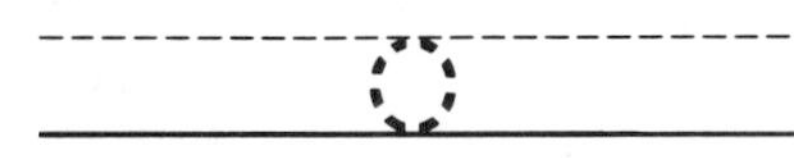

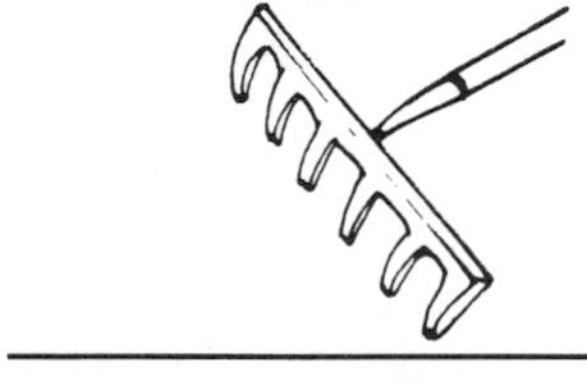

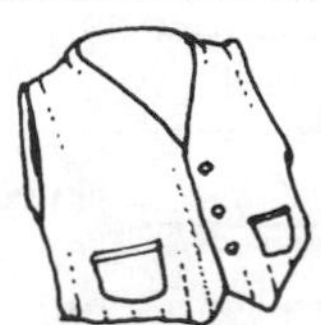

Short O

Name ______________________

Read the words and look at the pictures. Draw a line from each word to the picture it tells about.

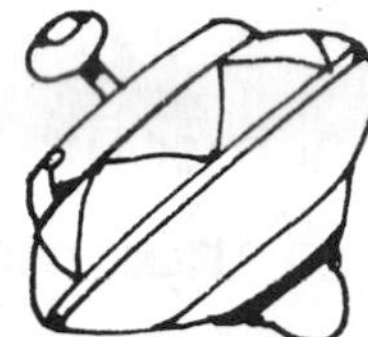

top

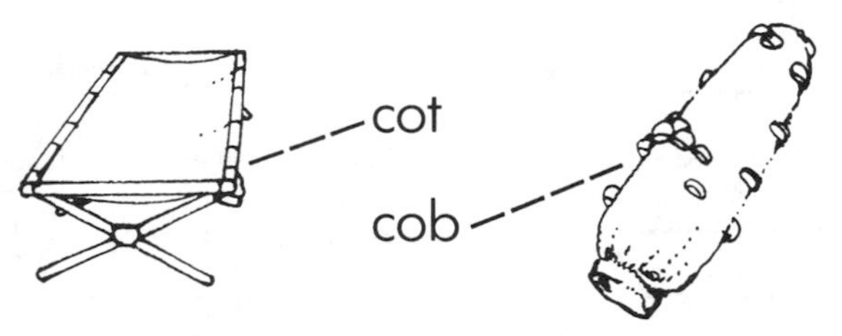

cot

cob

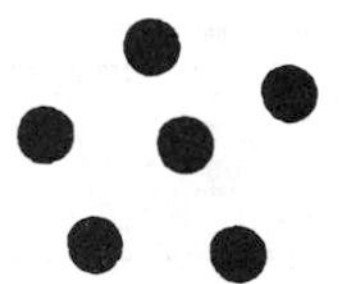

doll

dots

pot

spot

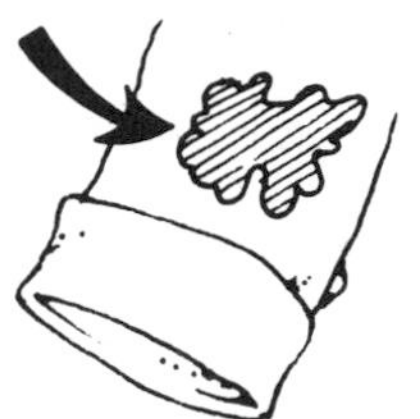

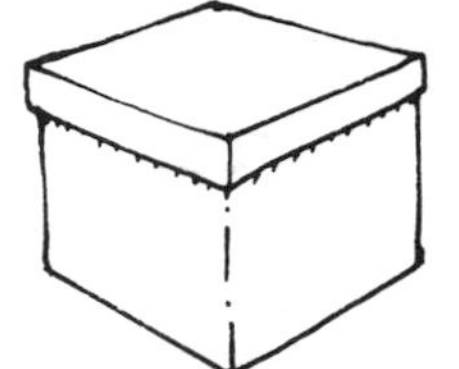

box

ox

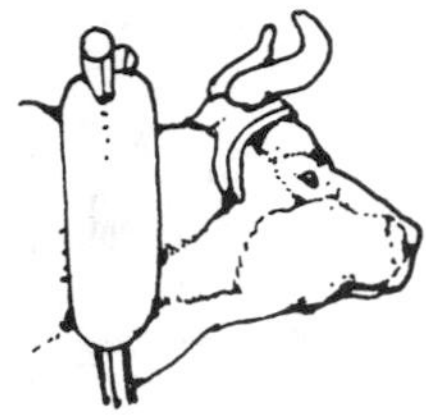

mop

chop

hog

fox

rod

top

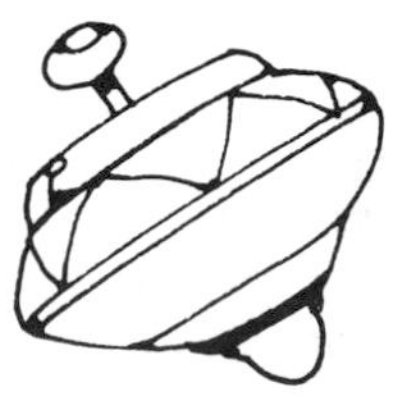

hot

hop

Short O

Name ______________________

Read each sentence and the words beside it. Write the word that makes sense in each sentence.

top 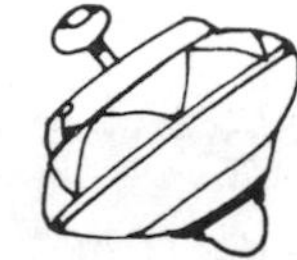

1. The doll is in a ___box___. — ox / box / mop
2. Don will mop the wet ________. — spot / cob / chop
3. That ________ is too hot. — pot / rot / dot
4. Bob will ________ hold a frog. — hop / not / nod
5. I got some ________ milk for Tom. — lot / hop / hot
6. The ________ ate the cob. — rod / log / hog
7. Dot is not sleeping on her ________. — hop / cot / rod
8. I saw the rabbit ________ by me. — hop / hot / hog
9. Alma plays with a ________. — dots / doll / stop

Short *E*

Name

Bed has the short-**e** sound. This sound is usually spelled by the letter **e.**

bed 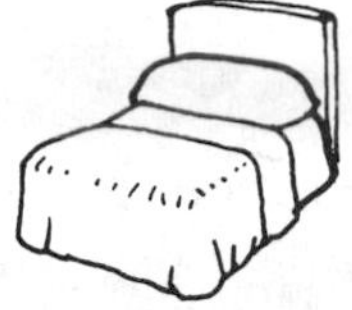

Name the pictures. Write **e** below each picture whose name has the short-**e** sound.

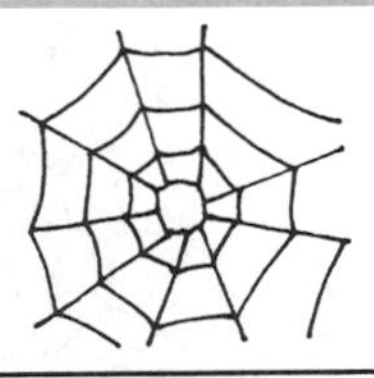

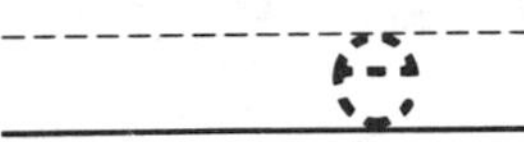

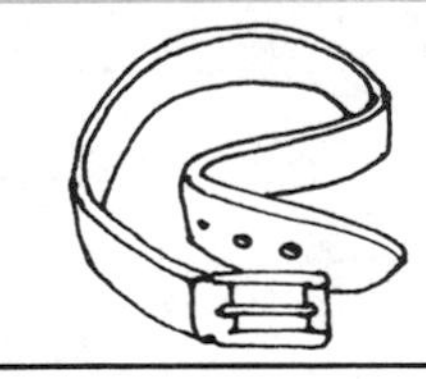

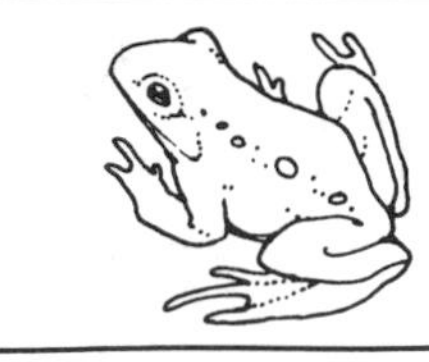

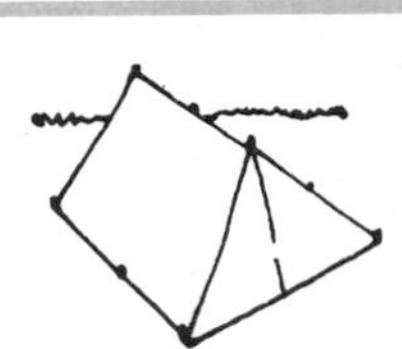

Short *E*

Name

Read the words and look at the pictures. Draw a line from each word to the picture it tells about.

bed

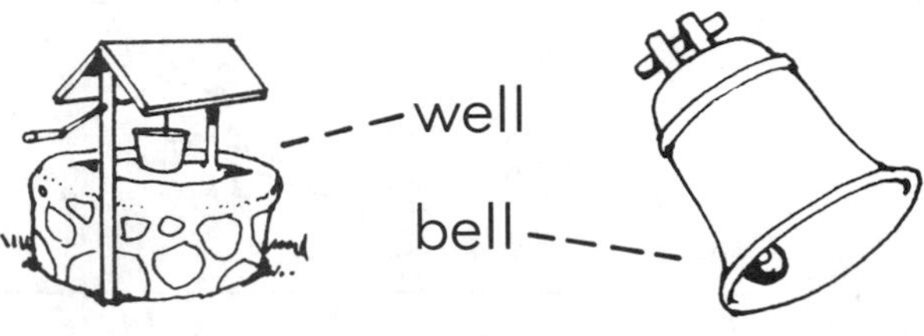

well

bell

web

wet

ten

hen

net

nest

leg

beg

pet

jet

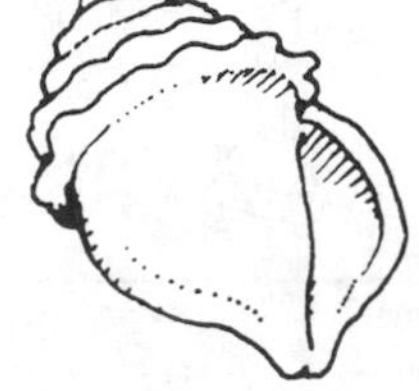

smell

shell

sled

step

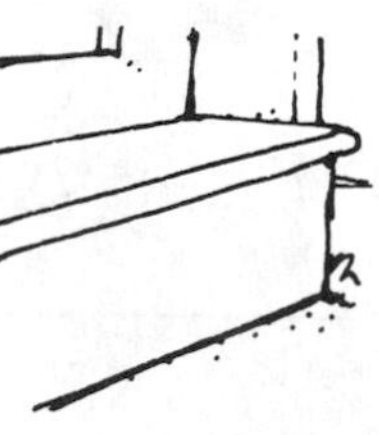

Short *E*

Name ______________________

Read each sentence and the words beside it. Write the word that makes sense in each sentence.

bed 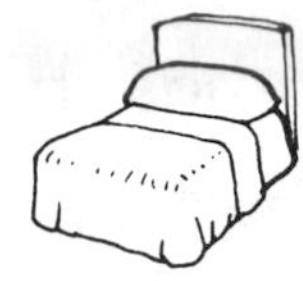

1. Ben ___fed___ his pet.	fed fell beg
2. My new sled is ______________.	bed red fed
3. Nell will fly on a ______________.	wet let jet
4. The pen made a ______________ on her dress.	mess men met
5. Ted let Ned ring the ______________.	bet bell bed
6. One of the men ______________ on the step.	less fell bell
7. Bess ______________ Fred at school.	men met net
8. Jed has a ______________ pig.	pen pet peg
9. Maria will sleep in a ______________.	tell ten tent

Short *U*

Name

Cup has the short-**u** sound. This sound is usually spelled by the letter **u.**

c**u**p

Name the pictures. Write **u** below each picture whose name has the short-**u** sound.

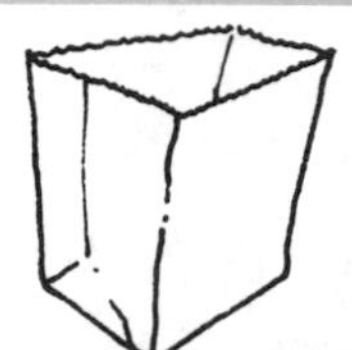

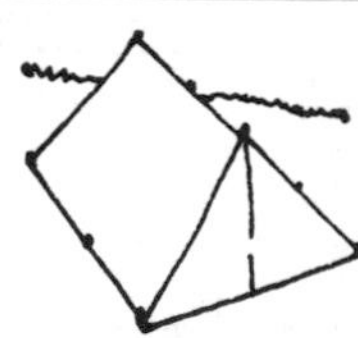

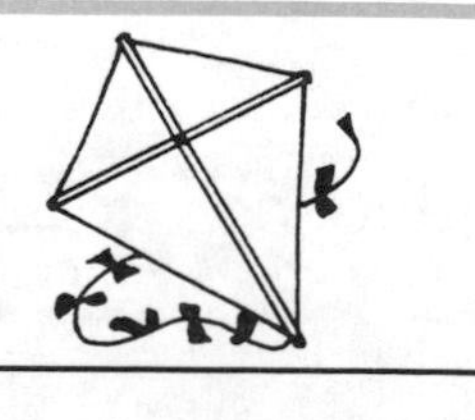

Short *U*

Name

Read the words and look at the pictures. Draw a line from each word to the picture it tells about.

c**u**p

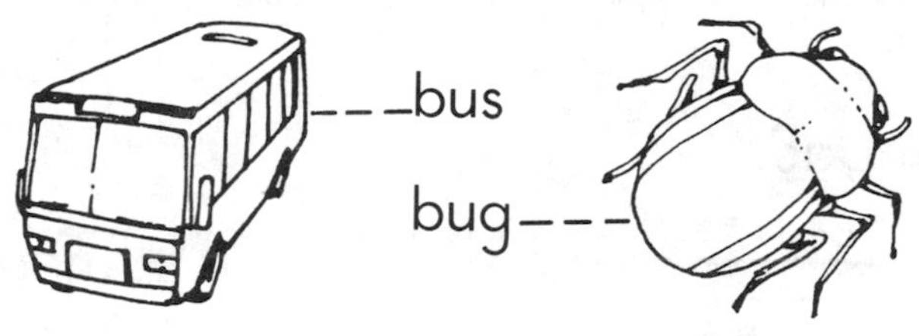

bus

bug

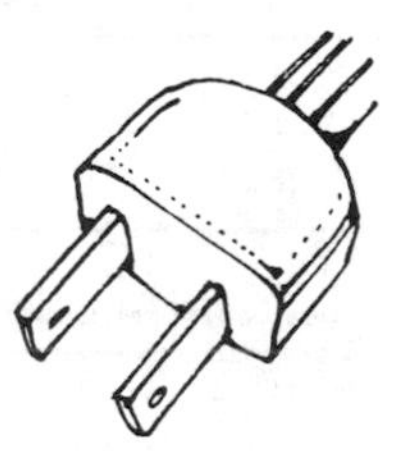

pup

plug

bun

sun

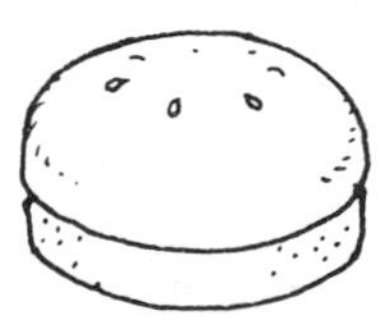

cub

cut

rug

run

jump

drum

hug

mug

tub

truck

Short *U*

Name ____________________

Read each sentence and the words beside it. Write the word that makes sense in each sentence.

cup

1. Jill takes her drum on the bus.	jump drum dug
2. Ted got a ____________ from Dad.	hug hum dug
3. The pup is playing on the ____________.	mug rug plug
4. Ann will not run from a ____________.	bun sun bug
5. Pat pulled the plug from the ____________.	tub nut tug
6. The bug sits in the hot ____________.	sun run rug
7. The little brown ____________ can run.	cup cut cub
8. The car is in some ____________.	mud much mug
9. Playing this game is ____________.	run fun full

Short Vowels

Name ___________________________

Read the words and name the pictures. Draw a line from each picture to the word that names it.

him hem ham ____ hum	tip tap top tan	cob cub cup cap
cap cup cut cat	sit six sat sip	bit bet but bat
mop top map tap	hen pen pan him	wet web will well
beg bed bad bag	peg pen pig pin	fit fix fox box

Review of symbol-sound association of short vowels.

Short Vowels

Name ____________________

Name the pictures. Write the letter that stands for the vowel sound in each picture name.

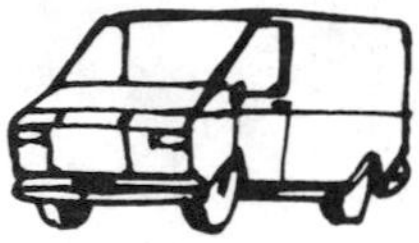

v a n	s n	b d
m p	p g	m n
b b	r g	j t
b x	c t	s x

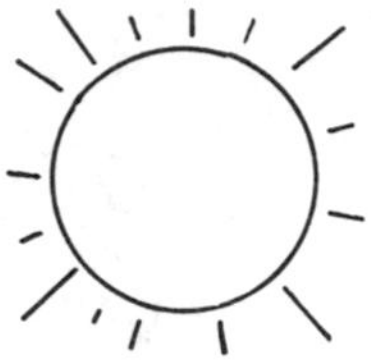

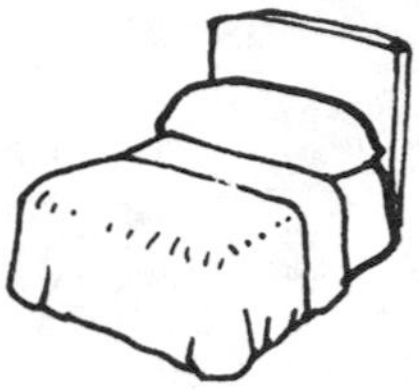

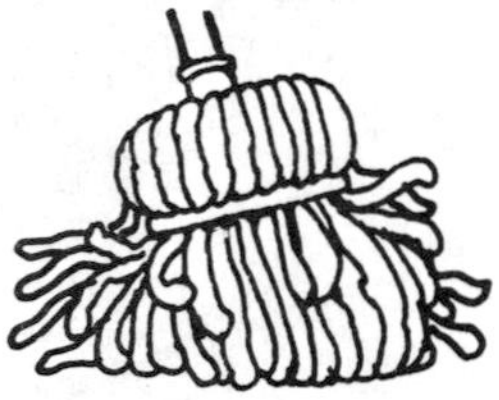

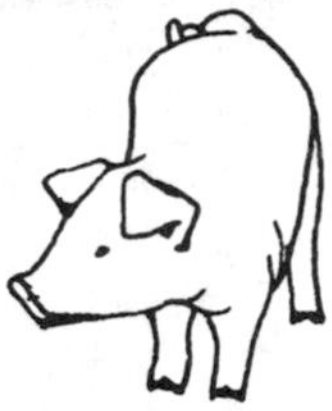

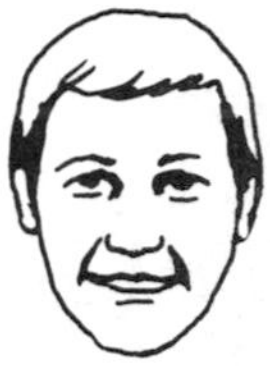

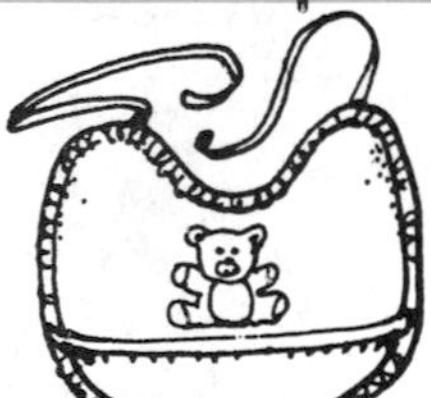

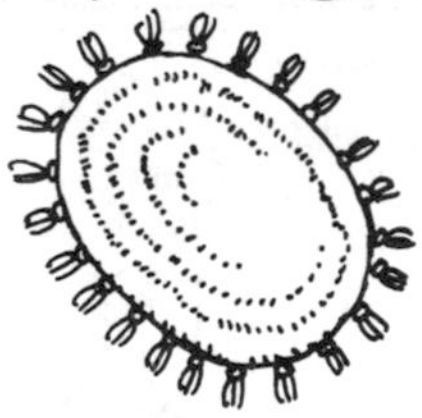

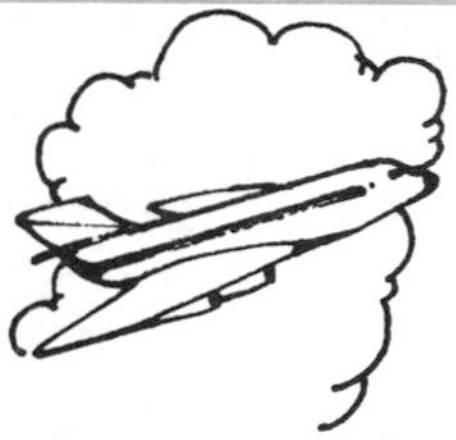

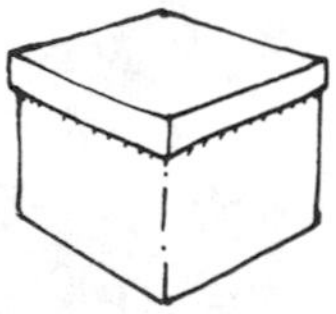

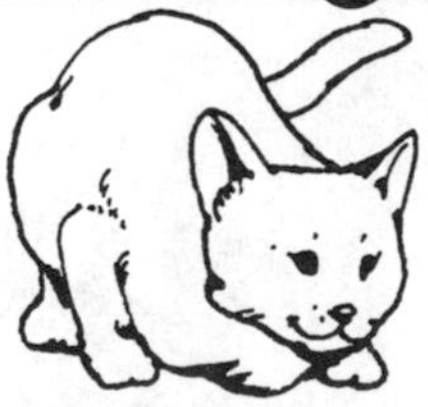

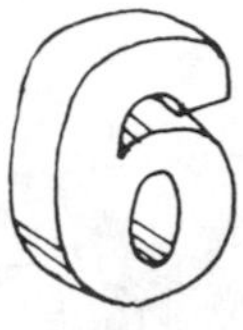

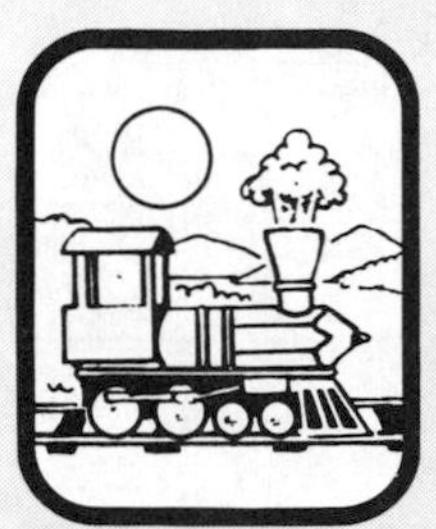

Long *A*

Name ______________________

Rake has the long-**a** sound. This sound is often spelled by **a** and silent **e.**

r**ake** f**a**n

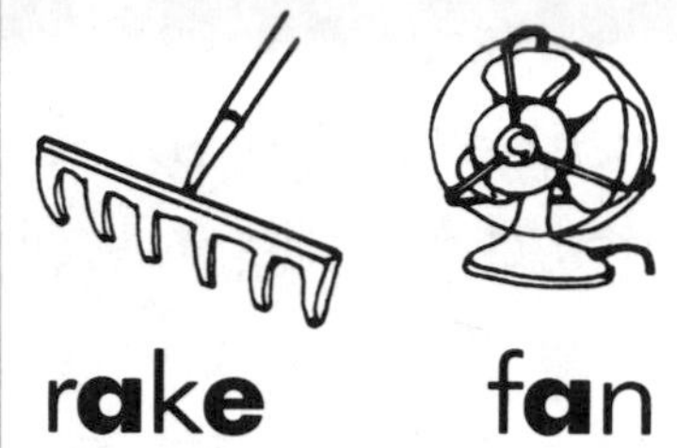

Read the words and name the pictures. Draw a line from each word to the picture it names.

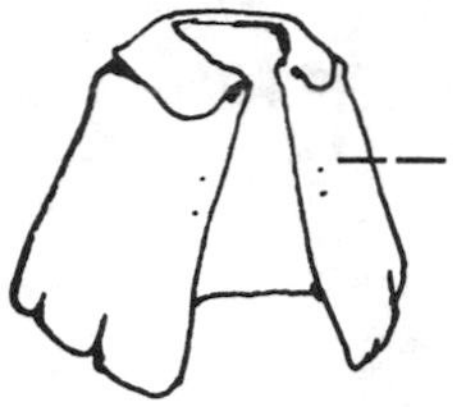

cape

cap

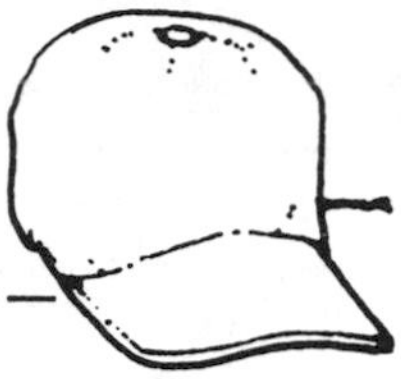

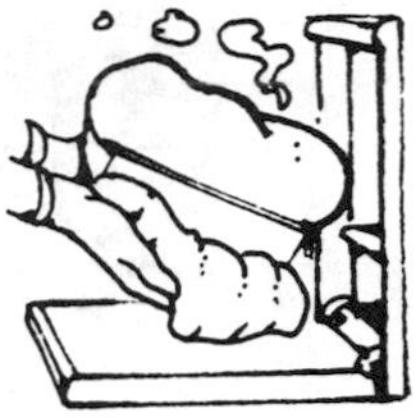

bake

bat

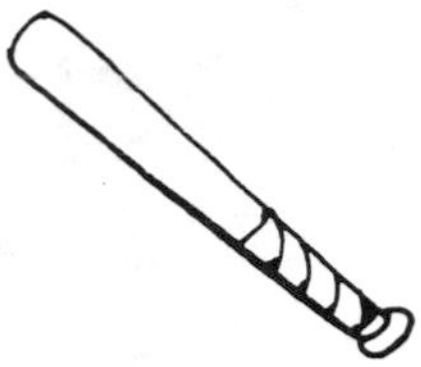

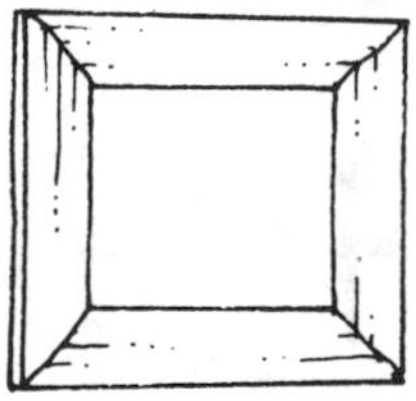

frame

flame

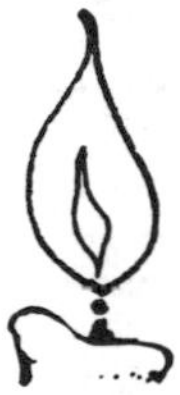

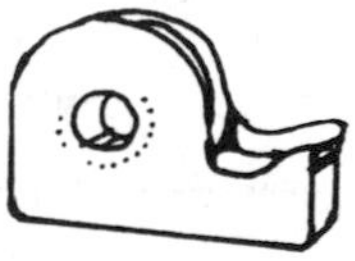

ape

tape

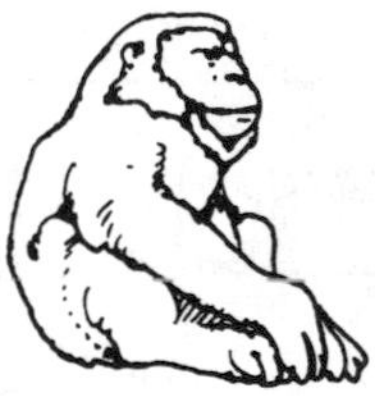

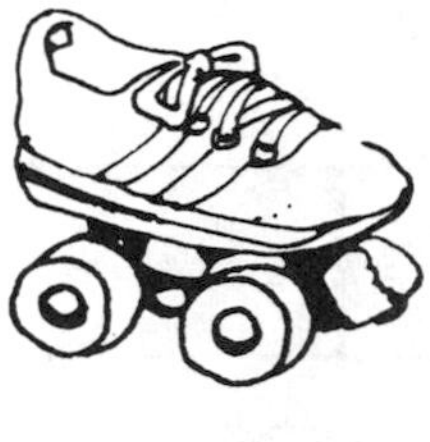

safe

skate

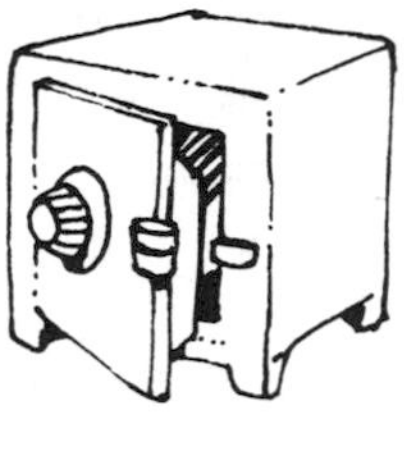

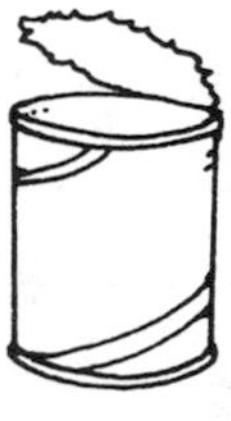

can

cane

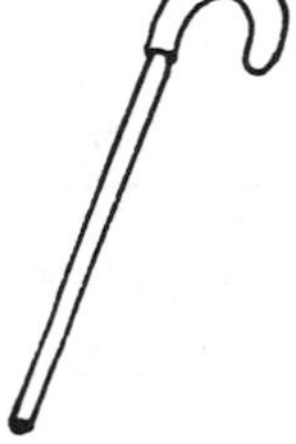

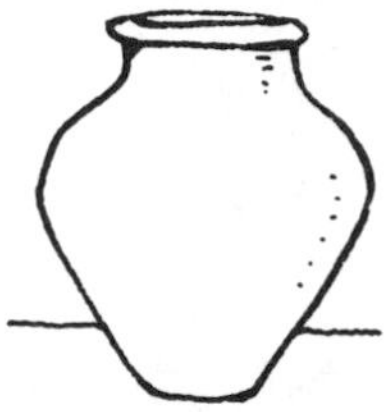

vase

van

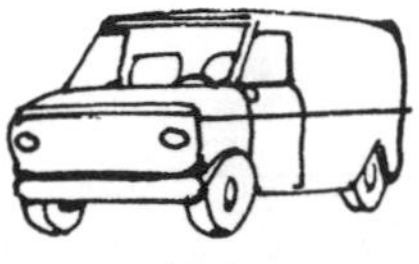

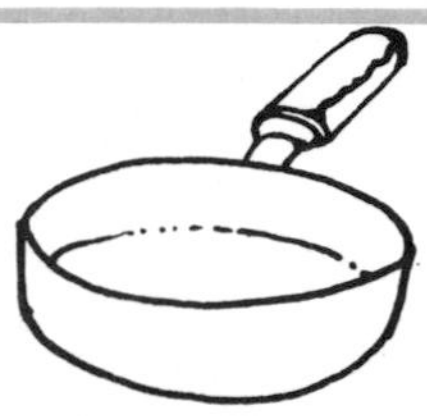

pan

plate

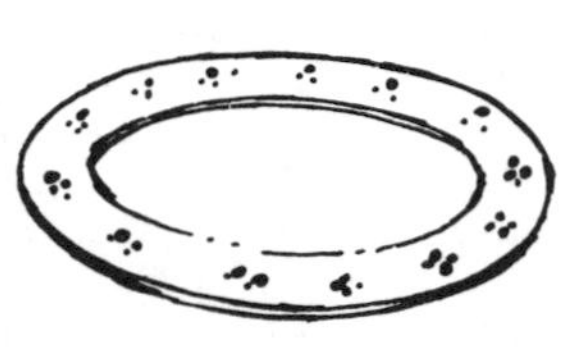

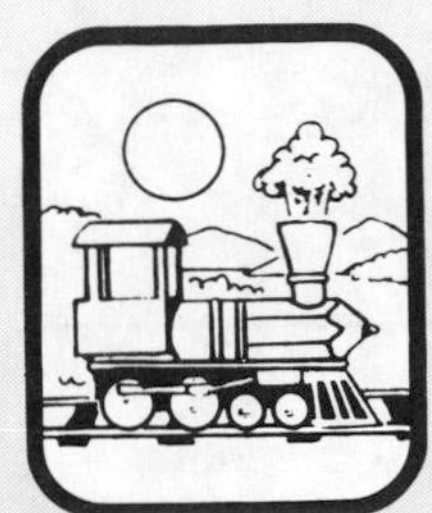

Long A

Name

Name the pictures. Write the letter or letters that stand for the vowel sound in each picture name.

rake

fan

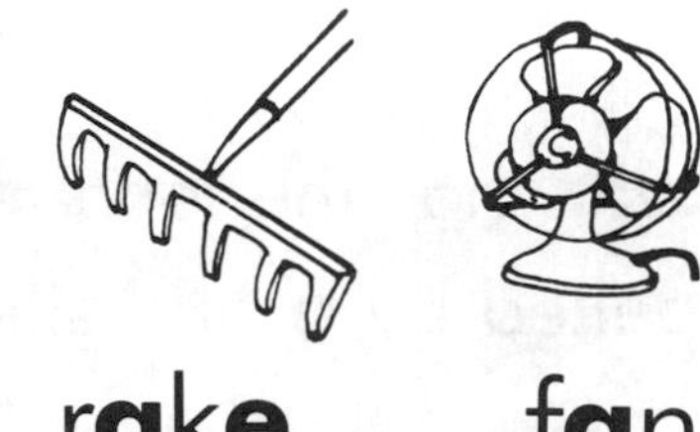

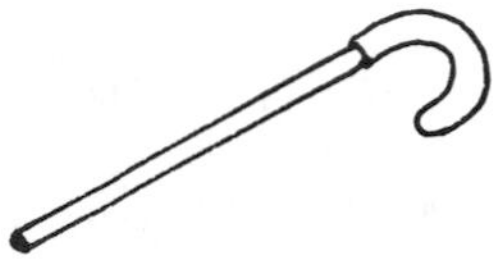

cane

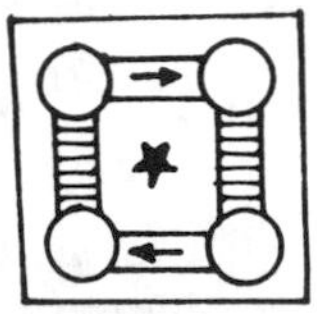

g m

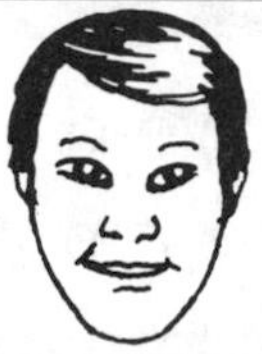

m n

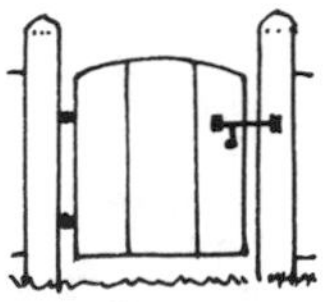

g t

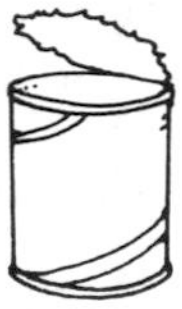

c n

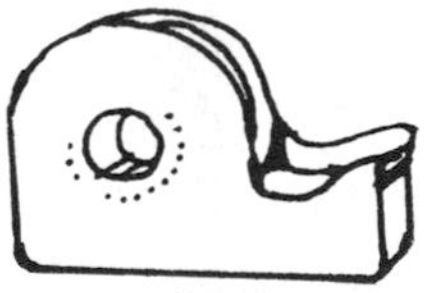

t p

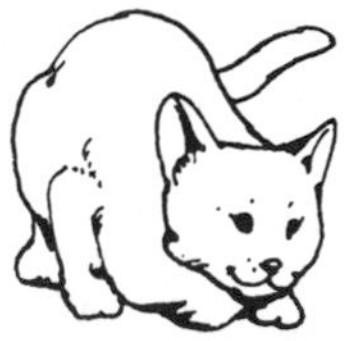

c t

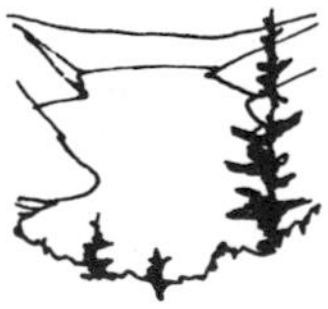

l k

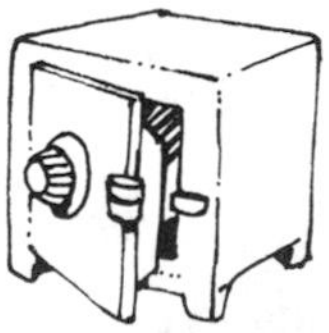

s f

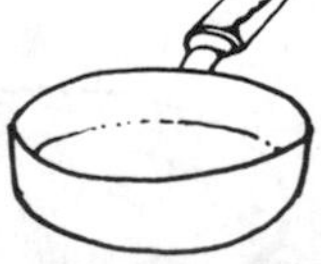

p n

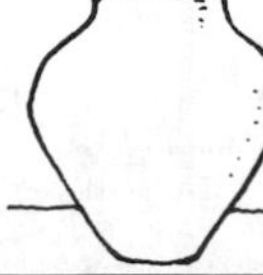

v s

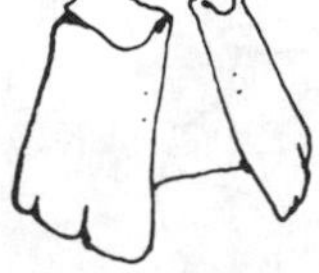

c p

Long *A*

Name ______________________

Read each sentence and the words beside it. Write the word that makes sense in each sentence.

1.	Jane ran by the ~~lake~~ ______________.	lake late lap
2.	Dale saw an ______________ at the zoo.	ate at ape
3.	Sam is the ______________ of my dog.	name same nap
4.	Kate put on a new ______________.	can cape cane
5.	Jan can play the ______________.	gate game gas
6.	Dan put a red bud in the ______________.	vase case has
7.	I gave Dad the ______________.	tap tape tan
8.	Ann ran to first ______________.	bat base case
9.	We ride to school in our ______________.	vase van case

Long *I*

Name ____________________

Kite has the long-**i** sound. This sound is often spelled by **i** and silent **e.**

k**i**te

b**i**b

Read the words and look at the pictures. Draw a line from each word to the picture it tells about.

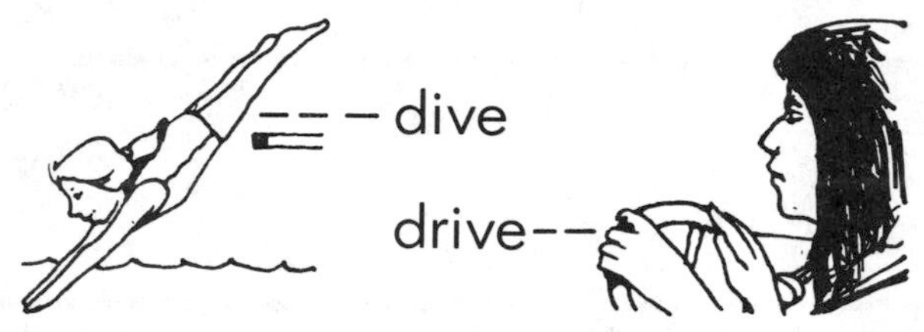

bite

bike

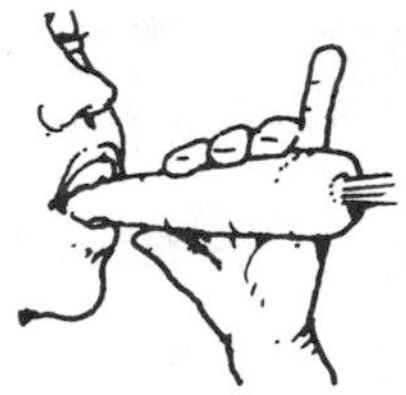

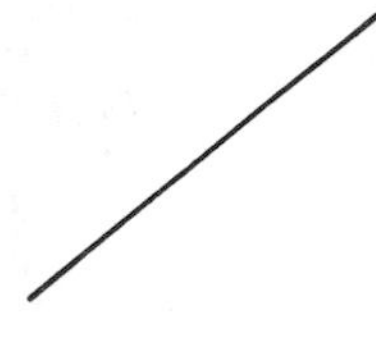

vine

line

hive

hide

pine

pin

six

slide

ride

crib

fish

five

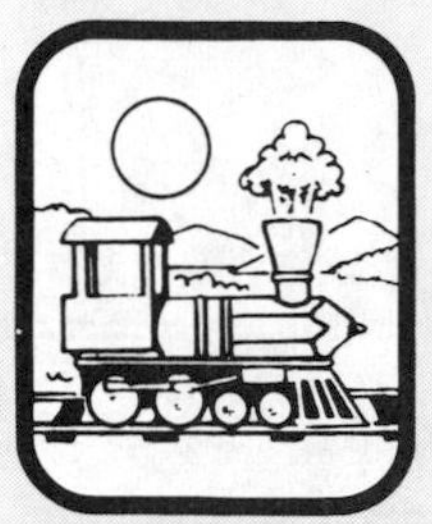

Long *I*

Name ____________________

Name the pictures. Write the letter or letters that stand for the vowel sound in each picture name.

kite

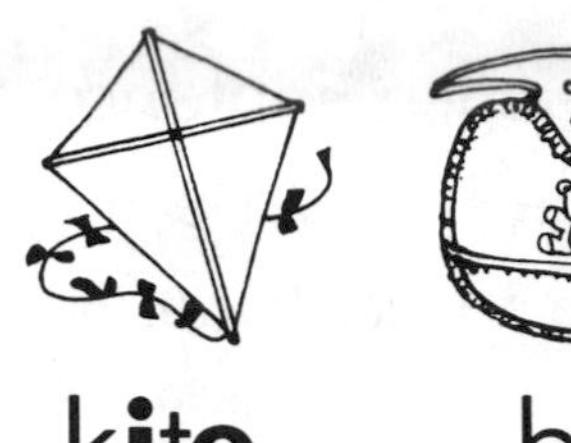

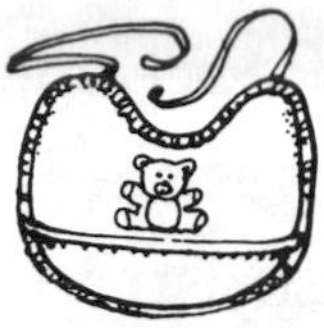

bib

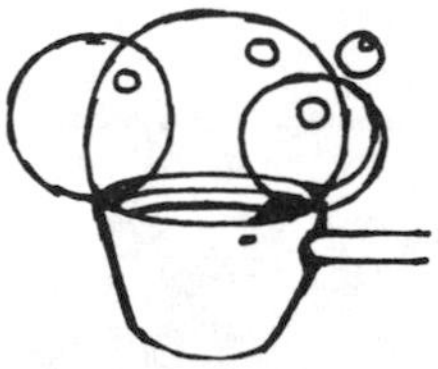

p i p e

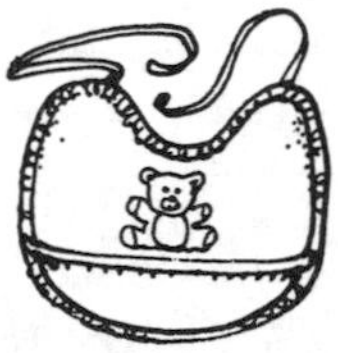

b b

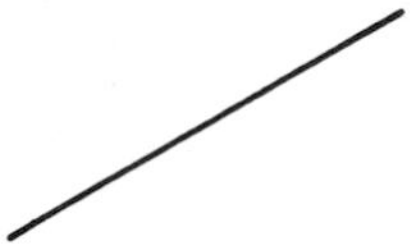

l n

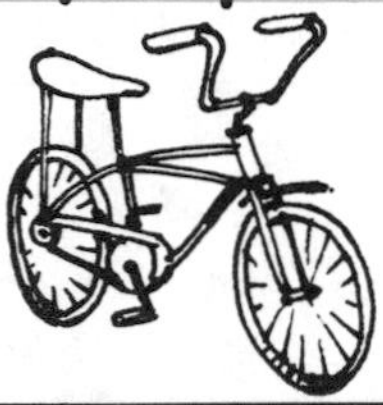

b k

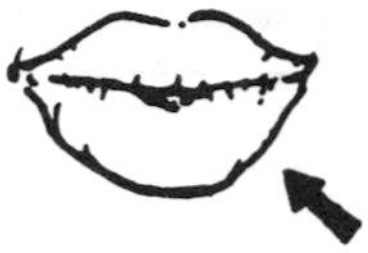

l p

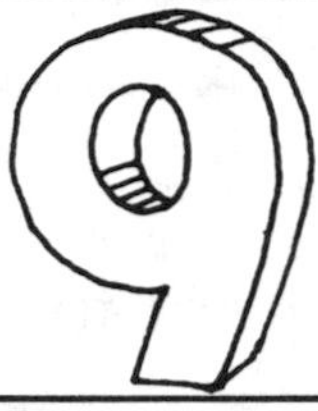

n n

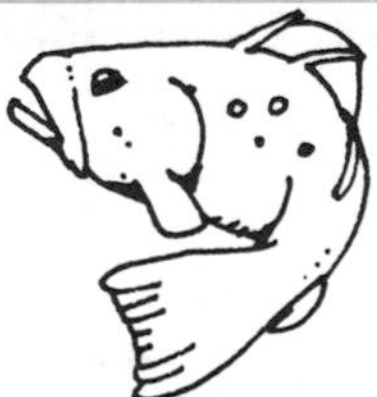

f sh

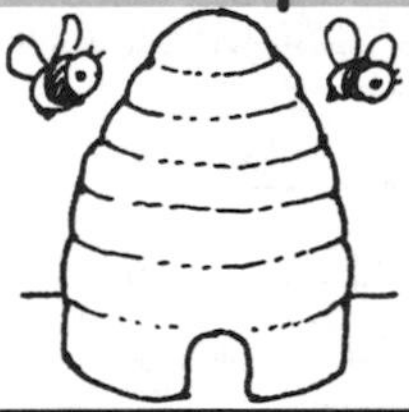

h v

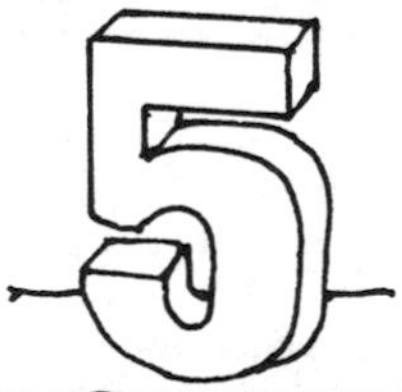

f v

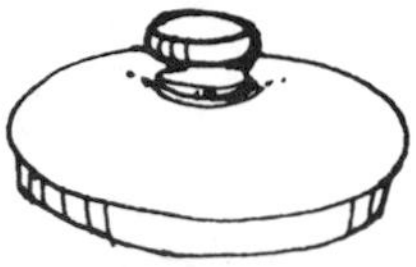

l d

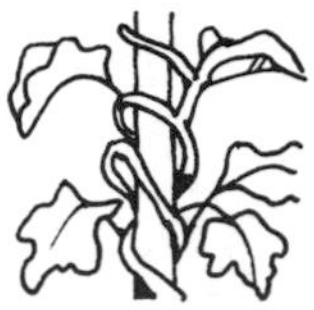

v n

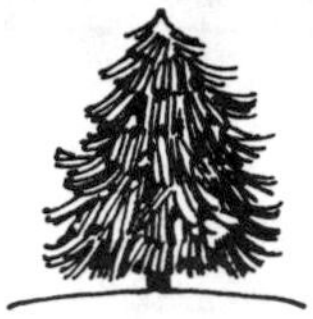

p n

Long *I*

Name ______________________

Read each sentence and the words beside it. Write the word that makes sense in each sentence.

kite **bib**

1.	Bill can ride a ___bike___.	bite big bike
2.	Jim took a __________ in the woods.	hit hike hide
3.	Jill likes to __________.	dive bit five
4.	Sis went for a __________ on a horse.	ride rid bride
5.	Kim got to school on __________.	time dime nine
6.	Mike put a __________ on the pan.	like line lid
7.	We have __________ new cats.	fire five file
8.	Tim __________ his lip.	bike big bit
9.	The baby is sleeping in her __________.	ride rid crib

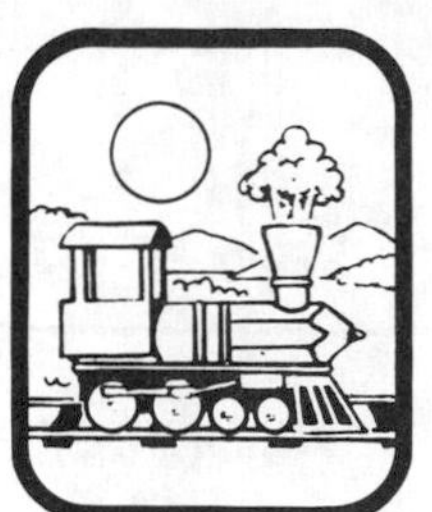

Long O

Name ______________________

Bone has the long-**o** sound. This sound is often spelled by **o** and silent **e.**

b**o**ne t**o**p

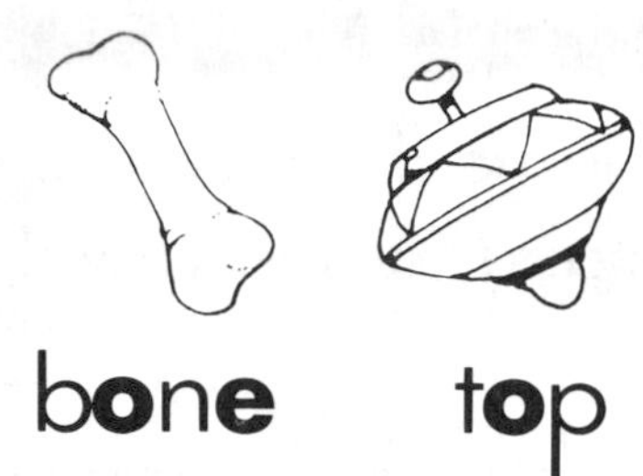

Read the words and name the pictures. Draw a line from each word to the picture it names.

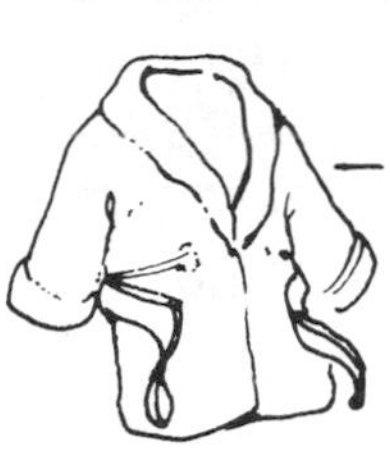

robe

rose

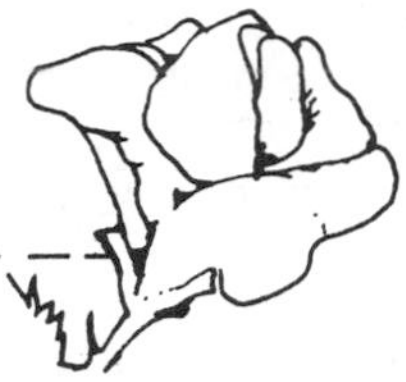

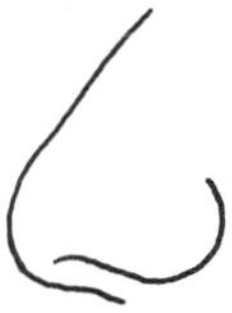

note

nose

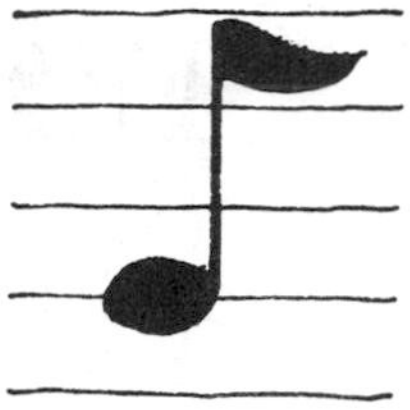

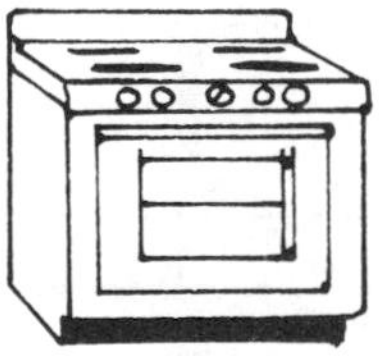

stove

stone

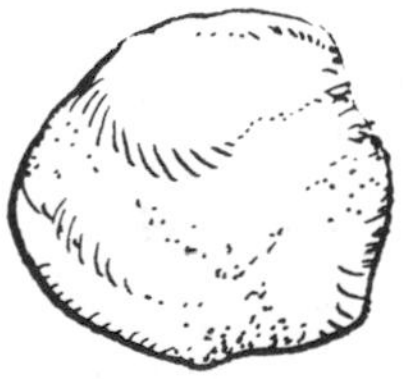

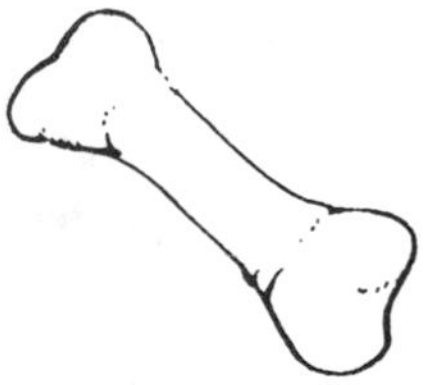

bone

box

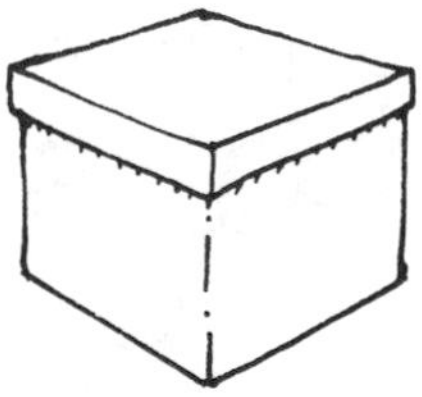

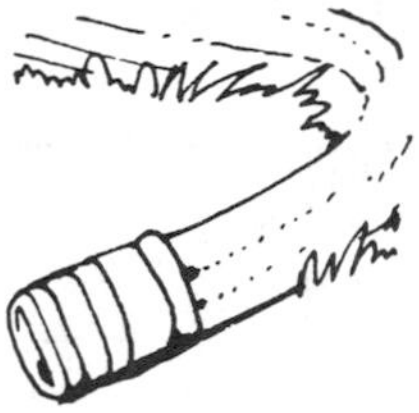

hose

hog

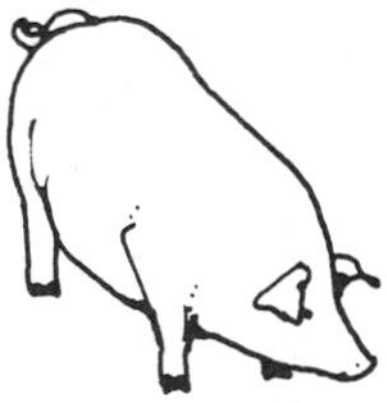

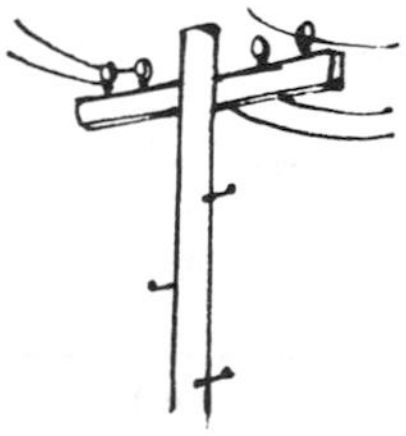

pot

pole

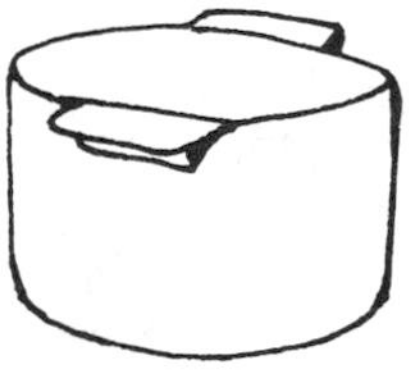

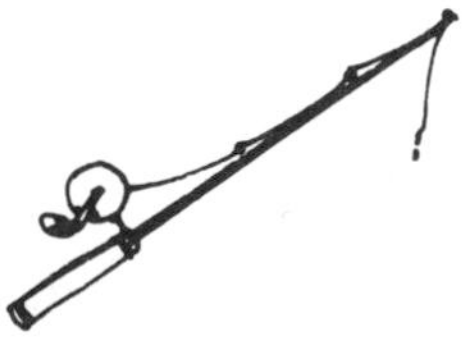

rod

rope

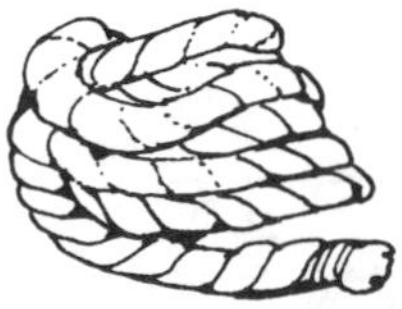

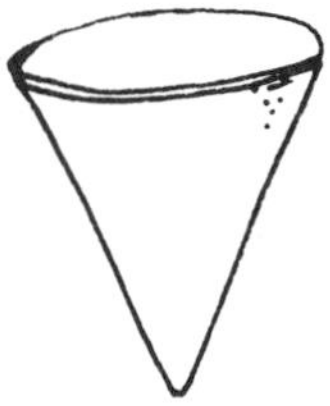

cot

cone

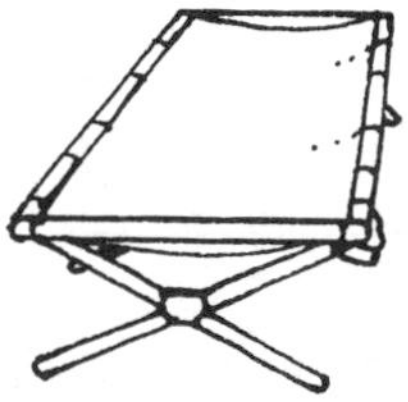

Long O

Name

Name the pictures. Write the letter or letters that stand for the vowel sound in each picture name.

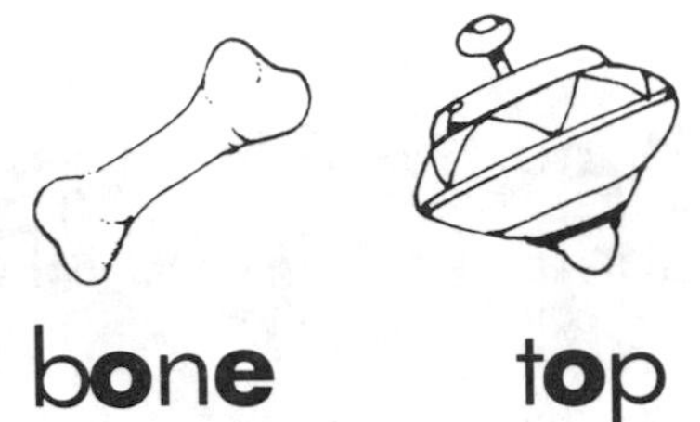

n o t e

r p

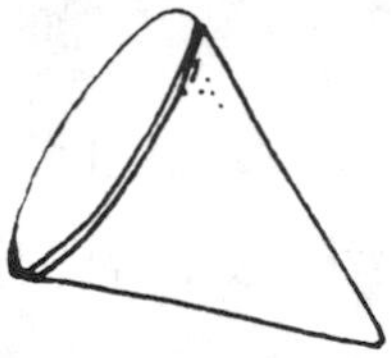

c n

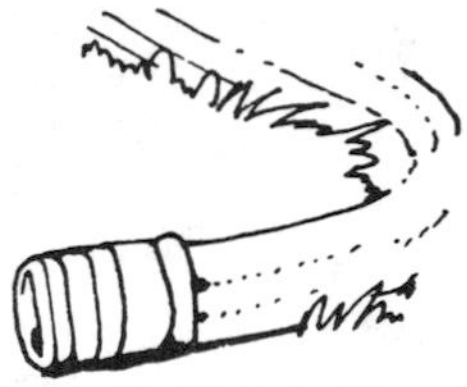

h s

d ll

r s

f x

n s

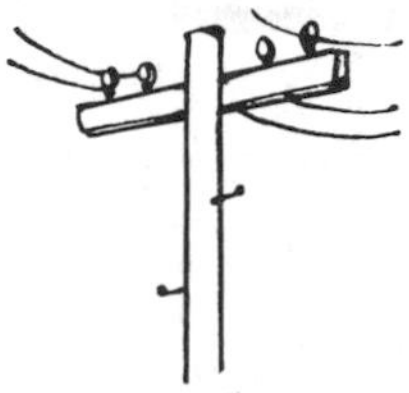

p l

r b

r d

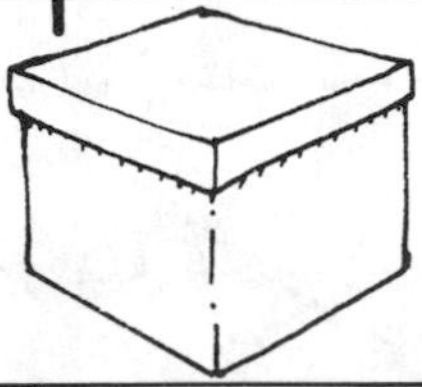

b x

Sound-symbol association of long-*o* words

Long O

Name ______________________

Read each sentence and the words beside it. Write the word that makes sense in each sentence.

bone **top**

1. Mom can grow a ___rose___.	rose robe rod
2. That ______________ is for the garden.	hop hose hot
3. Rose pats the dog on its ______________.	not note nose
4. Dot will read the ______________.	nose note not
5. The ______________ poked a hole in its pen.	fog hose hog
6. Don put on an old ______________.	robe rob roll
7. The ______________ got a new home.	box fox ax
8. Where is my fishing ______________?	rod rode rose
9. Bob can ______________ on one foot.	home hop hole

Long *U*

Name ______________________

Tube has the long-**u** sound. This sound is often spelled by **u** and silent **e.**

tube cup

Read the words and look at the pictures. Draw a line from each word to the picture it tells about.

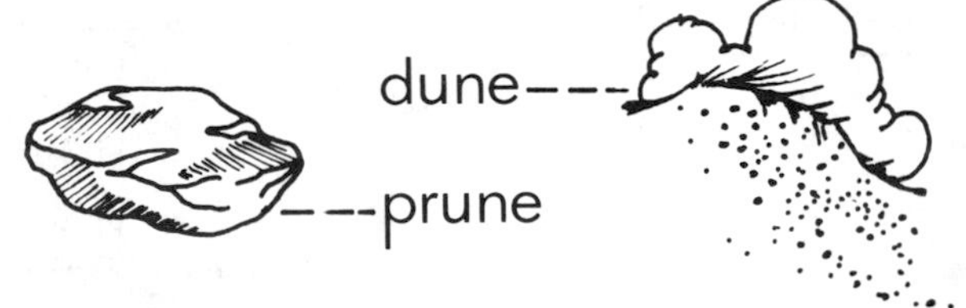

dune---

---prune

tube

tune

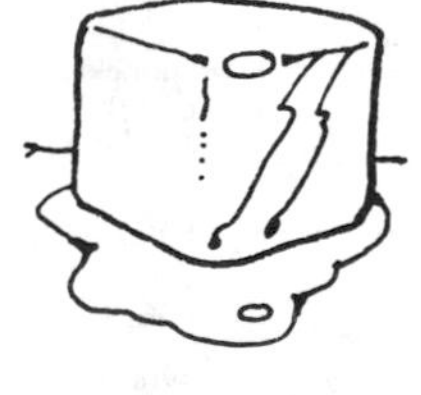

cub

cube

cute

cut

flute

lunch

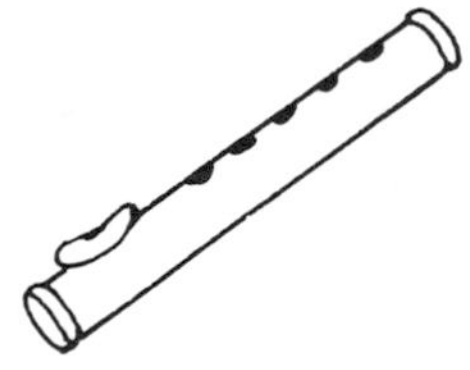

mule

mug

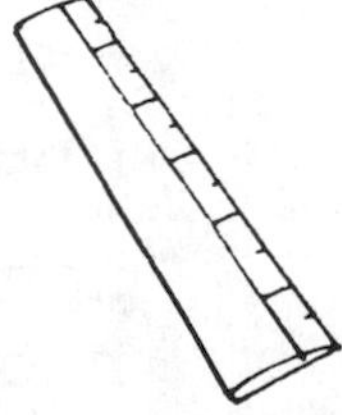

ruler

rug

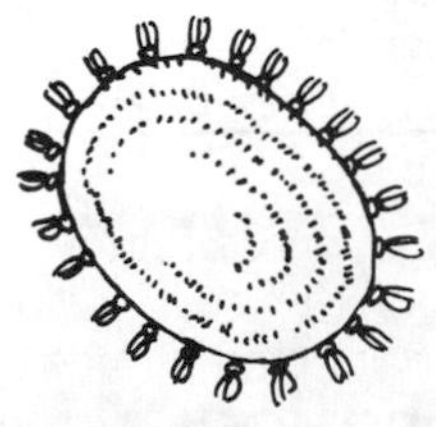

cup

cubes

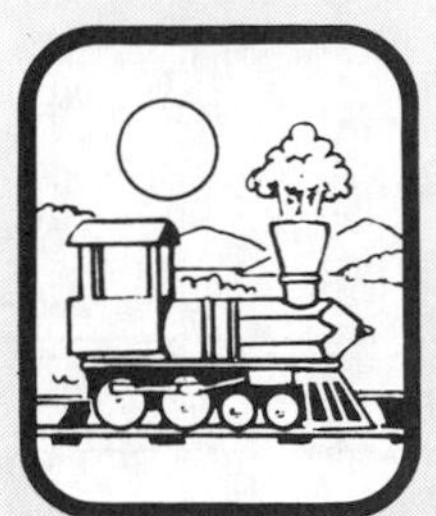

Long *u*

Name ______________________

Name the pictures. Write the letter or letters that stand for the vowel sound in each picture name.

tube

cup

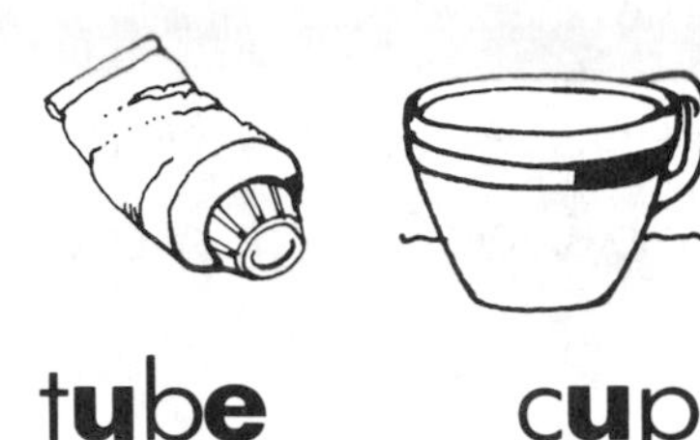

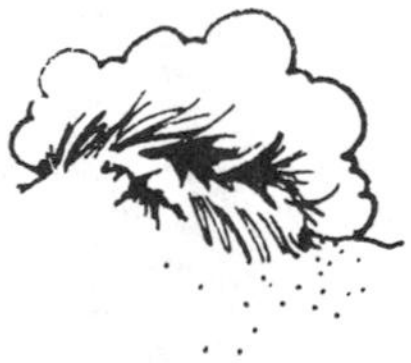

dune

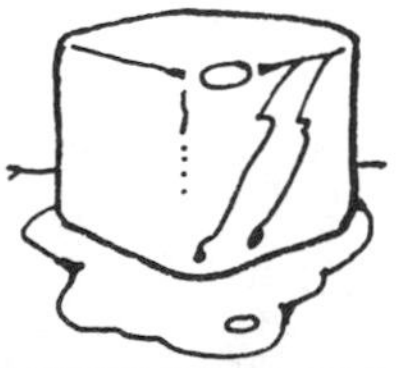

c b

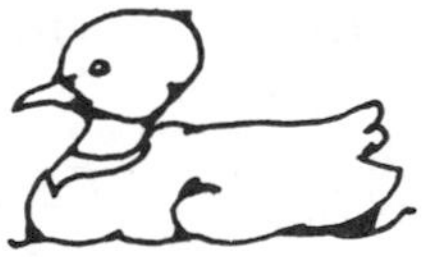

d ck

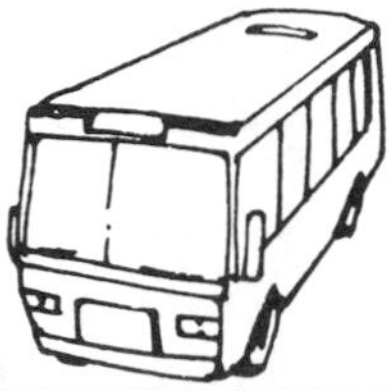

b s

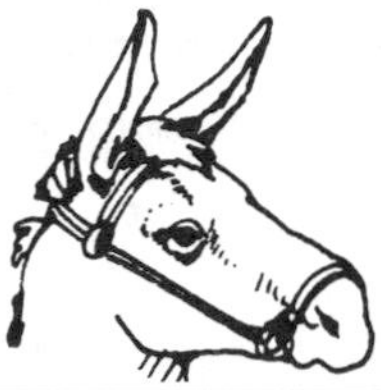

m l

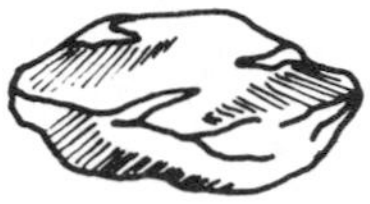

pr n

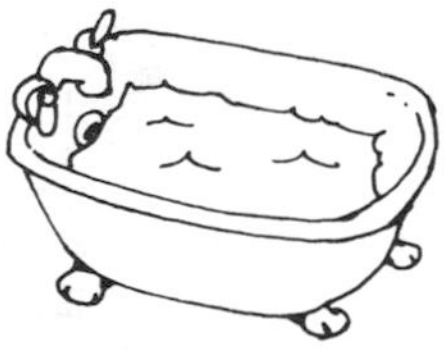

t b

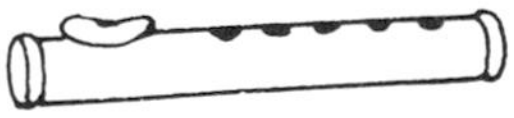

fl t

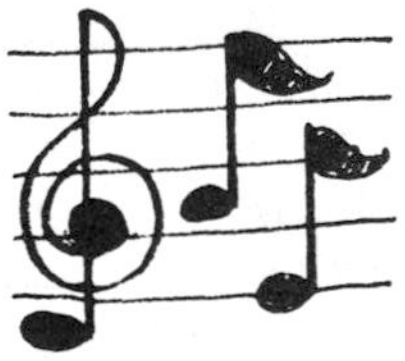

t n

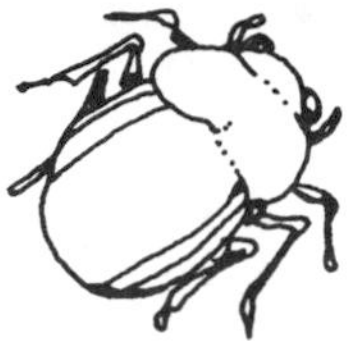

b g

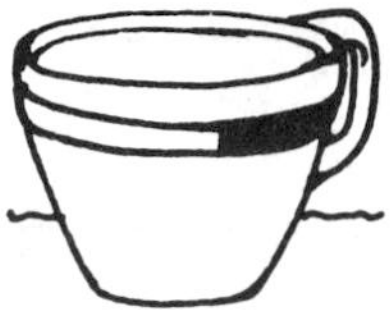

c p

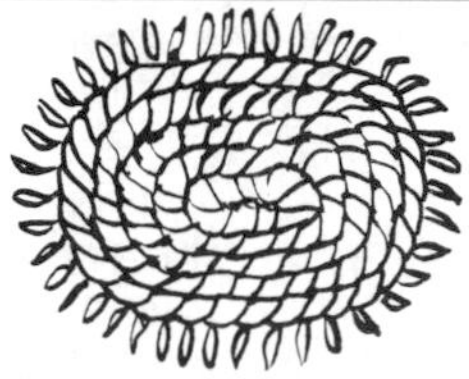

r g

Long *U*

Name ______________________

Read each sentence and the words beside it. Write the word that makes sense in each sentence.

tube 

 **cup**

1.	Ruth can play the flute.	flute jump June
2.	I ate a __________ with my lunch.	pup prune put
3.	Luke is looking for the school __________.	bus use bug
4.	Read every __________ before the game.	rule rub rug
5.	Did you hear Suzy hum a __________?	tub tune tug
6.	The __________ works on a farm.	mug mud mule
7.	An ice __________ makes water cold.	cub cube cute
8.	We walked along the sand __________.	tune dune duck
9.	That baby is __________.	cube cute tube

Long Vowels

Name

Read the words and name the pictures. Circle the word that names each picture.

hive hide had dive	can cone cane came	cub cube tub tube
male mile mule mole	pin pan pane pine	like lit lake luck
cute cut cob cone	tap tape tub tube	rule run rope rod
gate game date dune	note not nut nose	rid ride rode red

Long Vowels

Name

Look at the pictures. Write the letters that stand for the vowel sound in each picture name.

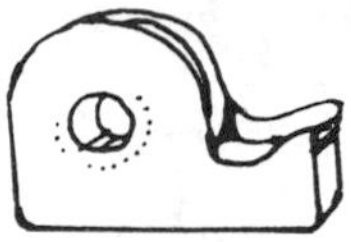

tape	b k	h s
c b	v n	k t
b n	t b	r k
m l	g t	r b

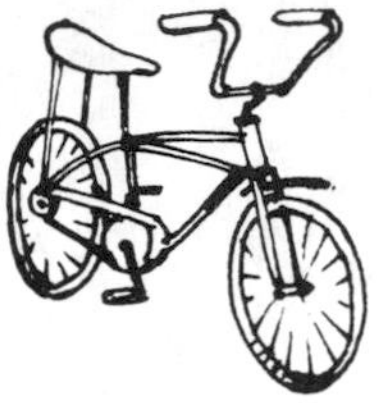

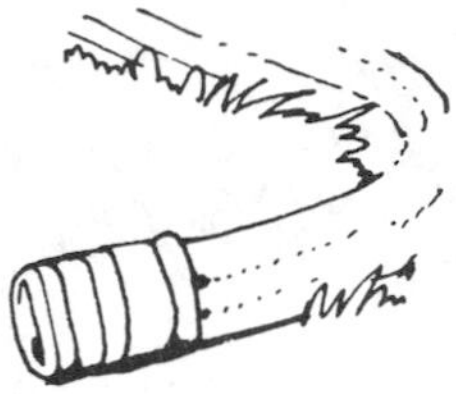

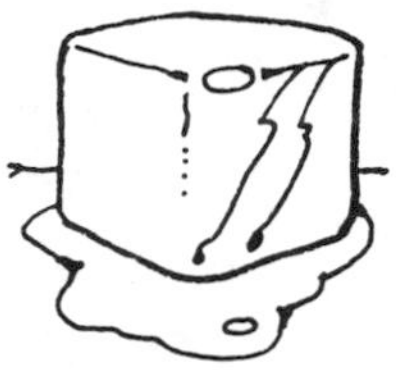

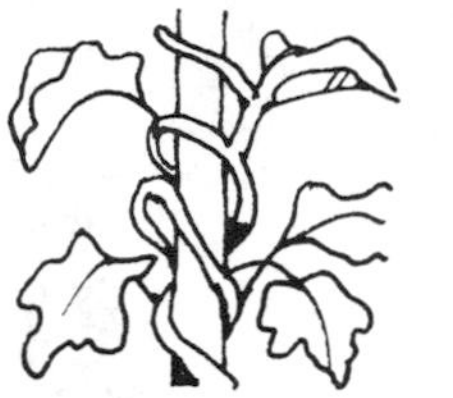

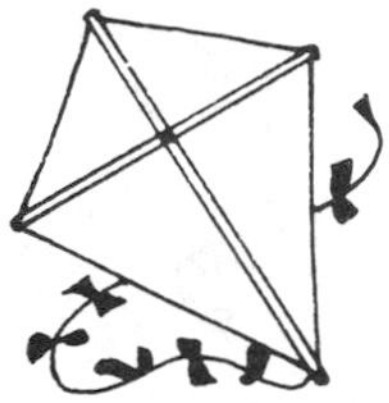

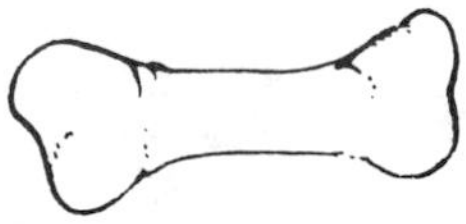

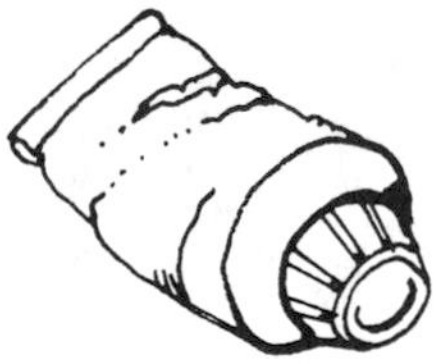

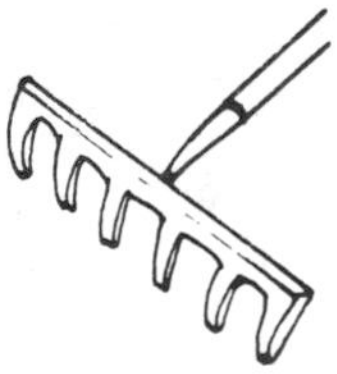

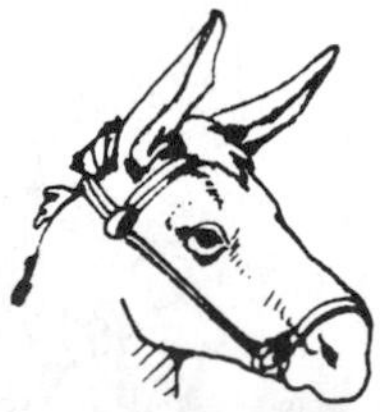

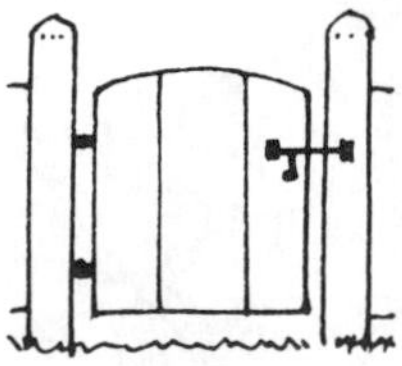

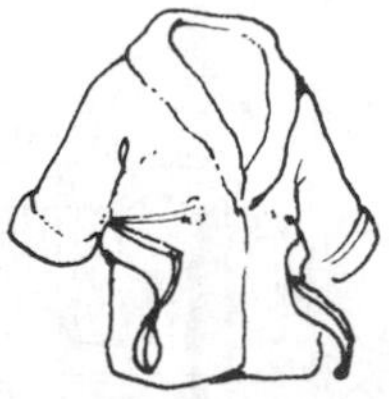

Short and Long Vowels

Name ______________________

Read the words and name the pictures. Circle the word that names each picture. Then write the word in the blank.

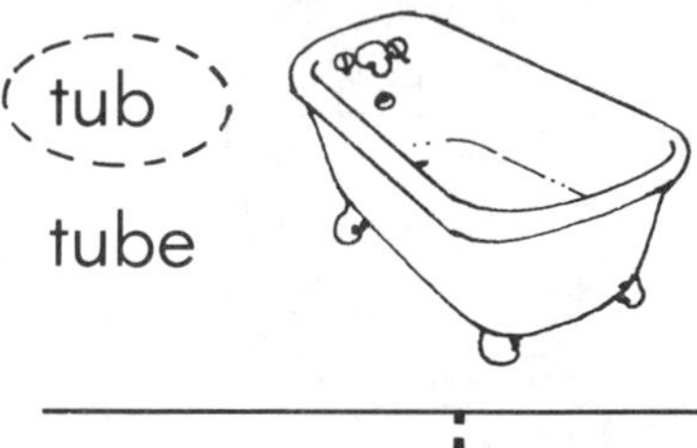

tub

tube

tub

cap

cape

fix

five

box

bone

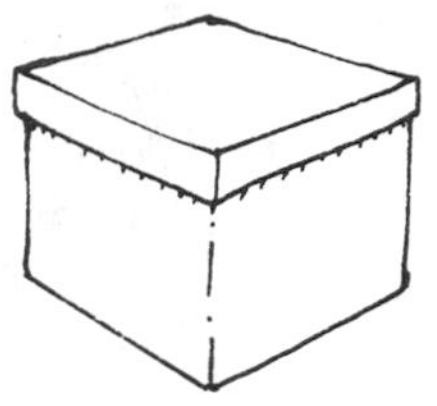

mug

mule

bib

bike

bag

bake

sad

safe

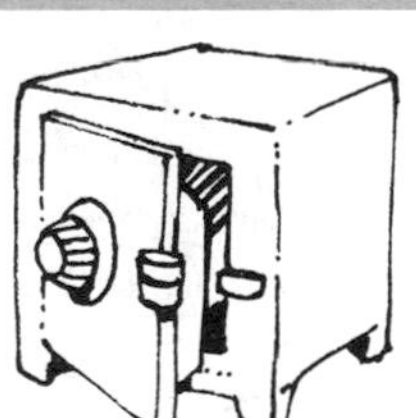

hog

hose

pin

pine

rod

robe

cub

cube

Short and Long Vowels

Name ______________________

Name the pictures. Write the letter or letters that stand for the vowel sound in each picture name.

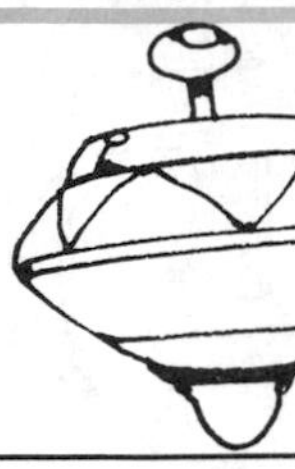

t _ p	k _ t	b _ k
t _ b	b _ g	p _ n
n _ s	b _ d	r _ p
s _ x	p _ l	h _ m

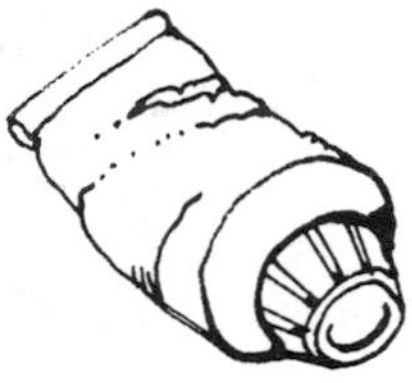

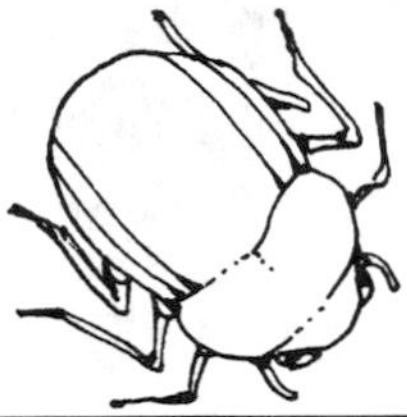

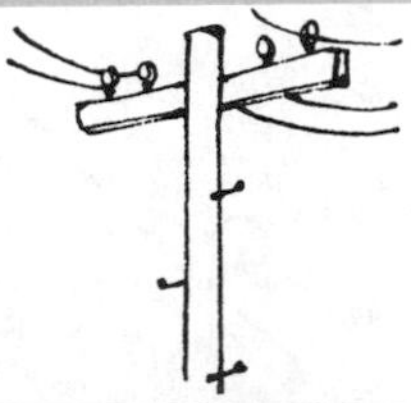

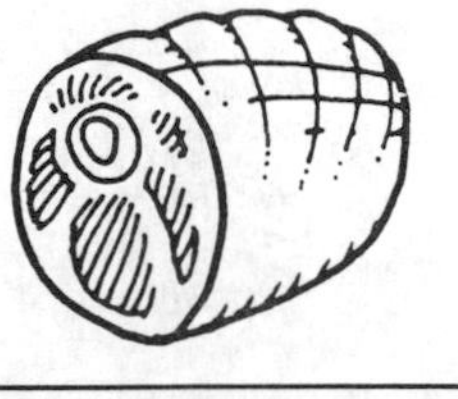

Short and Long Vowels

Name ______________________

Read each sentence and the words beside it. Circle the word that makes sense in the sentence. Then write the word in the blank.

1.	Gus rides the ___bus___ to school.	bus base
2.	Dave ____________ a dive into the water.	mad made
3.	The old dog likes to eat a good ____________.	bone broke
4.	Bess put the ____________ into a box.	robe rob
5.	Jan went for a swim in the ____________.	like lake
6.	Who lost the ____________ to the pan?	line lid
7.	I put my dog in the ____________.	tub tube
8.	Kate will write a ____________.	not note
9.	Did Nate ____________ his bed today?	map make

Short and Long Vowels

Name ____________________

Read the words and name the pictures. Circle the word that names each picture. Then write the word that names the picture.

tap
tape

tape

pot
pole

bike
bit

fish
fine

rod
robe

can
cane

tub
tube

lip
line

cup
cube

not
nose

mule
mug

bat
bake

Short and Long Vowels

Name ______________________

Read each sentence and the words beside it. Write the word that makes sense in the sentence.

1.	Did Mom buy a new ___rug___ for my room?	rob rug rule
2.	I ______________ to swim.	line lid like
3.	The ______________ ran into its cave.	fix fox five
4.	My ______________ has a flat tire.	bib bite bike
5.	Did you hear a ______________ on the window?	tape tap tan
6.	I want to go ______________ now.	home hog hose
7.	Jimmy can play a pretty ______________.	tub tube tune
8.	The children ran down the ______________.	hill hide hive
9.	Rosa sleeps on a little ______________.	cone cot cane

Short and Long Vowels

Name ______________________

Read the words and name the pictures. Draw a line from each picture to the word that names it.

pin pat pan pine	ham hand hat hate	robe rod rode rose
rug run rub rule	sale sat safe sad	well wet web wed
fun flute fuss flat	find fire fine fin	bib bike bite bid
bag bat base bake	pole pop pod pot	mud mug mule must

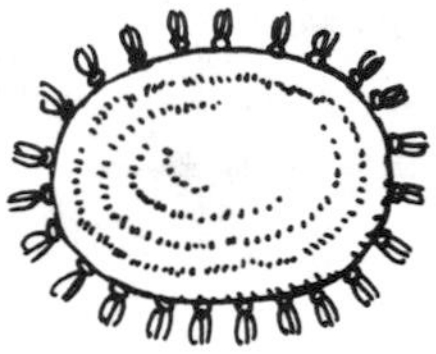

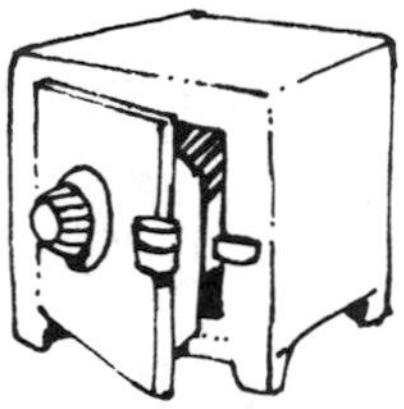

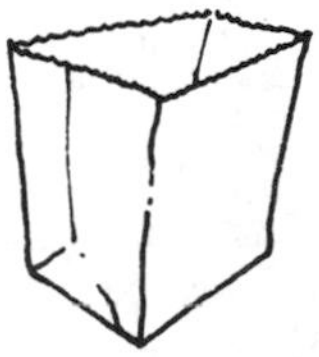

Short and Long Vowels

Name ____________________

Name the pictures. Write the letter or letters that stand for the vowel sound in each picture name.

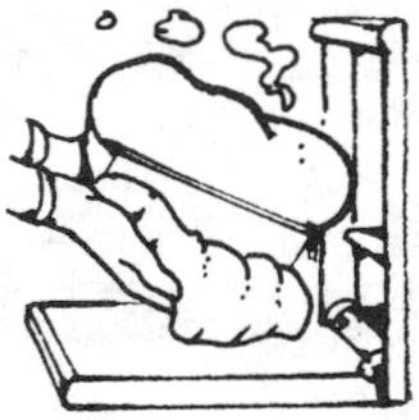

b _ k _

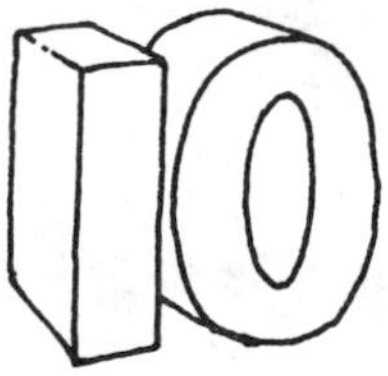

t _ n

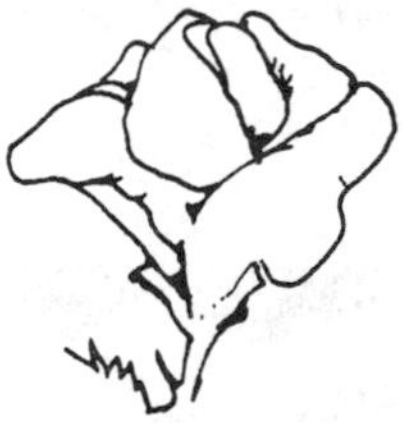

r _ s

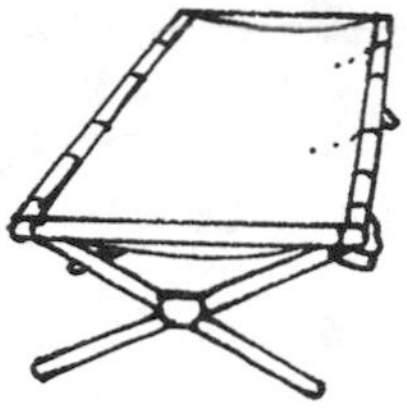

c _ t

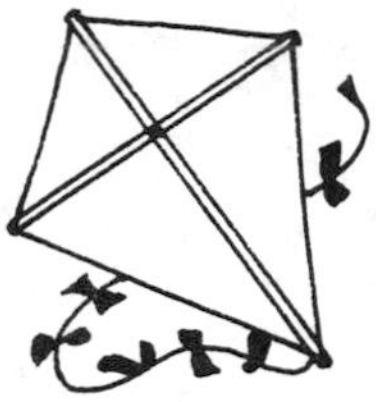

k _ t

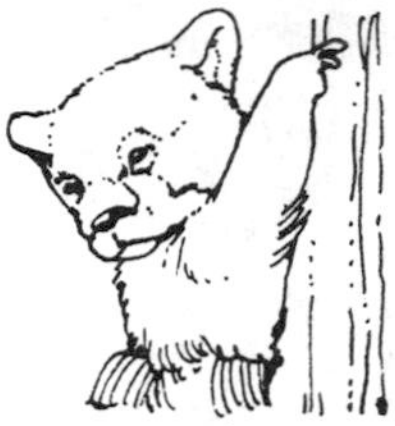

c _ b

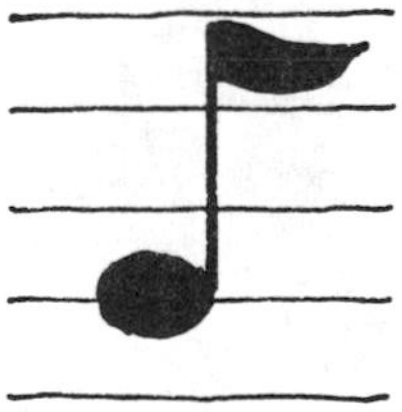

n _ t

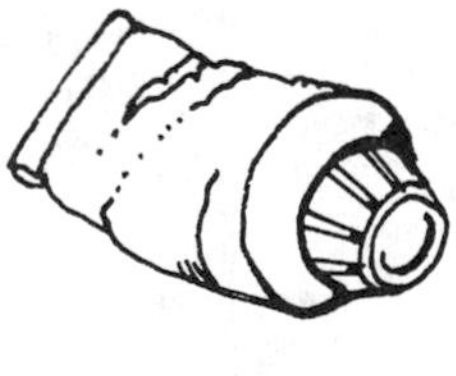

t _ b

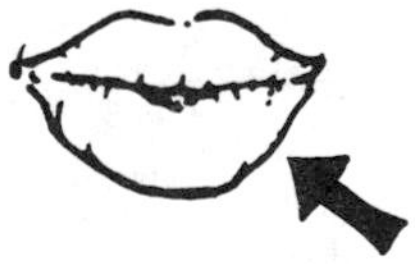

l _ p

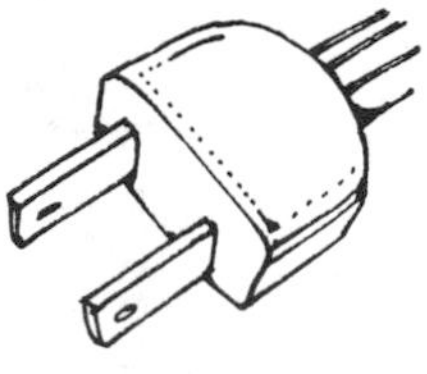

pl _ g

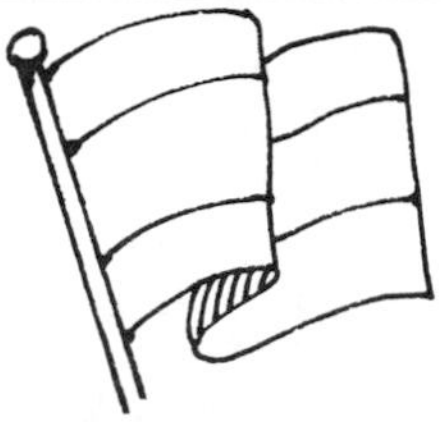

fl _ g

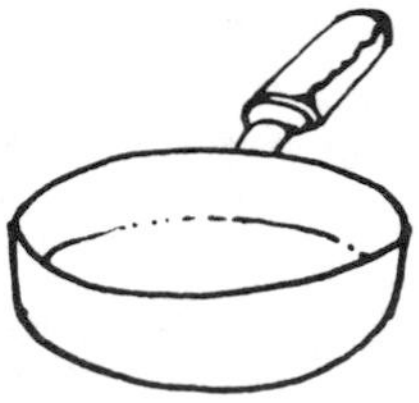

p _ n

Hard C and G

Name ______________________

The letter **c** can stand for the **k** sound, as in **cat.** This is called the hard-**c** sound. The letter **g** can stand for the **g** sound, as in **wagon.** This is called the hard-**g** sound.

cat

(hard **c**)

wa**g**on

(hard **g**)

Read the words and name the pictures. Draw a line from each word to the picture it names.

coat

goat

wig

cup

pig

cap

cow

garden

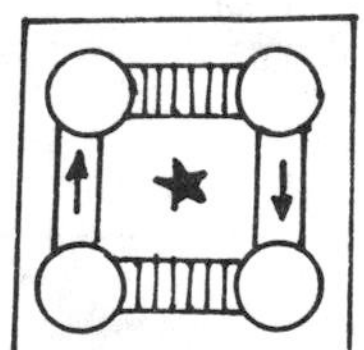

game

calf

cot

wagon

gas

cab

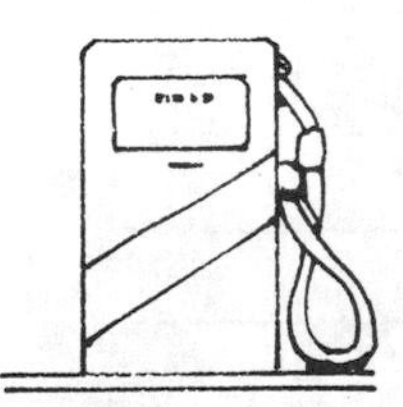

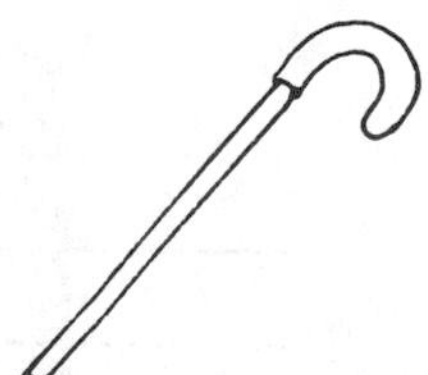

cane

gate

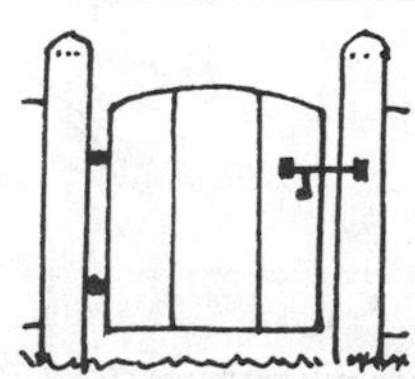

Hard C and G

Name

Read the words in the list below. Then name the pictures. Write the word from the list that names each picture.

cane	car	cup	cat	garden
gate	gas	cow	goat	

cat (hard **c**)

wa**g**on (hard **g**)

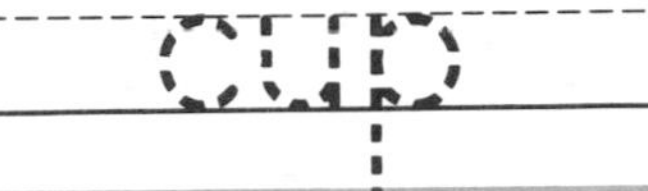

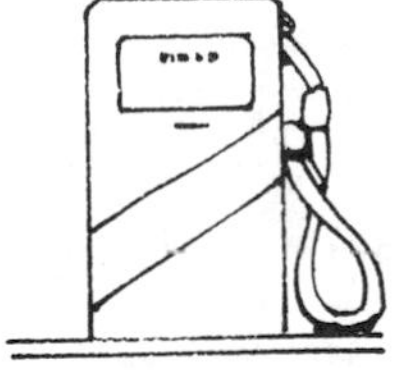

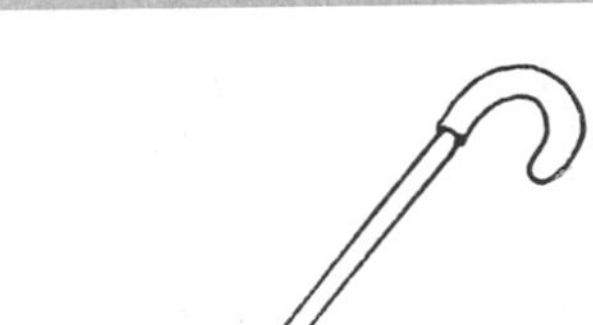

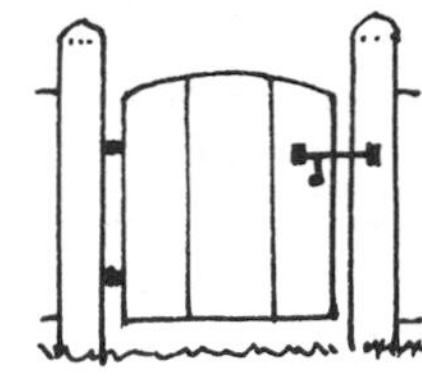

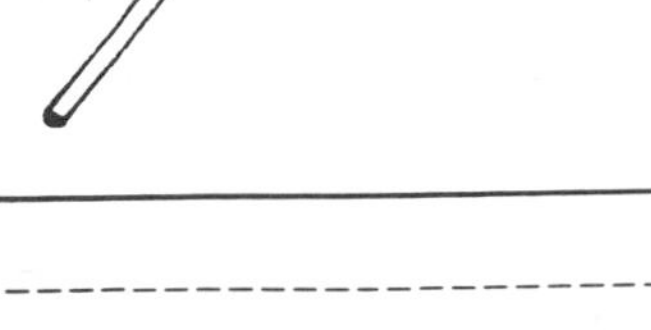

Hard C and G

Name ____________________

Read each sentence and the words beside it. Write the word that makes sense in each sentence.

cat (hard **c**) 

wa**g**on (hard **g**) 

1. Can you play this guessing game?	gave gate game
2. Beth has cold milk in the ____________.	cube cup cute
3. Some grass was growing in the ____________.	goose games garden
4. She found a ____________ of old paint.	calf can cane
5. Chang likes to drive his new ____________.	cat car can
6. My ____________ won a prize at the state fair.	wig pig dig
7. The ____________ has a baby calf.	color coming cow
8. Mother filled the car with ____________.	gardens gas gave
9. Carlos will buy a new ball ____________.	cab cup cap

Soft C and G

Name ____________________

The letter **c** followed by **e, i,** or **y** usually stands for the soft-**c** sound, as in **cent.** The letter **g** followed by **e, i,** or **y** usually stands for the soft-**g** sound, as in **page.** The letters **dge** also stand for the soft-**g** sound.

cent
(soft **c**)

pa**g**e
(soft **g**)

Read the words and name the pictures. Draw a line from each word to the picture it names.

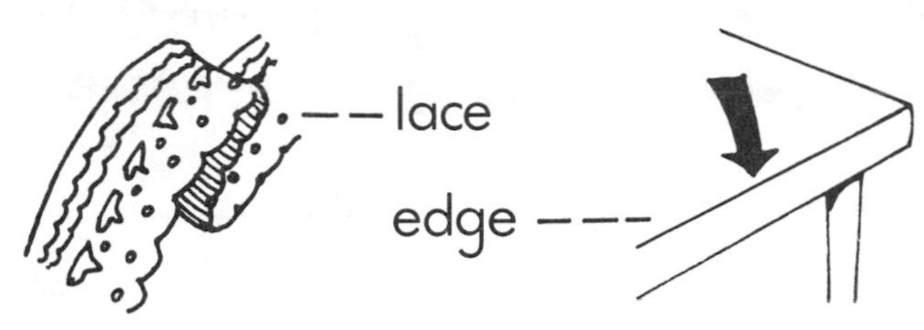

lace
edge

judge
ice

page
pencil

circus
bridge

stage
city

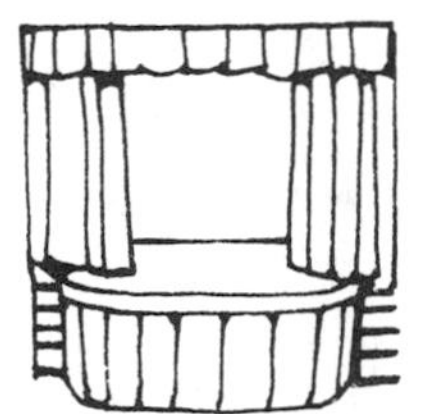

mice
cage

fence
judge

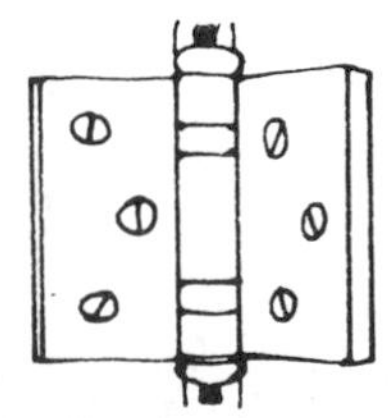

face
hinge

Soft C and G

Name ____________________

Read the words in the list below. Then name the pictures. Write the word from the list that names each picture.

fence	pencil	city	page	ice
edge	circus	cage	stage	

cent (soft **c**)

pa**g**e (soft **g**)

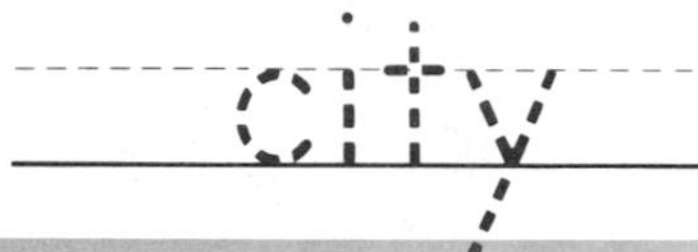

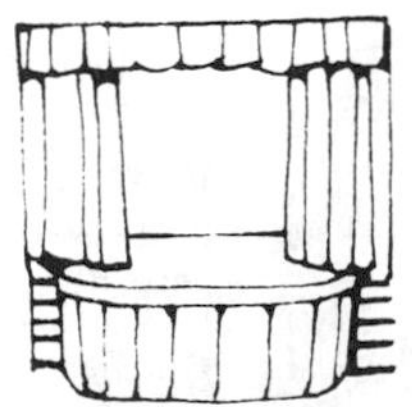

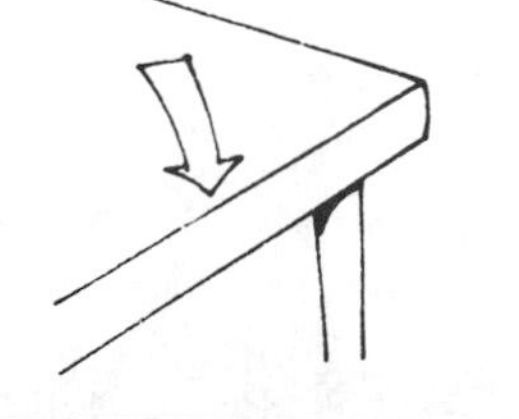

Soft C and G

Name ______________________

Read each sentence and the words beside it. Write the word that makes sense in each sentence.

cent
(soft **c**)

pa**g**e
(soft **g**)

1. Gus walked over the bridge.	bridge page change
2. Can you jump over the ______?	dance trace fence
3. Greg tore a ______ from the notebook.	judge cage page
4. Bruce will come to our ______.	rice city nice
5. Ginny put the bird in a big ______.	cage stage page
6. Our class show will be on the ______.	hinge stage judge
7. We can see clowns at the ______.	pencil circus face
8. I saw the cat clean its ______.	face race lace

Hard and Soft C and G

Name

Read the words and name the pictures. Circle the word that names each picture.

cat lace  cab face 	cap place car face 	page gas cage gate 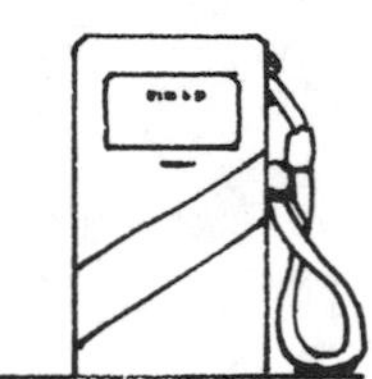
egg edge beg bridge 	page peg cage wig 	fence can face cob 
gate tag stage sag 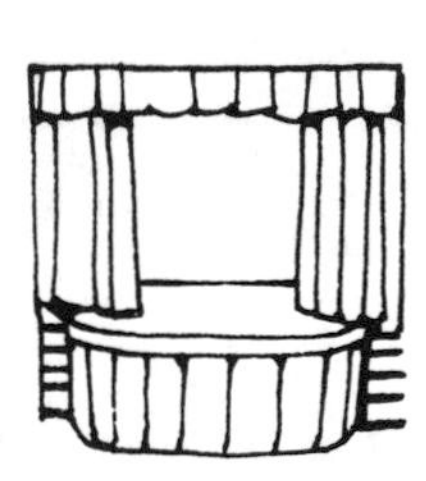	place cap trace cat 	bridge beg badge bug 
bridge bug badge bag 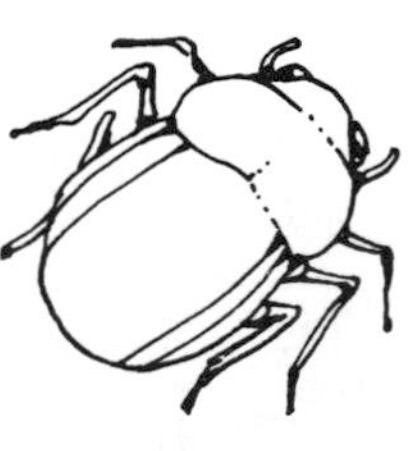	city car cent cat 	race cube place cup 

Review of symbol-sound association of hard- and soft-*c* and *g* words

Hard and Soft C and G

Name ______________________

Read each sentence and the words beside it. Circle the word that belongs in the sentence. Then write the word in the blank.

1.	Vince got his hair __cut__.	(cut) lace
2.	Mom got ________ for the car.	edge gas
3.	Bruce has a smile on his ________.	cab face
4.	My cat ate fish from a ________.	race can
5.	Gus is a ________ for the pet show.	judge hug
6.	Gene gave his ________ a pat.	dog stage
7.	We saw the children run the ________.	race cane
8.	Mother fixed a ________ for Nina.	nice coat
9.	I keep my bird in a ________.	wig cage

Reading and Writing Wrap-Up

Name ______________________________

Two Mice in a Cage

There once were two mice in a cage
Who wanted to go on the stage.
One could dance with a cane,
One could sing in the rain.
So they went on the stage in their cage.

A Goat in a Boat

There once was a funny brown goat
Who wanted to row in a boat.
So a boat she did make
And rowed out on a lake.
But the boat of the goat would not float.

1. Circle the words that tell about the mice.
   They could dance and sing.
   They wanted to go on the stage.
   They wanted new hats and coats.

2. Circle the words that tell about the goat.
   She wanted gas for her boat.
   She was a funny brown goat.
   She wanted to be a cow.

Literature

Name ______________________________

3. In each box, circle the two words that sound the same.

stage	cage	two	went	goat	float
rain	wanted	cane	make	once	lake

4. Circle the words that mean the same as *stage.*

   a place to sing and dance

   a place to eat good food

   a place to play games

5. Circle the words that mean the same as *float.*

   to row a boat

   to stay on top of the water

   to ride in a parade

6. Write a story about the mice in the cage or the goat in the boat. Tell about some other things the mice or the goat did. Make your story fun to read.

S Blends

Name

In some words, the letter **s** comes before another consonant. To say these words, blend the sound of **s** with the sound of the consonant that follows it.

scare **sp**in **sw**im
smile **st**op **sl**eep
skate **sn**ap **sq**uirrel

Read the words and look at the pictures. Draw a line from each word to the picture it tells about.

smile
steps

skates
sled

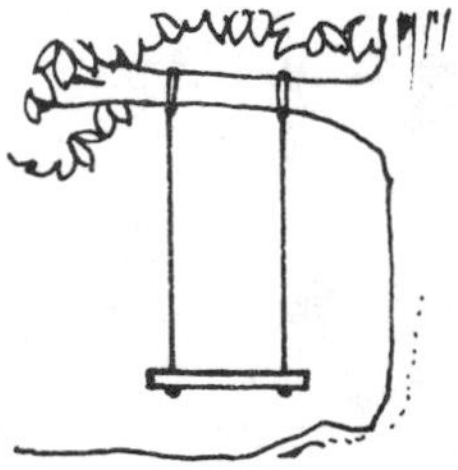

scale
swing

snap
square

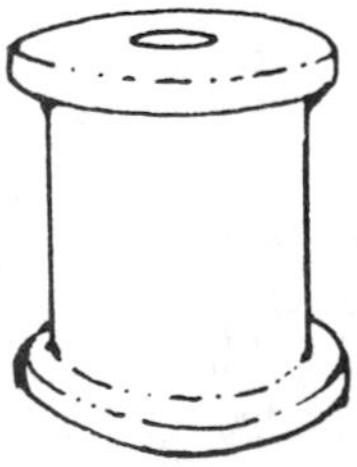

spool
squirrel

snail
smoke

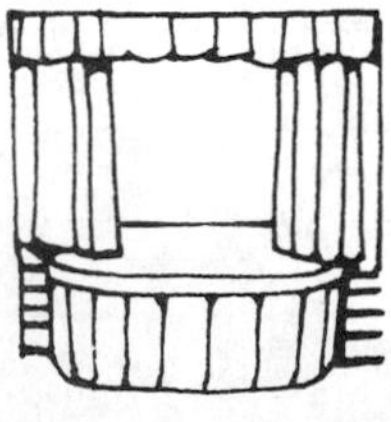

scare
stage

sleep
spoon

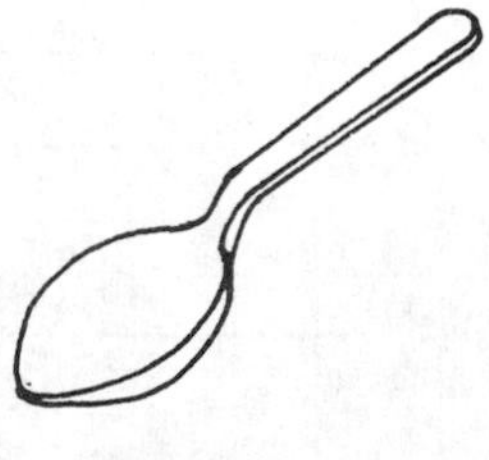

Symbol-sound association of words containing *s* blends: *st, sm, sk, sl, sc, sw, sn, sp*

S Blends

Name

Look at the pictures. Write the letters that stand for the beginning sound of each picture name.

skates	eep	one
oop	oon	ake
ing	oke	ide
uare	ore	ool

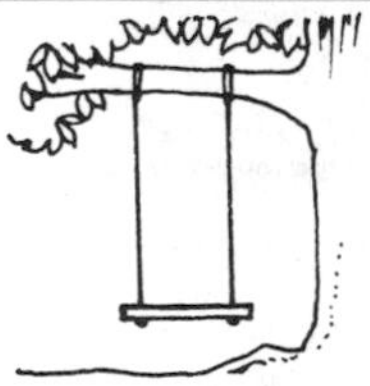

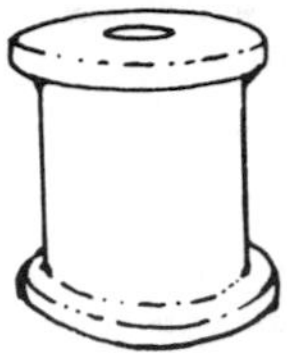

S Blends

Name ____________________

Read each sentence and the words beside it. Write the word that makes sense in each sentence.

1.	Skip went for a swim in the pool.	slim swim skim
2.	A ________ slid down the path.	stake snake scare
3.	This brown bread is ________.	scale stale snail
4.	Do you have a dime to ________?	spare stare square
5.	Try not to ________ on the ice.	snip skid swim
6.	Stella has a ________ on her face.	squirrel speak smile
7.	The fire made much ________.	slope smoke spoke
8.	Do you like to ________ rope?	slip skip snip
9.	Rosa likes to ice ________.	skate slate stake

Words containing s blends in context: *st, sm, sk, sl, sc, sw, sn, sp, sq*

L Blends

Name ______________________

In some words, the letter **l** follows another consonant. To say these words, blend the sound of the first consonant with the sound of **l.**

flower **bl**ue
play **gl**ad
clown

Read the words and look at the pictures. Draw a line from each word to the picture it tells about.

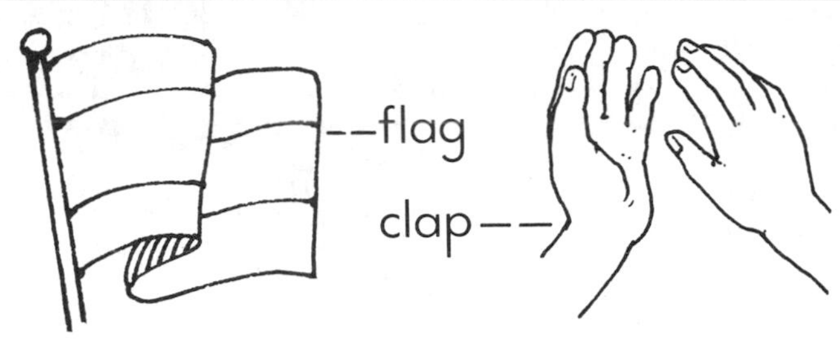

flag
clap

flame
clam

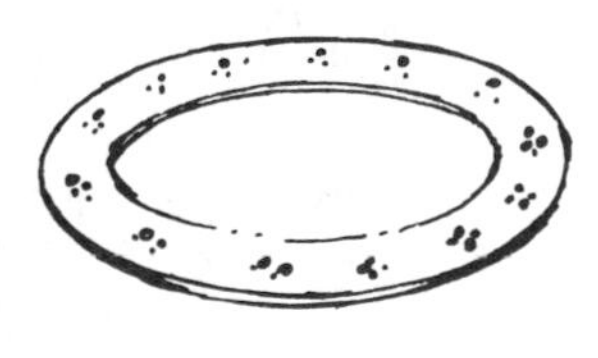

glass
plate

globe
float

clown
blow

flower
glow

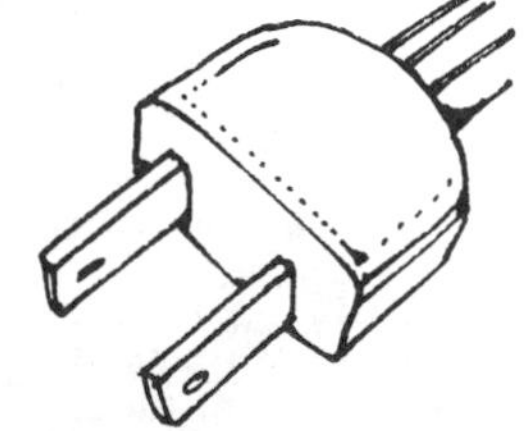

plug
club

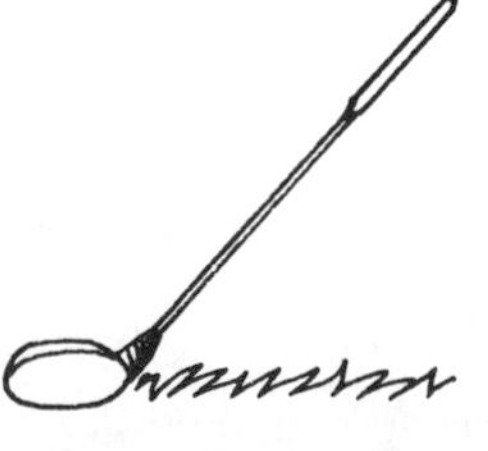

flute
fly

L Blends

Name

Look at the pictures. Write the letters that stand for the beginning sound of each picture name.

fl ag	ug	own
ate	obe	ow
ame	ip	ap
ant	ock	ute

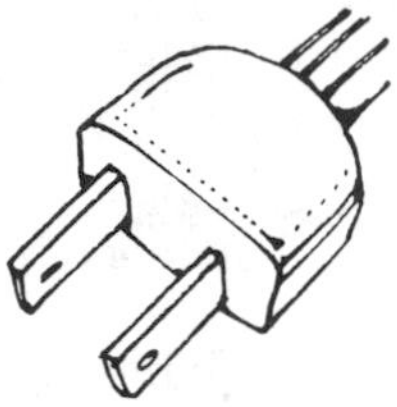

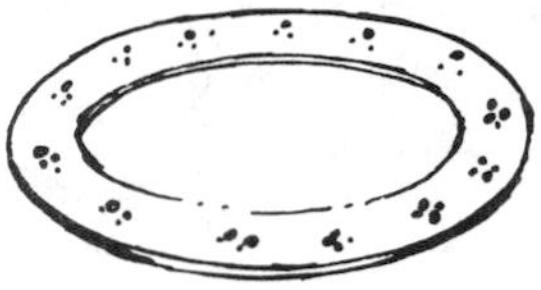

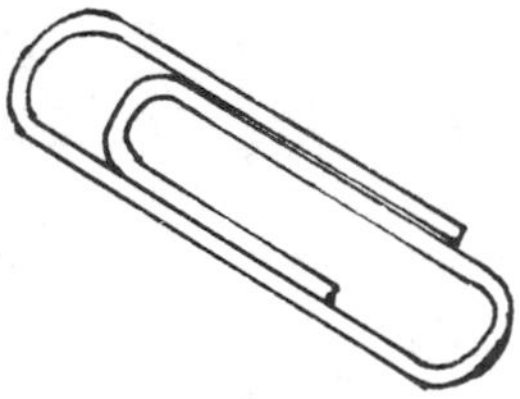

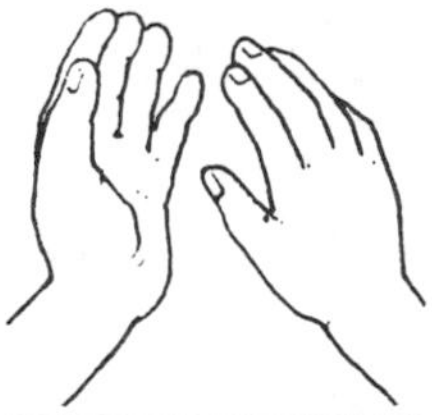

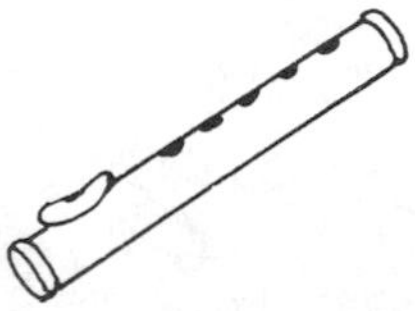

Sound-symbol association of words containing *l* blends: *fl, pl, cl, bl, gl*

L Blends

Name ______________________

Read each sentence and the words beside it. Write the word that makes sense in each sentence.

1.	Glen plays the flute.	flute club plug
2.	Our ______ flew at the top of a pole.	glad flag clam
3.	Please fill my ______ with milk.	class flash glass
4.	Cliff likes his ______ boat.	glue blue clue
5.	I have friends in my ______.	flat class glass
6.	Our class will ______ in this game.	clay glad play
7.	Is your ______ blue or green?	plate clam blame
8.	I am so ______ to see you.	glad flag play
9.	The light ______ in the night.	blows glows flows

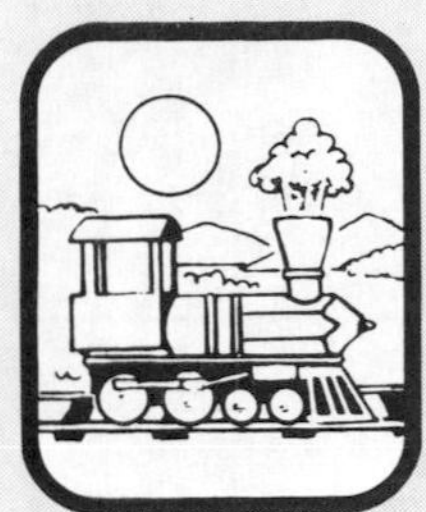

R Blends

Name ____________________

In some words, the letter **r** follows another consonant. To say these words, blend the sound of the first consonant with the sound of **r.**

frog **dr**ess
brown **pr**etty
green **tr**ee
cry

Read the words and look at the pictures. Draw a line from each word to the picture it tells about.

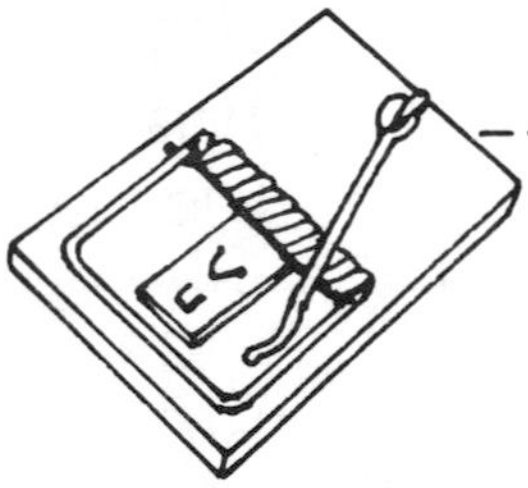
trap
crayon
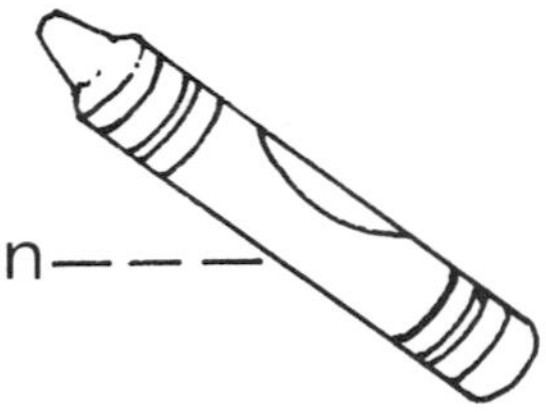

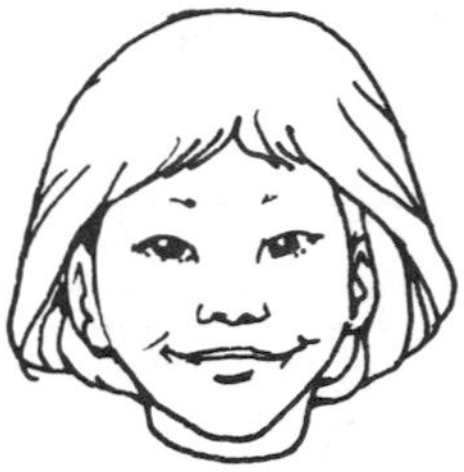
drum
grin
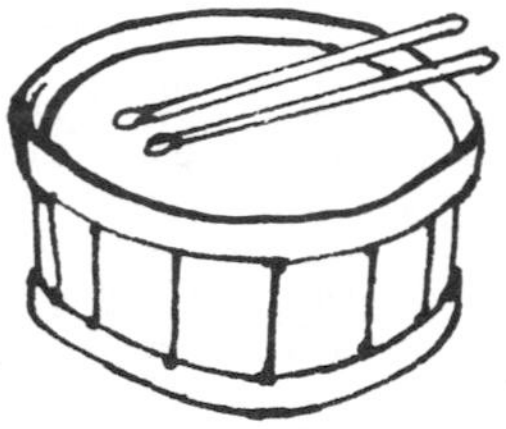

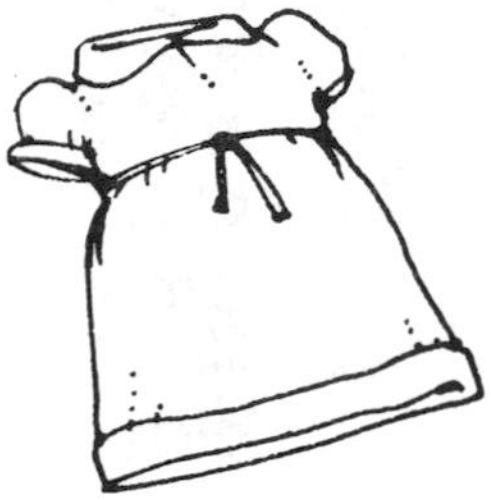
truck
dress
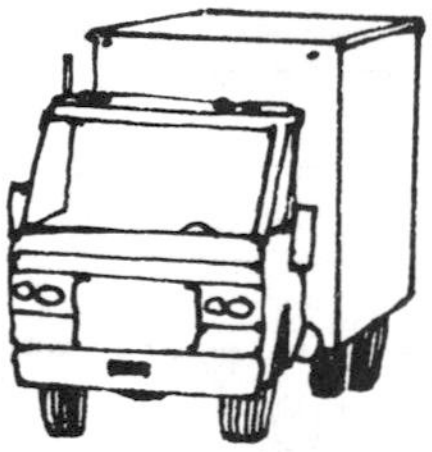

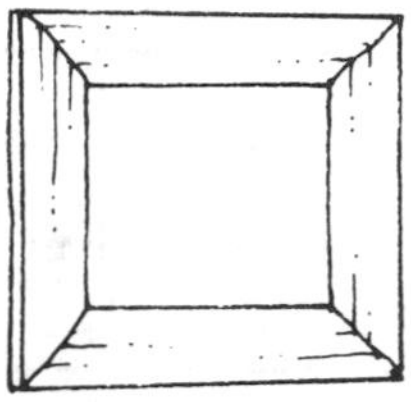
frame
prize
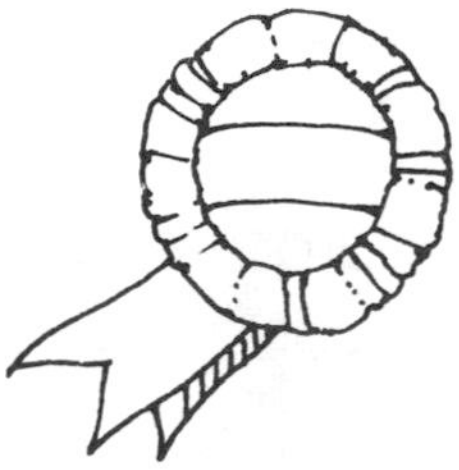

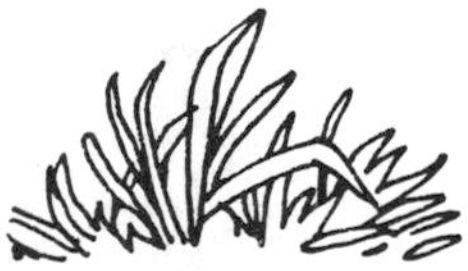
grass
tray
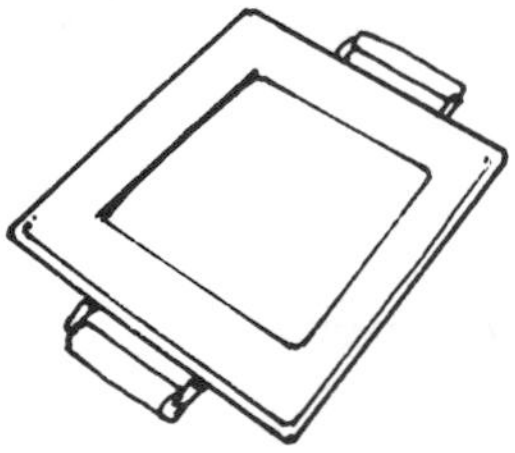

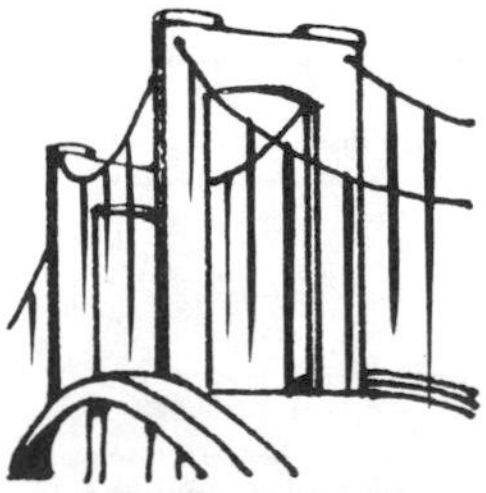
crow
bridge
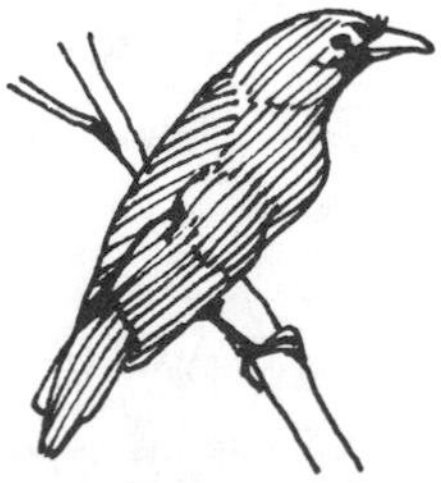

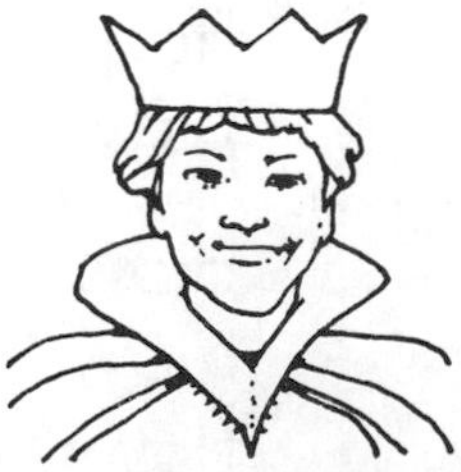
prince
crab
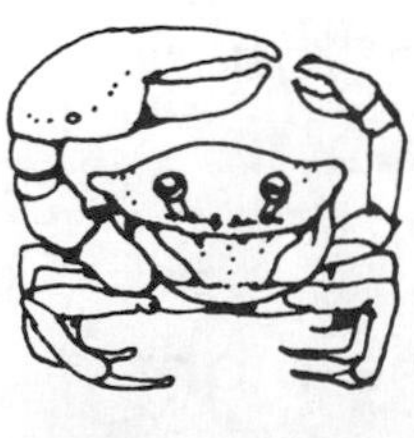

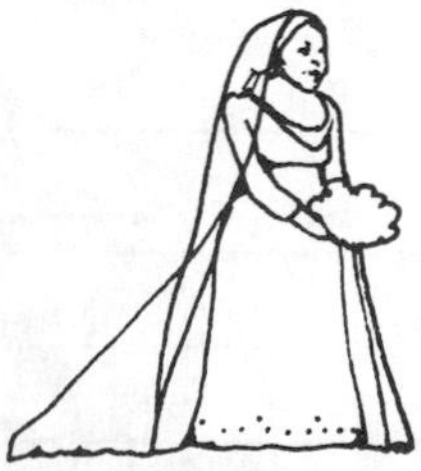
bride
frog
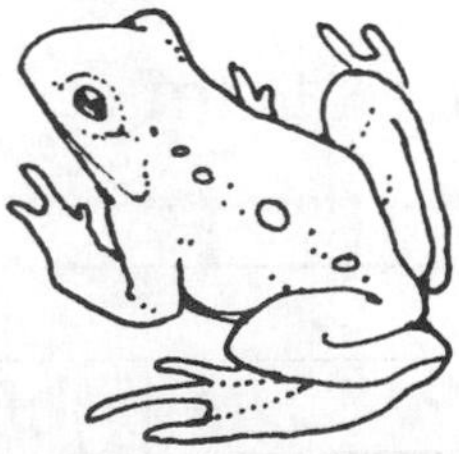

Symbol-sound association of words containing *r* blends: *fr, br, gr, cr, dr, pr, tr*

R Blends

Name

Name the pictures. Write the letters that stand for the beginning sound of each picture name.

broom	ib	og
ape	um	ize
ee	ame	idge
ow	uck	ess

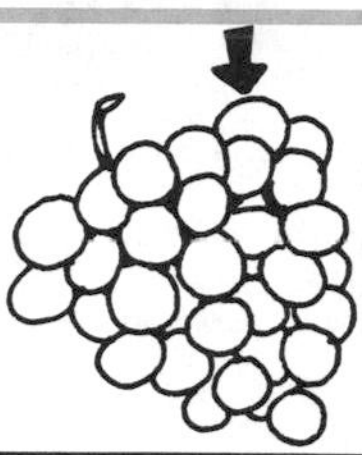

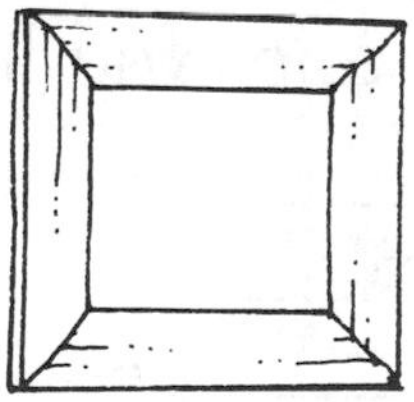

R Blends

Name

Read each sentence and the words beside it. Write the word that makes sense in each sentence.

1.	Fran took a trip on the train.	train drain brain
2.	My friend got first ________ for a painting.	press dress prize
3.	We took a ________ to the park.	trip drip grip
4.	Did the baby ________ in his crib?	cry try dry
5.	Is ________ the color you like best?	tray pray gray
6.	I broke my ________ pencil.	crown drown brown
7.	I saw a green ________ jump over a log.	frog trot from
8.	Juan likes ________ jam and bread.	price grape bride
9.	My mother can ________ a truck.	drive broke prize

S, L, and R Blends

Name ______________________

Read the words and look at the pictures. Circle the word that tells about each picture.

traps grapes globe slope 	price slice plate crate 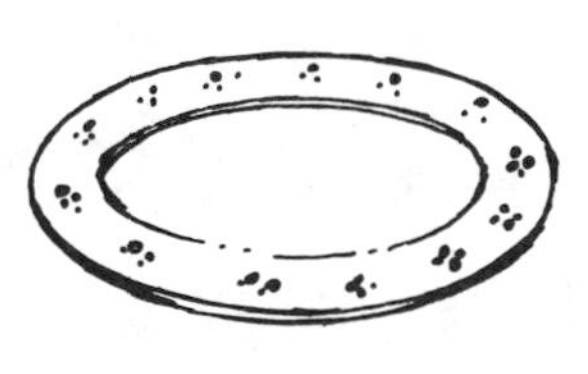	skin slip still swim 
stage scare stare square 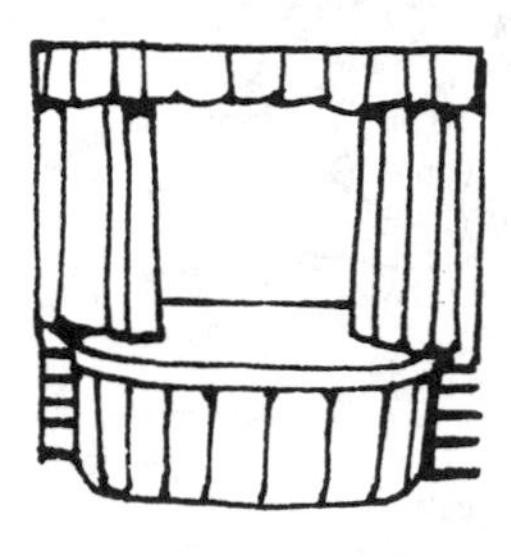	crow grow globe float 	crab clap slap glad 
snag flag smog frog 	skin spice smile slide 	free grow brown tree 
stake slate snake skate 	grin drip bridge blade 	blame frame squirrel float 

Ending Blends

Name ______________________

At the end of some words, the letter **s** comes before another consonant. To say these words, blend the sound of **s** with the sound of the consonant that follows it.

la**st**
de**sk**

Read the words and look at the pictures. Circle the word that tells about each picture.

toast tusk	most mask
dust desk	roast risk
fist task	husk chest
nest mask	cast ask

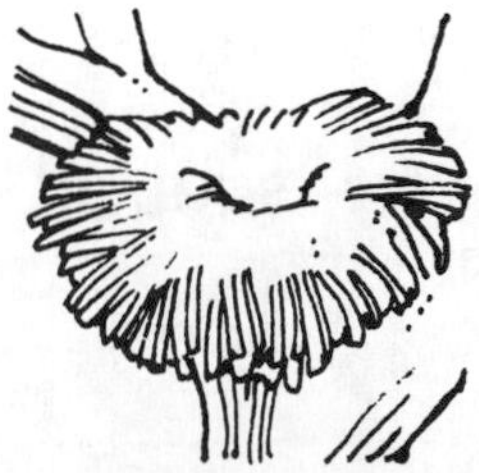

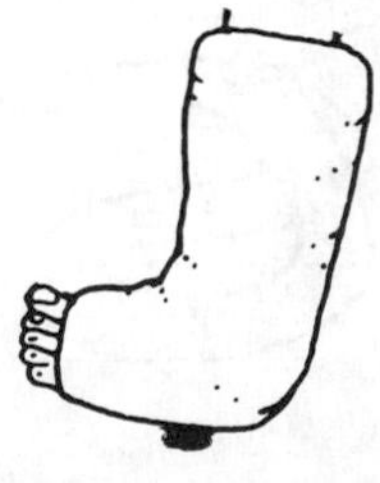

Symbol-sound association of words containing final blends: *st, sk*

Ending Blends

Name ______________________

Name the pictures. Write the letters that stand for the ending sound of each picture name.

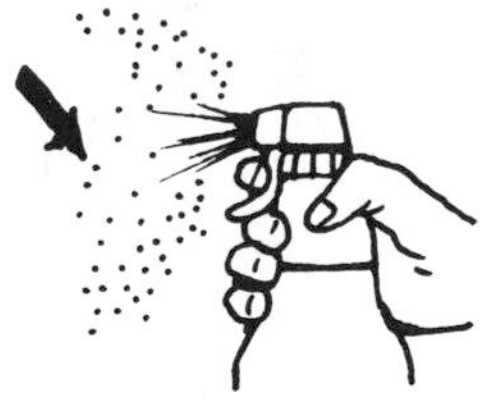

mist	ve	de
ne	ma	che
ca	fi	toa
tu	roa	li

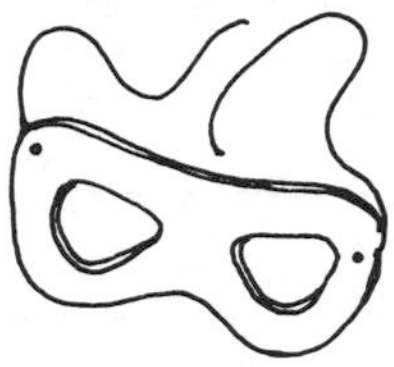

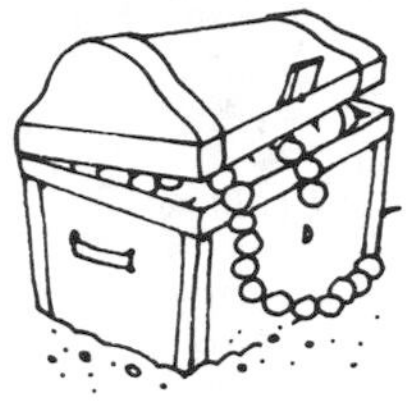

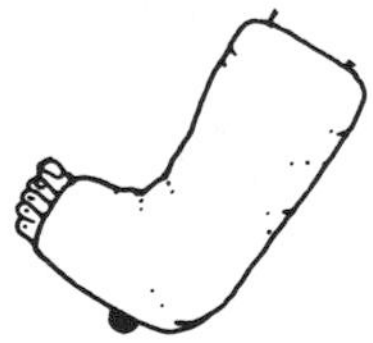

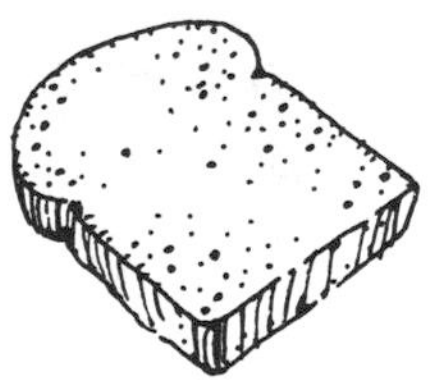

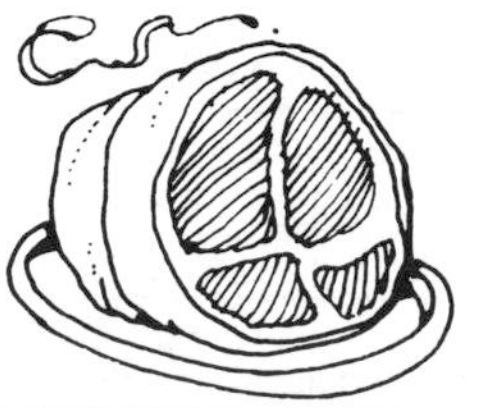

Ending Blends

Name ______________________

Read each sentence and the words beside it. Write the word that makes sense in each sentence.

1.	Lin made a ___list___ of her jobs.	last list lost
2.	James has the book on his ____________.	mask desk most
3.	Della filled the ____________ with books.	cast chest tusk
4.	I like to eat eggs and ____________.	toast tusk task
5.	Jane made a funny ____________ for the party.	ask desk mask
6.	Wendy hit the ball with her ____________.	fist risk fast
7.	Did you ____________ your friends for help?	mast mask ask
8.	I fed the bird a ____________ of bread.	crust risk cast
9.	The old toys were full of ____________.	desk dust most

Ending Blends

Name ______________________

Read the words and name the pictures. Circle the word that names each picture.

cost (cast) most mask	dust desk mask most	vest test tusk most
task tusk test nest	crust roast toast tusk	last lost list tusk
tusk crust cast cost	dust desk mask must	mask must most nest
chest crust tusk test	fast task fist tusk	toast roast test task

Ending Blends

Name ________________________

At the end of some words, two consonants appear together. To say these words, blend the sounds of the two consonants together.

ha**nd**
ba**nk**
se**nt**
sta**mp**

Read the words and look at the pictures. Draw a line from each word to the picture it tells about.

stand

stamp

pond

plant

band

bank

stump

skunk

paint

pump

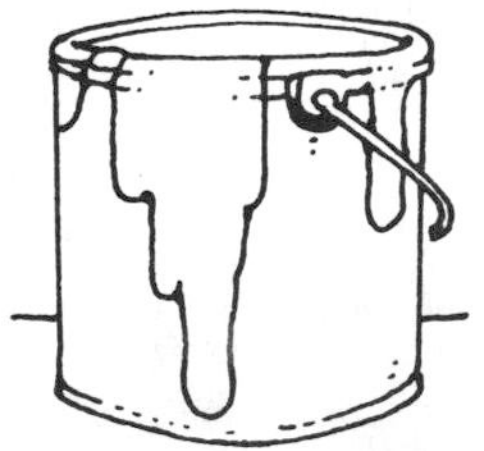

wind

wink

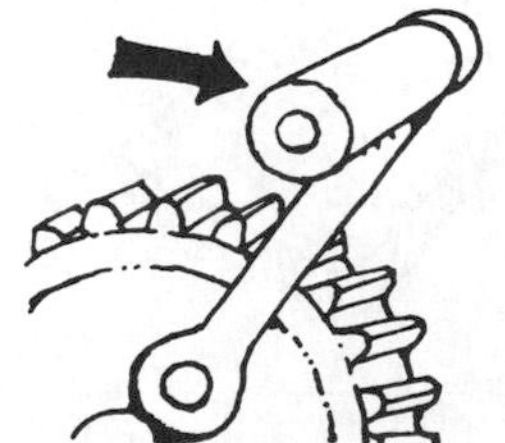

crank

cent

stamp

sink

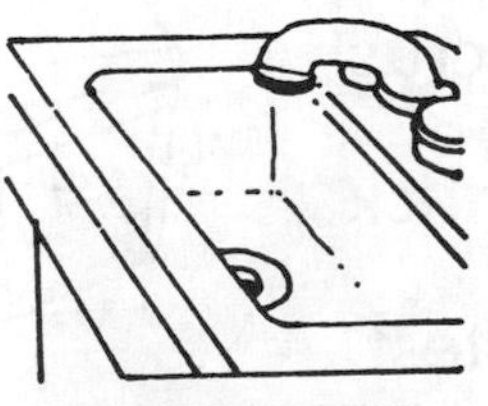

Symbol-sound association of words containing final blends: *nd, nk, nt, mp*

Ending Blends

Name ______________________

Name the pictures. Write the letters that stand for the ending sound of each picture name.

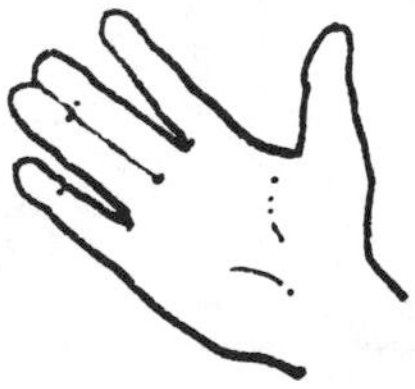 hand	 ba	 a
 la	 po	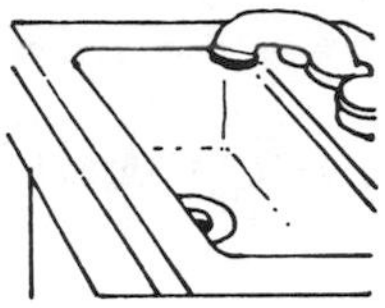 si
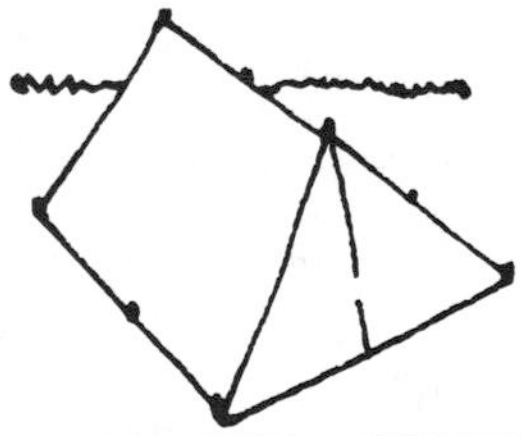 te	 ce	 sta
 wi	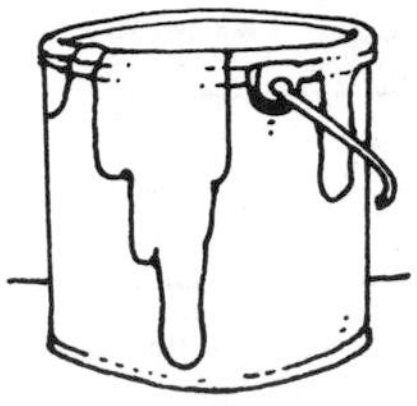 pai	 pu

Sound-symbol association of words containing final blends: *nd, nk, nt, mp*

Ending Blends

Name ______________________

Read each sentence and the words beside it. Write the word that makes sense in each sentence.

1.	Ling went into her ___tent___.	mend tent damp
2.	Please put the plates in the ______.	sink send sent
3.	Nancy will be going to ______ this year.	hand camp cent
4.	The breeze feels cool blowing over my ______.	hint honk hand
5.	Ken hunts for the best seeds to ______.	paint plant tent
6.	A ______ lights the ramp near the door.	lamp pond pink
7.	The penny went clink inside my ______.	band bank wink
8.	Did you put a ______ on the letter?	stand stamp skunk
9.	The ______ blew all night.	wink wind went

Words containing final blends in context: *nd, nk, nt, mp*

Ending Blends

Name ______________________________

Read the words and name the pictures. Circle the word that names each picture.

pink plant past pond 	bump blast band bank 	pest pond paint pump 
mend mint most mask 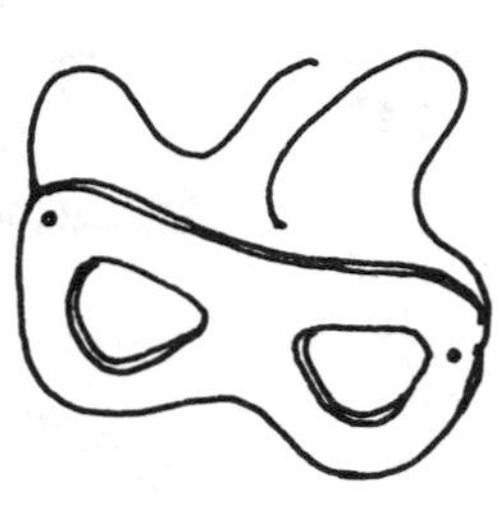	vest desk bend cent 	skunk stump stand slant 
sent sand stamp skunk 	tank task test tent 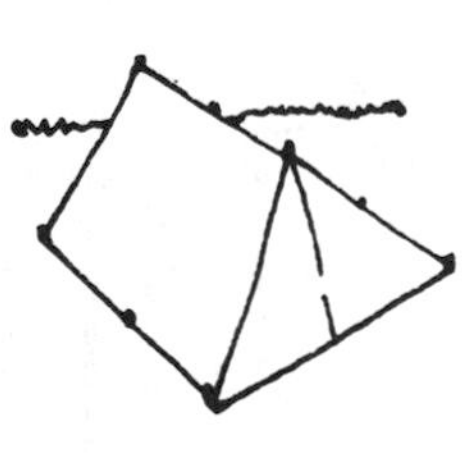	hand hump honk hint 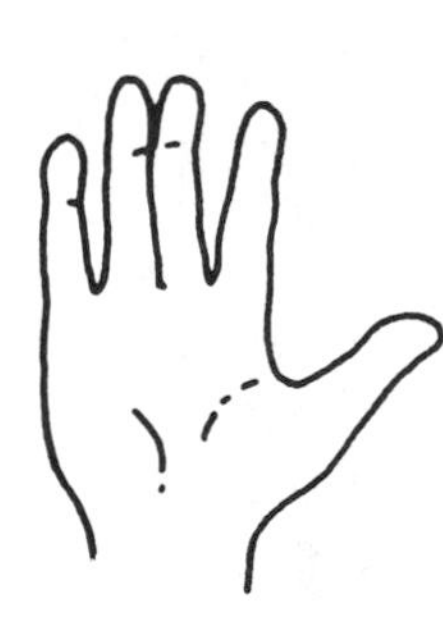
crust crank cramp cast 	dust desk drink damp 	best sent mend nest 

Review of symbol-sound association of words containing final blends: *st, sk, nd, nk, nt, mp*

Ending Blends

Name ______________________

At the end of some words, two consonants appear together. To say these words, blend the sounds of the two consonants together.

be**lt**
wo**lf**
gi**ft**

Read the words and look at the pictures. Draw a line from each word to the picture it tells about.

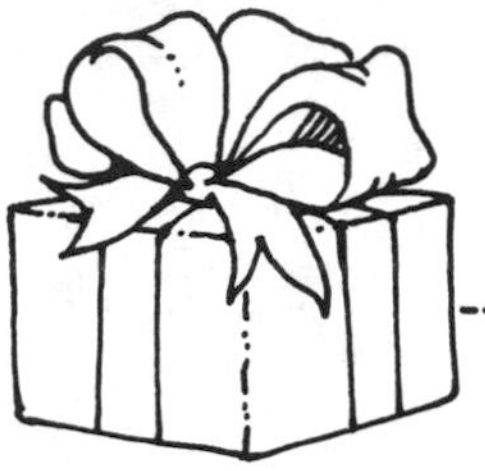

raft	gift	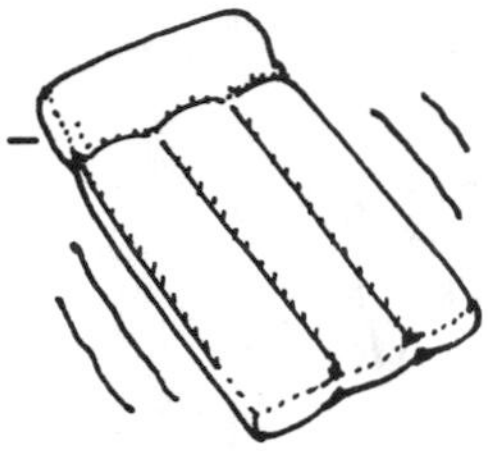
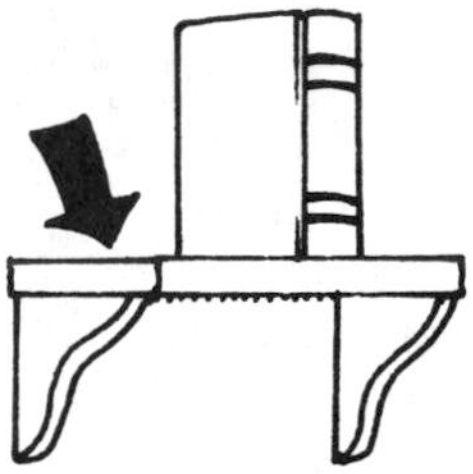	shelf	elf
	wilt	quilt
	gift	lift
	wolf	elf
	melt	belt
	golf	shelf
	lift	raft

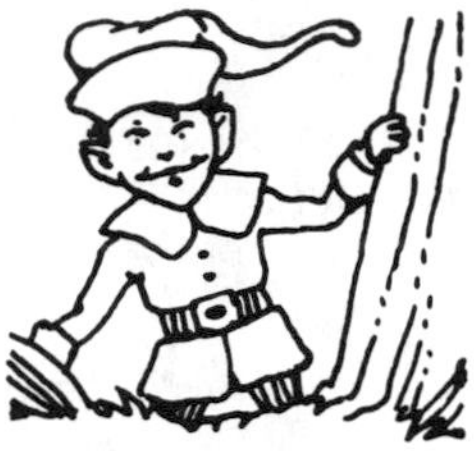

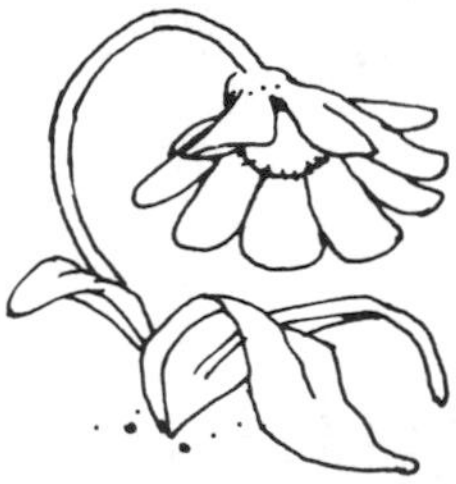

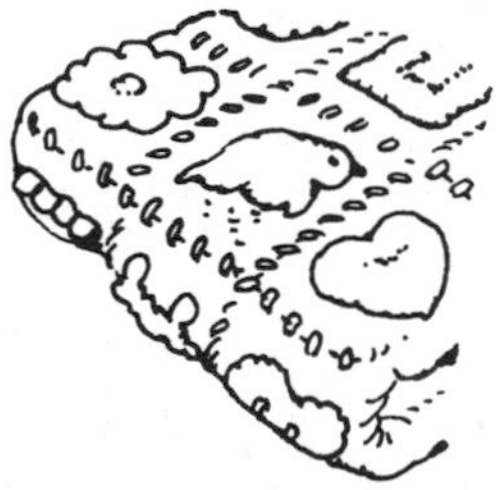

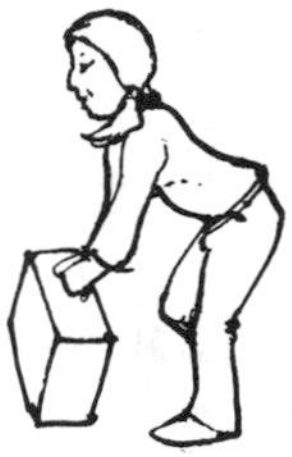

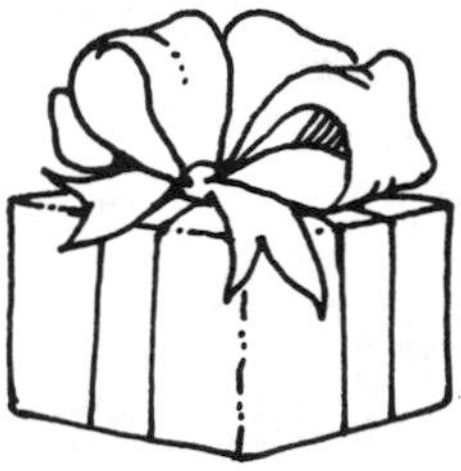

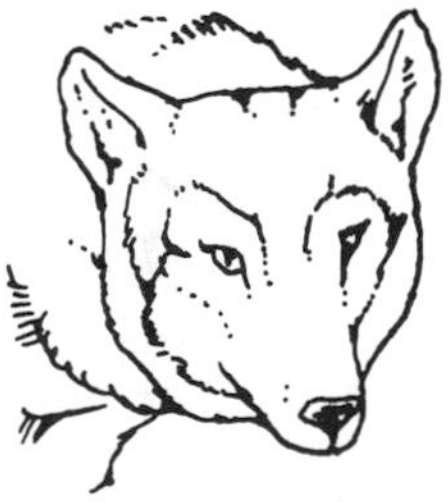

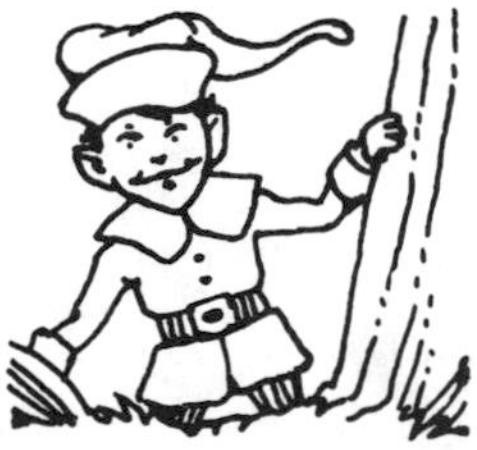

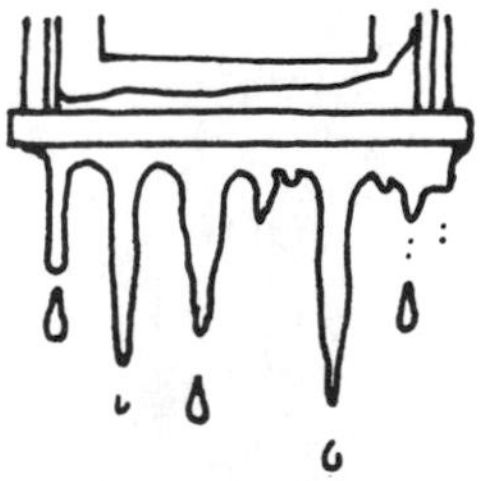

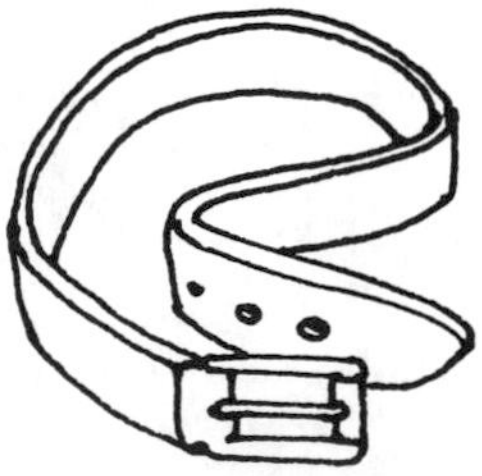

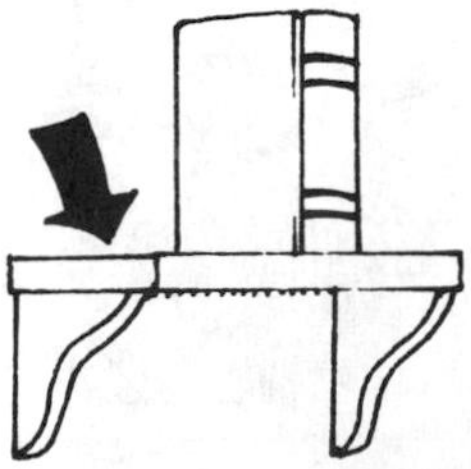

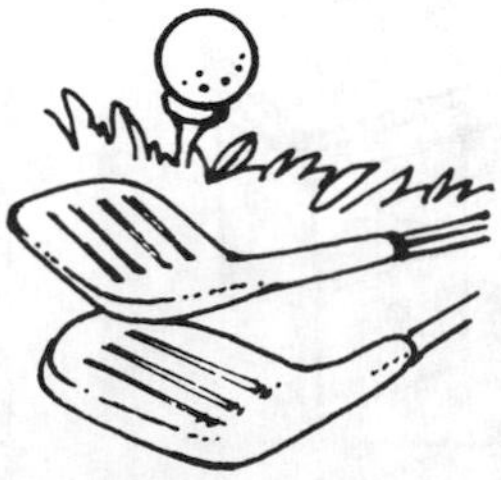

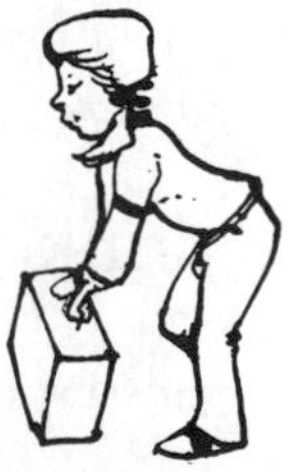

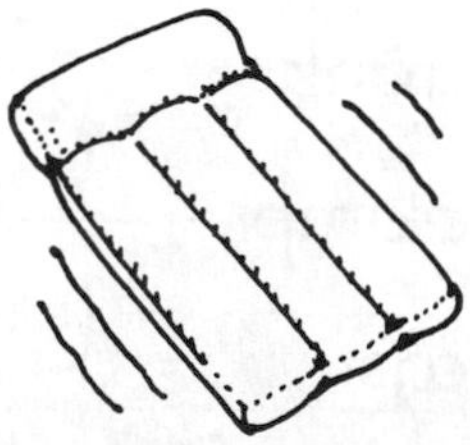

Ending Blends

Name

Look at the pictures. Write the letters that stand for the ending sound of each picture name.

quilt

gi

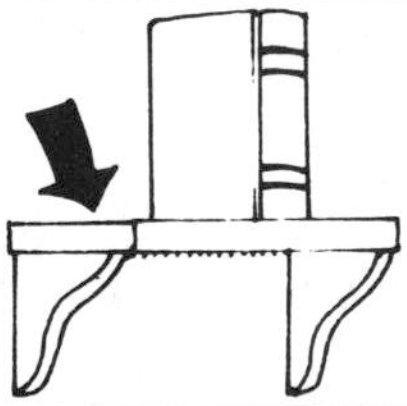

she

e

go

be

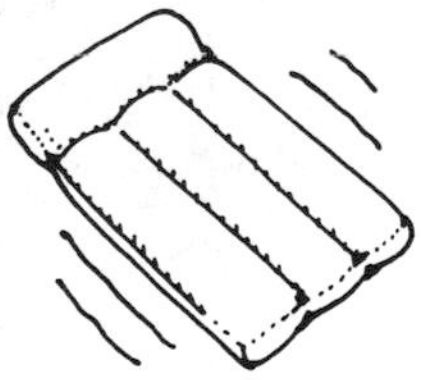

ra

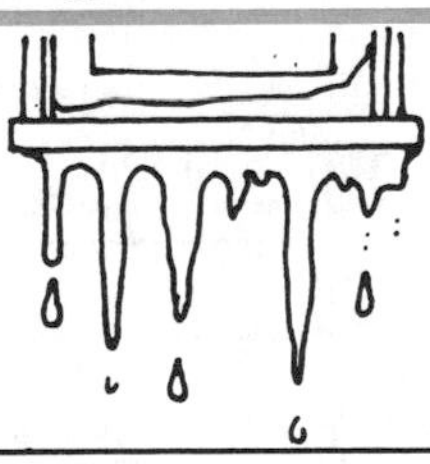

me

li

wo

wi

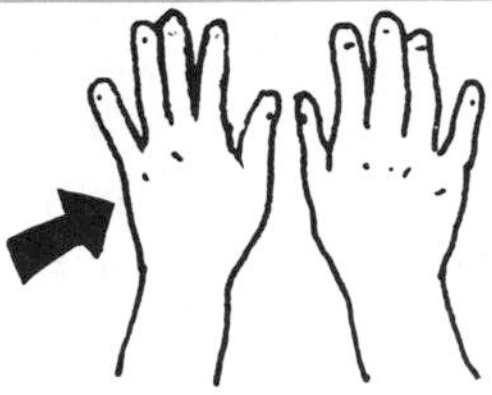

le

Ending Blends

Name ______________________

Read each sentence and the words beside it. Write the word that makes sense in each sentence.

1.	We will float down the creek on a raft.	golf gift raft
2.	Fran played ______________ all day long.	left golf soft
3.	My new ______________ fits well.	elf belt help
4.	Jane can ______________ that box from the shelf.	lift left felt
5.	The grass felt ______________ under my feet.	soft shelf melt
6.	Bobby got a raft for a birthday ______________.	left golf gift
7.	Did all of the ice ______________?	felt left melt
8.	Dad made a new ______________ for my books.	shift melt shelf
9.	We found a baby ______________ in the woods.	wolf golf lift

Words containing final blends in context: *lt, lf, ft*

Ending Blends

Name

Read the words and look at the pictures. Circle the word that tells about each picture.

belt wilt quilt (melt) 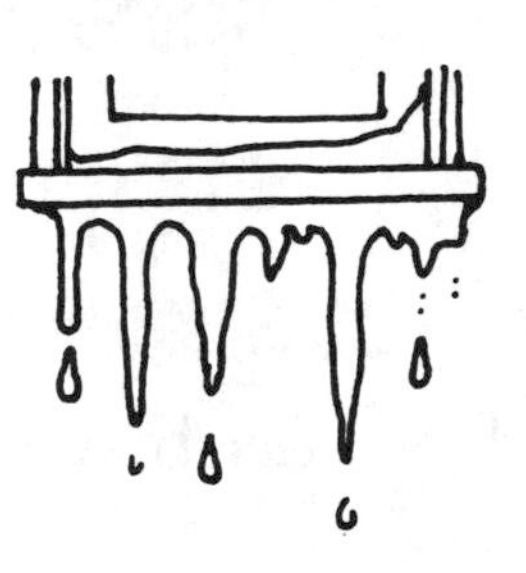	elf wolf golf shelf 	golf elf shelf soft 
lift left gift golf 	sift soft golf gift 	quilt gift shelf shift 
elf belt melt wolf 	felt melt belt soft 	soft sift gift raft 
felt belt shelf shift 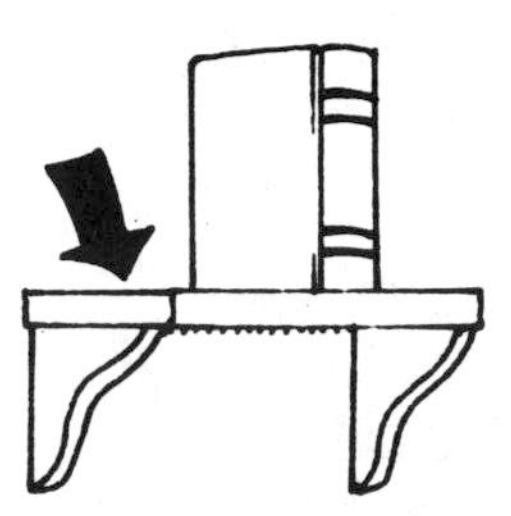	craft drift lift gift 	shelf elf self golf 

Review of symbol-sound association of words containing final blends: *lt, lf, ft*

Three-Letter Blends

Name ______________________

In some words, the letter **s** comes before other consonants. To say these words, blend the sound of **s** with the sounds of the consonants that follow it.

split
spring
scream
strip

Read the words and look at the pictures. Draw a line from each word to the picture it tells about.

spring
string

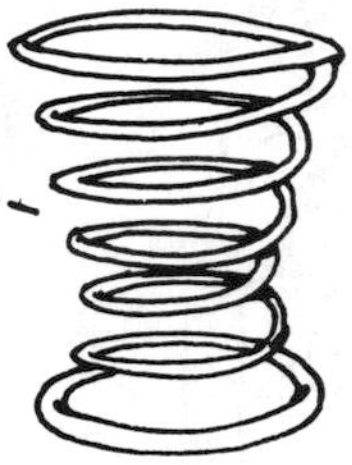

street
scream

spray
strap

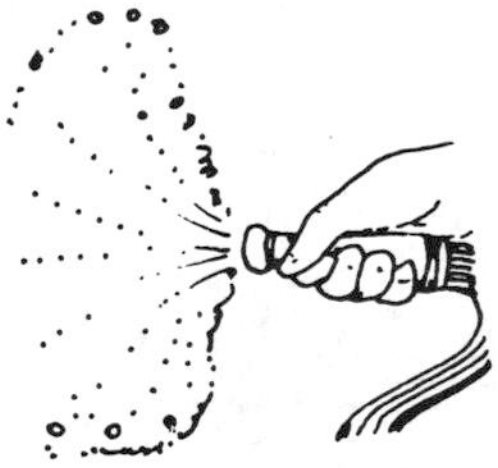

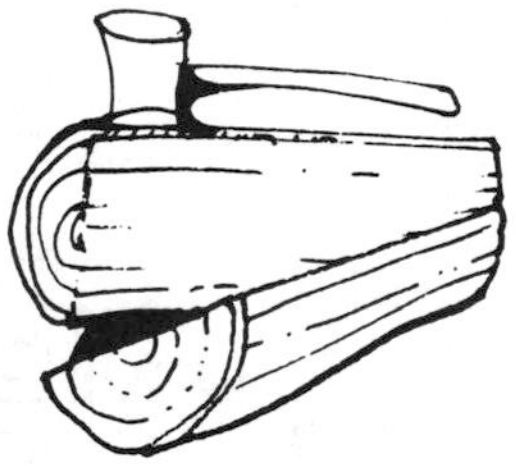

sprain
split

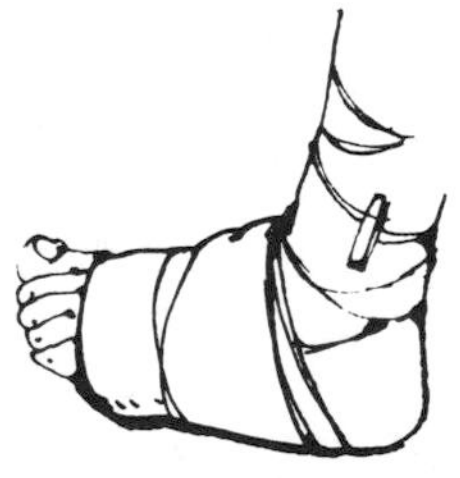

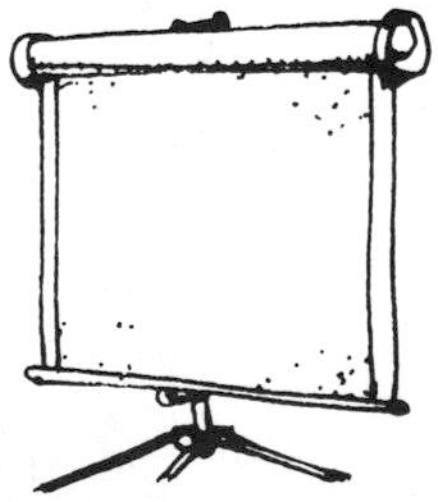

screen
stream

splash
stripes

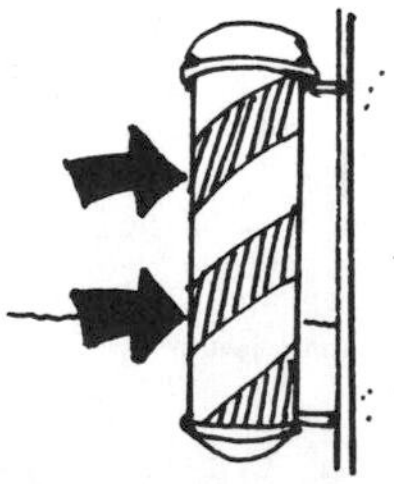

scrape
strong

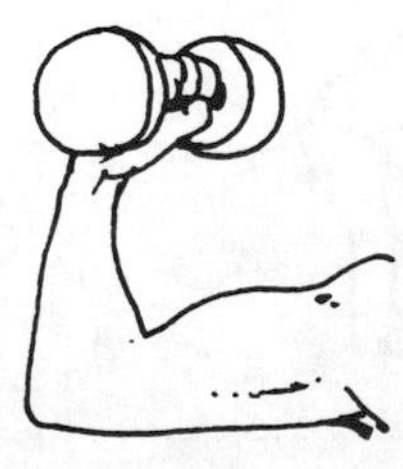

scrub
strap

Symbol-sound association of words containing three-letter blends: *spl, spr, scr, str*

Three-Letter Blends

Name ______________________

Look at the pictures. Write the letters that stand for the beginning sound of each picture name.

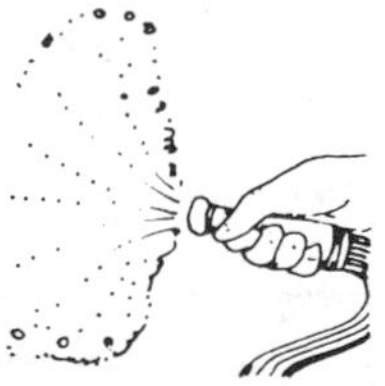

spray	___it	___ub
___ipe	___ing	___ain
___een	___ash	___ing
___eam	___ape	___eet

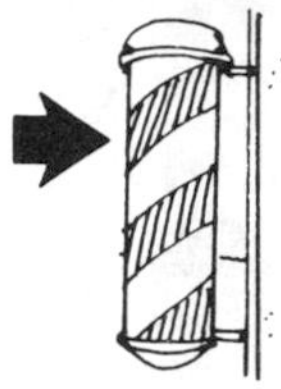

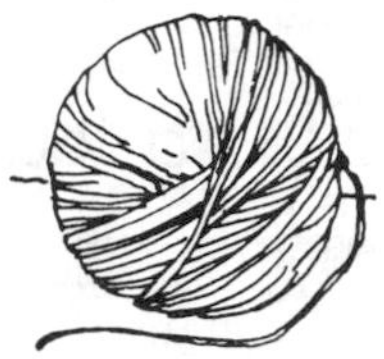

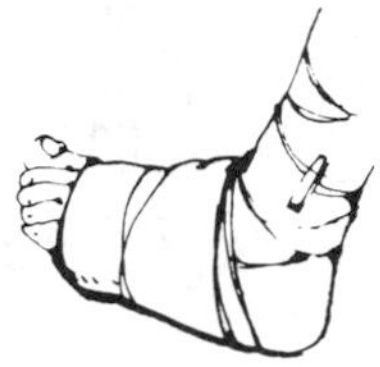

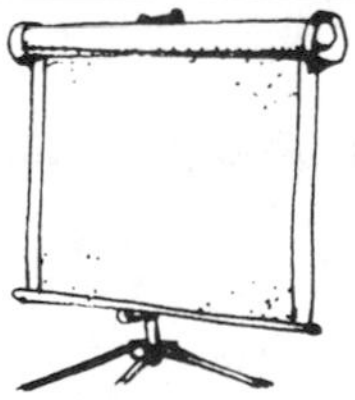

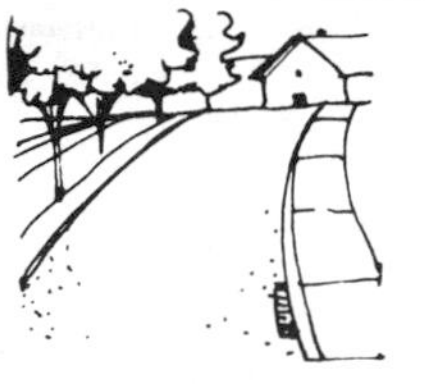

Three-Letter Blends

Name ______________________________

Read each sentence and the words beside it. Write the word that makes sense in each sentence.

1.	Some stripes were painted down the street.	spring street scream
2.	The ____________ on my helmet had stripes.	scrap strap spray
3.	An ax can ____________ a log in two.	strap scrub split
4.	A screw came out of our window ____________.	screen scream stream
5.	Does Dad ____________ water on the garden?	strap stray spray
6.	Jan springs into the pool with a ____________.	split splash strap
7.	I like to see the flowers in ____________.	string spring split
8.	Chan has a ____________ on his hand.	strange scratch scrub
9.	Ben found a big ball of ____________.	spring string scream

Three-Letter Blends

Name ______________________________

Read the words and look at the pictures. Circle the word that tells about each picture.

stray spray spring string	scrap scrub strap strip	strip string split splash
strap scrap strange scrape	spring strap stray spray	streak street screen scream
string split stripe spring	screen scream streak stream	sprain strain street screen
scrape scrap strange strap	string stripe split splash	sprain spray stray strange

Review of symbol-sound association of words containing three-letter blends: *spl, spr, scr, str*

Blends

Name

Read the words in the list below. Then read the clues that follow. Write a word from the list to match each clue.

mask	street	tent	crib	bank	cost
spring	spoon	glass	lift	lamp	crow

1. a bed for a baby
   crib
2. something to drink from
3. a tool used for eating
4. a road in a town or city
5. the time of year before summer
6. something that gives light
7. a thing to hide the face
8. something to live in at camp
9. to pick something up
10. a place to keep money
11. the price of something
12. a black bird

Silent Consonants

Name ____________________

In some words, two consonants stand for one sound. The letters **kn** usually stand for the sound of **n,** as in **knot.** The letters **wr** usually stand for the sound of **r,** as in **write.**

knot

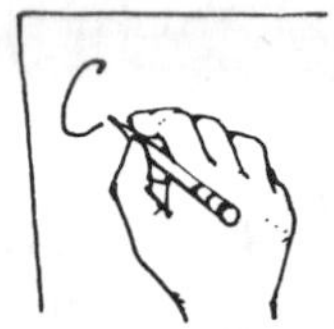

write

Look at the pictures. Circle the letter or letters that stand for the beginning sound in each picture name.

wr w	kn k	kn k
wr w	wr w	kn k
kn k	kn k	wr w
wr w	kn k	kn k

Silent Consonants

Name ______________________

Read the words and look at the pictures. Circle the word that tells about each picture.

 knit kit 	wrist wagon 	knob kite 
wrist wish 	knee key 	know king 
wrote well 	write wing 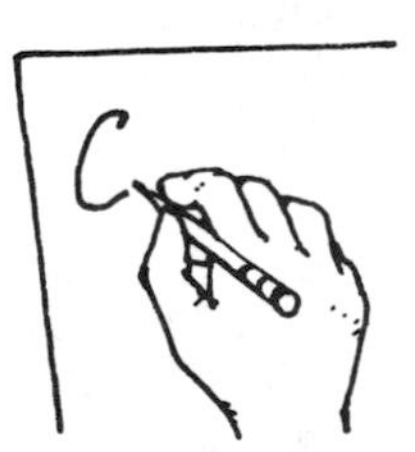	kneel keep 
knot kitten 	wrap wag 	wrong water 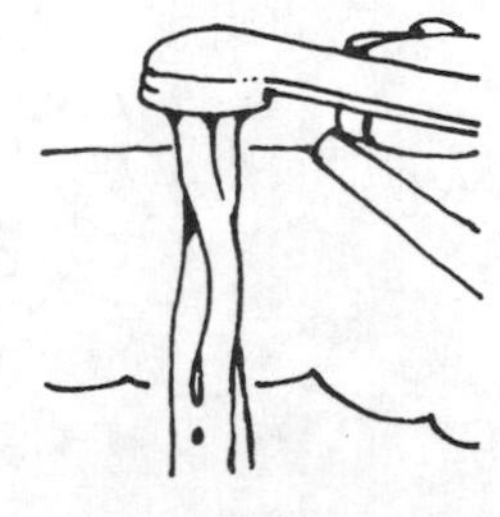

Symbol-sound association of words containing silent consonants: *kn, wr*

Silent Consonants

Name ______________________

Read each sentence and the words beside it. Write the word that makes sense in each sentence.

knot **wr**ite

1.	I fell and scraped my knee.	knee knot know
2.	We drove down the ______________ street.	wrap wrong wrist
3.	The ______________ on that door is old.	knob knot knee
4.	Did you find a ______________ in the rope?	knot knit knob
5.	Kate will ______________ a letter.	wrist wrote write
6.	We need a ______________ to cut the apple.	knob knife knot
7.	I hurt my left ______________.	write wrap wrist
8.	We heard a ______________ on the door.	knock know knit
9.	Will you help me ______________ the gift?	wrap wrong wrote

Silent Consonants

Name ______________________________

In some words, two consonants stand for one sound. The letters **ck** usually stand for the sound of **k,** as in **duck.**

du**ck**

Read the words and name the pictures. Circle the word that names each picture.

truck trick	pack pick	tack track
deck dock	clock click	luck lock
pocket jacket	rock rack	brick block
stack sack	track truck	sock sick

Silent Consonants

Name ______________________

Read the words in the list below. Then name the pictures. Write a word from the list that names each picture.

check	rock	pocket	brick	lock
duck	chick	rocket	clock	

du**ck**

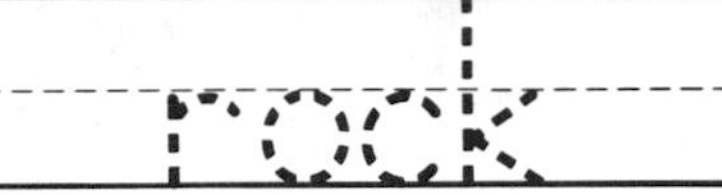

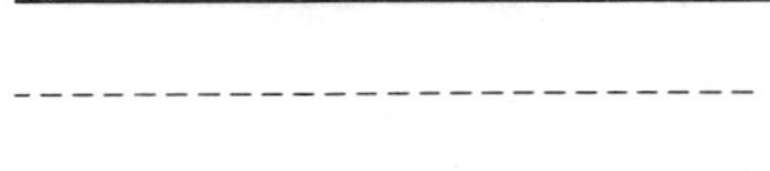

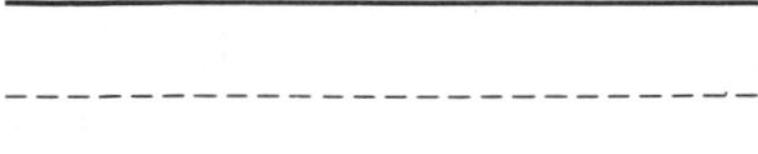

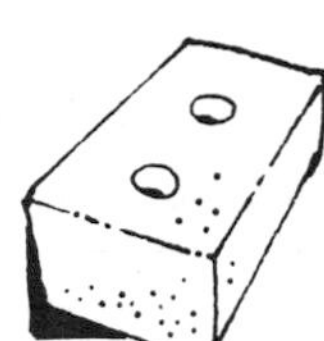

Silent Consonants

Name ____________________

Read each sentence and the words beside it. Write the word that makes sense in each sentence.

du**ck**

1.	A __duck__ sat on the boat dock.	deck duck peck
2.	Rick put his ____________ into a sack.	snack stack smack
3.	Please check the time on the ____________.	clock click cluck
4.	Put that ____________ back in the stack.	black back brick
5.	You will find the book on this ____________.	rack back lock
6.	Pam put a ____________ on the bike rack.	lock lack lick
7.	Ice was ____________ and slick on the steps.	trick thick brick
8.	The train is coming down the ____________.	trick track black
9.	See the six baby ____________!	chicks sticks thicks

Silent Consonants

Name ______________________________

When the letters **gh** appear together in a word, both the **g** and the **h** are usually silent.

ni**gh**t

Read the words and look at the pictures. Circle the word that tells about each picture.

fright

bright

night

light

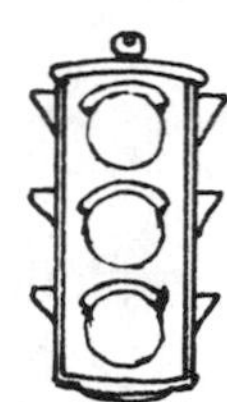

eighty

tight

fight

knight

high

sigh

eight

might

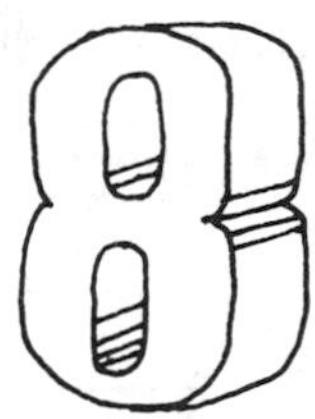

sight

night

straight

light

Silent Consonants

Name ______________________________

Read each sentence and the words beside it. Write the word that makes sense in each sentence.

1.	Birds fly ___high___ over our heads.	sight sigh high
2.	My blue shirt is too ____________.	bright flight tight
3.	Our class sits in ____________ lines.	sight straight sigh
4.	Mrs. Wright will stay for ____________ days.	eight night tight
5.	Becky can see the moon at ____________.	right night sight
6.	Jim reads by the ____________ over his bed.	flight light might
7.	A ____________ light showed us the path.	bright right fight
8.	The birds took ____________ to a tree.	bright flight night
9.	Is a brave ____________ in the story?	bright knight high

Silent Consonants

Name ______________________

Read the words below. Then read the sentences. Write the word that makes sense in each sentence.

tight	right	high	might	sigh
night	light	eight	sight	

1. Shane likes to read a story each night.
2. My puppy is ______________ weeks old.
3. The bird flew ______________ in the sky.
4. Please turn on a ______________.
5. My black shoes are too ______________.
6. We ______________ go with you.
7. Do you have the ______________ answer?
8. We like to catch ______________ of a deer.
9. Meg heard a loud ______________.

Silent Consonants

Name

Read the words and look at the pictures. Circle the word that tells about each picture.

check chick click clock	knob knot knock know	wrist wrote write wrong
light tight night sight	rack rock sock stuck	locket rocket jacket pocket
rock sock lock dock	knit knob knee kneel	wrist wrote wrong wrap
knock knob knit knee	wrong wrap wrist write	knife knight bright fright

Review of symbol-sound association of words containing silent consonants: *kn, wr, ck, gh*

Silent Consonants

Name ____________________

Read the words in the list below. Then read the clues that follow. Write a word from the list to match each clue.

snack	clock	knee	night	knife	wrong
kneel	rock	duck	write	eight	light

1. a bird that likes to swim

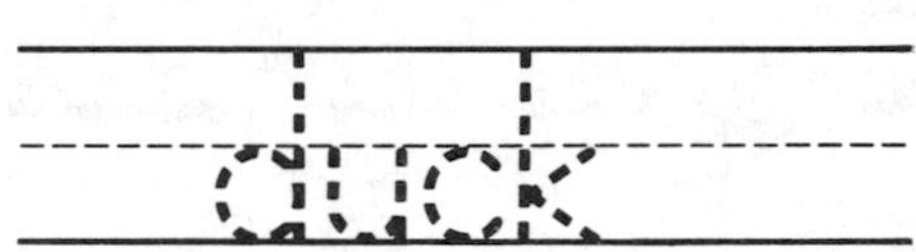

2. the time when it is dark

3. a stone

4. the middle of the leg

5. to put words on paper

6. something to eat

7. a thing that tells the time

8. a tool used to cut meat

9. not right

10. four plus four

11. opposite of dark

12. to get down on the knees

Vowel Pairs: *AI* and *AY*

Name ______________________________

In some words, two vowels together stand for the sound of the first vowel. **Train** has the long-**a** sound spelled **ai. Hay** has the long-**a** sound spelled **ay.**

tr**ai**n

h**ay**

Read the words and look at the pictures. Circle the word that tells about each picture.

train tray	tail stay	say sail
stain spray	clay chain	hail hay
paint pay	may mail	rain ray

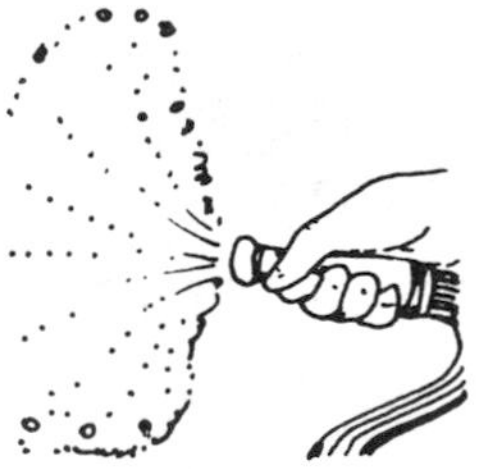

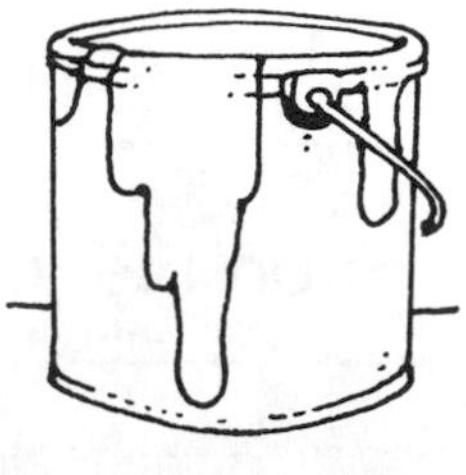

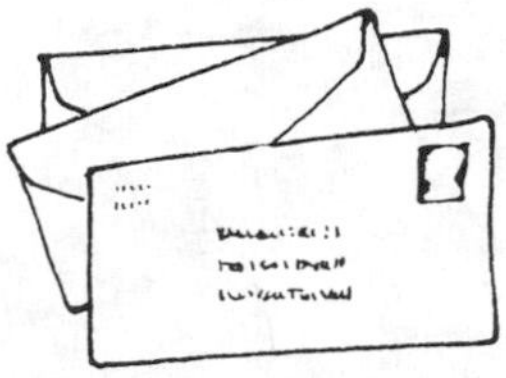

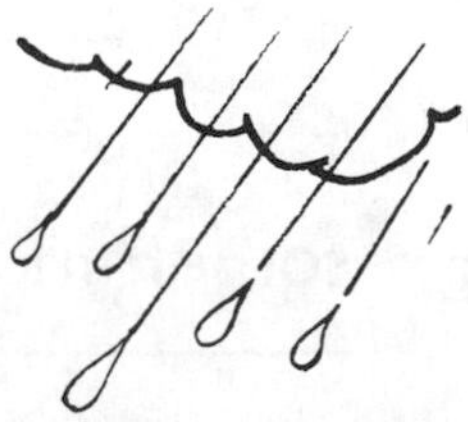

Symbol-sound association of words containing vowel digraphs: *ai, ay*

Vowel Pairs: *AI* and *AY*

Name ______________________________

Read the list of words below. Then look at the pictures. Write the word from the list that tells about each picture.

snail	stain	pail	pay	hay
clay	rain	tray	chain	

tr**ai**n h**ay**

stain

Vowel Pairs: *AI* and *AY*

Name ______________________

Read each sentence and the words beside it. Write the word that makes sense in each sentence.

train  hay 

1.	The store will have a ___chain___ for my bike.	chain train clay
2.	Jane has a boat with a big ______________.	stay sail say
3.	The horse ate ______________ all day long.	hay say sail
4.	Pat gets good ______________ for her work.	pay pail plain
5.	The ______________ runs on the tracks.	tray train trail
6.	Gail likes to play with ______________.	stay clay claim
7.	Did our mail get wet in the ______________?	main rain ray
8.	Jane knows how to ______________ hair.	braid brain grain
9.	Please ______________ at my house.	stay stain away

Vowel Pairs: *EE* and *EA*

Name ______________________________

In some words, two vowels together stand for the sound of the first vowel. **Bee** has the long-**e** sound spelled **ee.** **Bean** has the long-**e** sound spelled **ea.** **Bread** has the short-**e** sound spelled **ea.**

b**ee**
b**ea**n
br**ea**d

Read the words and look at the pictures. Circle the word that tells about each picture.

tree team	fear feet	sleep steam
seem seal	bean beef	seat seed
thread three	heel head	bread bead

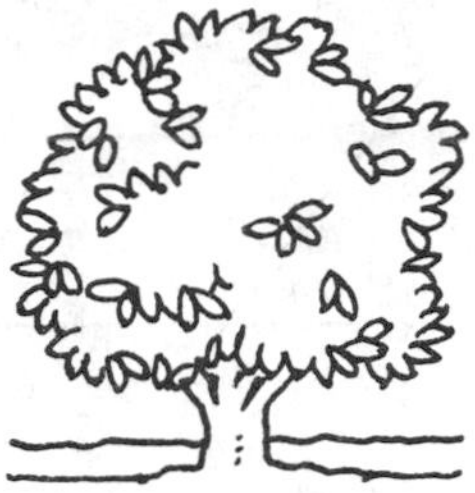

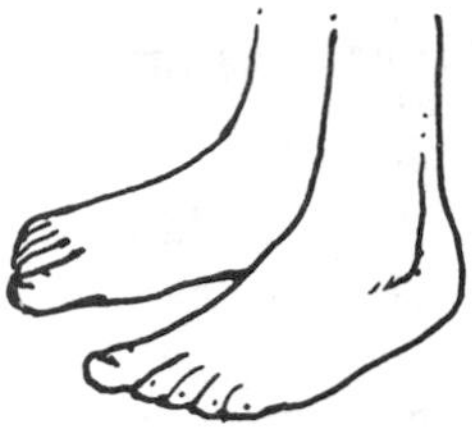

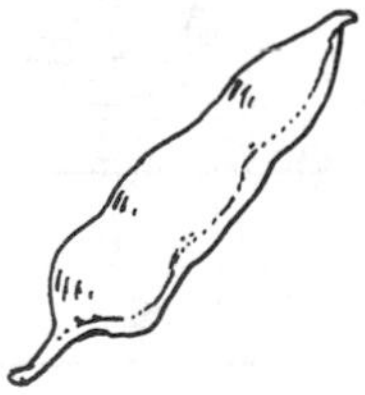

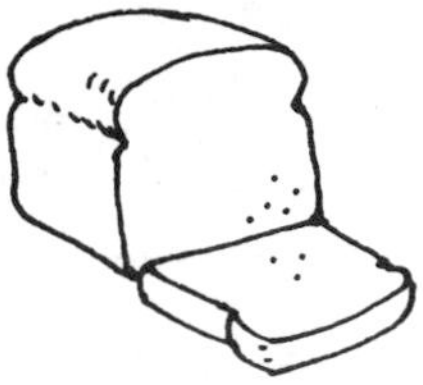

Vowel Pairs: *EE* and *EA*

Name

Read the words in the list below. Then name the pictures. Write the word from the list that names each picture.

leaf	beads	heel	feet	thread
steam	head	screen	bread	

head

Vowel Pairs: *EE* and *EA*

Name ______________________________

Read each sentence and the words beside it. Write the word that makes sense in each sentence.

1. I need a new ___heel___ on my boot.	heel heat heap
2. There are ten ______________ for each team.	seems seats seams
3. Three cows were eating in the ______________.	meeting meatball meadow
4. Dee put a bean ______________ into the clay pot.	seal seed seek
5. We need to sweep the ______________.	leap leaves leak
6. Jean saw sixteen ______________ on the farm.	sleep cheap sheep
7. Lee likes to eat wheat ______________.	bread beads beach
8. I like to swim at the ______________.	been beach beak
9. Do you like roast ______________?	beef bead break

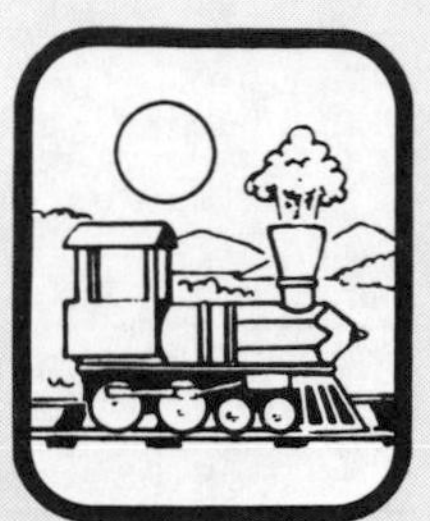

Vowel Pairs: *OA* and *OW*

Name ______________________________

In some words, two vowels together stand for the sound of the first vowel. **Coat** has the long-**o** sound spelled **oa. Window** has the long-**o** sound spelled **ow.**

co**oa**t windo**w**

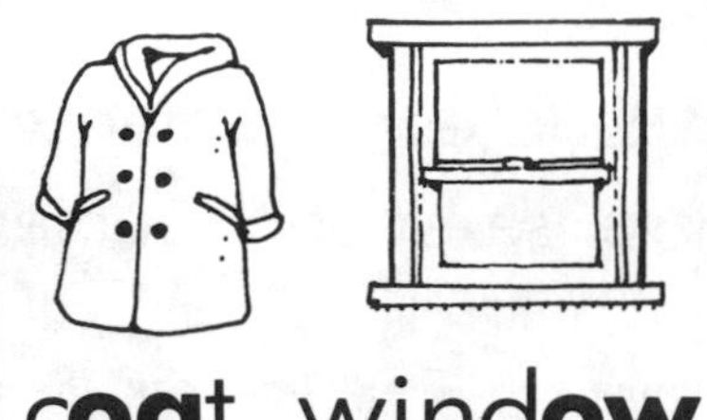

Read the words and look at the pictures. Circle the word that tells about each picture.

toast
tow

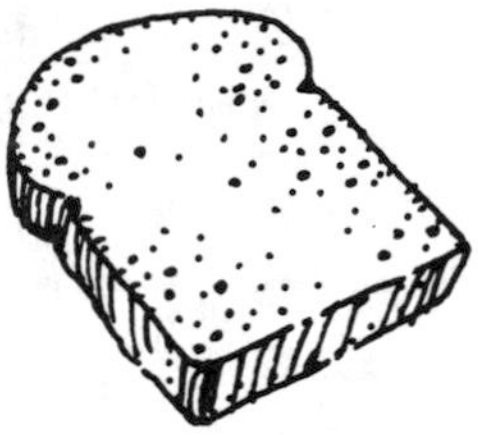

soap
soak

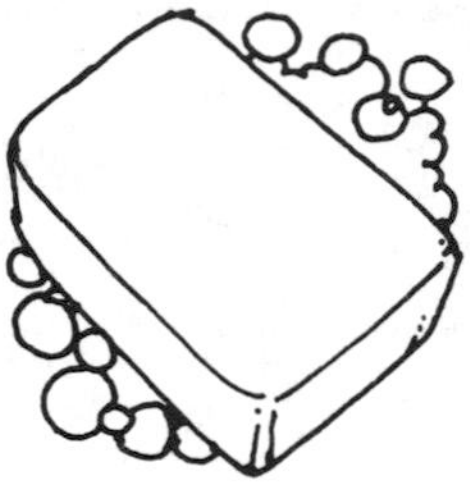

row
road

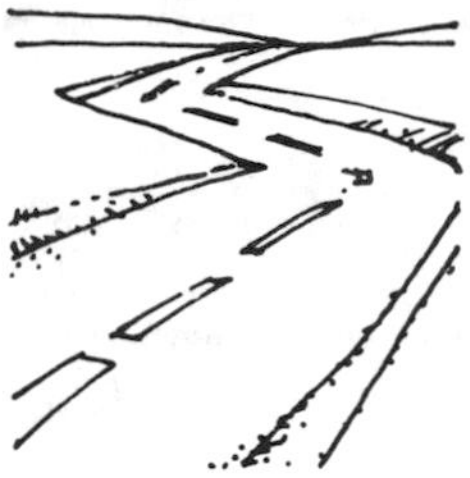

slow
snow

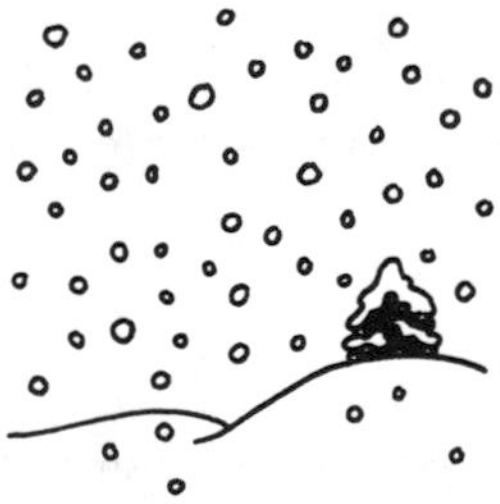

boat
blow

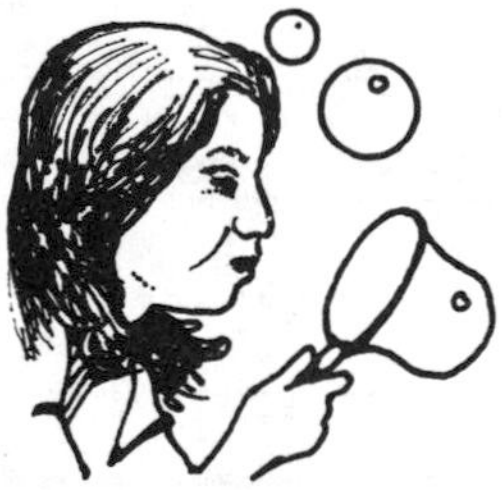

croak
crow

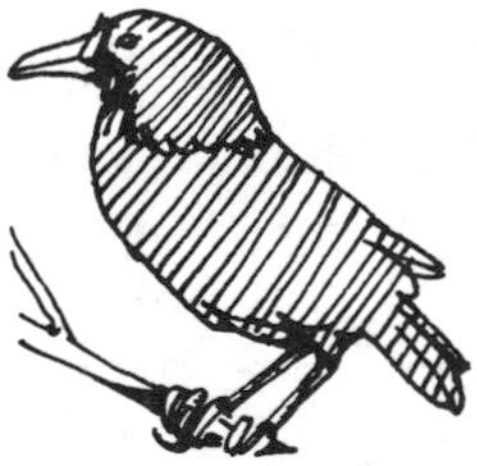

boat
bowl

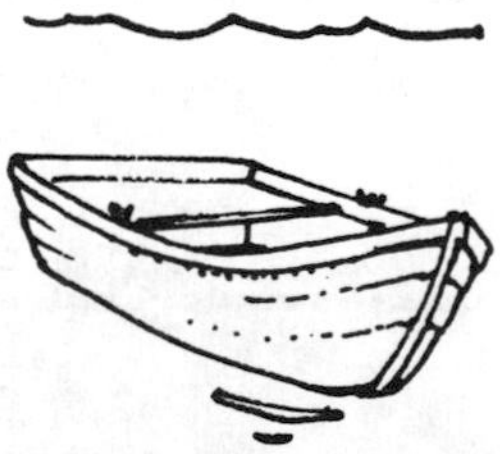

pillow
window

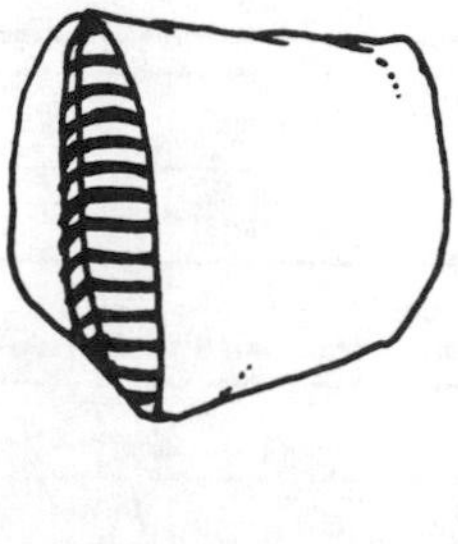

goat
glow

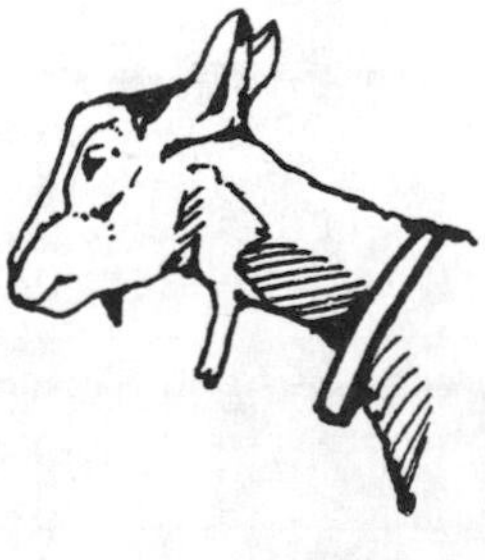

Symbol-sound association of words containing vowel digraphs: *oa, ow*

Vowel Pairs: *OA* and *OW*

Name ______________________

Read the words in the list below. Then name the pictures. Write the word from the list that names each picture.

toad	soap	pillow	snow	toast
goat	crow	bowl	boat	

c**oa**t window**ow**

toast

Vowel Pairs: *OA* and *OW*

Name ______________________

Read each sentence and the words beside it. Write the word that makes sense in each sentence.

c**oa**t  wind**ow** 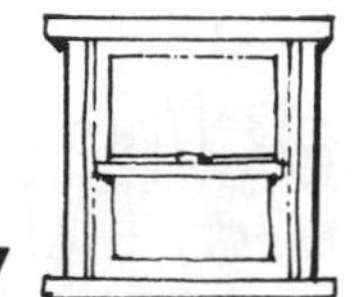

1.	Lee saw a ___crow___ in the sky.	coal coat crow
2.	Rest your head on the ______.	pillow shadow boast
3.	Joan ate ______ and eggs.	toad toast tow
4.	I like to ______ in a boat.	goat float grown
5.	Dan did not know if there would be ______.	soak slow snow
6.	The ______ ate my soap.	glow groan goat
7.	A flower grows by my ______.	window coast shadow
8.	How far can you ______ the ball?	throw throat toast
9.	Mom drives the van down the ______.	road roast row

Vowel Pairs

Name ______________________

Read the words and look at the pictures. Circle the word that tells about each picture.

chain cheek cheap cheese	tray train tree treat 	hay heap head heel 
trail tray thread tree 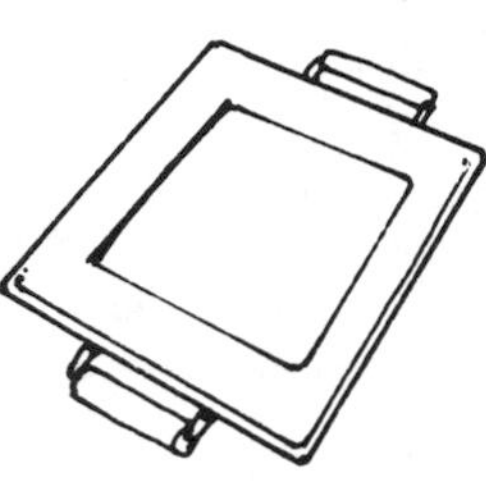	team tail toad tea 	bean bee bread beak 
spread stream sprain stray 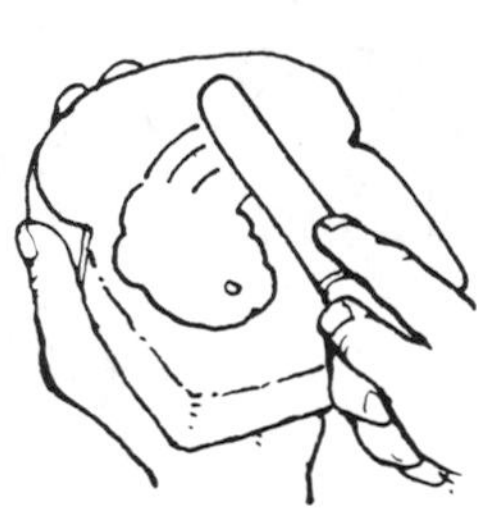	ray rain read road 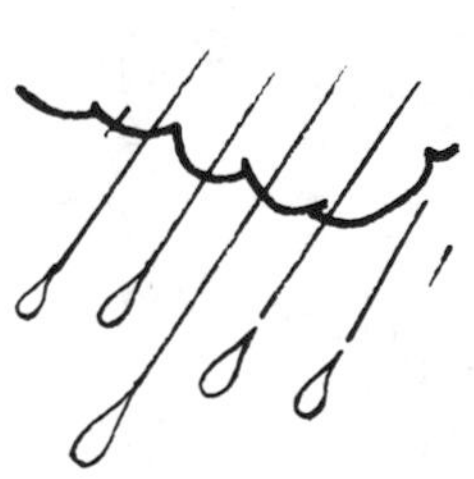	chain clay coat crow 
beat boat bay bow 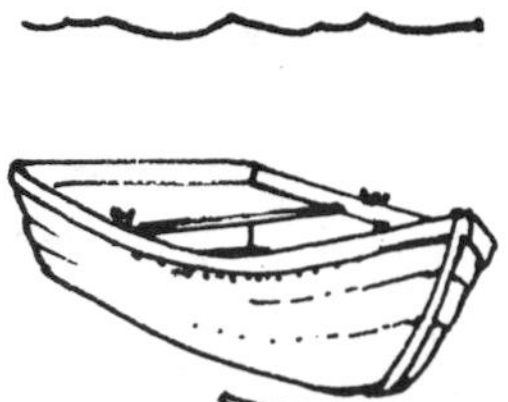	three thread throat throw 	spray sprain street stream 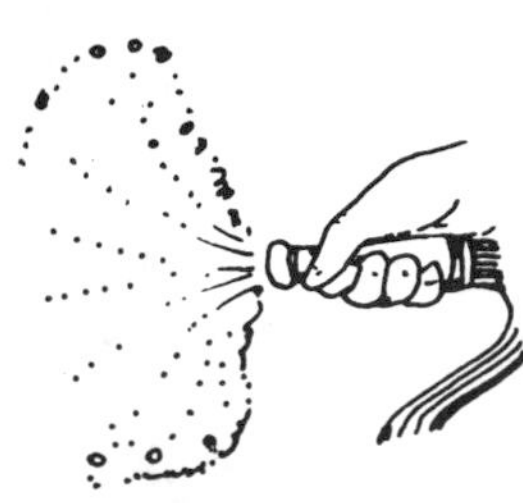

Review of symbol-sound association of words containing vowel digraphs: *ai, ay, ee, ea, oa, ow*

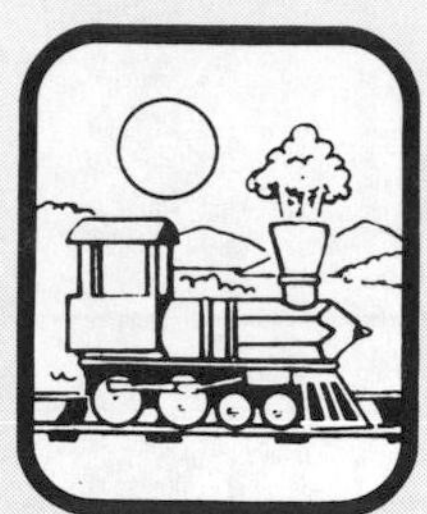

Sounds of OO

Name ______________________________

The letters **oo** can stand for the sound you hear in the middle of **moon.** The letters **oo** can also stand for the sound you hear in the middle of **book.**

m**oo**n b**oo**k

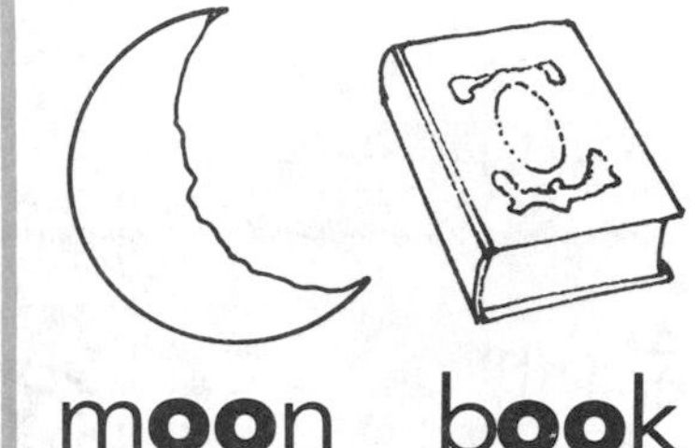

Read the words and name the pictures. Draw a line from each word to the picture it names.

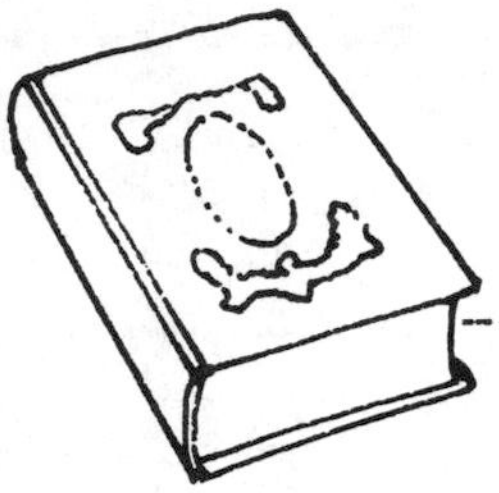
boot
book
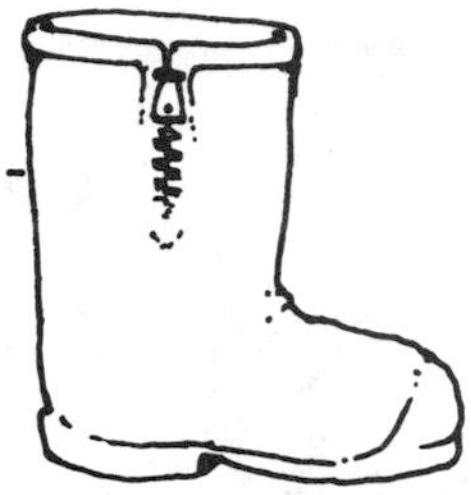

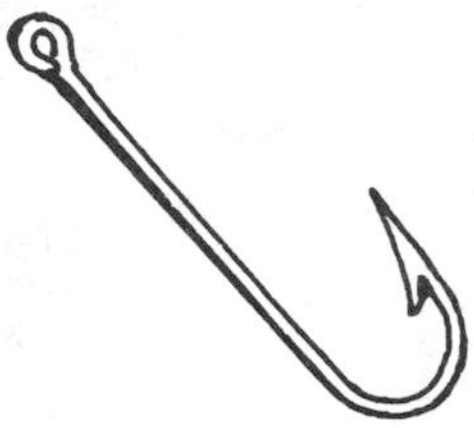
hook
hoop
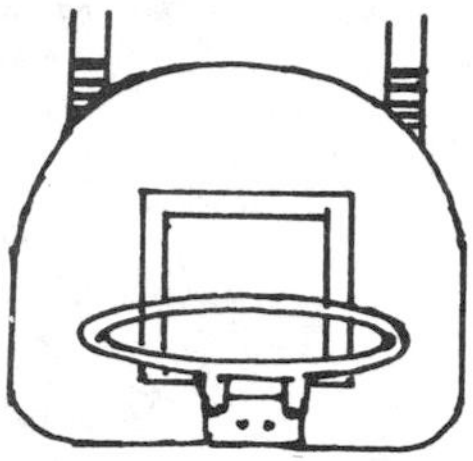

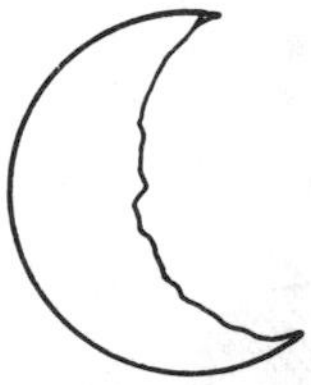
moon
wood
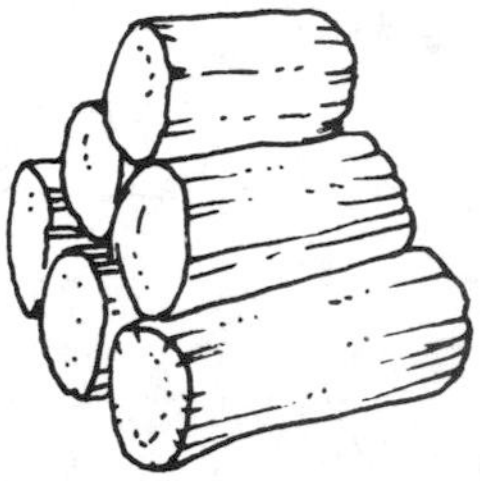

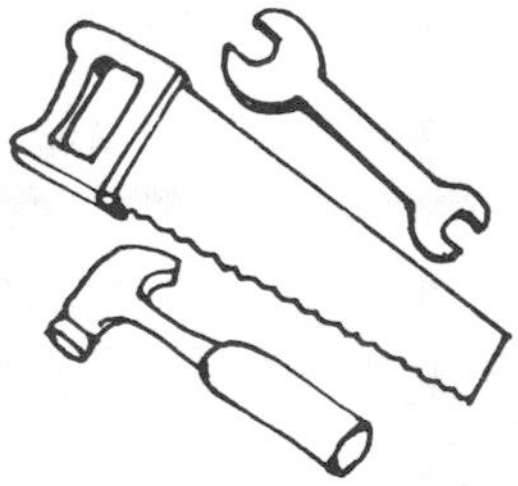
tooth
tools
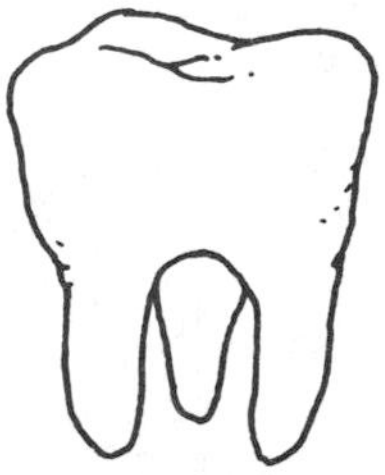

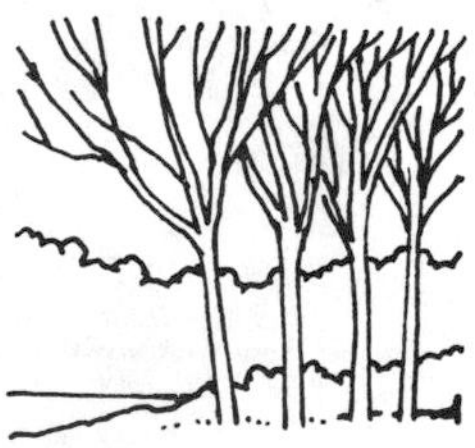
woods
moose
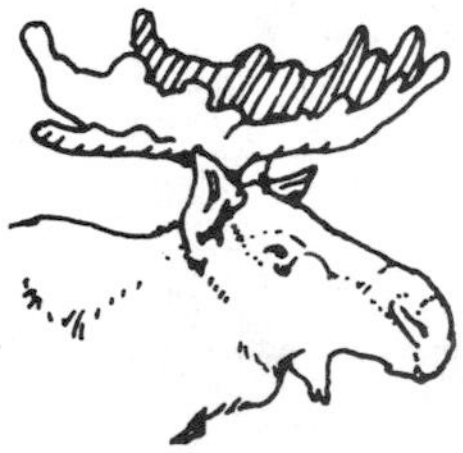

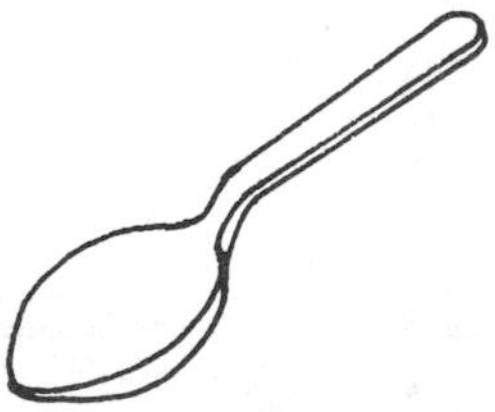
spool
spoon
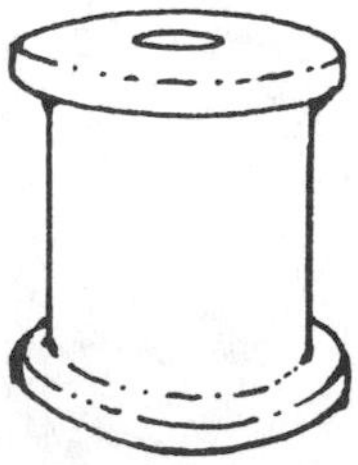

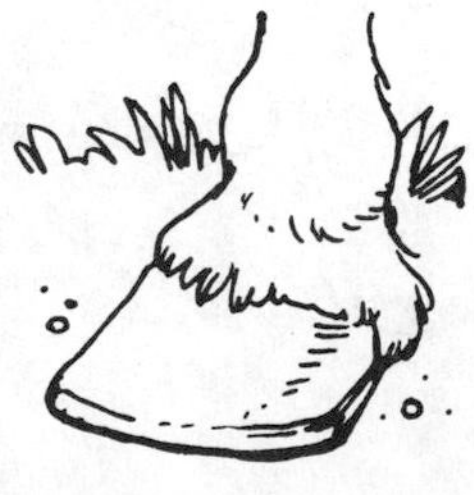
hood
hoof
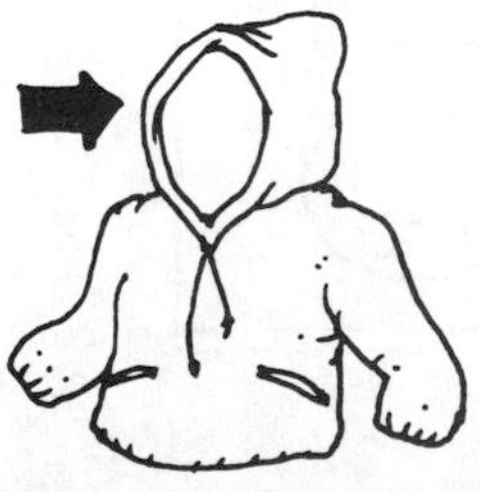

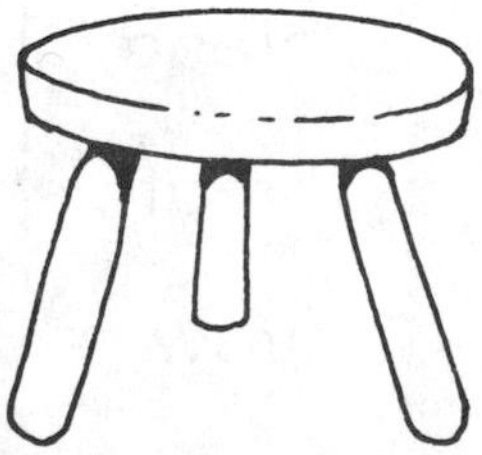
stool
pool
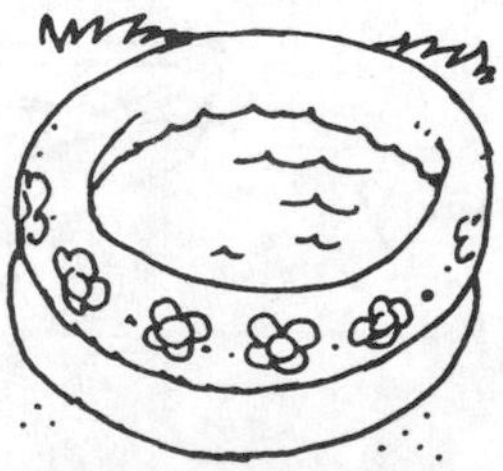

Symbol-sound association of words containing *oo*

Sounds of OO

Name ______________________

Read the words in the list below. Then name the pictures. Write the word from the list that names each picture.

hood	foot	boot	broom	tooth
wood	spoon	hook	stool	

m**oo**n b**oo**k

tooth

Sounds of OO

Name ______________________

Read each sentence and the words beside it. Write the word that makes sense in each sentence.

moon **book**

1.	Our troop will cook over a fire.	coop cook cool
2.	The baby eats with a ____________.	spoon stool stoop
3.	Gail saw a ____________ in the woods.	soon moon moose
4.	Ray ____________ in line at the zoo.	stood stool stoop
5.	Hang your coat on a ____________.	hoop hook hood
6.	Fay will ____________ up the words in a book.	loom loop look
7.	I like my wool coat with the ____________.	hood hoop hook
8.	Will likes to ____________ his own lunch.	pool cook shook
9.	We learn many things in ____________.	school spool spoon

Vowel Pairs: *AU* and *AW*

Name ______________________________

The sound you hear at the beginning of **auto** is spelled by the letters **au.** The sound you hear at the end of **saw** is spelled by the letters **aw.**

Read the words and look at the pictures. Draw a line from each word to the picture it tells about.

sauce
shawl

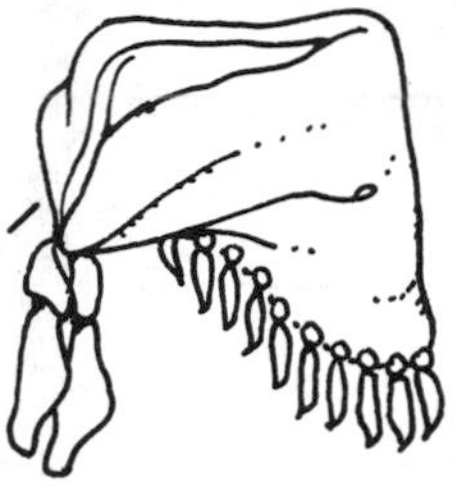

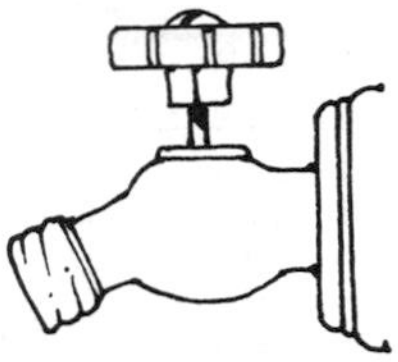

faucet
fawn

lawn
laundry

auto
claw

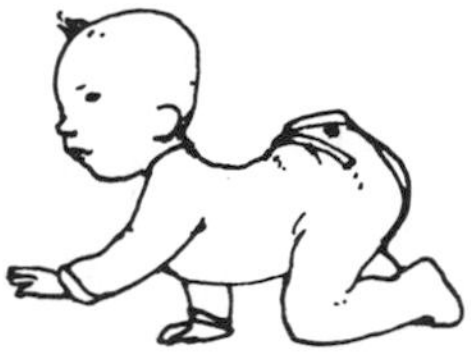

crawl
caught

straw
sauce

yawn
auto

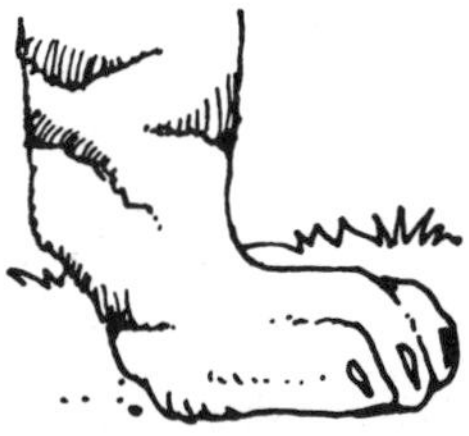

paw
faucet

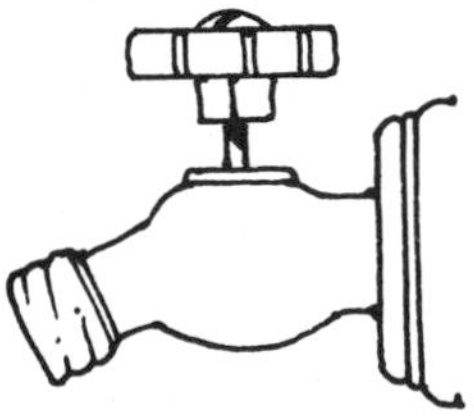

Vowel Pairs: *AU* and *AW*

Name ______________________

Read the words in the list below. Then name the pictures. Write the word from the list that names each picture.

claw laundry crawl paw faucet
straw shawl fawn sauce

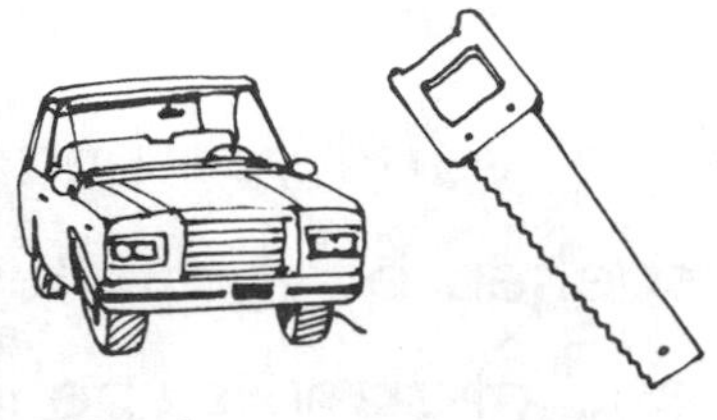

auto **s**aw

fawn

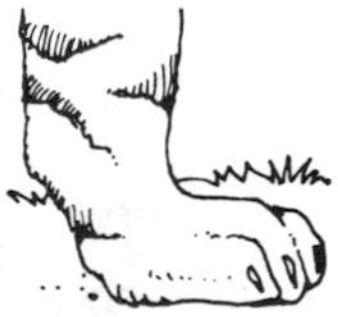

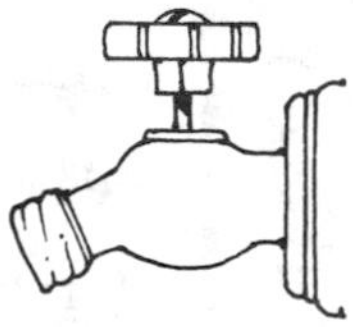

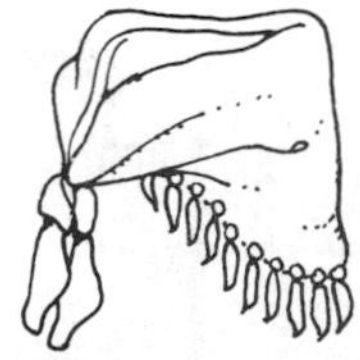

Vowel Pairs: *AU* and *AW*

Name ______________________________

Read each sentence and the words beside it. Write the word that makes sense in each sentence.

auto  s**aw** 

1. Paula put ___sauce___ on the meat.	sauce straw cause
2. Dawn can ______________ very well.	claw draw caught
3. Put a ______________ in each glass.	sauce crawl straw
4. I hear a drip from that ______________.	faucet fawn fault
5. I ______________ when I am sleepy.	lawn yawn fawn
6. Paul will do the ______________.	laundry hawk faucet
7. A ______________ feels good when I am cold.	haul straw shawl
8. What was the ______________ of the fire?	shawl cause sauce
9. One of the cat's ______________ was caught.	paws cause laws

Vowel Pairs: *EW*

Name ______________________

The letters **ew** can stand for the sound you hear in the middle of **news.**

news

Read the words and name the pictures. Circle the word that names each picture.

jewelry crew few dew	flew stew grew blew
mew few dew news	chew new screw drew

Read the sentences and word choices. Circle the word that makes sense in each sentence.

1. Roses (grew, flew) in the garden.
2. We read (mew, new) words in class.
3. A work (crew, stew) fixed the street.
4. Ling (dew, drew) a picture of Bob.
5. A (flew, few) friends met after school.

Vowel Pairs: *EW*

Name ______________________

Read each sentence and the words beside it. Write the word that makes sense in each sentence.

1.	Mark got a ___new___ book today.	drew new crew
2.	Drops of ____________ are on the grass.	dew few new
3.	I like to ____________ red apples.	blew crew chew
4.	A ____________ fell out of the door.	screw stew flew
5.	Linda is my ____________ friend.	dew new news
6.	Mandy ____________ the ball to Steve.	few stew threw
7.	The pine tree ____________ to be big.	grew dew chew
8.	Juan ____________ a pretty picture.	chew grew drew
9.	We ate beef ____________ for lunch.	screw crew stew

Vowel Pairs: *EW*

Name ______________________

Read the words in the list below. Then read the clues that follow. Write a word from the list to match each clue.

jewelry	flew	stew	dew	mew
new	chew	few	blew	

1. makes the grass wet 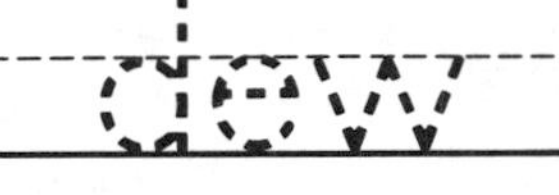
2. something to eat ______________
3. rings, necklaces, and bracelets ______________
4. not old ______________
5. sound a kitten makes ______________
6. not very many ______________
7. what you do to food ______________
8. what the wind did ______________
9. what the birds did ______________

Vowel Pairs

Name ______________________

Read the words and name the pictures. Circle the word that names each picture.

book boot blew drew	saw auto boot stew	jaw jewelry grew groom
sauce saw straw stew	foot food fool few	news paw pool haul
moon mew news noon	chew claw crawl crew	stew saw sauce spoon
hoop haul hook hawk	sauce spoon straw screw	straw stew saw sauce

Review of symbol-sound association of words containing vowel digraphs: *oo, au, aw, ew*

Two Sounds of *Y*

Name ______________________

The letter **y** at the end of some words can stand for the long-**i** sound, as in **fly.** The letter **y** at the end of some words can stand for the long-**e** sound, as in **pony.**

Read the words and look at the pictures. Circle **long e** or **long i** to show which sound **y** makes in each word.

bunny — long e / long i	cry — long e / long i	penny — long e / long i
fry — long e / long i	city — long e / long i	puppy — long e / long i
baby — long e / long i	sky — long e / long i	fly — long e / long i
pony — long e / long i	story — long e / long i	dry — long e / long i

Symbol-sound association of words containing *y* as a vowel

Two Sounds of *Y*

Name ____________________

Read the words and look at the pictures. Circle the word that tells about each picture.

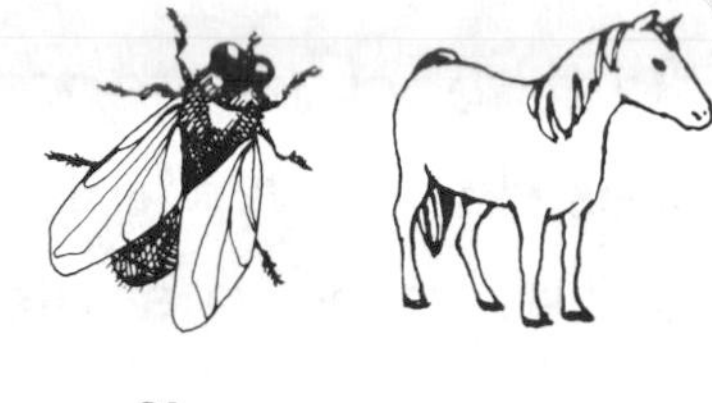

skinny sky 	cry city 	dry dusty 
by bunny 	funny fly 	my muddy 
story spy 	fry fifty 	baby by 
dizzy dry 	sky silly 	spy skinny 

Two Sounds of *Y*

Name ______________________________

Read each sentence and the words beside it. Write the word that makes sense in each sentence.

fl**y** pon**y**

1.	The baby did not ___cry___ for long.	cry fry spy
2.	We moved from a farm to the ______________.	city kitty party
3.	Tracy is ______________ when she plays ball.	happy penny puppy
4.	Did you see many birds in the ______________?	sky sly spy
5.	My ______________ has black and white spots.	muddy penny puppy
6.	Ron will help ______________ the plates.	fly dry cry
7.	Jan will ______________ to win the game.	fry dry try
8.	Please read us a ______________.	silly story city
9.	Our boots are ______________.	party muddy puppy

Words containing *y* as a vowel in context

Vowel Pairs and Sounds of *Y*

Name ______________________________

Read the sentences below. Circle the word that makes sense in each sentence.

1. Do you hear (rain, rays) on the roof?
2. James likes to bake (beads, bread).
3. Rose floats a toy (boat, blow) in the tub.
4. The horse hit its (heat, hoof) on a fence.
5. Our cat licked one of its (pays, paws).
6. This (saw, stew) tastes good.
7. Sandy will (try, tray) to win the game.
8. Our club met a (flow, few) times after school.
9. Are there (many, my) pages in the book?
10. I will (feed, fear) the cats from a bowl.
11. Mr. Jones (taught, toot) the class about deer.
12. How (seen, soon) can you be ready to go?
13. The gift has a (bow, boat) on top.
14. I will cut the (meat, mew) for our meal.
15. Are you going to (plain, play) ball with us?
16. I (caught, crow) a fish with my net.
17. We went to a (fly, party).
18. I have a (spray, pain) in my foot.

Consonant Pairs

Name ______________________

In some words, two or more consonants together stand for one sound. Some consonants that stand for one sound are **sh, ch, th, thr,** and **wh.**

shoe **thr**ee
chair **wh**eel
thin

Read the words and look at the pictures. Draw a line from each word to the picture it tells about.

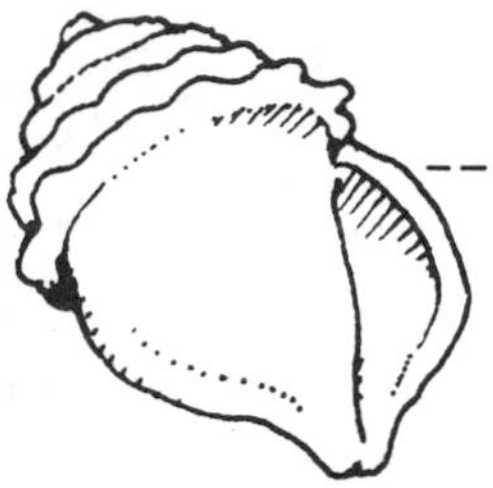

---shell wheel---	 chick think
 check thread	three sheep
 whip ship	 whale chain
 thin chin	 chop shop

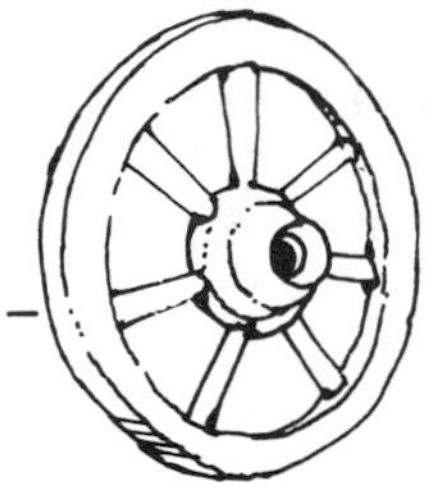

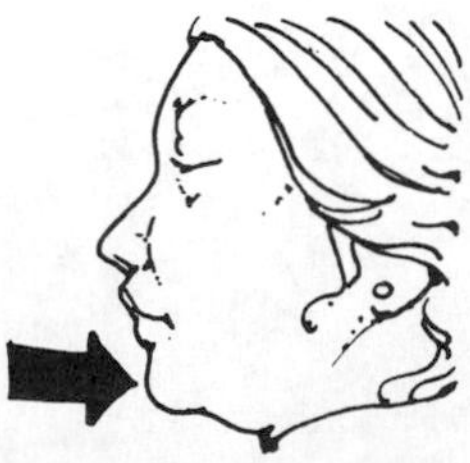

Symbol-sound association of words containing initial consonant digraphs: *sh, ch, th, thr, wh*

Consonant Pairs

Name ______________________

Look at the pictures. Write the letters that stand for the beginning sound of each picture name.

thin	eese	elf
eek	ale	air
ip	ink	eel
ead	oe	oat

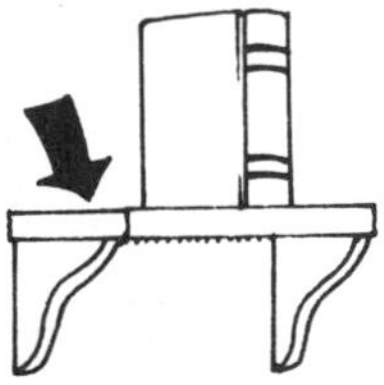

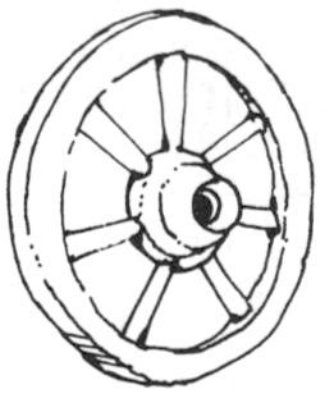

Consonant Pairs

Name ______________________

Read each sentence and the words beside it. Write the word that makes sense in each sentence.

1.	A heavy <u>chain</u> keeps the gate shut.	thin when chain
2.	Shane put his books on the ______________.	cheap shelf thrill
3.	A ______________ swims in the sea.	chain shake whale
4.	Chuck ate a ______________ slice of meat.	which thick chick
5.	Ann took a walk with ______________ friends.	cheese three wheel
6.	Do not skate on ______________ ice.	chin thin shin
7.	My wagon needs a new ______________.	wheel sheep cheese
8.	We keep our wood in that ______________.	shed thread check
9.	Jim ______________ the wood with an ax.	shops chops whips

Words containing initial consonant digraphs in context: *sh, ch, th, thr, wh*

Consonant Pairs

Name ______________________

At the end of some words, two or more consonants together stand for one sound. Some consonants that stand for one sound are **sh, ch, tch, th,** and **ng.**

wi**sh** wi**th**
ea**ch** ri**ng**
ca**tch**

Read the words and look at the pictures. Draw a line from each word to the picture it tells about.

wash watch	string stitch
bath bang	ditch dish
ring ranch	splash scratch
brush branch	bush bench

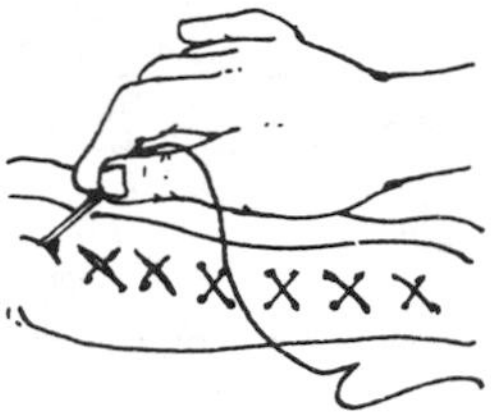

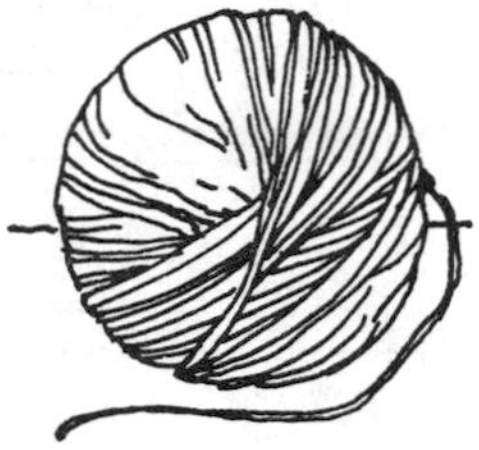

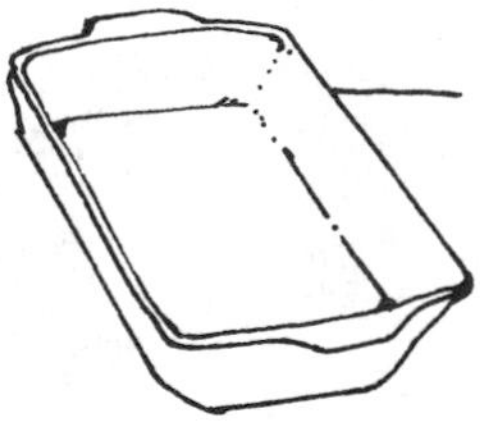

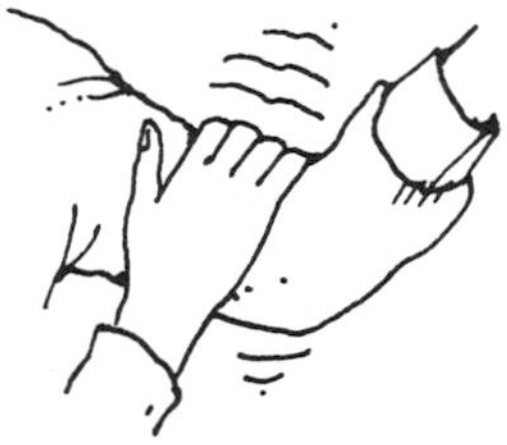

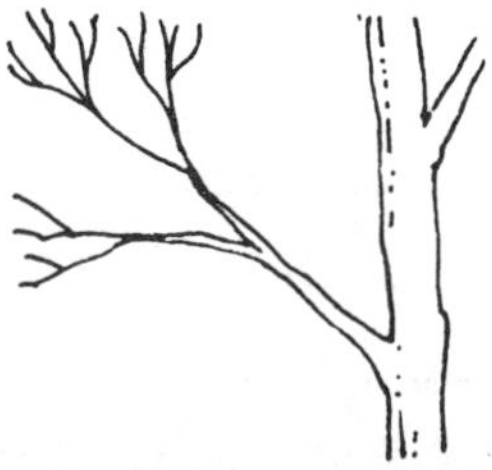

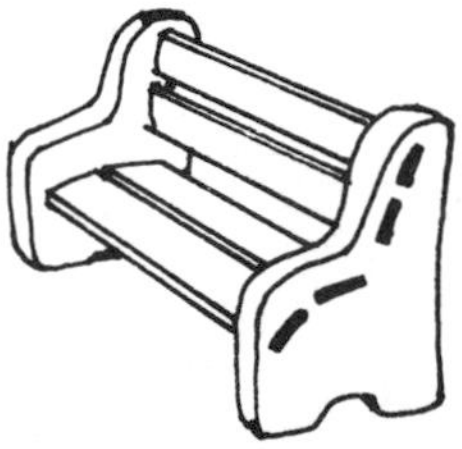

Consonant Pairs

Name

Read the words in the list below. Then look at the pictures. Write the word from the list that tells about each picture.

string	path	tooth	fish	beach
ring	branch	switch	dish	

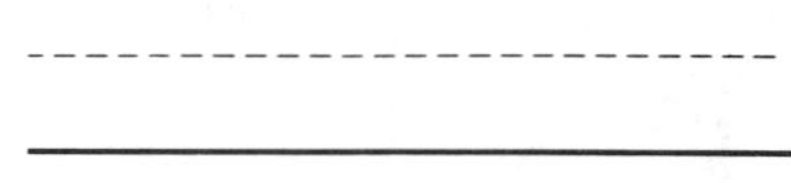

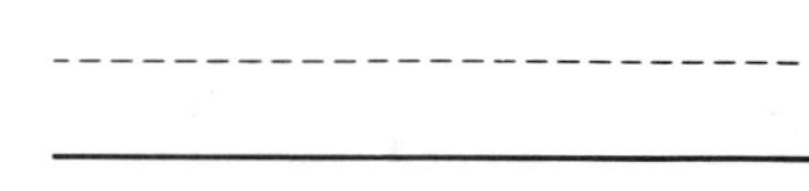

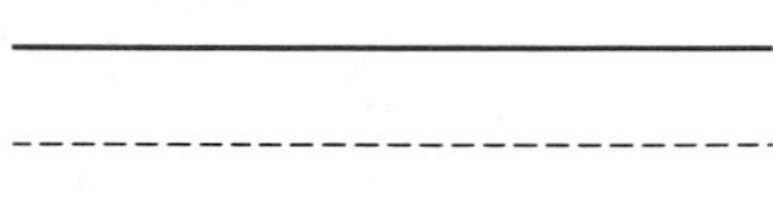

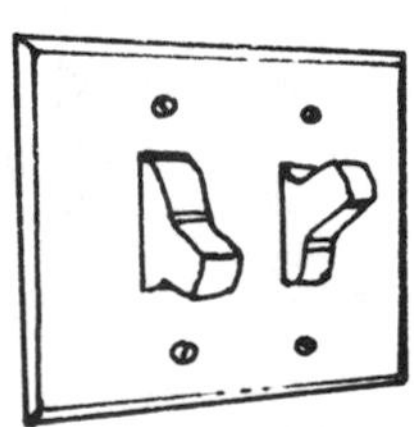

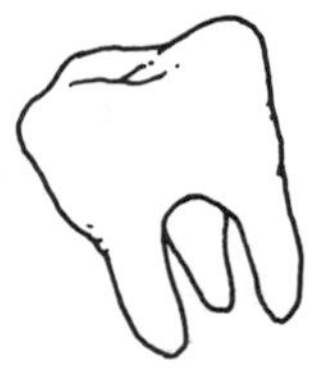

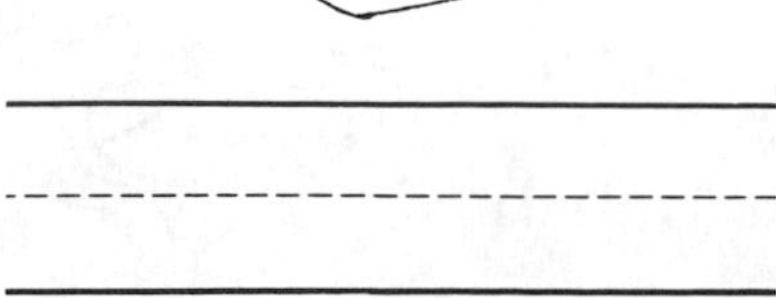

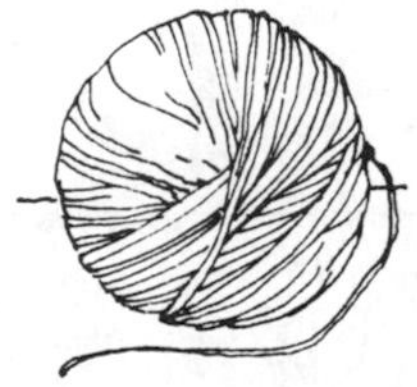

Symbol-sound association of words containing final consonant digraphs: *sh, ch, tch, th, ng*

Consonant Pairs

Name ______________________

Read each sentence and the words beside it. Write the word that makes sense in each sentence.

1. Ruth will give her dog a <u>bath</u>.	batch bush bath
2. I looked at the time on my new ________.	swing watch wash
3. My cat ate fish from a ________.	watch dish with
4. Did you hear that bell ________?	rich ring sting
5. We will sit and rest on this ________.	bench catch bang
6. Brush your ________ after every meal.	teach scratch teeth
7. Jane needs a new ________ for her paint set.	branch brush bush
8. The rope on my tree ________ broke.	wish switch swing
9. We walked down a ________ in the woods.	peach splash path

Consonant Pairs

Name ______________________

Read the words and look at the pictures. Circle the word that tells about each picture.

chick (ship) thin white 	chain shake whale that 	chip while shift think 
watch wish wrong wreath 	shone whole shop throne 	bath bush bring branch 
thin chain shake whale 	wish wing watch wreath 	bench bath bang bush 
sheet wheel cheek three 	pitch path push patch 	rush rich ring rash 

Review of symbol-sound association of words containing consonant digraphs: *sh, ch, th, thr, wh, tch, ng*

Consonant Pairs

Name ______________________________

Read the sentences below. Circle the word that makes sense in each sentence.

1. Chuck ate a (chunk, shut) of cheese with his lunch.
2. Shane put his new book on the (check, shelf).
3. The (branch, bring) of the tree will scratch the window.
4. I think this slice of meat is too (which, thick).
5. Who can fix the (wheel, cheek) on my bike?
6. Ling wants to (sing, such) for our class.
7. I wish our (bath, bush) would bloom soon.
8. A pinch made the pig (squeal, wheel).
9. We took a hike on that (patch, path).
10. I like to (watch, wash) the birds fly.
11. Ruth has (squeeze, three) new friends.
12. Sit down on the (bang, bench) and rest.
13. The clay is in the (shape, chase) of a ball.
14. Please go (with, witch) me to a show.
15. I had to (chase, shade) my dog last night.
16. Did you (bring, brush) your new books?
17. I (wish, with) we could go out to play.
18. The (squirrel, wheel) ran up a tree.

Reading and Writing Wrap-Up

Name ____________________

Growing Up

When you were a baby, there were many things you could not do. You could not walk or talk. You could not dress without help, and you could not eat without help. Your family dressed you. They gave you good things to eat. They played with you and made you laugh. Your family was there to help you when you were a baby.

Now you are older. Your family is not around to help you all the time. You can do many things you could not do when you were a baby. You are growing up.

A. Tell two things a baby can not do that you can do.

1. ____________________

2. ____________________

B. Tell two things the family does to help a baby.

1. ____________________

2. ____________________

C. What can a baby do? What can you do? Circle the things a baby can do. Draw a box around the things you can do that a baby can not do.

cry ride a bike read sleep go to school

make a bed smile see write add two and two

Name

D. Tell what "growing up" means.

E. Write a story about growing up.
Tell something you can do now that you could not do when you were a baby. Tell how your family helped you.

AR and *ER*

Name

A vowel that is followed by **r** stands for a special sound that is neither long nor short. The sound at the end of **jar** is spelled by the letters **ar.** The sound in the middle of **fern** is spelled **er.**

Read the words and name the pictures. Draw a line from each word to the picture it names.

harp hammer	slipper star
paper park	fern farm
dart dancer	camper car
yard yarn	ladder letter

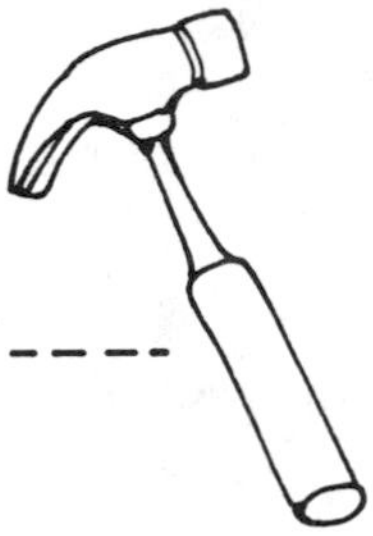

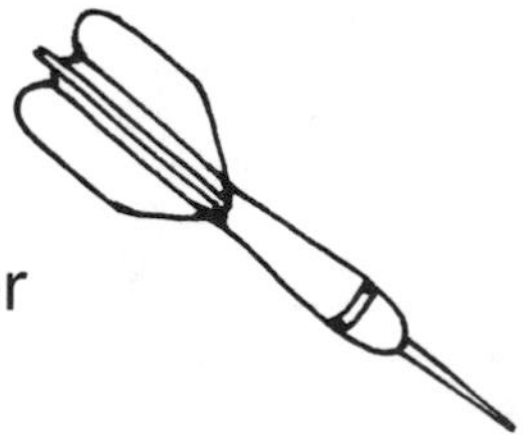

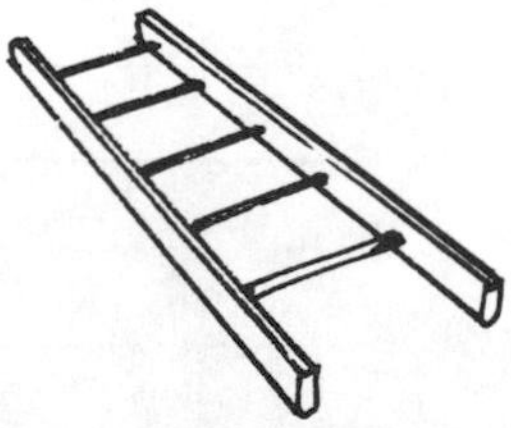

Symbol-sound association of words containing *r*-controlled vowels: *ar, er*

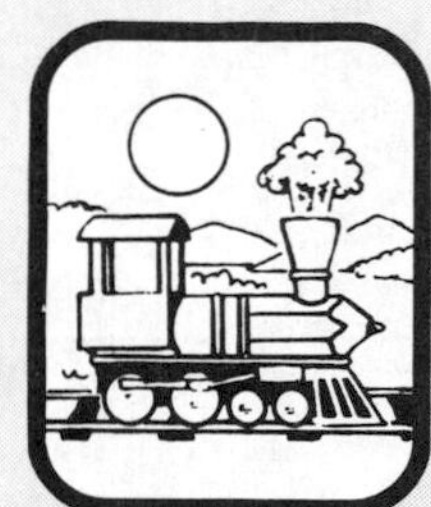

AR and *ER*

Name

Name the pictures. Write the letters **ar** or **er** to complete each picture name.

j**ar** f**er**n

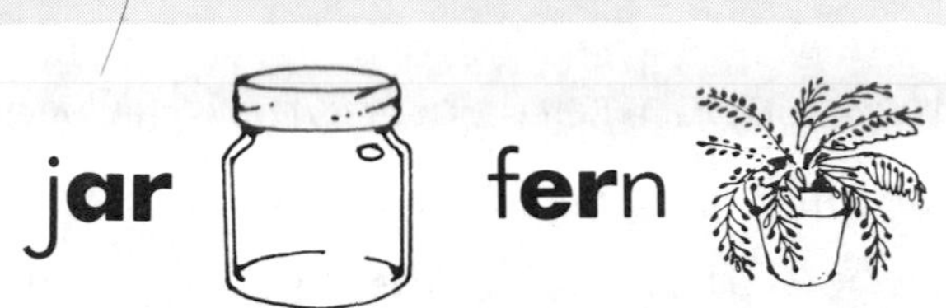

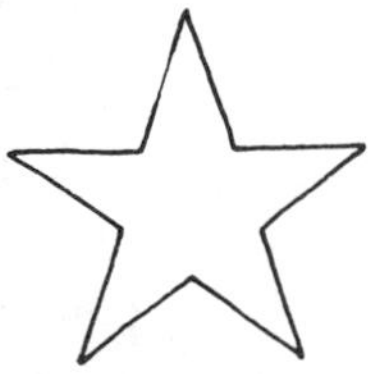
star

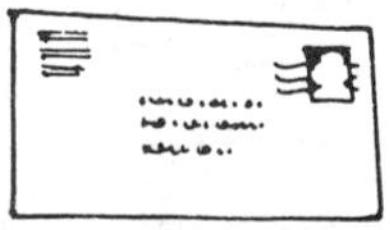
lett

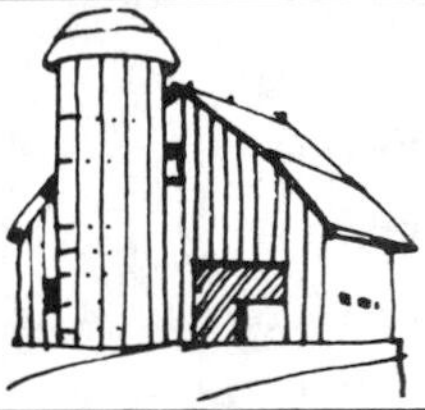
b n

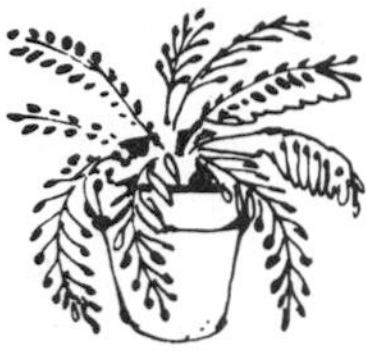
f n

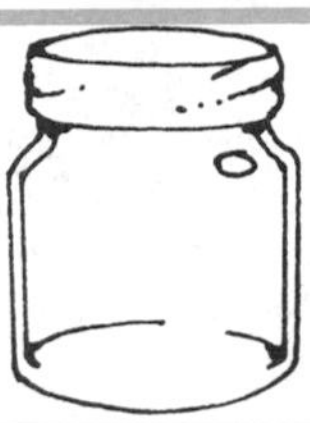
j

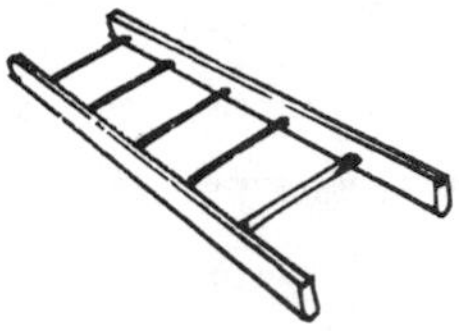
ladd

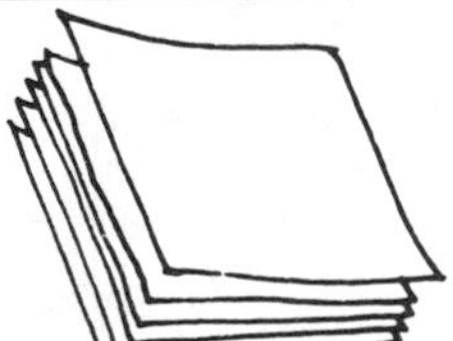
pap

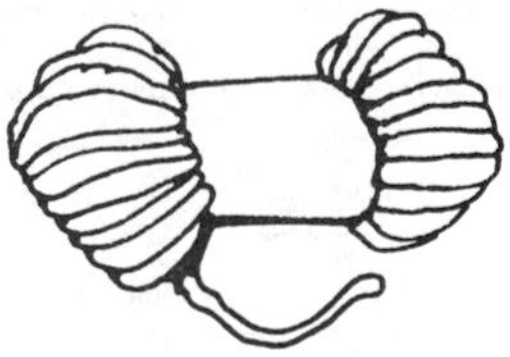
y n

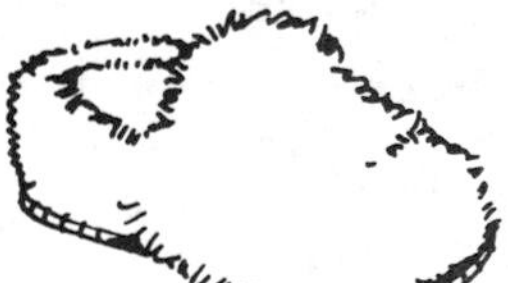
slipp

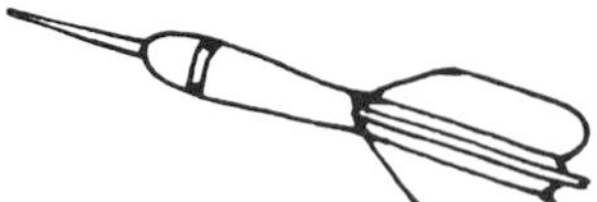
d t

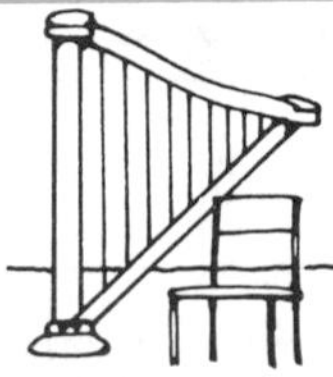
h p

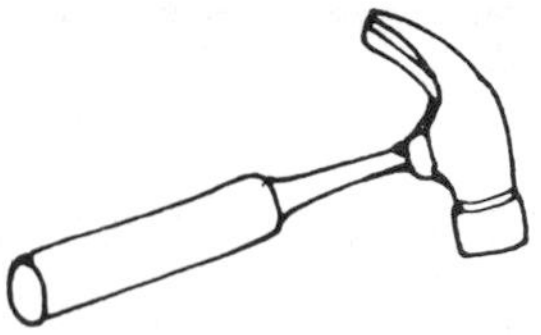
hamm

AR and ER

Name ________________________

Read each sentence and the words beside it. Write the word that makes sense in each sentence.

1.	Bert will park his ___car___ by the yard.	fern arm car
2.	Our team pitcher is player ________ three.	farm number lumber
3.	A ________ lives in deep water.	shark star slipper
4.	I put the ________ into a pot.	far farm fern
5.	Mark sent a ________ to his mother.	cart card camper
6.	Spray some ________ on the roses.	shark star water
7.	The friends played out in the ________.	germ yarn yard
8.	Farm animals stay in the ________.	germ barn flower
9.	Please give everyone a sheet of ________.	slipper zipper paper

IR and *OR*

Name ______________________

A vowel that is followed by **r** stands for a special sound that is neither long nor short. The sound in the middle of **bird** is spelled by the letters **ir.** The sound in the middle of **horn** is spelled by the letters **or.**

Read the words and look at the pictures. Draw a line from each word to the picture it tells about.

shirt
squirt

bird
dirt

skirt
storm

fork
fort

girl
horn

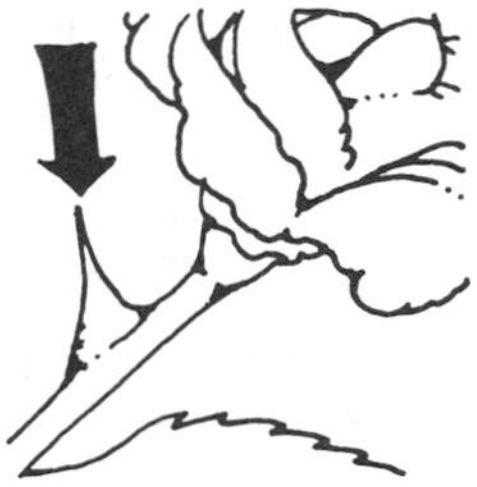

thirty
thorn

30

cork
corn

short
shirt

IR and *OR*

Name ______________________

Look at the pictures. Write the letters **ir** or **or** to complete the word that tells about each picture.

sh ir t

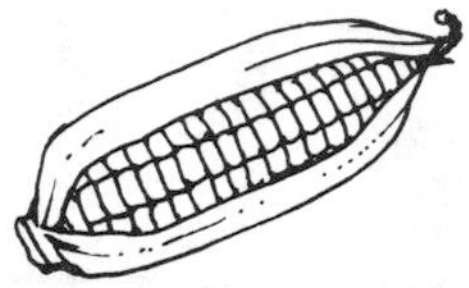

c n

st m

c k

d t

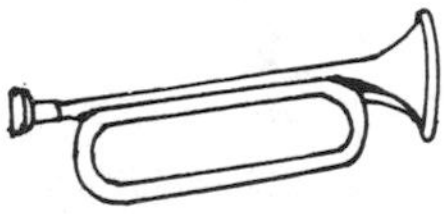

h n

b d

th n

sk t

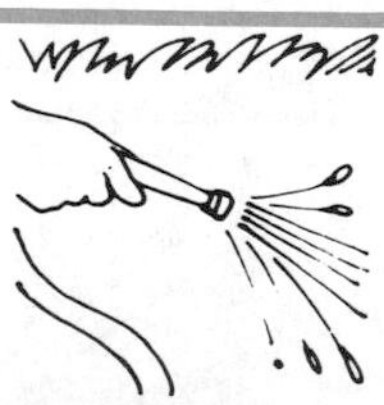

squ t

h se

g l

Sound-symbol association of words containing *r*-controlled vowels: *ir, or*

IR and *OR*

Name ______________________

Read each sentence and the words beside it. Write the word that makes sense in each sentence.

1. The funny clown wears a red shirt.	short shirt storm
2. Is your sister in the ______ grade?	torn thorn third
3. The little chicks like to eat ______.	corn cork circus
4. Jill will write a ______ story.	short shirt skirt
5. There was a ______ next to each plate.	fort fork first
6. Watch out for the ______ on that rose.	torn thorn third
7. The ______ ate seeds from the dirt.	shirt cord bird
8. There is a dark ______ cloud in the sky.	storm store squirt
9. Please do not ______ the stew.	stir storm shirt

UR

Name

A vowel that is followed by **r** stands for a special sound that is neither long nor short. The sound in the middle of **burn** is spelled by the letters **ur.**

b**ur**n

Read the words and look at the pictures. Draw a line from each word to the picture it tells about.

fur ----

---fort

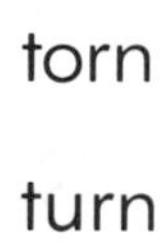

torn

turn

card

curb

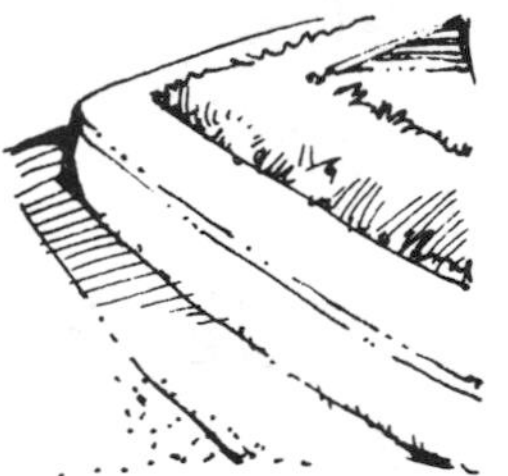

cord

curl

barn

burn

horn

hurt

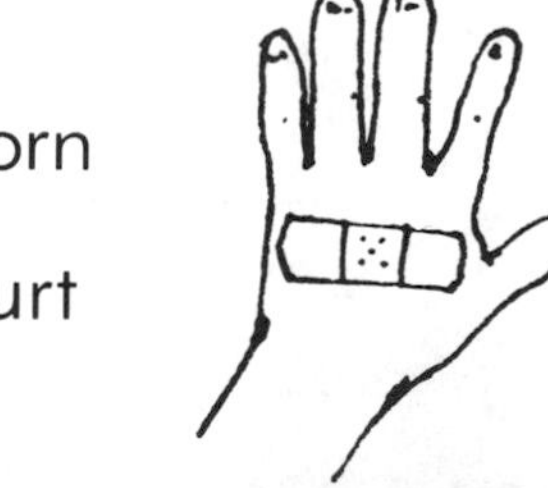

star

turn

fork

fur

UR

Name ______________________________

Look at the pictures. Write the letters **ur, ar,** or **or** to complete the word that tells about each picture.

b**ur**n

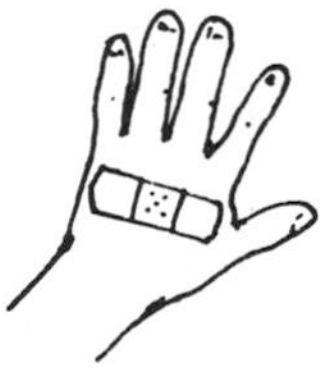

hurt

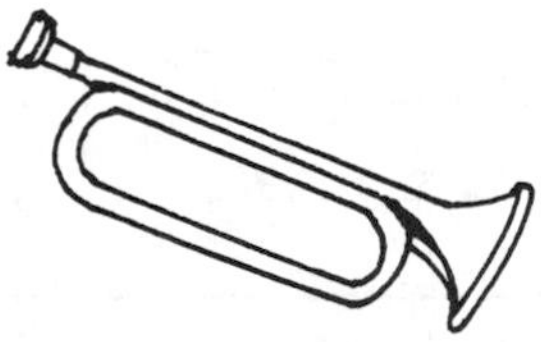

h__n

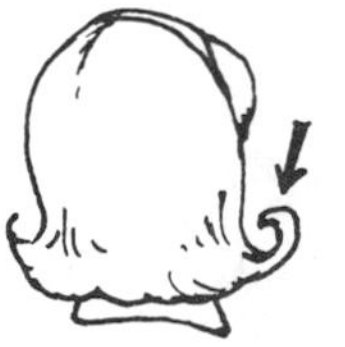

c__l

f__

c__

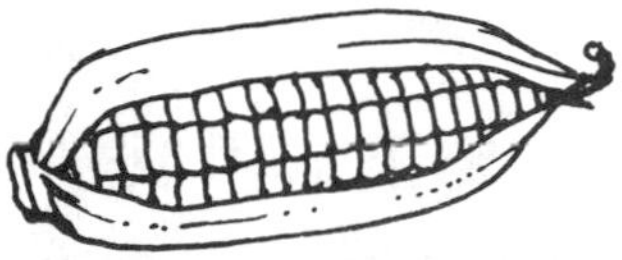

c__n

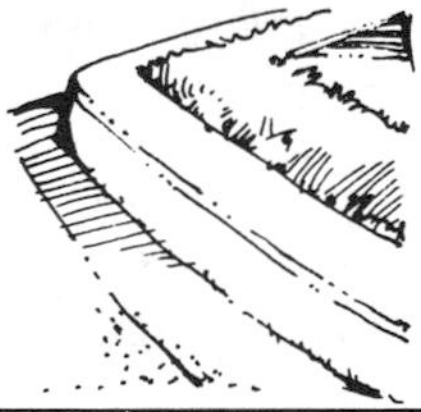

c__b

c__k

b__n

st__

b__n

f__k

Vowels With *R*

Name ______________________

Read each sentence and the words beside it. Write the word that makes sense in each sentence.

burn 

1.	I parked the car by the street curb.	card curb corn
2.	Bert ate his corn with a ______.	fort fork fern
3.	The farmer put lumber in the ______.	bird born barn
4.	Mark will wait in line for his ______.	torn tar turn
5.	When the dogs ______, they wake me up.	barn bark bird
6.	The baby had a ______ on his head.	curb curl cart
7.	A thorn on the rose ______ my hand.	hurt horn harp
8.	I sent Joe a ______ on his birthday.	curb card curl
9.	My dog has thick, black ______.	for fur far

Words containing *r*-controlled vowels in context: *ar, er, ir, or, ur*

Vowels With *R*

Name ________________________

Read the words and look at the pictures. Circle the word that tells about each picture.

bird burn born barn 	fur fork fern farm 	bark born barn bird 
harp horn herd hurt 	curl corn curb cork 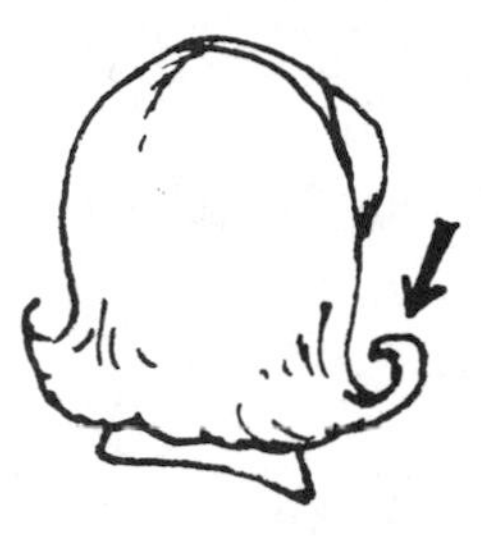	stir star shirt short 
hurt harp horn herd 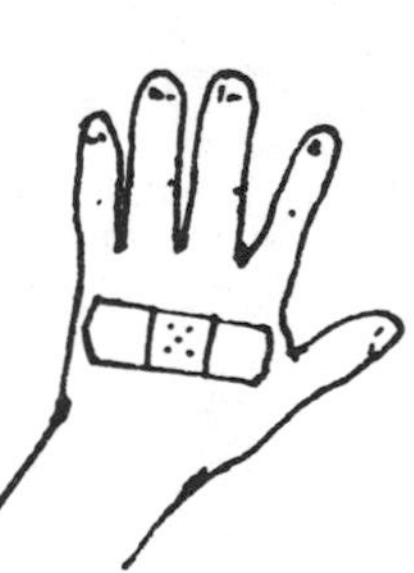	shirt short sharp skirt 	fort form farm fork 
letter lantern turn torn 	card cord cart car 	burn barn born bark 

Vowels With *R*

Name ______________________

Read the sentences below. Circle the word that makes sense in each sentence.

1. I like a little butter on my (car, corn).
2. Jean took a short walk in the (pork, park).
3. Our town had each street (curb, cord) painted yellow.
4. Mark needs to wash the (dirt, dart) off his car.
5. This (fern, form) grows best in a large pot.
6. The (hard, herd) of cows is on the hill.
7. Marge drew a star and a flying (bird, born) on her paper.
8. Stir the sauce in that (jar, jerk).
9. Sis likes to play the (cork, horn).
10. The cat licks its (fur, far).
11. Our horse stays in the (burn, barn).
12. I will sweep the (perch, porch).
13. She put on her new (sharp, shirt).
14. You can get a (born, burn) in the sun.
15. It is my (torn, turn) to wash the car.
16. Spot likes to dig in the (dirt, dart).
17. A baby (bark, bird) is in the nest.
18. My grandmother lives on a (farm, fern).

Assessment of words containing *r*-controlled vowels in context *ar, er, ir, or, ur*

OI and OY

Name ______________________

The sound in the middle of **coin** is spelled by the letters **oi.** The sound in the middle of **toys** is spelled by the letters **oy.**

Read the words and look at the pictures. Circle the word that tells about each picture.

oyster (circled) / noise 	toys / foil 	choice / coins 
soil / spoil 	boil / boy 	boil / coil 
coin / coil 	oil / oyster 	joy / toy 
boil / point 	join / boys 	foil / voice 

Symbol-sound association of words containing diphthongs: *oi, oy*

OI and OY

Name

Read the words in the list below. Then look at the pictures. Write the word from the list that tells about each picture.

boys	foil	toys	coin	boy
boil	oil	soil	point	

coin

toys

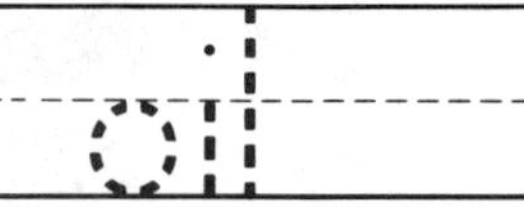

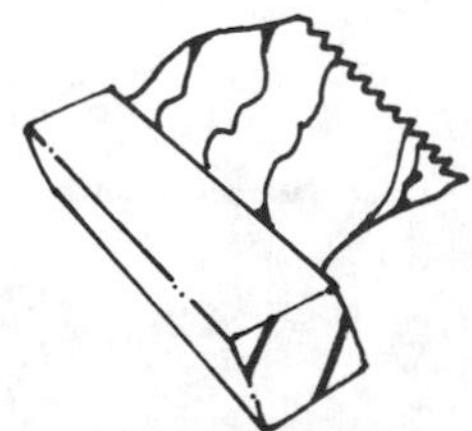

OI and OY

Name ______________________________

Read each sentence and the words beside it. Write the word that makes sense in each sentence.

coin   toys 

1.	A boy with a low ___voice___ will sing the song.	choice toys voice
2.	The gift put a look of ______________ on Roy's face.	joins joy boys
3.	Will you ______________ the coin club?	joy join point
4.	The baby likes to play with her ______________.	toys joys joins
5.	I ______________ eating boiled eggs.	choice joy enjoy
6.	Did you hear that funny ______________?	joins coins noise
7.	Please ______________ to the oil can.	soil spoil point
8.	Heat the water to a ______________.	oil boil oyster
9.	Dad likes to save old ______________.	coins boils enjoys

OU and OW

Name ______________________

The sound in the middle of **cloud** is spelled by the letters **ou.** The sound at the end of **cow** is spelled by the letters **ow.**

cl**ou**d

c**ow**

Read the words and look at the pictures. Circle the word that tells about each picture.

blouse brown	pound power	how house
count cow 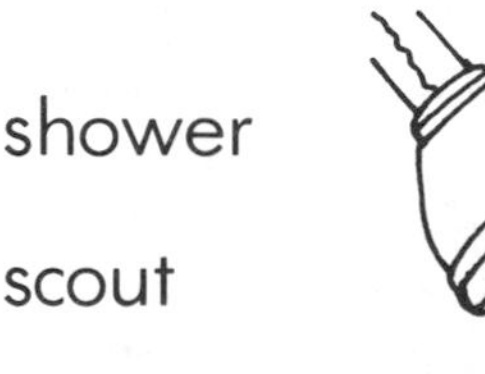	shower scout 	flower found 
clouds clown 	crown count 	plow pound 
bounce brown 	frown found 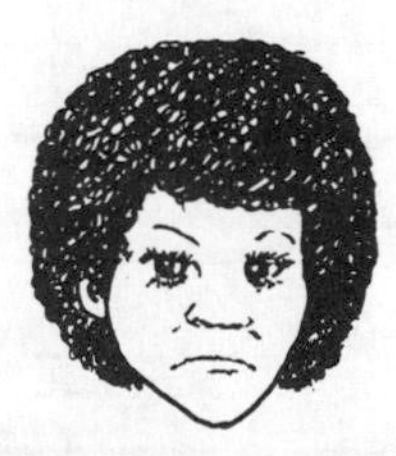	ground gown 

OU and OW

Name ________________________

Read the words in the list below. Then look at the pictures. Write the word from the list that tells about each picture.

crown	house	owl	mouth	blouse
pound	frown	clown	plow	

cl**ou**d c**ow**

owl

OU and OW

Name ____________________

Read each sentence and the words beside it. Write the word that makes sense in each sentence.

cl**ou**d c**ow**

1.	The cow opened its ___mouth___ for food.	mouse mouth flower
2.	I picked a ____________ for you.	flower tower cloud
3.	The ____________ had pretty lace trim.	ground gown town
4.	Our hound can ____________ a ball.	brown blouse bounce
5.	The sky was filled with rain ____________.	clowns clouds counts
6.	Please ____________ this nail into the wood.	power pound plow
7.	The clown took a ____________ as we cheered.	ouch cow bow
8.	The little gray ____________ ran away.	power mouse mouth
9.	I have a new ____________ and skirt.	drown blouse brown

OI, OY, OU, and OW

Name ____________________

Read the words and look at the pictures. Circle the word that tells about each picture.

boy brown boil bounce	boy boil pound power	pound point power proud
town toys boys boil	frown flower found foil	boys boil bounce bow
cow clown cloud count	cow coin count coil	down how house blouse
owl oil bow boil	cow coil count clown	foil frown found flower

OI, OY, OU, and OW

Name ______________________________

Read the sentences below. Circle the word that makes sense in each sentence.

1. Ling made a (tower, flour) of blocks.
2. Ann pointed to a chest filled with (town, toys).
3. No one found a (clown, cloud) in the sky.
4. I saw a cow walk (down, bounce) the road.
5. Joyce gave a (down, coin) to her sister.
6. Roy gave his toy to another (brown, boy).
7. You may (join, joy) the club of your choice.
8. I found a (power, pound) of flour.
9. Can you make that ball (boil, bounce)?
10. The man's face is full of (join, joy).
11. Rain came down in a (shout, shower).
12. Help me (count, down) the people in the crowd.
13. Wrap the meat in (foil, found).
14. Will you (pound, power) this nail for me?
15. There is a new (boil, boy) in our class.
16. This spinning top is my best (toy, town).
17. The (couch, cow) is eating grass.
18. My new coat is (brown, broil).

Assessment of words containing diphthongs in context: *oi, oy, ou, ow*

Endings: *-ED* and *-ING*

Name ________________________________

When a word ends with a consonant, and is preceded by a vowel, double the consonant before adding -**ed** or **ing.**

hop
hopp**ed**
hopp**ing**

Read each sentence and the word beside it. Add -**ed** or -**ing** to the word to complete the sentence. Write the word in the blank.

1.	I batted the ball.	bat
2.	Who is ____________ next to you in class?	sit
3.	I was ____________ to catch the bus.	run
4.	Tess is ____________ at the lake.	fish
5.	Andy ____________ the cat on its head.	pat
6.	Jean ____________ the fence at our school.	paint
7.	Pablo is ____________ Father.	help
8.	Mother ____________ a blue glass.	drop

Endings: *-ED* and *-ING*

Name ______________________________

When a word ends with **e,** drop the **e** before adding -**ed** or -**ing.**

smile
smil**ed**
smil**ing**

Read each sentence and the word beside it. Add -**ed** or -**ing** to the word to complete the sentence. Write the word in the blank.

1. Luke ___baked___ a good loaf of bread. bake
2. Fran is ______________ the door. close
3. I will be ______________ my room soon. clean
4. Fay enjoys ______________ to her friends. write
5. Rick ______________ a good meal for us. cook
6. Beth ______________ the ball ten times. bounce
7. Rosa is ______________ the leaves now. rake
8. Sue is ______________ on the stage. dance

Dropping final *e* before adding *-ed* or *-ing* to verbs in context

Endings: *-ED* and *-ING*

Name ______________________________

When a word ends in **y**, simply add **-ing** to the word. When a word ends in **y** and is preceded by a vowel, just add **-ed**. When a word ends in **y** and is preceded by a consonant, change the **y** to **i** before adding **-ed.**

fry	fry**ing**
play	play**ed**
fry	fri**ed**

Read each sentence and the word beside it. Add **-ed** or **-ing** to the word to complete the sentence. Write the word in the blank.

1. Bob washed and ___dried___ the dishes. dry
2. We ______________ in the house when it rained. stay
3. My sister is ______________ for a new job. look
4. Stan ______________ to get his work done. hurry
5. Dave ______________ an egg for me. fry
6. Frank is ______________ the books for us. carry
7. We ______________ your party very much. enjoy
8. Mom is ______________ a new dress. buy

Base Words and Endings

Name ____________________

A word to which an ending is added is called a base word. Read the list of words and base words in the box at the right.

Word	Base Word
popping	pop
smiling	smile
carried	carry

Read each word below. Then write its base word in the blank.

1. rubbed rub
2. crying ______
3. missed ______
4. smiled ______
5. taking ______
6. tried ______
7. stopped ______
8. clapping ______
9. played ______
10. tapped ______
11. writing ______
12. liked ______
13. carried ______
14. hummed ______
15. dried ______
16. talked ______

Endings: *-S* and *-ES*

Name ____________________

Many words can be formed by adding **-s** to other words. When a word ends in **s, ss, sh, ch,** or **x,** add **-es.**

sing**s** catch**es** pass**es** fix**es** wash**es**

Read each word below. Add **-s** or **-es** to form a new word. Write the new word in the blank.

1. rush rushes
2. miss ____________
3. help ____________
4. catch ____________
5. guess ____________
6. jump ____________
7. watch ____________
8. think ____________
9. reach ____________
10. work ____________
11. wax ____________
12. toss ____________
13. ask ____________
14. push ____________
15. talk ____________
16. wish ____________

Endings: *-S* and *-ES*

Name ______________________

When a word ends with a consonant followed by **y,** change the **y** to **i** and add -**es.** When a word ends in a vowel followed by **y,** just add -**s.**

cry cri**es**
play play**s**

Read each word below. Add -**s** or -**es** to form a new word. Write the new word in the blank.

1. try tries
2. say ______
3. study ______
4. buy ______
5. fly ______
6. hurry ______
7. tray ______
8. marry ______
9. fry ______
10. lay ______
11. stay ______
12. copy ______
13. dry ______
14. enjoy ______
15. carry ______
16. pay ______

Endings: *-S* and *-ES*

Name ______________________

Read each sentence and the word beside it. Add -**s** or -**es** to the word to complete the sentence. Write the word in the blank.

1. Fran ___carries___ her lunch to work every day. carry
2. My puppy ______________ for bones. beg
3. Gail ______________ her teeth after each meal. brush
4. Our team always ______________ to play its best. try
5. Our club ______________ toys for friends. fix
6. The bus ______________ us to school in the morning. take
7. Rick ______________ water on the garden. spray
8. Our band ______________ in big parades. march
9. Mrs. Smith ______________ first grade. teach
10. The bell ______________ every night. ring

Endings: *-ER* and *-EST*

Name ______________________

The ending -**er** sometimes means "more." For example, **smaller** means "more small." The ending -**est** means "most." For example, **smallest** means "most small."

small
small**er**
small**est**

Look at the pictures and read the words. Draw a line from each word to the picture it tells about.

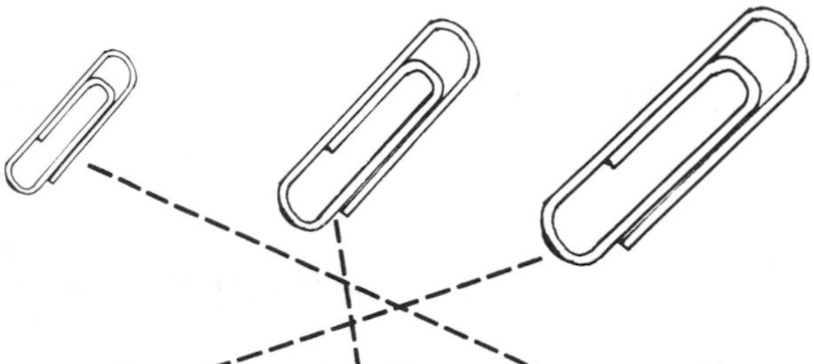

small smaller smallest

tall taller tallest

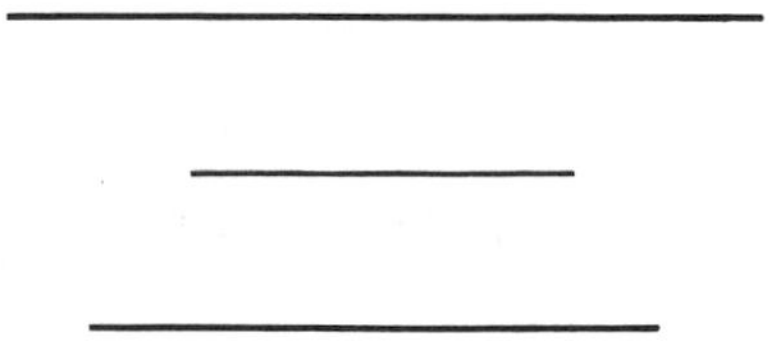

long longer longest

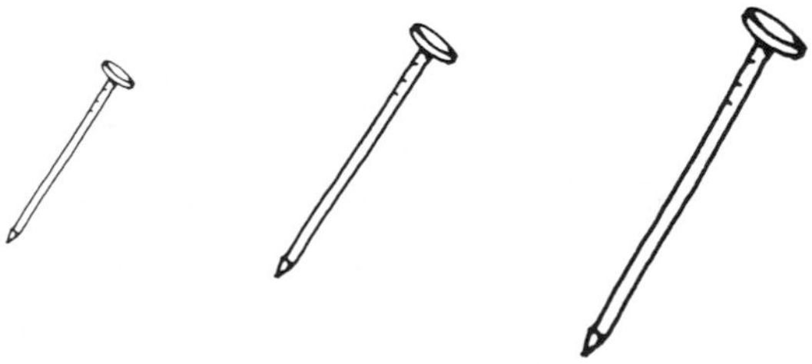

short shorter shortest

little littler littlest

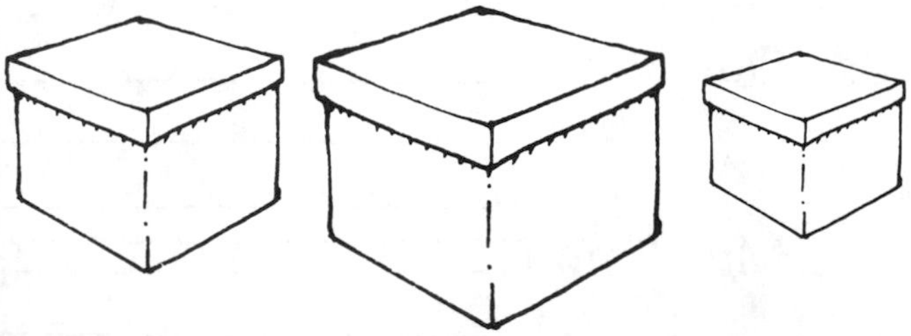

large larger largest

Endings: *-ER* and *-EST*

Name ____________________

The ending -**er** can be used to compare two things. The ending -**est** can be used to compare more than two things.

Read each sentence and the words beside it. Write the word that makes sense in each sentence.

1.	The tree is __taller__ than a house.	tall taller
2.	My cat is a ____________ color than my dog.	light lighter
3.	That is the ____________ tree in these woods.	older oldest
4.	My hair is ____________ than yours.	dark darker
5.	The blue car is the ____________ of all.	smaller smallest
6.	Tom's turtle was ____________ than mine.	slow slower
7.	Sam is the ____________ boy in the class.	faster fastest
8.	The lake is ____________ than the pond.	deeper deepest

Endings: *-ER* and *-EST*

Name ______________________

Read each sentence and the word beside it. Add -**er** or -**est** to the word to complete the sentence. Write the word in the blank.

1. Our team was the slower of the two. slow
2. The lake is ______________ than the pond. near
3. This plant is the ______________ in my garden. tall
4. I will take ______________ walks than before. long
5. Ted's pillow is ______________ than mine. soft
6. Play the ______________ note in this song. high
7. This test is the ______________ one of all. hard
8. I read the ______________ story in my book. short
9. Chad's shirt looks ______________ than mine. clean
10. The river is ______________ than the stream. wide

Endings

Name

Read each word below. Add the ending shown beside the word to form a new word. Write the new word in the blank.

1. wash + s or es =

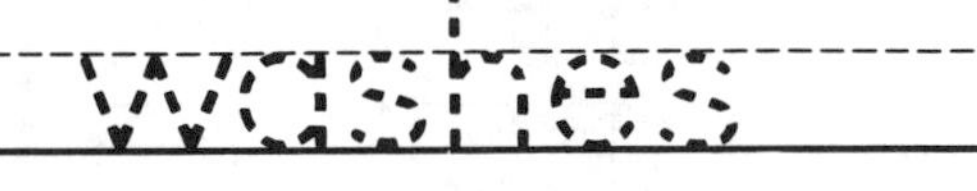

2. carry + s =
3. dark + er =
4. smile + ing =
5. come + ing =
6. near + est =
7. stop + ing =
8. match + s or es =
9. close + ed =
10. smart + est =

Endings

Name ______________________________

Read each sentence and the word beside it. Add an ending from the list below to the word. Write the word in the blank. You may use an ending more than once. **-ed** **-ing** **-s** **-es** **-er** **-est**

1.	Mom hurried to work this morning.	hurry
2.	The puppy ______________ the ball.	drop
3.	This is the ______________ hill in our town.	steep
4.	A free pencil ______________ with the paper.	come
5.	Jim ______________ the ball for our team.	catch
6.	Mandy is ______________ at me.	smile
7.	Is your pen ______________ than mine?	new
8.	Marsha will be ______________ her flute to school.	carry
9.	Ben ______________ the dishes after dinner.	dry
10.	Anna will be ______________ her nap soon.	take

Assessment of adding endings to base words in context

Plurals: -S and -*ES*

Name ______________________________

You can make many words mean "more than one" by adding **-s** to base words. When a word ends in **s, ss, sh, ch,** or **x,** add **-es** to make it mean "more than one."

lid**s**	wish**es**
bus**es**	patch**es**
dress**es**	fox**es**

Read the list of words below. Then look at the pictures. Add **-s** or **-es** to a word from the list to name the pictures in each box. Write the word in the blank.

watch	rake	bird	ax	hand
glass	bus	duck	mop	peach

birds ______________________________

____

____

____

____

____

____

____

____

____

Plurals: -S and -ES

Name ______________________

When a word ends in a consonant followed by **y,** change the **y** to **i** and add -**es** to make it mean "more than one." When a word ends in a vowel followed by **y,** just add -**s.**

story stor**ies**
boy boy**s**

Read the words below. Change each word to make it mean "more than one." Write the new word in the blank.

1. baby babies
2. key ______
3. pony ______
4. bunny ______
5. toy ______
6. watch ______
7. daisy ______
8. day ______
9. wish ______
10. book ______
11. fox ______
12. party ______
13. frog ______
14. penny ______
15. tray ______
16. dress ______

Plurals: -*S* and -*ES*

Name ______________________________

Read each sentence and the word beside it. Change the word to make it mean "more than one." Write the new word in the blank.

1.	Bob put ten ___cans___ of food onto the shelf.	can
2.	May likes sliced ______________ with cream.	peach
3.	Our class was standing in two ______________.	line
4.	The frogs like to eat ______________.	fly
5.	A big town can have many ______________.	park
6.	Sam has two ______________ in his hand.	penny
7.	Two wild ______________ ran into the woods.	fox
8.	All three of those ______________ sing well.	boy
9.	Did Carmen buy two new ______________?	dress
10.	The ______________ were hopping down the trail.	bunny

Plurals

Name

Read each sentence and the words beside it. Change one of the words to make it mean "more than one." Write the word in the blank. The word you write must make sense in the sentence.

1. We stacked the dishes on a shelf. — dish / door
2. Two ________ made a nest in the tree. — bird / bike
3. I put six ________ into the bank. — penny / party
4. Many ________ pass my home each day. — bus / bag
5. We rested on ________ after the game. — bench / bush
6. Pam went to three birthday ________. — party / pony
7. We use ________ for chopping wood. — ax / ash
8. I had two ________ for my lunch. — watch / peach
9. We told ________ and sang songs. — story / spray

Plurals

Name ______________________________

Read the words. Change each word to make it mean "more than one." Write the new word in the blank.

1. watch watches
2. bunny ______
3. game ______
4. city ______
5. wish ______
6. key ______
7. peach ______
8. penny ______
9. hand ______
10. cup ______
11. fly ______
12. fox ______
13. daisy ______
14. match ______
15. toy ______
16. box ______
17. goat ______
18. dress ______
19. bed ______
20. party ______

Adding 'S

Name ______________________

To show that something belongs to a person or thing, add **'s** to the end of the word that names the owner.

girl**'s** hat

Read each group of words below. Then add **'s** to the underlined word that names the owner. Write both underlined words in the blank.

1. the robe of Dad ______ Dad's robe ______
2. the bone of the dog ______________________
3. a sled that the girl has ______________________
4. the cat that Ray owns ______________________
5. the thorn of the rose ______________________
6. a pen that Ann has ______________________
7. the sister of Pat ______________________
8. the smile of the boy ______________________

Adding 'S

Name ______________________________

Read each sentence and the words beside it. Write the word that makes sense in each sentence.

1.	My **bike's** tire has gone flat.	bikes	bike's
2.	The ________ walked to school.	girls	girl's
3.	Her ________ hat fits just right.	dads	dad's
4.	My ________ coat is just like mine.	friends	friend's
5.	The ________ are closed.	bank's	banks
6.	My ________ eyes are brown.	mothers	mother's
7.	Those ________ have the same shirts.	boy's	boys
8.	That ________ car is new.	man's	mans
9.	My ________ toy is lost.	sister's	sisters

Adding 'S

Name ______________________

Read each sentence and the words beside it. Add **'s** to one of the words so it makes sense in the sentence. Write the word in the blank.

1.	Did Jane's cat run away?	Jane Jump Jam
2.	I like to watch the ______ new chicks.	head hen help
3.	The ______ cup is too full.	bone bow boy
4.	The ______ pages are torn.	book boot boom
5.	______ home is on my street.	Took Top Tom
6.	Is the ______ water dish blue?	door dot dog
7.	I will hang ______ coat on a hook.	Bill Bike Big
8.	Our ______ cage is clean.	bone bird book
9.	The ______ arm is in a cast.	give girl gate

Adding 'S

Name ______________________

Read each group of words below. Then add **'s** to the underlined word that names the owner. Write both underlined words in the blank.

1. the <u>tail</u> of the <u>kite</u> kite's tail
2. the <u>hat</u> that <u>Dan</u> has ______
3. the <u>paw</u> of the <u>cat</u> ______
4. a <u>book</u> that <u>Mom</u> owns ______
5. the <u>leg</u> of the <u>chair</u> ______
6. a <u>bike</u> that <u>Ben</u> has ______
7. the <u>flute</u> of <u>Amy</u> ______
8. the <u>game</u> of the <u>girl</u> ______
9. the <u>arm</u> of the <u>boy</u> ______
10. the <u>kitten</u> that <u>Bob</u> owns ______

Adding 'S

Name ______________________

Read each sentence and the words beside it. Add **'s** to one of the words so it makes sense in the sentence. Write the word in the blank.

1.	Our __town's__ stores are big.	too tune town
2.	This ____________ counter is full of toys.	stop shop spot
3.	The ____________ color is dark red.	ash apple at
4.	My ____________ painting is pretty.	fatter father feather
5.	That ____________ head is huge.	lion lean leaf
6.	The ____________ ears are long and floppy.	dot dog dig
7.	____________ coat is the same color as mine.	Jump Jill Jeep
8.	The ____________ tail was made of red string.	kit kite kick
9.	The ____________ leaves are falling.	trap tree trot

Assessment of forming singular possessives in context

Compound Words

Name ______________________

A compound word is formed by joining two smaller words together.

tea + pot = teapot

Read each compound word below. Write the two words that form each compound word.

1. baseball base ball
2. doghouse
3. snowflake
4. flashlight
5. popcorn
6. raincoat
7. bathtub
8. sailboat

Compound Words

Name ______________________

Read the words in each list. Draw lines to show words that form compound words.

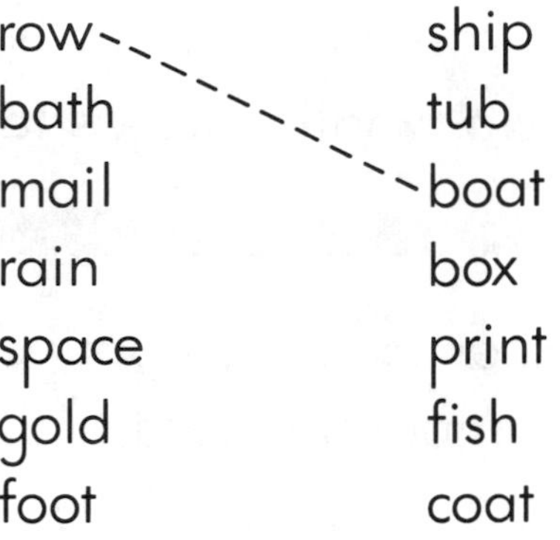

Read the sentences below. Write a compound word from the exercise above to complete each sentence.

1. A rowboat was on the lake.
2. Nell filled the ______________ with water.
3. A ______________ took off for the moon.
4. Jack put a letter in the ______________.
5. Each step left my ______________ in the sand.
6. A big ______________ swims in the pond.
7. Charlie wore his yellow ______________.

Compound Words

Name ______________________

Read each sentence below. Use two words from the sentence to form a compound word. Write the word in the blank.

1. A bird that is blue is a bluebird.
2. A burn from the sun is a ______________.
3. A drop of rain is a ______________.
4. The end of a week is a ______________.
5. A boat with a sail is a ______________.
6. A room where a class meets is a ______________.
7. A pole where a flag flies is a ______________.
8. A ball you kick with your foot is a ______________.
9. A knob on a door is a ______________.

Compound Words

Name ____________________

Read each sentence below. Use two words from the sentence to form a compound word. Write the word in the blank.

1. A coat worn in the rain is a raincoat.
2. The print your foot makes is a ____________.
3. A shell from the sea is a ____________.
4. A paper that tells news is a ____________.
5. A fish that is gold is a ____________.
6. The day of your birth is your ____________.
7. A plane that flies in the air is an ____________.
8. A box that holds sand is a ____________.
9. The long bone in your back is the ____________.

Compound Words

Name ______________________

Read the words in each list. Then read the sentences that follow. Choose a word from list **A** and a word from list **B** to form a compound word that completes each sentence. Write the word in the blank.

A	B
rain	noon
base	house
flash	end
after	light
dog	storm
pop	corn
week	ball

1. Last night's rainstorm soaked the garden.
2. Rover ran into his ______________.
3. My ______________ let us see the best path.
4. Two classes will play a game of ______________.
5. Our class reads in the ______________.
6. The ______________ tastes good.
7. I will see you at the game next ______________.

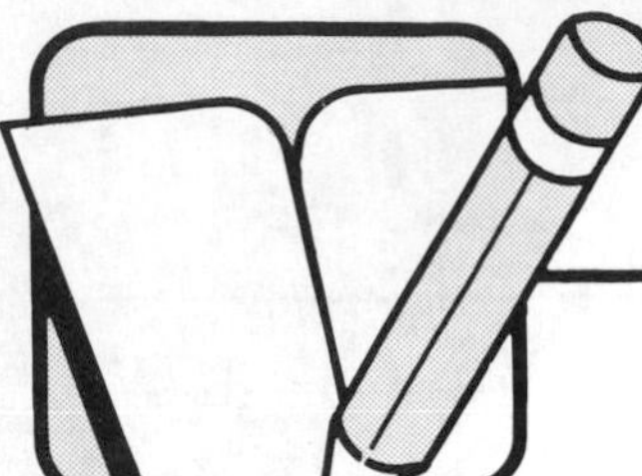

Reading and Writing Wrap-Up

Name ______________________

Your Five Senses

Every day you use your five senses to help you understand the things around you.

You use your [eyes] to see things. Think about the way the sun looks when it rises in the morning. Think about the color of a bright red fire truck.

You use your [ears] to hear things. Some sounds are loud, like a balloon popping—BANG! Some sounds are soft, like a penny dropping—PING.

You use your [nose] to smell things. You can smell the logs burning in a fireplace. You can smell the fresh paint on a bookcase.

You use your [mouth] to taste things. Some foods taste sweet. Other foods are sour.

You use your [hand] to feel things. Your skin tells you if something is smooth or if it will scratch. You can feel if something is wet or dry or warm or cold.

1. Look at the pictures in the first row. Which one of your five senses would best help you understand each thing? Draw a line to join each picture in the first row with the best picture in the next row.

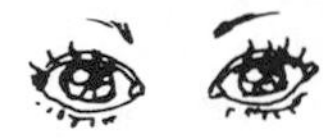

Science

Name

2. Read each word in the box. Then write each word in the best list.

rainbow	honey	laugh	fur	stars
butter	cold	gas	smoke	noise

Taste **Feel** **Smell**

Hear **See**

3. Choose one of the words in the box. Tell how it looks, feels, smells, tastes, and sounds.

water	apple	popcorn	gum

Contractions

Name

A contraction is a short way to write two words. It is written by putting two words together and leaving out a letter or letters. An apostrophe takes the place of the letter or letters that are left out. The word **won't** is a special contraction made from the words **will** and **not.**

is + not = **isn't**
I + am = **I'm**
let + us = **let's**
will + not = **won't**

Read the list of words below. Then read the word pairs that follow. Write a contraction from the list for each word pair.

hasn't	can't	let's	isn't	won't	haven't
weren't	I'm	aren't	wasn't	didn't	doesn't

1. have not haven't
2. was not
3. let us
4. will not
5. does not
6. has not
7. are not
8. is not
9. did not
10. can not
11. I am
12. were not

Contractions

Name

Read each contraction below. Then write the two words for which each contraction stands.

I + will = **I'll**
we + are = **we're**

1. she'll — she — will
2. they're
3. we'll
4. he'll
5. you're
6. I'll
7. we're
8. they'll
9. you'll

Contractions

Name ______________________

Read each sentence below. Write the contraction for the words shown under the blank in each sentence.

I + have = **I've**
it + is = **it's**

1. Linda said she's your friend.
(she is)

2. James thinks ______ going to the show.
(he is)

3. It seems ______ studied for a long time.
(you have)

4. ______ been playing baseball today.
(They have)

5. ______ easy to write my name.
(It is)

6. ______ been reading a good book.
(I have)

7. ______ been gone a long time.
(We have)

8. ______ been sick for three days.
(You have)

Contractions

Name ______________________________

Read each sentence below. Write the contraction for the words shown below the blank in each sentence.

1. Barb __won't__ be late for school.
   (will not)
2. Joyce and Bob said ____________ see us later.
   (they will)
3. Fran says ____________ going to her friend's house.
   (she is)
4. ____________ need a rest stop after the long hike.
   (We will)
5. You ____________ swim by yourself.
   (should not)
6. ____________ going to see snow falling soon.
   (We are)
7. The blue swimsuit ____________ my first choice.
   (was not)
8. ____________ glad to see you.
   (I am)
9. Sam ____________ going to sing for us.
   (is not)

Contractions

Name

Read each pair of words below. Write the contraction for each word pair.

1. did not didn't
2. she is
3. he will
4. I have
5. you will
6. they are
7. she will
8. has not
9. we are
10. it is
11. let us
12. I am
13. will not
14. is not
15. are not
16. you are
17. they have
18. they will
19. was not
20. we have

Prefixes

Name ______________________________

A prefix is a letter or group of letters that can be added to the beginning of a word. The prefix **re**- means "again." For example, the word **refill** means "fill again."

re + fill = **re**fill

Read each word below. Add the prefix **re**- to form a new word. Write the new word in the blank.

1. make remake
2. paint ______________
3. do ______________
4. play ______________
5. tell ______________
6. draw ______________

Read each sentence and the words beside it. Write the word that makes sense in each sentence.

1.	We will replant our garden.	repaint replant
2.	Please ______________ the story.	refold reread
3.	Dad will ______________ the cold meat.	rewrite reheat
4.	Ling will ______________ the glass.	retell refill

Prefixes

Name ______________________

The prefix **un**- means "not" or "the opposite of." For example, the word **unlock** means "the opposite of lock."

un + lock = **un**lock

Read each word below. Add the prefix **un**- to form a new word. Write the new word in the blank.

1. fair unfair
2. wrap ______________
3. happy ______________
4. pack ______________
5. lock ______________
6. dress ______________

Read each sentence and the words beside it. Write the word that makes sense in each sentence.

1.	Will you help me untie this knot?	undress untie
2.	The little girl looked ______________.	unhappy unlocked
3.	Did Carlos ______________ his gift yet?	unwrap unfair
4.	Mom will ______________ the box of dishes.	unsafe unpack

Forming words with prefix *un*-; Using words containing *un*- in context

Prefixes

Name ____________________

Read each sentence and the word beside it. Add **re**- or **un**- to the word to complete each sentence. The word you form must make sense in the sentence.

1.	I must reread this book.	read
2.	Was Pablo ____________ to you?	kind
3.	I will ____________ this story.	tell
4.	Can you ____________ the picture?	draw
5.	Jimmy must ____________ his work.	write
6.	The new rule of the game is ____________.	fair
7.	Did Ramona ____________ her house?	paint
8.	It is ____________ to throw away your paper.	wise
9.	Driving too fast is ____________.	safe
10.	The ____________ bill is a week late.	paid

Suffixes

Name ______________________

A suffix is a letter or group of letters that can be added to the end of a word. The suffix -**ful** usually means "full of." For example, the word helpful means "full of help."

help + **ful** = help**ful**

Read each word below. Add the suffix -**ful** to form a new word. Write the new word in the blank.

1. color colorful
2. care ______
3. use ______
4. pain ______
5. hope ______
6. thank ______

Read each sentence and the words beside it. Write the word that makes sense in each sentence.

1. I was thankful to get home. — useful / thankful
2. The falling leaves are very ______. — colorful / careful
3. My cut hand is ______. — playful / painful
4. I have a ______ smile on my face. — joyful / useful

Suffixes

Name ______________________

The suffix **-ly** can be added to some words. For example, something done in a **nice** way is done **nicely.**

nice + **ly** = nice**ly**

Read each word below. Add the suffix **-ly** to form a new word. Write the new word in the blank.

1. soft 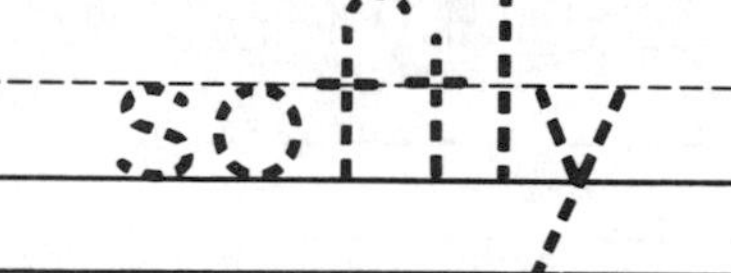
2. friend ______________
3. slow ______________
4. brave ______________
5. tight ______________
6. quick ______________

Read each sentence and the words beside it. Write the word that makes sense in each sentence.

1. Dress 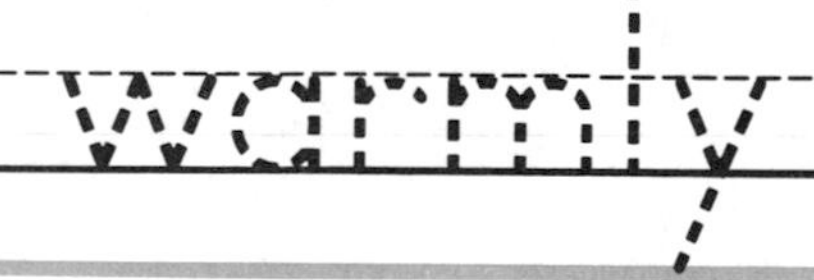 when it is cold. — warmly / badly
2. The gloves fit too ______________. — tightly / slowly
3. The little girl pet the kitten ______________. — softly / nearly
4. Chang ran ______________ down the street. — quickly / fairly

Suffixes

Name ______________________

Read each sentence and the word beside it. Add -**ful** or -**ly** to the word to complete each sentence. The word you form must make sense in the sentence.

1.	I am hopeful of winning the prize.	hope
2.	The wind blew __________ on my face.	soft
3.	Be sure to write your name __________.	neat
4.	Be __________ when you cross the street.	care
5.	Stan plays the horn __________.	loud
6.	Jose __________ gave up his turn.	glad
7.	Our new puppy is very __________.	play
8.	I like your __________ smile.	friend
9.	Alma wants to go home very __________.	bad
10.	We study many __________ things in school.	use

Prefixes and Suffixes

Name ______________________________

Read the list of prefixes and suffixes below. Then add one of the prefixes or suffixes to the underlined word in each group of words. Write the new word in the blank.

re- **un-** **-ful** **-ly**

1. to fill again ______ refill
2. the opposite of happy ______
3. in a quick way ______
4. full of hope ______
5. the opposite of pack ______
6. full of pain ______
7. in a safe way ______
8. the opposite of fair ______
9. full of cheer ______
10. to read again ______

Prefixes and Suffixes

Name ____________________

Read the list of words below. Underline the prefix or suffix in each word.

1. rewrap
2. fairly
3. repaint
4. cheerful
5. neatly
6. unfair
7. redo
8. gladly
9. rewrap
10. helpful
11. softly
12. restful
13. unpack
14. careful
15. unhappy
16. hopeful
17. unlock
18. retell
19. useful
20. colorful

Read the list of words below. Then read the sentences that follow. Write the word from the list that makes sense in each sentence.

careful	cheerful	retell
unlock	refill	bravely

1. A sunny day always makes Mary feel .
2. Do you have the key to ____________ the door?
3. I like to hear Mother ____________ that story.
4. Be ____________ of that top step.
5. Please ____________ my glass.
6. John ____________ said he would go first.

 Assessment of identifying prefixes and suffixes; Using words containing prefixes and suffixes in context

Syllables

Name ______________________

Many words are made of small parts called syllables. Because each syllable has one vowel sound, a word has as many syllables as it has vowel sounds. The word **stone** has one vowel sound, so it has one syllable. The word **raincoat** has two vowel sounds, so it has two syllables.

Name the pictures. Write the number of syllables you hear in each picture name.

bathtub 2	umbrella ____	slipper ____
chick ____	fork ____	pocket ____
bird ____	garden ____	butterfly ____
valentine ____	frog ____	wagon ____

Syllables

Name

A compound word can be divided into syllables between the words that make it compound.

rain / bow

Read the list of compound words below. Write each compound word and draw a line between its syllables.

1. doorbell door / bell
2. sailboat
3. raincoat
4. popcorn
5. sunset
6. airplane
7. sunburn
8. backyard
9. birthday

Syllables

Name

A word that has a prefix or suffix can be divided into syllables between the prefix or suffix and the base word.

un / tie
help / ful

Read the list of words. Write each word and draw a line between its syllables.

1. refill re/fill
2. unfair
3. rewrap
4. gladly
5. unlock
6. painful
7. untie
8. retell
9. reread
10. unkind
11. restful
12. playful
13. loudly
14. hopeful
15. reheat
16. badly

Syllables

Name ______________________

Read each sentence below. Use two words from the sentence to form a compound word. Write the word in the blank and draw a line between its syllables.

1. A fish that is gold is a gold/fish.
2. The print your foot makes is a ______________.
3. A boat with a sail is a ______________.
4. The day of your birth is your ______________.

Read the list of prefixes and suffixes below. Then add one of the prefixes or suffixes to the underlined word in each group of words. Write the new word in the blank and draw a line between its syllables.

re- **un-** **-ful** **-ly**

1. full of <u>hope</u> hope/ful
2. in a <u>neat</u> way ______________
3. the opposite of <u>lock</u> ______________
4. to <u>read</u> again ______________

Review of forming compound words and words with prefixes and suffixes; Dividing words into syllables

Syllables

Name ______________________

Read the words below. Write each word and draw a line between its syllables.

1. airplane air / plane
2. lightly
3. useful
4. refill
5. unfair
6. glassful
7. raindrop
8. rewrap
9. lately
10. undress

Antonyms

Name ______________________

An antonym is a word that has the opposite meaning of another word.

yes—no
near—far
first—last

Read the words in each box. Draw a line to match each word with its antonym (opposite).

day	leave	thin	there
stay	shut	come	thick
open	night	here	go
hot	new	in	under
sick	cold	over	warm
old	well	cool	out
wet	far	fast	slow
near	quiet	light	push
noise	dry	pull	dark
strong	below	on	small
above	soft	after	off
hard	weak	large	before

Antonyms

Name ______________________

Read the words below. In each row, circle the word that is an antonym (opposite) for the first word.

1.	hard	deep	(soft)	free
2.	sink	float	trap	run
3.	right	less	hurt	wrong
4.	after	first	before	near
5.	fast	slow	many	pretty

Read each sentence and the words beside it. Write the word that is an antonym (opposite) for the word shown below each blank.

1. Turn a light ____on____ so we can see. (off) — around / on
2. The ______________ runner will win this race. (slowest) — fastest / oldest
3. The books are on a shelf ______________ my head. (below) — above / near
4. The little boy has a ______________ dog. (large) — quiet / small
5. Jan wore her ______________ coat. (old) — new / warm

Antonyms

Name ____________________

Read the list of words below. Then read the words that follow. Write an antonym (opposite) from the list for each word.

in	no	slow	bad	found	near
cry	stop	on	big	small	more
night	thin	last	cold	dry	after

1. fast slow
2. good ____
3. out ____
4. large ____
5. start ____
6. yes ____
7. far ____
8. day ____
9. less ____
10. hot ____
11. laugh ____
12. first ____
13. lost ____
14. off ____
15. wet ____
16. little ____
17. thick ____
18. before ____

Synonyms

Name ______________________

A synonym is a word that has the same or nearly the same meaning as another word.

small—little
sleep—nap
fast—quick

Read the words in each box. Draw a line to match each word with its synonym (word that has the same meaning).

shout	chilly	start	begin
big	large	sleep	look
cool	yell	see	rest

look	dad	under	city
pile	see	town	clean
father	stack	wash	below

sack	small	happy	road
little	bag	friend	pal
land	ground	street	glad

lift	speak	steps	close
talk	noisy	penny	stairs
loud	raise	shut	cent

Synonyms

Name ______________________

Read the words below. In each row, circle the word that is a synonym (word that has the same meaning) for the first word.

1.	friends	pals	boys	caps
2.	bag	stand	sack	paper
3.	big	new	free	large
4.	sniff	smell	pet	nose
5.	cool	good	chilly	high

Read each sentence and the words beside it. Write the word that is a synonym (word that has the same meaning) for the word shown below each blank.

1. Jeff's home is near mine. like / near
   (close to)
2. I made a ______________ trip to the store. quick / third
   (fast)
3. Kenny has a ______________ on his face. mark / smile
   (grin)
4. We need to ______________ our dog. wash / find
   (clean)
5. You may ______________ now. brook / begin
   (start)

Synonyms

Name ______________________

Read the list of words below. Then read the words that follow. Write a synonym (word that has the same meaning) from the list for each word.

happy	fix	small	shout	swift	song
cent	rock	near	throw	supper	fire
sniff	brook	noisy	grin	afraid	rest

1. mend fix
2. smell ______
3. tune ______
4. smile ______
5. dinner ______
6. sleep ______
7. fast ______
8. close ______
9. penny ______
10. pitch ______
11. stone ______
12. scared ______
13. stream ______
14. flame ______
15. tiny ______
16. loud ______
17. yell ______
18. glad ______

Homophones

Name

Homophones are words that sound the same but have different spellings and different meanings.

sea—see
to—two
right—write

Read the words in each box. Draw a line to match each word on the left with a word on the right that is pronounced the same.

meat	made	weak	road
maid	sail	here	week
sale	meet	rode	hear

flower	deer	pane	plain
to	flour	pail	pale
dear	two	plane	pain

right	waste	bare	be
would	write	buy	bear
waist	wood	bee	by

sent	sea	knot	knight
eye	cent	night	not
see	I	new	knew

Homophones

Name

Read the list of words below. Then read the words that follow. For each word write a word that is pronounced the same but spelled differently.

meat	here	waist	be	cent	two	deer	made
right	eye	knew	blue	sale	week	heal	road

1. dear deer
2. meet
3. waste
4. sail
5. to
6. blew
7. write
8. maid
9. weak
10. hear
11. bee
12. sent
13. new
14. I
15. heel
16. rode

Homophones

Name

Read the words below. In each row, circle the word that is pronounced the same as the first word.

1.	here	hear	head	heel
2.	cent	seed	sent	see
3.	week	weak	weed	weep
4.	sale	sail	safe	sat
5.	road	robe	roast	rode

Read each sentence and the words beside it. Write the word that is pronounced the same as the word shown below each blank.

1. Jane blew dust off the old book. (blue) — blew, beat
2. We saw ________ skunks in the woods. (too) — ten, two
3. There is a bug in my ________. (I) — eye, ear
4. Robin will ________ a story in class. (right) — write, read
5. I ________ like you to come to my party. (wood) — would, waist

Antonyms, Synonyms, and Homophones

Name ______________________________

Read the words in each box. Draw a line to match each word with its antonym (opposite).

wrong	last	slow	happy
before	right	sad	hot
first	dark	weak	fast
light	after	cold	strong

Read the words in each box. Draw a line to match each word with its synonym (word that has the same meaning).

smell	clean	small	close
wash	grin	talk	steps
smile	sick	stairs	little
ill	sniff	shut	speak

Read the words in each box. Draw a line to match each word with its homophone (word that is pronounced the same).

meet	road	deer	right
rode	sale	write	I
two	meat	eye	by
sail	too	buy	dear

PROGRESS CHECK

Antonyms, Synonyms, and Homophones

Name ______________________________

Read the questions below. Answer each question by circling two words.

1. Which two words are antonyms?
   cold small hot water
2. Which two words are synonyms?
   ill well glad sick
3. Which two words are homophones?
   spend sent cent penny
4. Which two words are antonyms?
   fast near slow race
5. Which two words are synonyms?
   big large small size

Read each pair of words below. Write **a** between each pair of antonyms. Write **s** between each pair of synonyms. Write **h** between words that are pronounced the same.

1. big __s__ large
2. dark ____ light
3. sail ____ sale
4. first ____ last
5. dear ____ deer
6. happy ____ sad
7. smile ____ grin
8. blue ____ blew
9. soft ____ hard
10. fast ____ quick
11. knew ____ new
12. lift ____ raise

Assessment of identification of antonyms, synonyms, homophones

Alphabetical Order

Name

You can put words in alphabetical order by writing the first letter of each word in alphabetical order.

bed
play
yard

Read each set of words below. Then look at the first letter of each word to write the words in alphabetical order.

talk bug horse

1. bug
2.
3.

rain feet zoo

1.
2.
3.

egg ice apple dog

1.
2.
3.
4.

dress sun noise pan

1.
2.
3.
4.

Alphabetical Order

Name ______________________

Read each set of words below. Then look at the first letter of each word to write the words in alphabetical order.

like work down

1. down
2.
3.

jump can stop

1.
2.
3.

wet miss fun ant

1.
2.
3.
4.

yard hen bag ox

1.
2.
3.
4.

Alphabetical Order

Name ______________________

When words begin with the same letter, use the second letters to put the words in alphabetical order.

d**o**g
d**i**sh
d**r**aw

Read each set of words below. Write the words in alphabetical order.

ax ask and

1. and
2. ______
3. ______

give gas get

1. ______
2. ______
3. ______

sun sack song set

1. ______
2. ______
3. ______
4. ______

east eye egg ever

1. ______
2. ______
3. ______
4. ______

Alphabetical Order

Name ______________________

Read each set of words below. Then write the words in alphabetical order. You may have to look at the second letter in some words.

truck lock gate

1. gate
2. ______
3. ______

bake brake blue

1. ______
2. ______
3. ______

stay scrub shell slip

1. ______
2. ______
3. ______
4. ______

up pass know cow

1. ______
2. ______
3. ______
4. ______

Alphabetical Order

Name ______________________

Read each set of words below. Then look at the first or second letter of each word to write the words in alphabetical order.

crab car clock

1. car
2. ______
3. ______

wash ring need

1. ______
2. ______
3. ______

pet bird duck cat

1. ______
2. ______
3. ______
4. ______

old one off open

1. ______
2. ______
3. ______
4. ______

Reading and Writing Wrap-Up

Name ______________________________

Milk

You drink milk every day. Have you stopped to think about where milk comes from and how it gets to you?

The milk you drink comes from cows. The cows feed on green grass. On some farms cows may eat other things, too. Corn plants that have been chopped up may be used as feed. Farmers may buy grain to feed their cows, too.

At night the cows come to the barn, where the farmer milks them. In the morning the cows are milked again. The milk goes into a steel tank that is kept very clean. Then the milk is checked to be sure it is good.

A milk truck comes to the farm to pick up the milk. The tank on the milk truck is just as clean as the milk tank on the farm. The milk truck takes the milk to the milk plant.

In the milk plant, the milk is heated. This makes it safe to drink. Then the milk is put into boxes and cases and the lids are sealed. The boxed milk is put onto another truck.

This truck takes the milk to the store where your family will buy it and bring it home for you to drink.

Milk has many uses. First of all, milk is a good food. Milk is used to make cheese and ice cream. But you may be surprised to know that milk is used in making paint and some kinds of dishes, too.

1. Check the two words that mean <u>feed</u>.

_____ grain _____ eat _____ buy

Name ______________________________

2. Write two things that are made from milk that are not foods.

______________________ ______________________

3. Write 1, 2, 3, and 4 to show what comes first, next, and so on.

_____ The milk is heated at the milk plant to make it safe to drink.

_____ The farmer milks the cows in the morning and at night.

_____ People buy the milk in stores.

_____ The cows eat grass, chopped corn, and other kinds of feed.

4. Find out something about another kind of food. Tell where it comes from and how it gets to you. Choose one of these foods or think of another one you would like to know more about.

apple drink ground beef bread oatmeal

Sounds and Letters

f**a**n

r**a**k**e**

tr**ai**n

j**ar**

auto

s**aw**

h**ay**

car

cent

chair

du**ck**

b**e**d

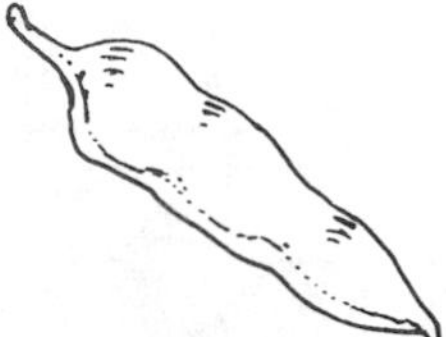

b**ea**n

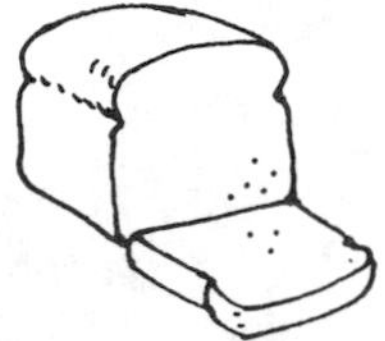

br**ea**d

b**ee**

Sounds and Letters

f**er**n	n**ew**s	**g**oat
		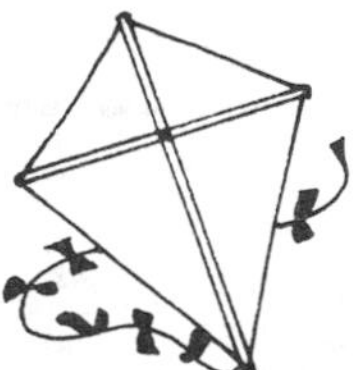
pa**g**e	b**i**b	k**i**t**e**

b**ir**d	**kn**ot	ri**ng**

t**o**p	c**oa**t	b**o**n**e**

c**oi**n	m**oo**n	b**oo**k

Sounds and Letters

h**or**n

cl**ou**d

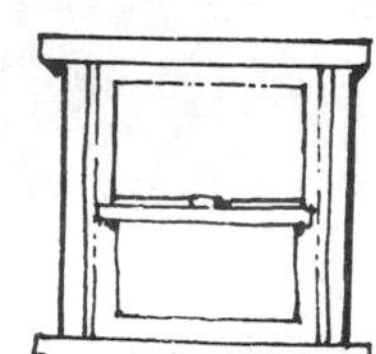

wind**ow**

c**ow**

t**oy**s

shoe

thin

three

c**u**p

t**u**b**e**

b**ur**n

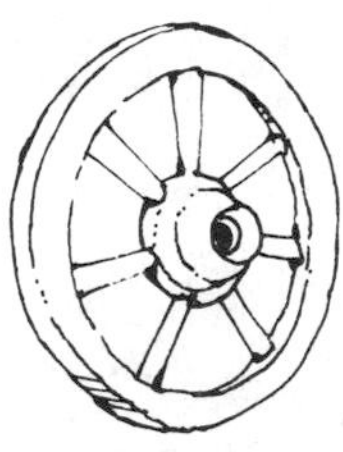

wheel

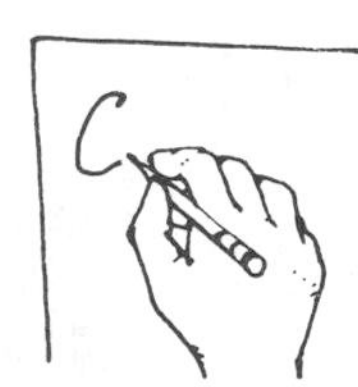

write

fl**y**

pon**y**

Beginning Sounds

Name ______ Words to use: ball, bank, bell, four, farm, fish, golf, watch, well, worm, wig, zoo, zero, gas, duck, desk, pan, pony, ring, red, rock, top, table, ten

Name the pictures. Write the letter that stands for the beginning sound of each picture name.

bat — b	fish — f	watch — w
zebra — z	dog — d	gate — g
pig — p	ring — r	top — t
six — s	nose — n	ham — h

Sound-symbol association of initial consonants 5

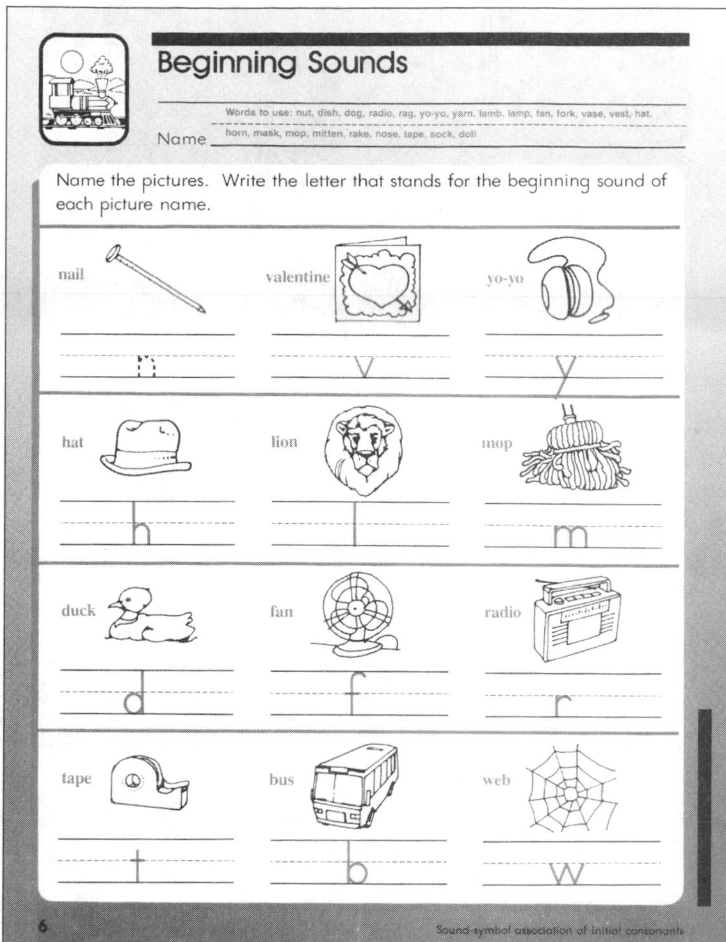

Beginning Sounds

Name ______ Words to use: nut, dish, dog, radio, rag, yo-yo, yarn, lamb, lamp, fan, fork, vase, vest, hat, horn, mask, mop, mitten, rake, nose, tape, sock, doll

Name the pictures. Write the letter that stands for the beginning sound of each picture name.

nail — n	valentine — v	yo-yo — y
hat — h	lion — l	mop — m
duck — d	fan — f	radio — r
tape — t	bus — b	web — w

6 Sound-symbol association of initial consonants

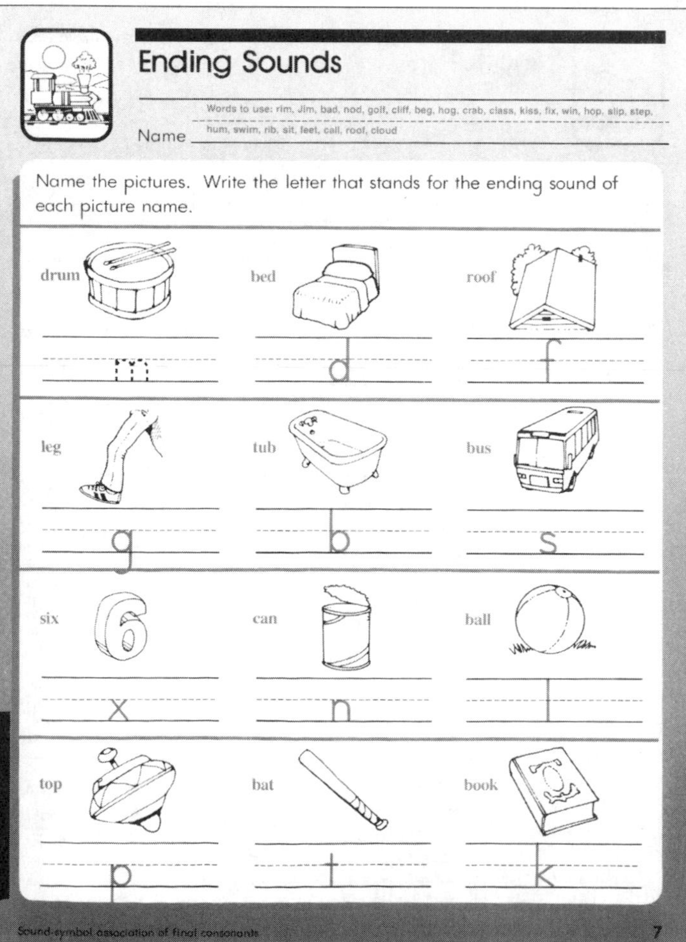

Ending Sounds

Name ______ Words to use: rim, Jim, bad, nod, golf, cliff, beg, hog, crab, class, kiss, fix, win, hop, slip, step, hum, swim, rib, sit, feet, call, roof, cloud

Name the pictures. Write the letter that stands for the ending sound of each picture name.

drum — m	bed — d	roof — f
leg — g	tub — b	bus — s
six — x	can — n	ball — l
top — p	bat — t	book — k

Sound-symbol association of final consonants 7

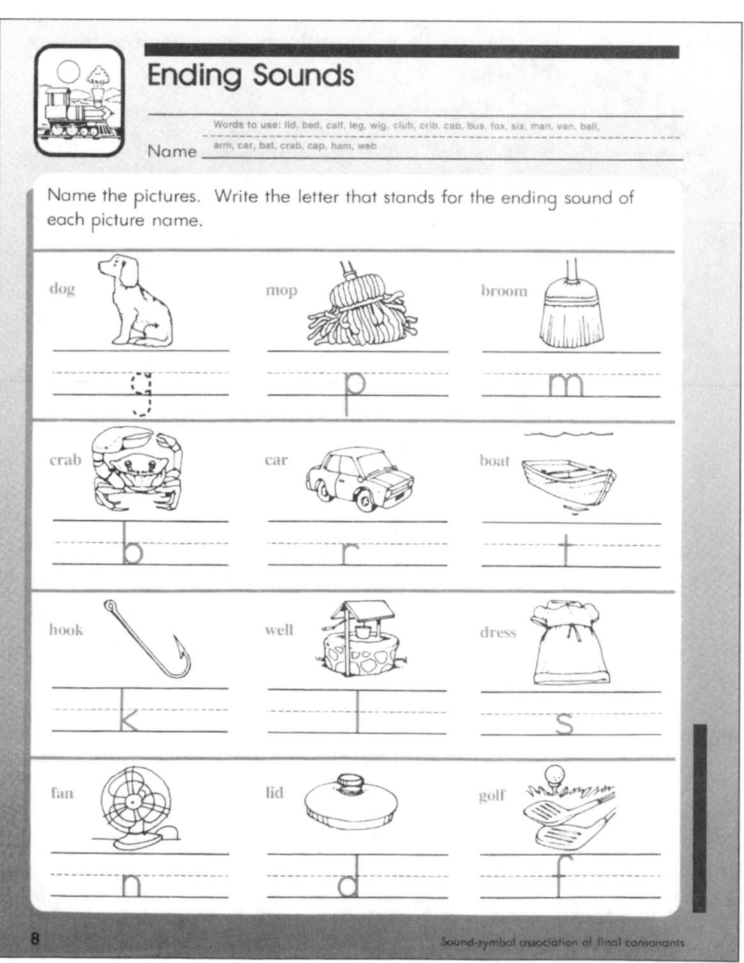

Ending Sounds

Name ______ Words to use: lid, bed, calf, leg, wig, club, crib, cab, bus, fox, six, man, van, ball, arm, car, bat, crab, cap, ham, web

Name the pictures. Write the letter that stands for the ending sound of each picture name.

dog — g	mop — p	broom — m
crab — b	car — r	boat — t
hook — k	well — l	dress — s
fan — n	lid — d	golf — f

8 Sound-symbol association of final consonants

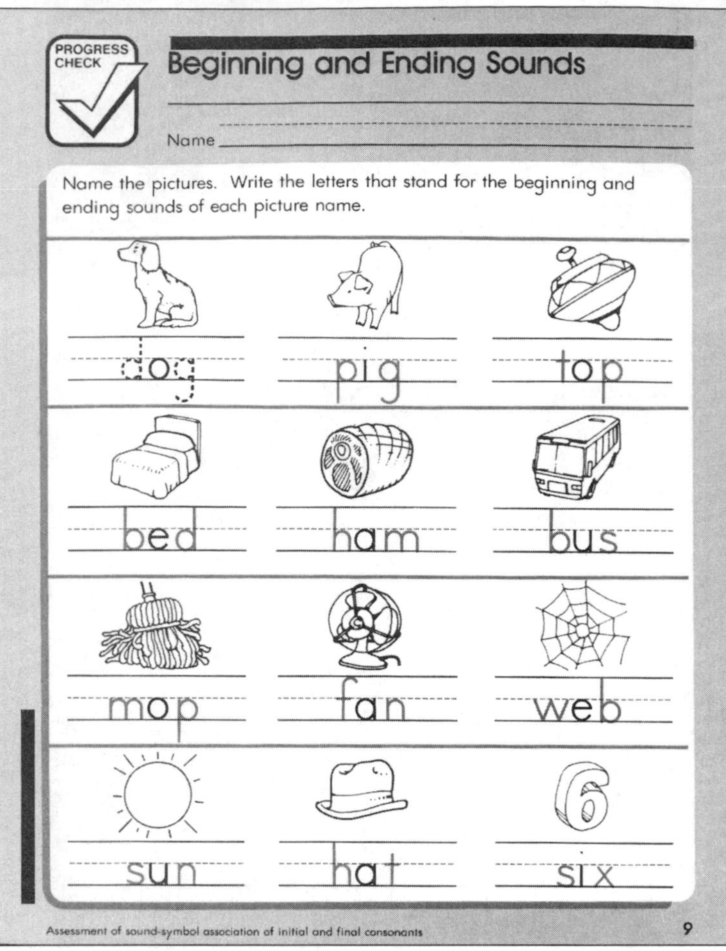

PROGRESS CHECK

Beginning and Ending Sounds

Name

Name the pictures. Write the letters that stand for the beginning and ending sounds of each picture name.

dog pig top

bed ham bus

mop fan web

sun hat six

Assessment of sound-symbol association of initial and final consonants 9

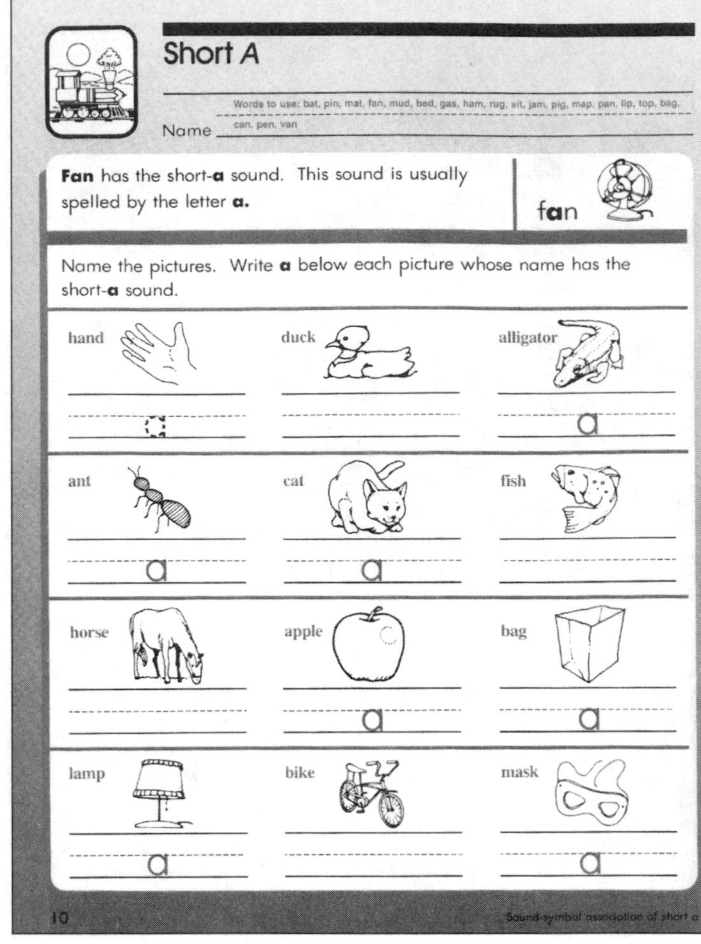

Short *A*

Words to use: bat, pin, mat, fan, mud, bed, gas, ham, rug, sit, jam, pig, map, pan, lip, top, bag, can, pen, van

Name

Fan has the short-**a** sound. This sound is usually spelled by the letter **a.**

f**a**n

Name the pictures. Write **a** below each picture whose name has the short-**a** sound.

hand	duck	alligator
a		a
ant	**cat**	**fish**
a	a	
horse	**apple**	**bag**
	a	a
lamp	**bike**	**mask**
a		a

10 Sound-symbol association of short a

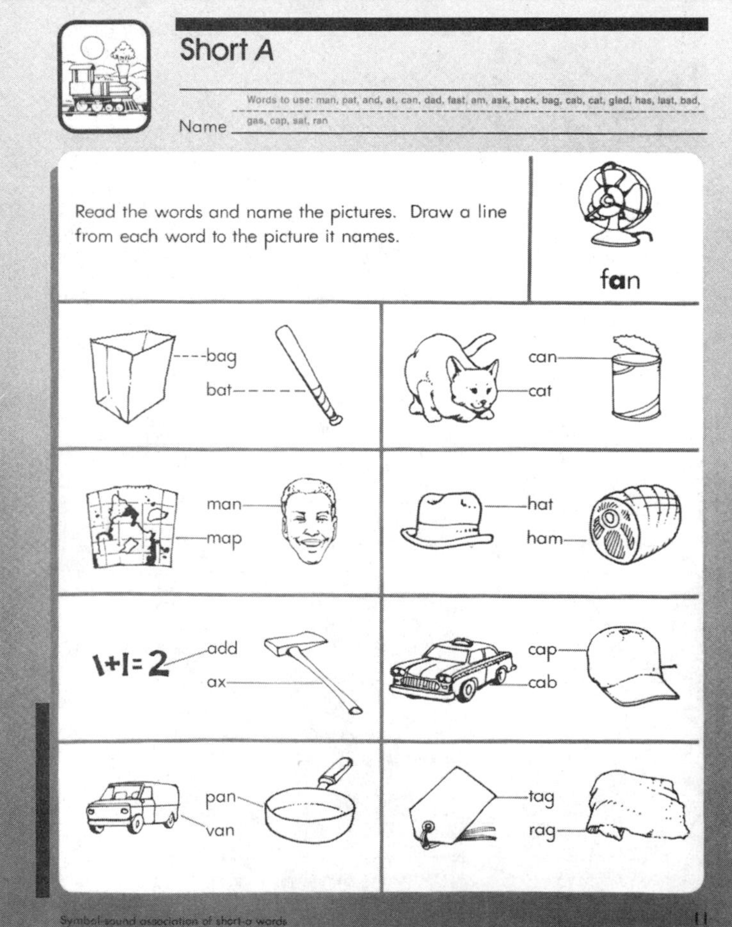

Short *A*

Words to use: man, pat, and, at, can, dad, fast, am, ask, back, bag, cab, cat, glad, has, last, bad, gas, cap, sat, ran

Name

Read the words and name the pictures. Draw a line from each word to the picture it names.

f**a**n

bag, bat

can, cat

man, map

hat, ham

\+I= 2 add, ax

cap, cab

pan, van

tag, rag

Symbol-sound association of short-a words 11

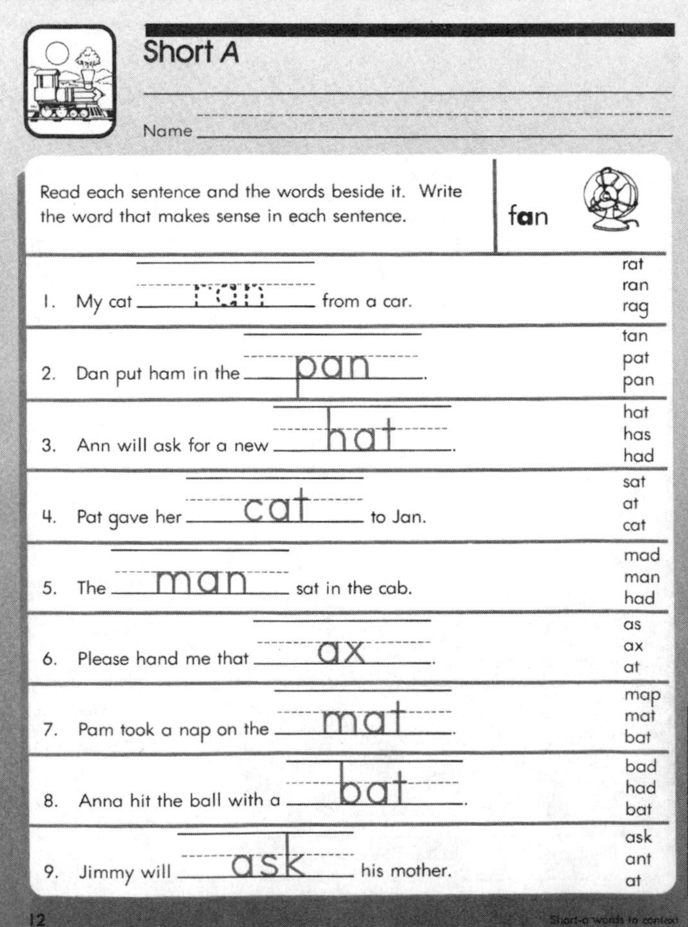

Short *A*

Name

Read each sentence and the words beside it. Write the word that makes sense in each sentence.

f**a**n

1. My cat ran from a car.	rat ran rag
2. Dan put ham in the pan.	tan pat pan
3. Ann will ask for a new hat.	hat has had
4. Pat gave her cat to Jan.	sat at cat
5. The man sat in the cab.	mad man had
6. Please hand me that ax.	as ax at
7. Pam took a nap on the mat.	map mat bat
8. Anna hit the ball with a bat.	bad had bat
9. Jimmy will ask his mother.	ask ant at

12 Short-a words in context

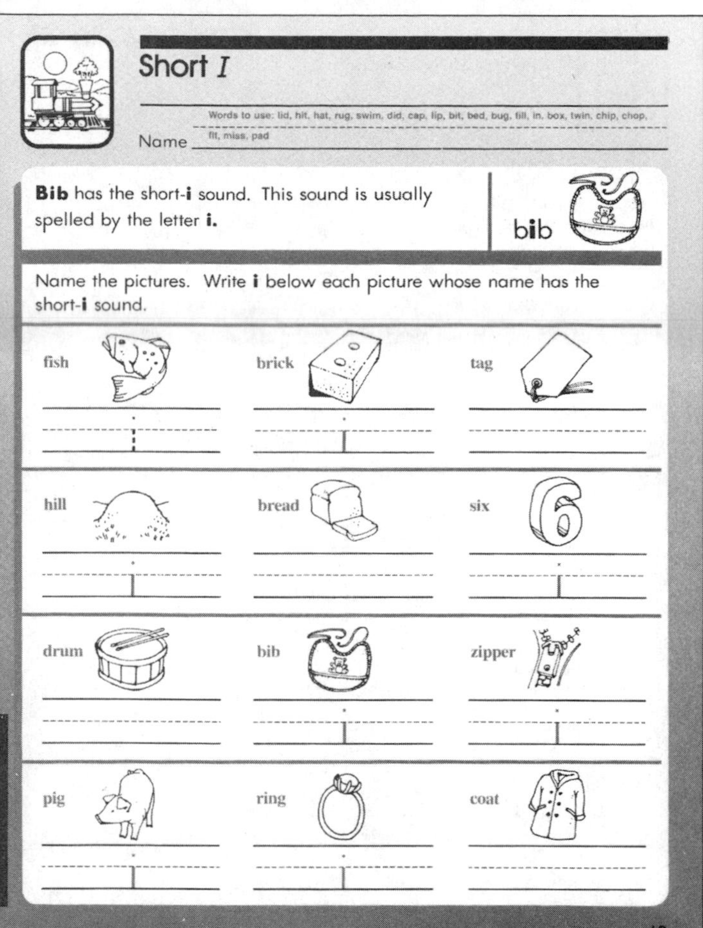

Short *I*

Name

Words to use: lid, hit, hat, rug, swim, did, cap, lip, bit, bed, bug, fill, in, box, twin, chip, chop, fit, miss, pad

Bib has the short-**i** sound. This sound is usually spelled by the letter **i.**

b**i**b

Name the pictures. Write **i** below each picture whose name has the short-**i** sound.

fish	brick	tag
hill	bread	six
drum	bib	zipper
pig	ring	coat

Sound-symbol association of short i

13

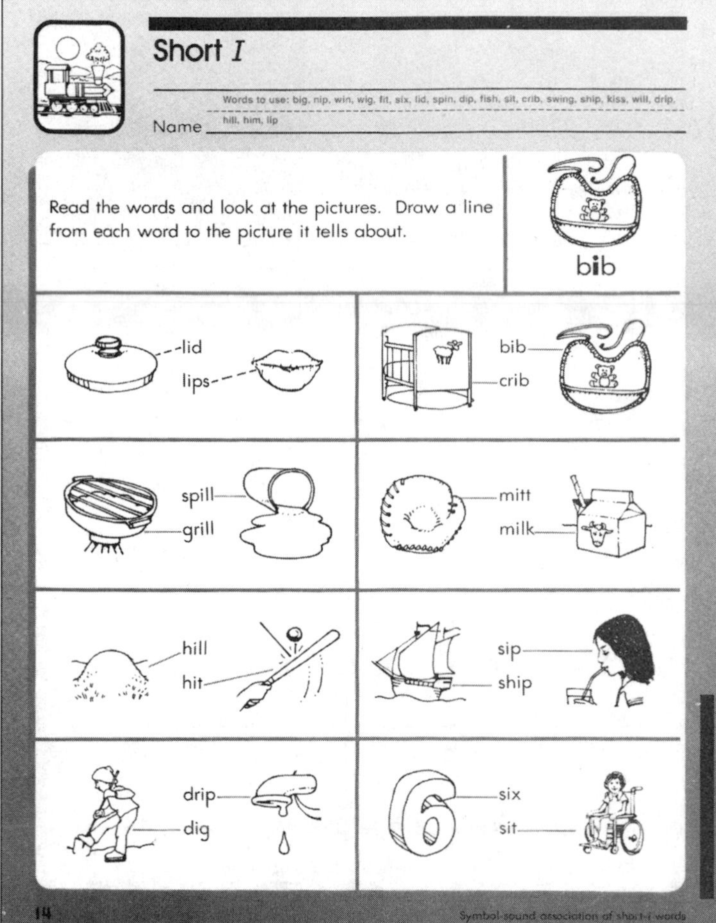

Short *I*

Name

Words to use: big, nip, win, wig, fit, six, lid, spin, dip, fish, sit, crib, swing, ship, kiss, will, drip, hill, him, lip

Read the words and look at the pictures. Draw a line from each word to the picture it tells about.

b**i**b

lid / lips	bib / crib
spill / grill	mitt / milk
hill / hit	sip / ship
drip / dig	six / sit

14

Symbol-sound association of short-i words

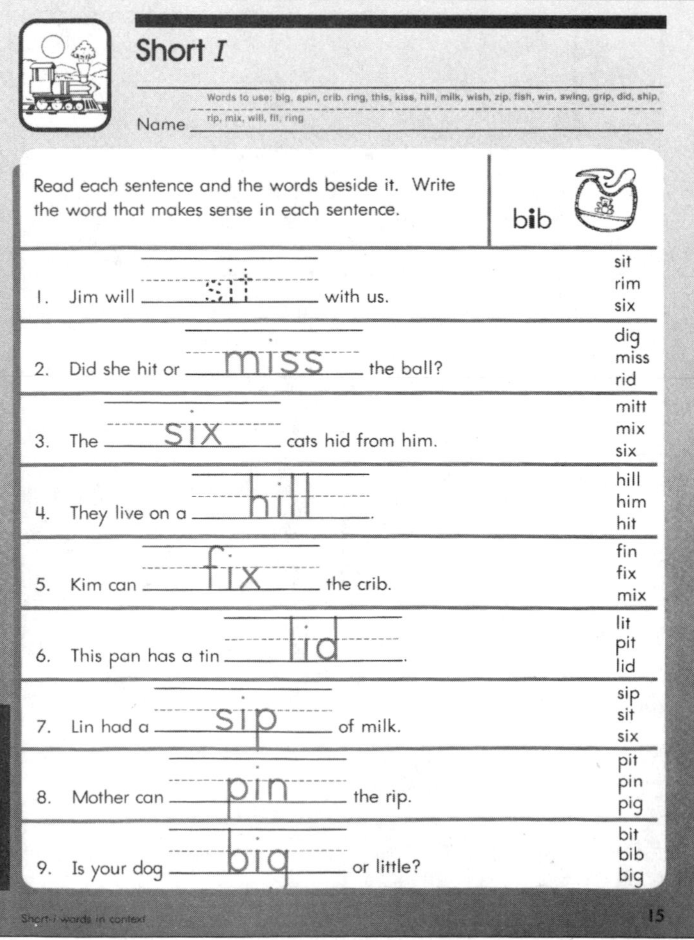

Short *I*

Name

Words to use: big, spin, crib, ring, this, kiss, hill, milk, wish, zip, fish, win, swing, grip, did, ship, rip, mix, will, fit, ring

Read each sentence and the words beside it. Write the word that makes sense in each sentence.

b**i**b

1. Jim will sit with us.	sit rim six
2. Did she hit or miss the ball?	dig miss rid
3. The six cats hid from him.	mitt mix six
4. They live on a hill.	hill him hit
5. Kim can fix the crib.	fin fix mix
6. This pan has a tin lid.	lit pit lid
7. Lin had a sip of milk.	sip sit six
8. Mother can pin the rip.	pit pin pig
9. Is your dog big or little?	bit bib big

Short-i words in context

15

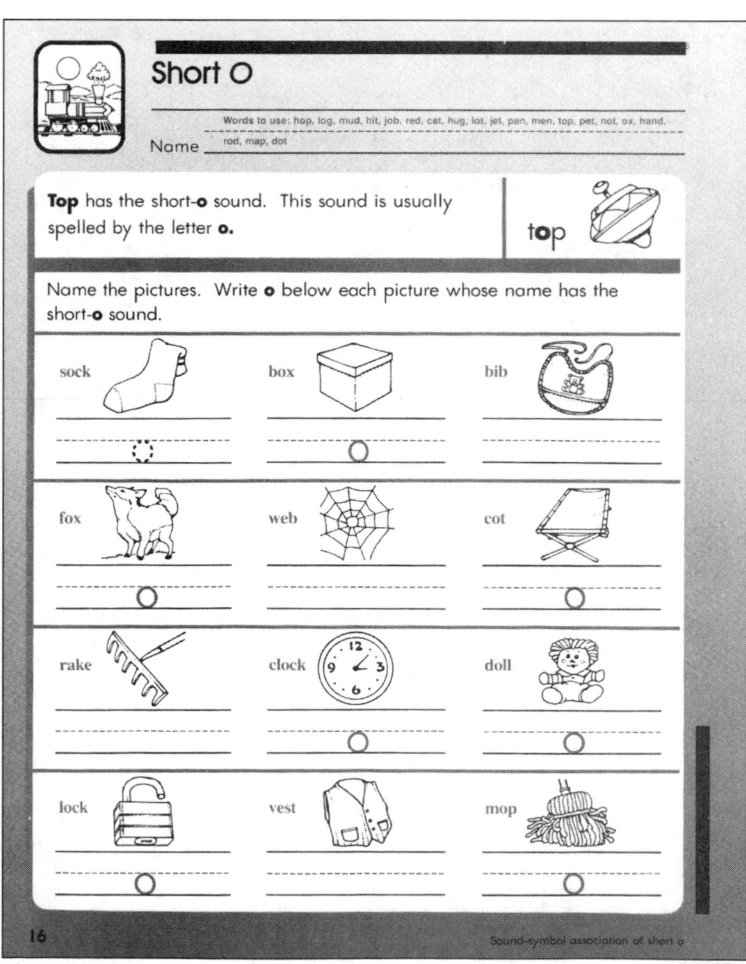

Short O

Name

Words to use: hop, log, mud, hit, job, red, cat, hug, lot, jet, pan, men, top, pet, not, ox, hand, rod, map, dot

Top has the short-**o** sound. This sound is usually spelled by the letter **o.**

t**o**p

Name the pictures. Write **o** below each picture whose name has the short-**o** sound.

sock	box	bib
fox	web	cot
rake	clock	doll
lock	vest	mop

16

Sound-symbol association of short o

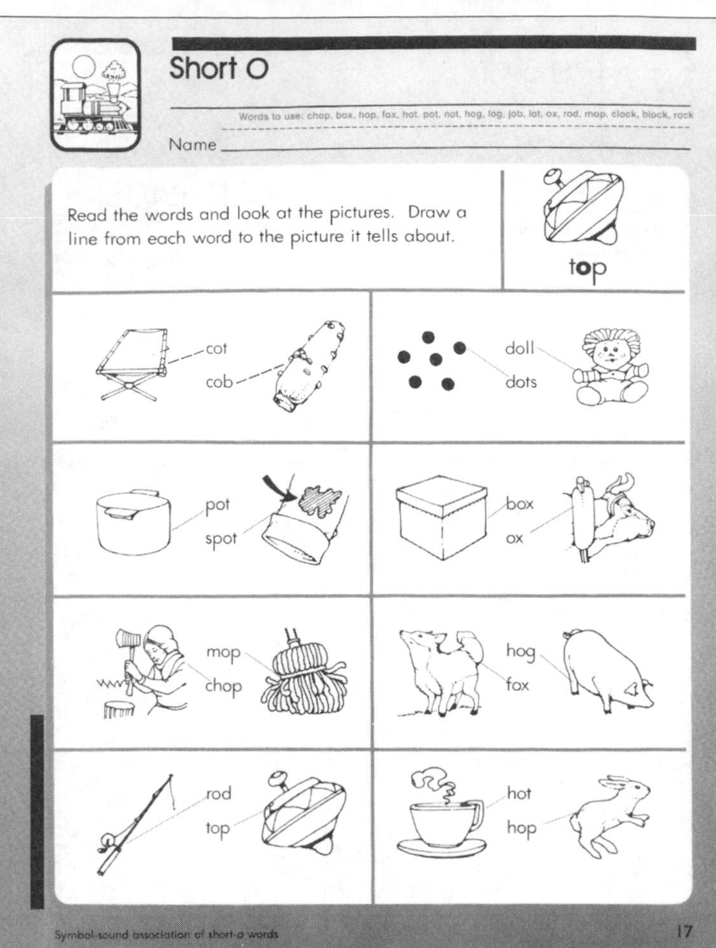

Short O

Words to use: chop, box, hop, fox, hot, pot, not, hog, log, job, lot, ox, rod, mop, clock, block, rock

Name ____________________

Read the words and look at the pictures. Draw a line from each word to the picture it tells about.

top

cot / cob	doll / dots
pot / spot	box / ox
mop / chop	hog / fox
rod / top	hot / hop

Symbol-sound association of short-*o* words 17

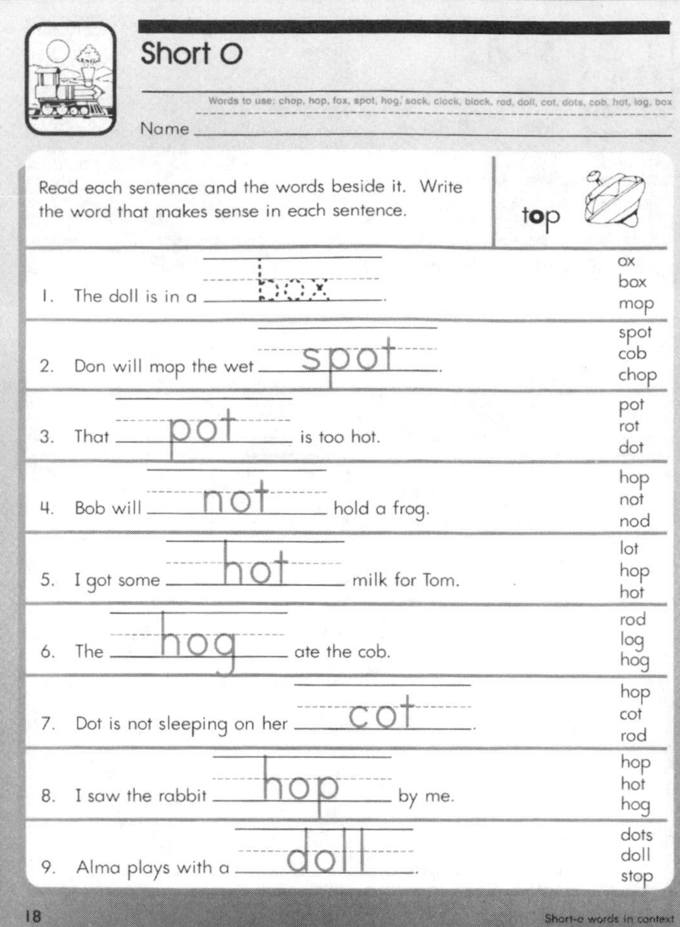

Short O

Words to use: chop, hop, fox, spot, hog, sock, clock, block, rod, doll, cot, dots, cob, hot, log, box

Name ____________________

Read each sentence and the words beside it. Write the word that makes sense in each sentence.

top

1. The doll is in a box.	ox / box / mop
2. Don will mop the wet spot.	spot / cob / chop
3. That pot is too hot.	pot / rot / dot
4. Bob will not hold a frog.	hop / not / nod
5. I got some hot milk for Tom.	lot / hop / hot
6. The hog ate the cob.	rod / log / hog
7. Dot is not sleeping on her cot.	hop / cot / rod
8. I saw the rabbit hop by me.	hop / hot / hog
9. Alma plays with a doll.	dots / doll / stop

18 Short-*o* words in context

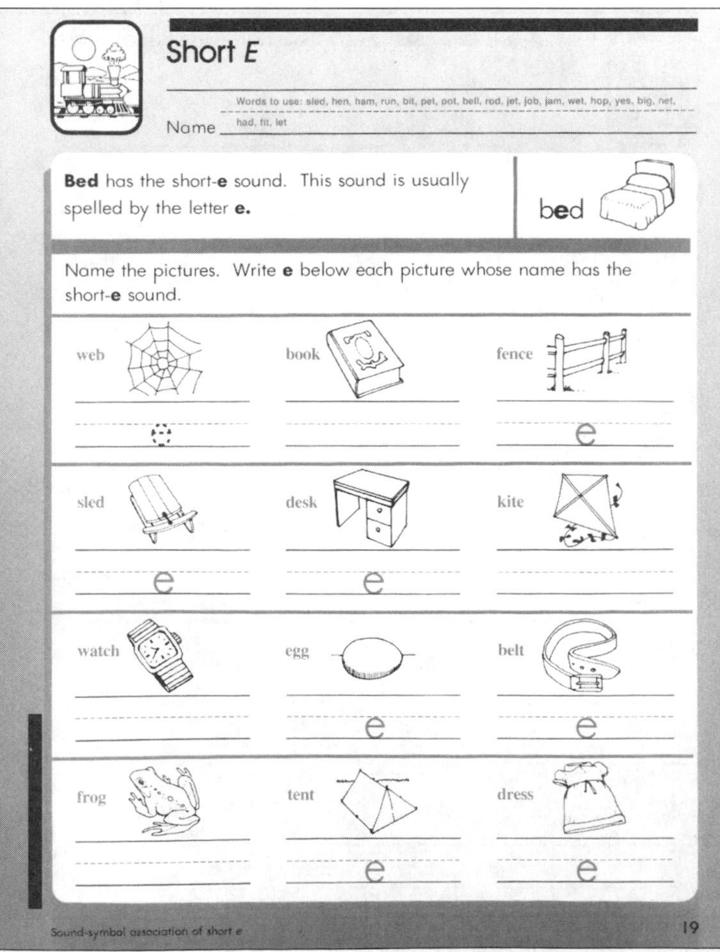

Short *E*

Words to use: sled, hen, ham, run, bit, pet, pot, bell, rod, jet, job, jam, wet, hop, yes, big, net, had, fit, let

Name ____________________

Bed has the short-**e** sound. This sound is usually spelled by the letter **e.**

bed

Name the pictures. Write **e** below each picture whose name has the short-**e** sound.

web: e	book:	fence: e
sled: e	desk: e	kite:
watch:	egg: e	belt: e
frog:	tent: e	dress: e

Sound-symbol association of short *e* 19

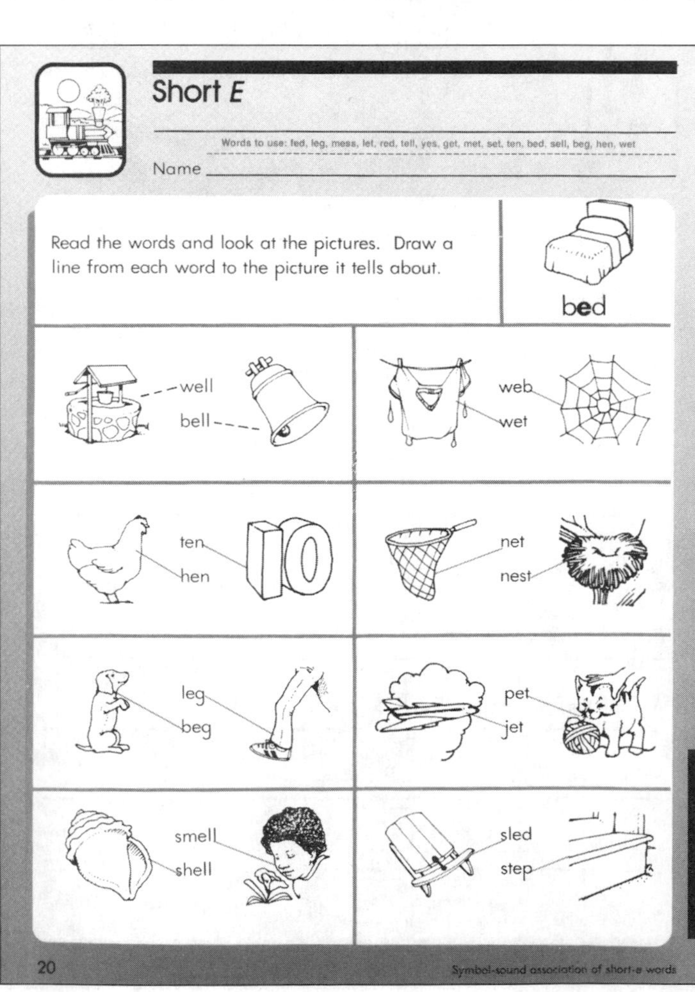

Short *E*

Words to use: fed, leg, mess, let, red, tell, yes, get, met, set, ten, bed, sell, beg, hen, wet

Name ____________________

Read the words and look at the pictures. Draw a line from each word to the picture it tells about.

bed

well / bell	web / wet
ten / hen	net / nest
leg / beg	pet / jet
smell / shell	sled / step

20 Symbol-sound association of short-*e* words

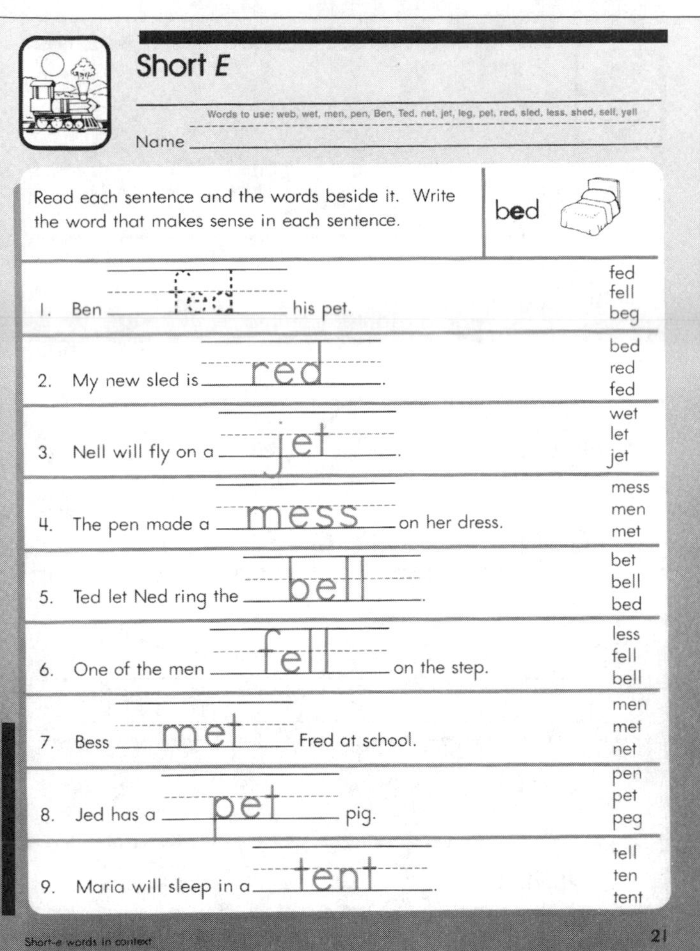

Short *E*

Words to use: web, wet, men, pen, Ben, Ted, net, jet, leg, pet, red, sled, less, shed, sell, yell

Name ______________________

Read each sentence and the words beside it. Write the word that makes sense in each sentence.

bed

1. Ben ___fed___ his pet. (fed, fell, beg)
2. My new sled is ___red___. (bed, red, fed)
3. Nell will fly on a ___jet___. (wet, let, jet)
4. The pen made a ___mess___ on her dress. (mess, men, met)
5. Ted let Ned ring the ___bell___. (bet, bell, bed)
6. One of the men ___fell___ on the step. (less, fell, bell)
7. Bess ___met___ Fred at school. (men, met, net)
8. Jed has a ___pet___ pig. (pen, pet, peg)
9. Maria will sleep in a ___tent___. (tell, ten, tent)

Short-e words in context 21

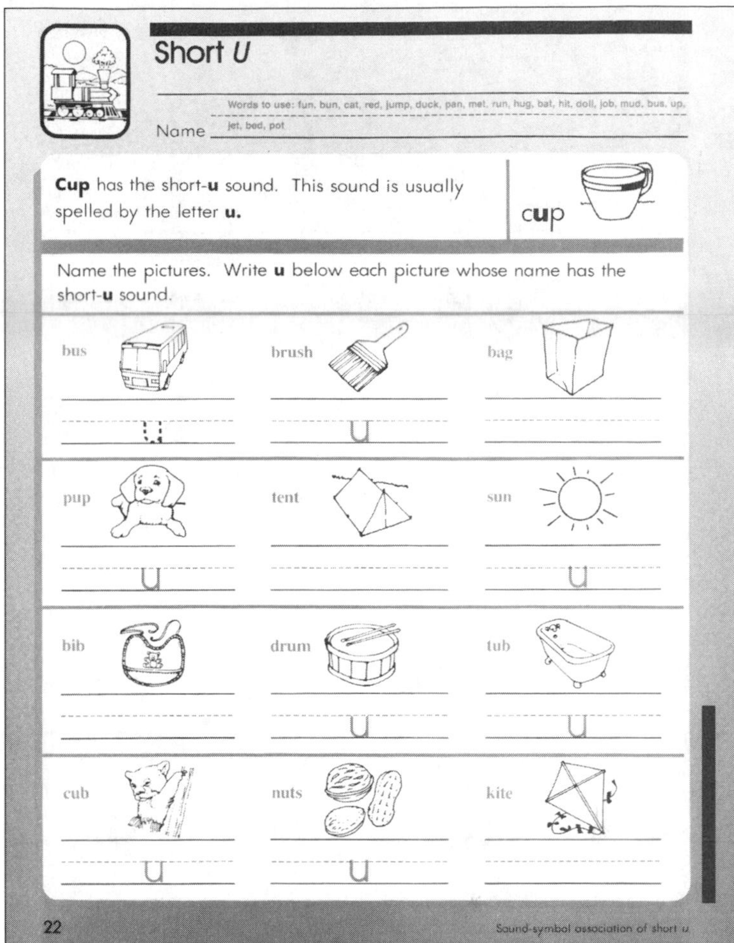

Short *U*

Words to use: fun, bun, cat, red, jump, duck, pan, met, run, hug, bat, hit, doll, job, mud, bus, up, jet, bed, pot

Name ______________________

Cup has the short-**u** sound. This sound is usually spelled by the letter **u.**

cup

Name the pictures. Write **u** below each picture whose name has the short-**u** sound.

bus — u	brush — u	bag
pup — u	tent	sun — u
bib	drum — u	tub — u
cub — u	nuts — u	kite

22 Sound-symbol association of short u

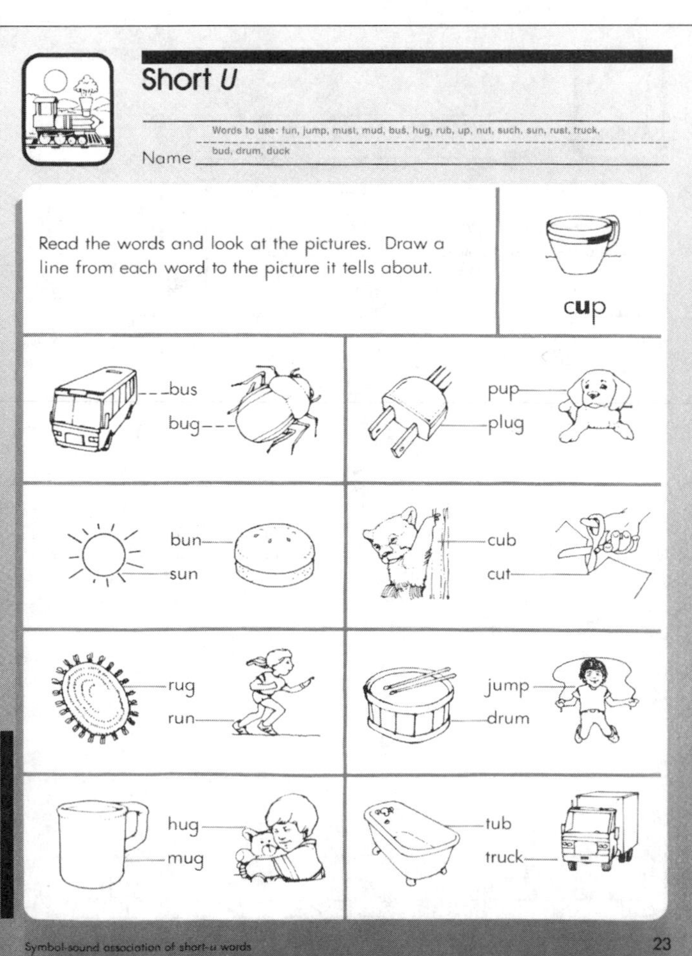

Short *U*

Words to use: fun, jump, must, mud, bus, hug, rub, up, nut, such, sun, rust, truck, bud, drum, duck

Name ______________________

Read the words and look at the pictures. Draw a line from each word to the picture it tells about.

cup

bus, bug	pup, plug
bun, sun	cub, cut
rug, run	jump, drum
hug, mug	tub, truck

Symbol-sound association of short-u words 23

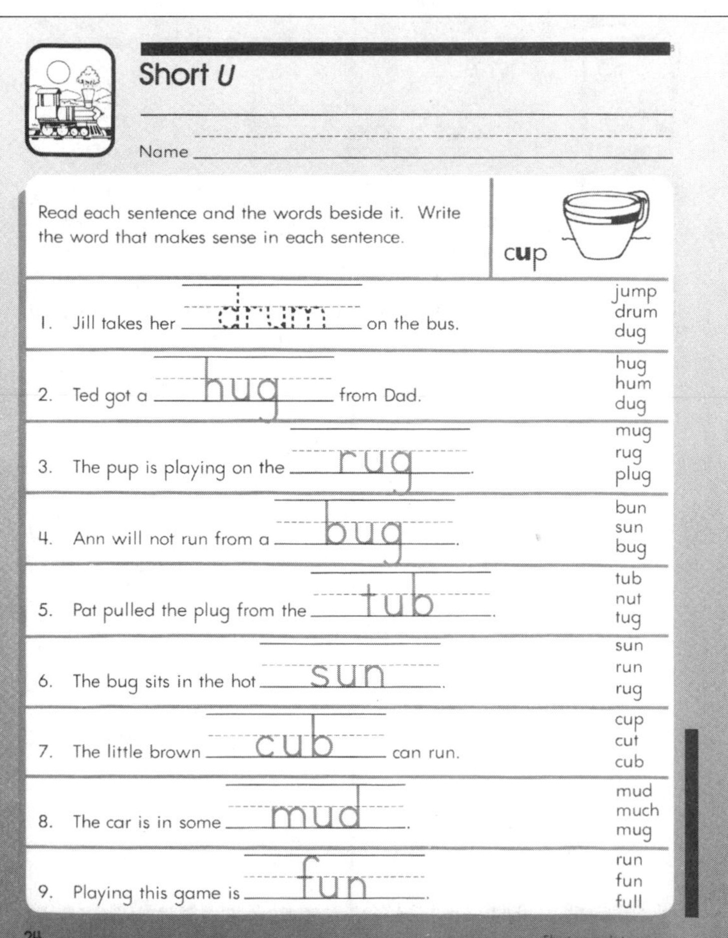

Short *U*

Name ______________________

Read each sentence and the words beside it. Write the word that makes sense in each sentence.

cup

1. Jill takes her ___drum___ on the bus. (jump, drum, dug)
2. Ted got a ___hug___ from Dad. (hug, hum, dug)
3. The pup is playing on the ___rug___. (mug, rug, plug)
4. Ann will not run from a ___bug___. (bun, sun, bug)
5. Pat pulled the plug from the ___tub___. (tub, nut, tug)
6. The bug sits in the hot ___sun___. (sun, run, rug)
7. The little brown ___cub___ can run. (cup, cut, cub)
8. The car is in some ___mud___. (mud, much, mug)
9. Playing this game is ___fun___. (run, fun, full)

24 Short-u words in context

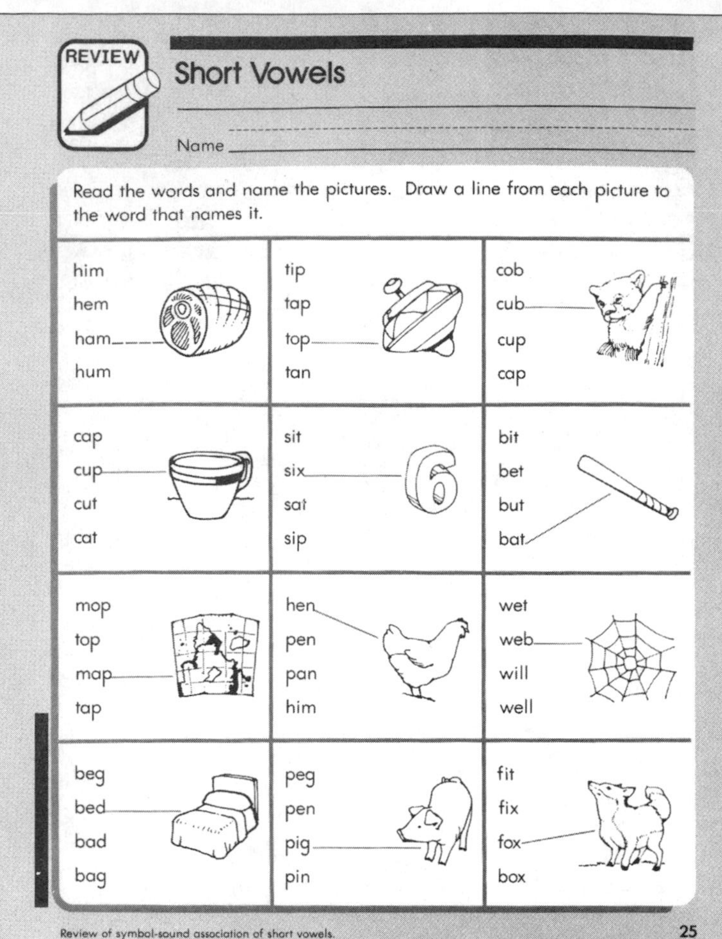

REVIEW

Short Vowels

Name

Read the words and name the pictures. Draw a line from each picture to the word that names it.

him hem ham hum	tip tap top tan	cob cub cup cap
cap cup cut cat	sit six sat sip	bit bet but bat
mop top map tap	hen pen pan him	wet web will well
beg bed bad bag	peg pen pig pin	fit fix fox box

Review of symbol-sound association of short vowels. 25

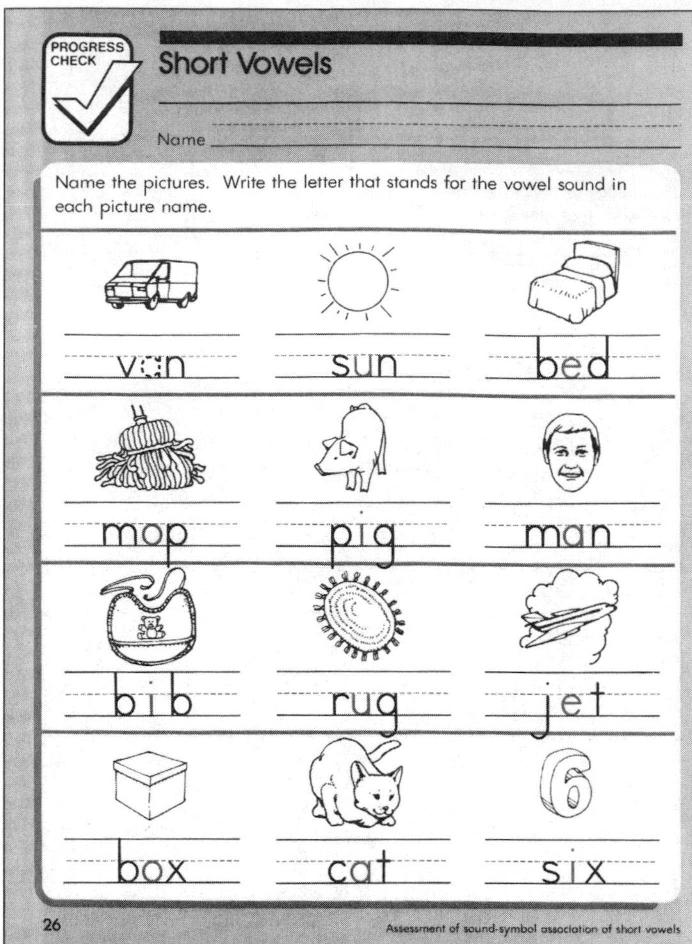

PROGRESS CHECK

Short Vowels

Name

Name the pictures. Write the letter that stands for the vowel sound in each picture name.

van	sun	bed
mop	pig	man
bib	rug	jet
box	cat	six

26 Assessment of sound-symbol association of short vowels

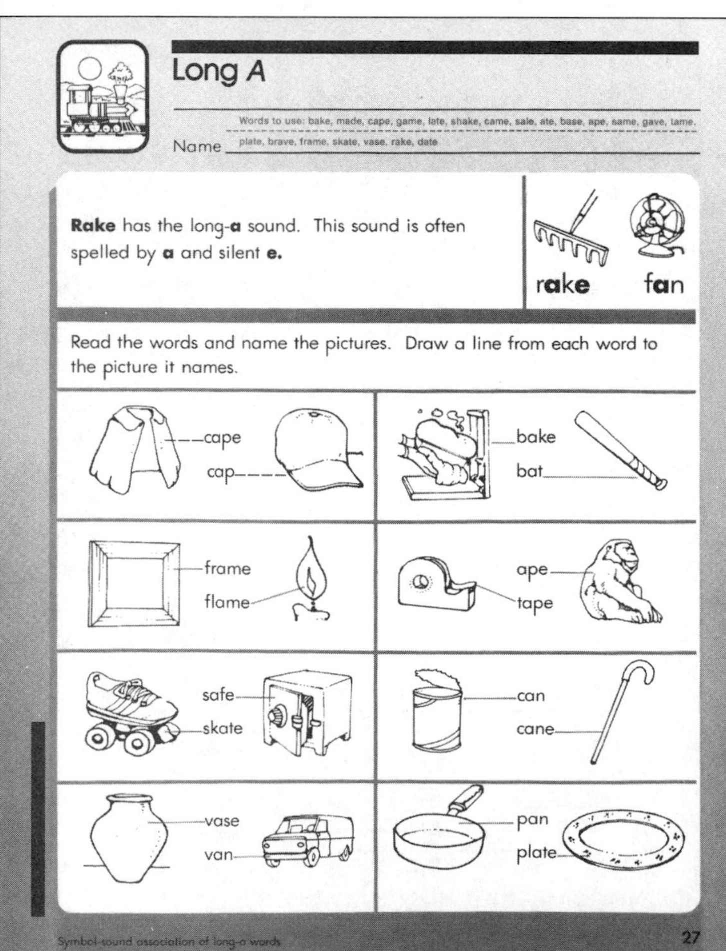

Long *A*

Words to use: bake, made, cape, game, late, shake, came, sale, ate, base, ape, same, gave, tame, plate, brave, frame, skate, vase, rake, date

Name

Rake has the long-**a** sound. This sound is often spelled by **a** and silent **e.**

rake fan

Read the words and name the pictures. Draw a line from each word to the picture it names.

cape cap	bake bat
frame flame	ape tape
safe skate	can cane
vase van	pan plate

Symbol-sound association of long-a words 27

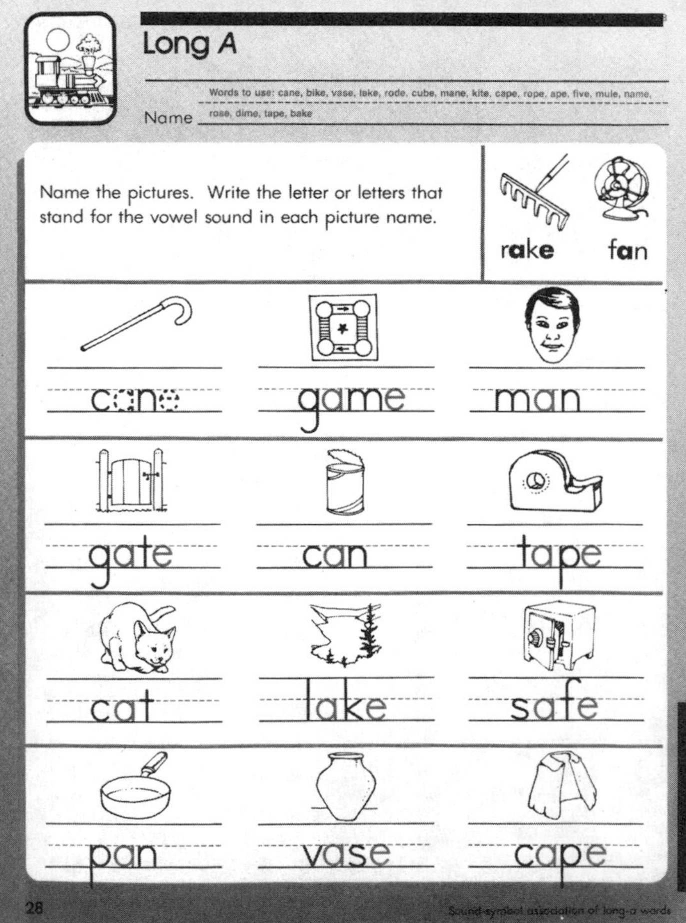

Long *A*

Words to use: cane, bike, vase, lake, rode, cube, mane, kite, cape, rope, ape, five, mule, name, rose, dime, tape, bake

Name

Name the pictures. Write the letter or letters that stand for the vowel sound in each picture name.

rake fan

cane	game	man
gate	can	tape
cat	lake	safe
pan	vase	cape

28 Sound-symbol association of long-a words

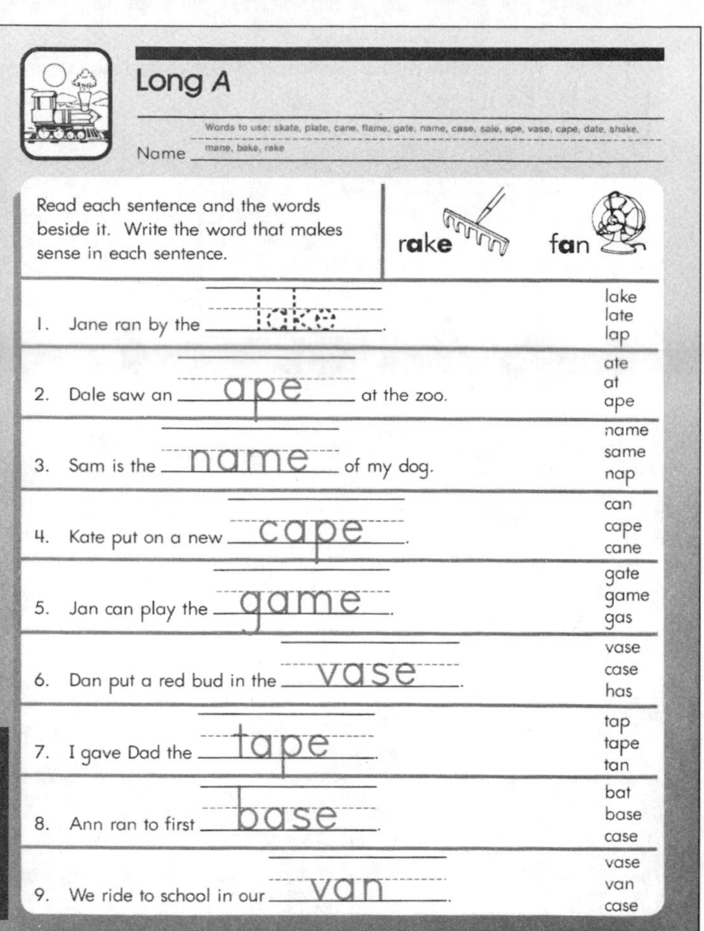

Long A

Words to use: skate, plate, cane, flame, gate, name, case, sale, ape, vase, cape, date, shake, mane, bake, rake

Name

Read each sentence and the words beside it. Write the word that makes sense in each sentence.

rake fan

1. Jane ran by the lake. (lake, late, lap)
2. Dale saw an ape at the zoo. (ate, at, ape)
3. Sam is the name of my dog. (name, same, nap)
4. Kate put on a new cape. (can, cape, cane)
5. Jan can play the game. (gate, game, gas)
6. Dan put a red bud in the vase. (vase, case, has)
7. I gave Dad the tape. (tap, tape, tan)
8. Ann ran to first base. (bat, base, case)
9. We ride to school in our van. (vase, van, case)

Long-a words in context 29

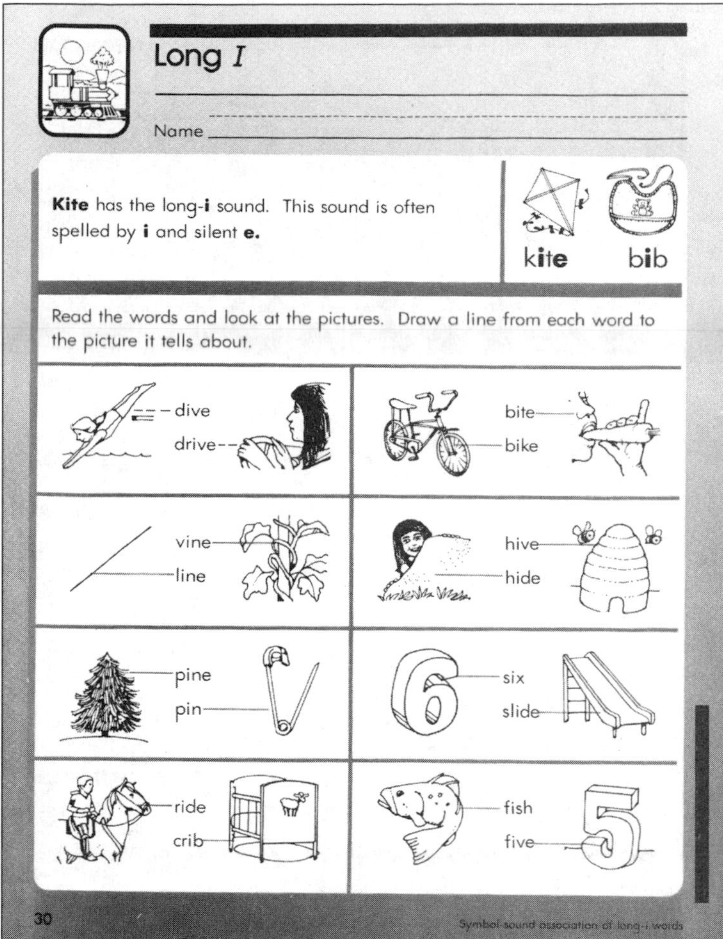

Long I

Name

Kite has the long-**i** sound. This sound is often spelled by **i** and silent **e.**

kite bib

Read the words and look at the pictures. Draw a line from each word to the picture it tells about.

dive, drive — bite, bike

vine, line — hive, hide

pine, pin — six, slide

ride, crib — fish, five

30 Symbol-sound association of long-i words

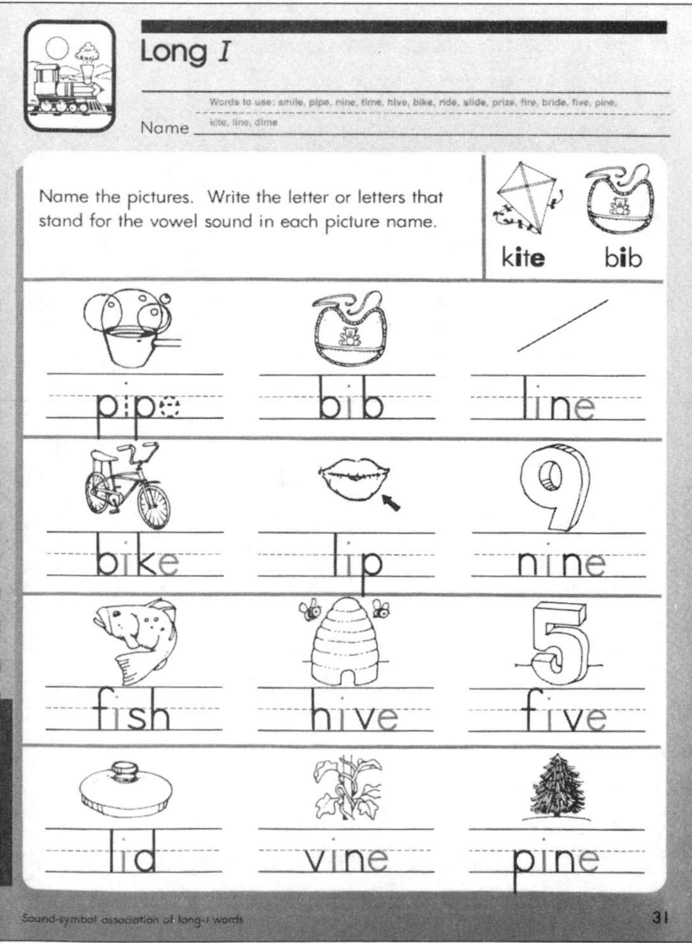

Long I

Words to use: smile, pipe, nine, time, hive, bike, ride, slide, prize, fire, bride, five, pine, kite, line, dime

Name

Name the pictures. Write the letter or letters that stand for the vowel sound in each picture name.

kite bib

pipe	bib	line
bike	lip	nine
fish	hive	five
lid	vine	pine

Sound-symbol association of long-i words 31

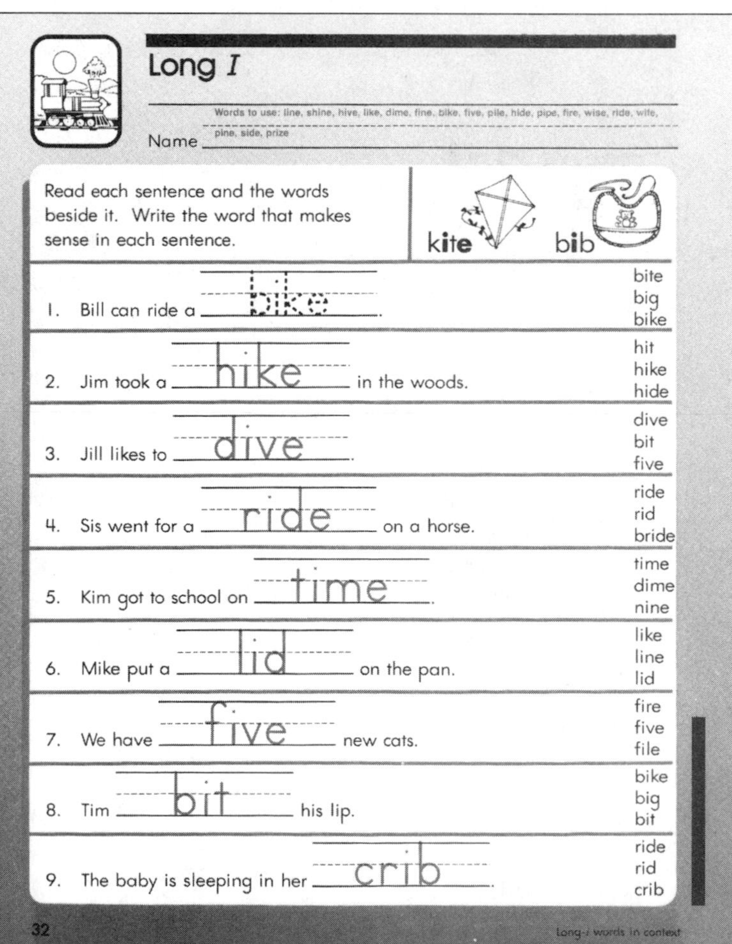

Long I

Words to use: line, shine, hive, like, dime, fine, bike, five, pile, hide, pipe, fire, wise, ride, wife, pine, side, prize

Name

Read each sentence and the words beside it. Write the word that makes sense in each sentence.

kite bib

1. Bill can ride a bike. (bite, big, bike)
2. Jim took a hike in the woods. (hit, hike, hide)
3. Jill likes to dive. (dive, bit, five)
4. Sis went for a ride on a horse. (ride, rid, bride)
5. Kim got to school on time. (time, dime, nine)
6. Mike put a lid on the pan. (like, line, lid)
7. We have five new cats. (fire, five, file)
8. Tim bit his lip. (bike, big, bit)
9. The baby is sleeping in her crib. (ride, rid, crib)

32 Long-i words in context

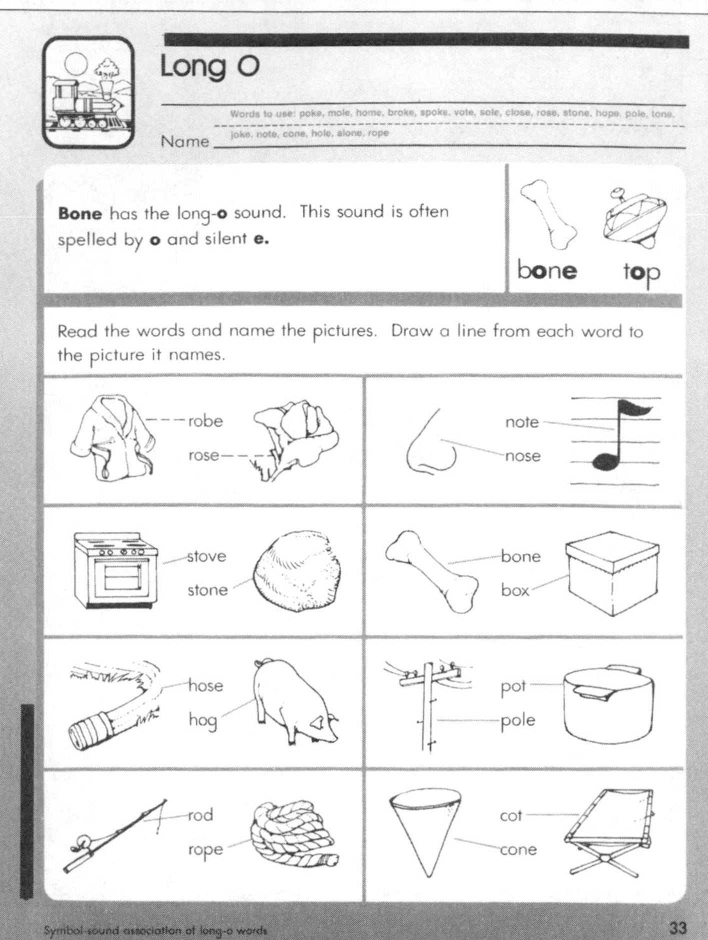
Long O

Name ____________ Words to use: poke, mole, home, broke, spoke, vote, sole, close, rose, stone, hope, pole, tone, joke, note, cone, hole, alone, rope

Bone has the long-**o** sound. This sound is often spelled by **o** and silent **e.**

b**o**ne t**o**p

Read the words and name the pictures. Draw a line from each word to the picture it names.

robe, rose	note, nose
stove, stone	bone, box
hose, hog	pot, pole
rod, rope	cot, cone

Symbol-sound association of long-o words 33

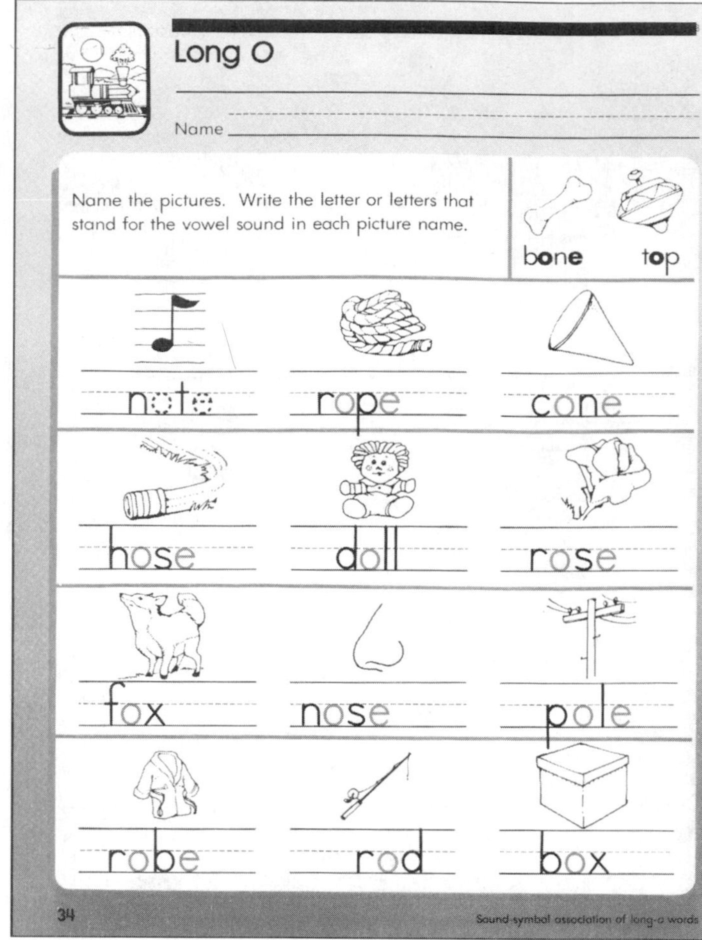
Long O

Name ____________

Name the pictures. Write the letter or letters that stand for the vowel sound in each picture name.

b**o**ne t**o**p

note	rope	cone
hose	doll	rose
fox	nose	pole
robe	rod	box

34 Sound-symbol association of long-o words

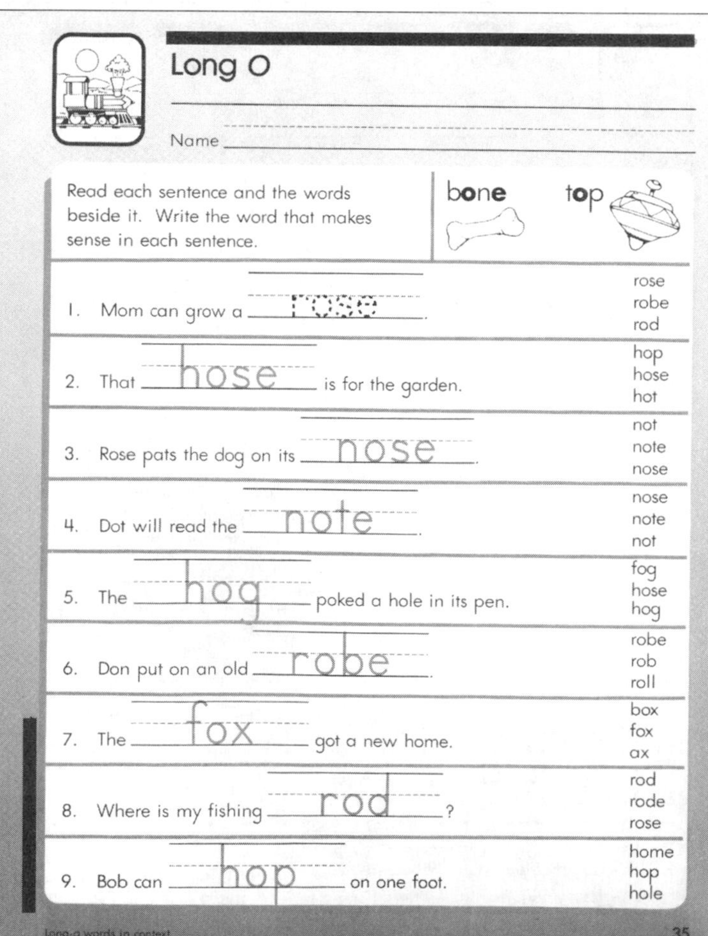
Long O

Name ____________

Read each sentence and the words beside it. Write the word that makes sense in each sentence.

b**o**ne t**o**p

1. Mom can grow a rose.	rose, robe, rod
2. That hose is for the garden.	hop, hose, hot
3. Rose pats the dog on its nose.	not, note, nose
4. Dot will read the note.	nose, note, not
5. The hog poked a hole in its pen.	fog, hose, hog
6. Don put on an old robe.	robe, rob, roll
7. The fox got a new home.	box, fox, ax
8. Where is my fishing rod?	rod, rode, rose
9. Bob can hop on one foot.	home, hop, hole

Long-o words in context 35

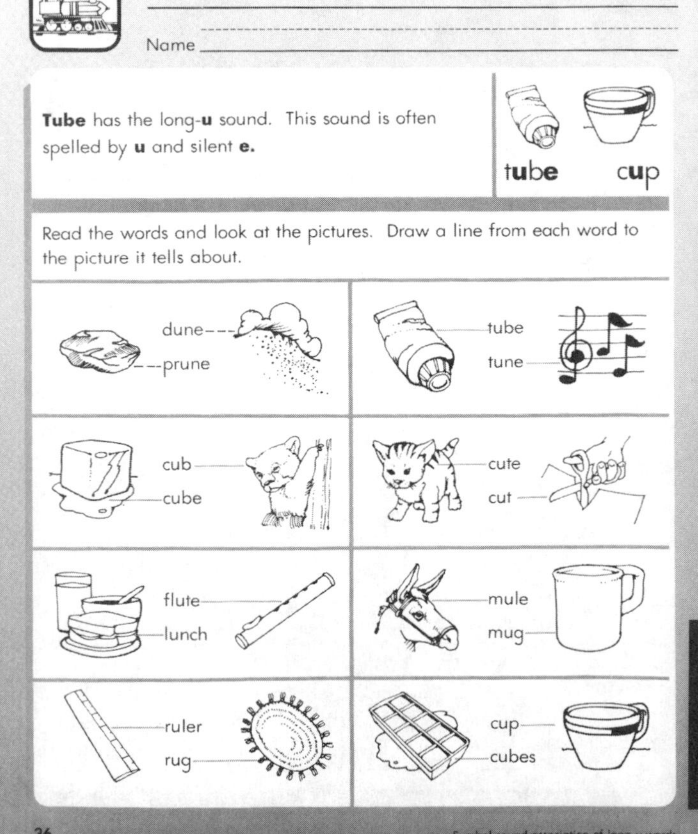
Long *U*

Name ____________

Tube has the long-**u** sound. This sound is often spelled by **u** and silent **e.**

t**u**be c**u**p

Read the words and look at the pictures. Draw a line from each word to the picture it tells about.

dune, prune	tube, tune
cub, cube	cute, cut
flute, lunch	mule, mug
ruler, rug	cup, cubes

36 Symbol-sound association of long-u words

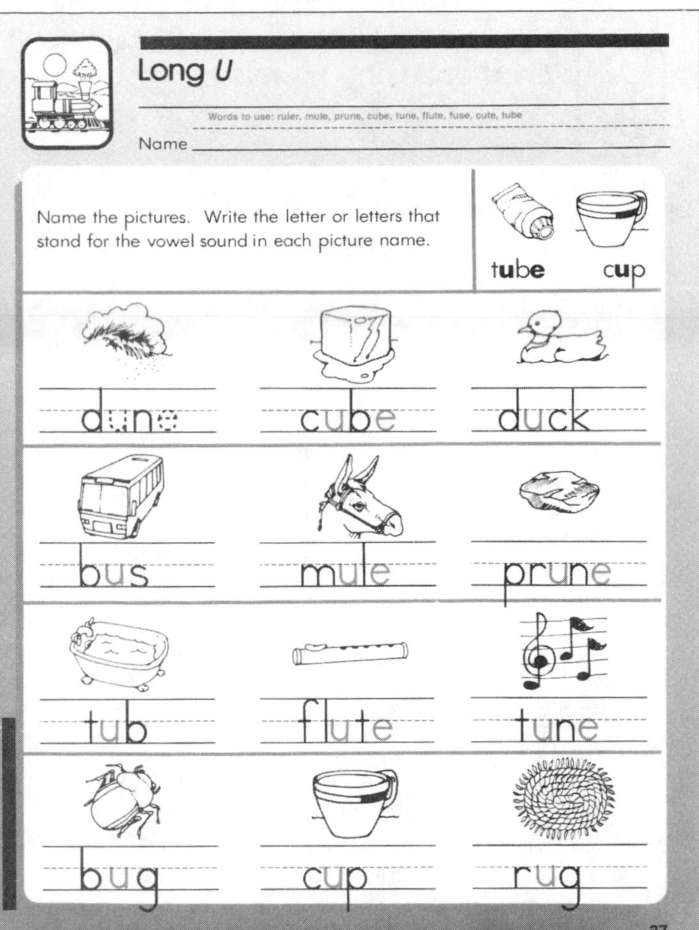

Long U

Words to use: ruler, mule, prune, cube, tune, flute, fuse, cute, tube

Name

Name the pictures. Write the letter or letters that stand for the vowel sound in each picture name.

tube cup

dune	cube	duck
bus	mule	prune
tub	flute	tune
bug	cup	rug

Sound-symbol association of long-u words 37

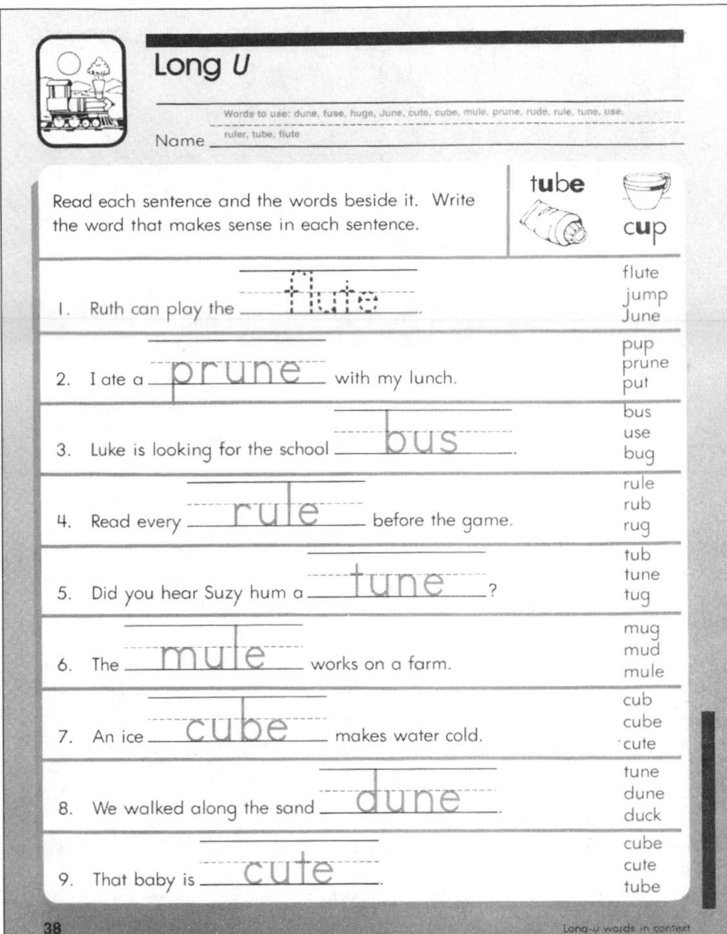

Long U

Words to use: dune, fuse, huge, June, cute, cube, mule, prune, rude, rule, tune, use, ruler, tube, flute

Name

Read each sentence and the words beside it. Write the word that makes sense in each sentence.

tube cup

1. Ruth can play the flute. (flute, jump, June)
2. I ate a prune with my lunch. (pup, prune, put)
3. Luke is looking for the school bus. (bus, use, bug)
4. Read every rule before the game. (rule, rub, rug)
5. Did you hear Suzy hum a tune? (tub, tune, tug)
6. The mule works on a farm. (mug, mud, mule)
7. An ice cube makes water cold. (cub, cube, cute)
8. We walked along the sand dune. (tune, dune, duck)
9. That baby is cute. (cube, cute, tube)

38 Long-u words in context

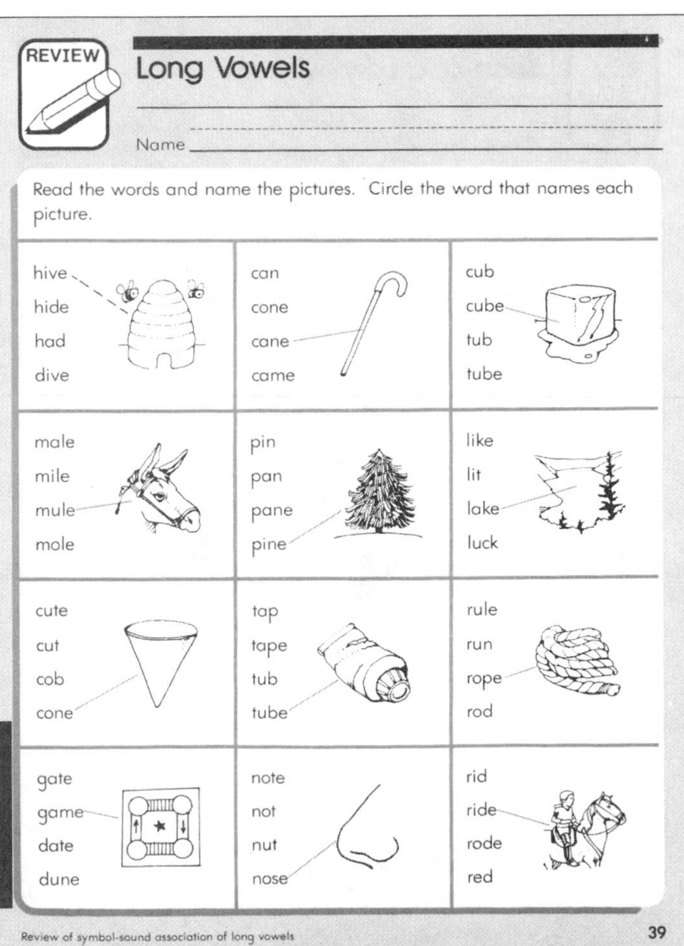

REVIEW

Long Vowels

Name

Read the words and name the pictures. Circle the word that names each picture.

hive hide had dive	can cone cane came	cub cube tub tube
male mile mule mole	pin pan pane pine	like lit lake luck
cute cut cob cone	tap tape tub tube	rule run rope rod
gate game date dune	note not nut nose	rid ride rode red

Review of symbol-sound association of long vowels 39

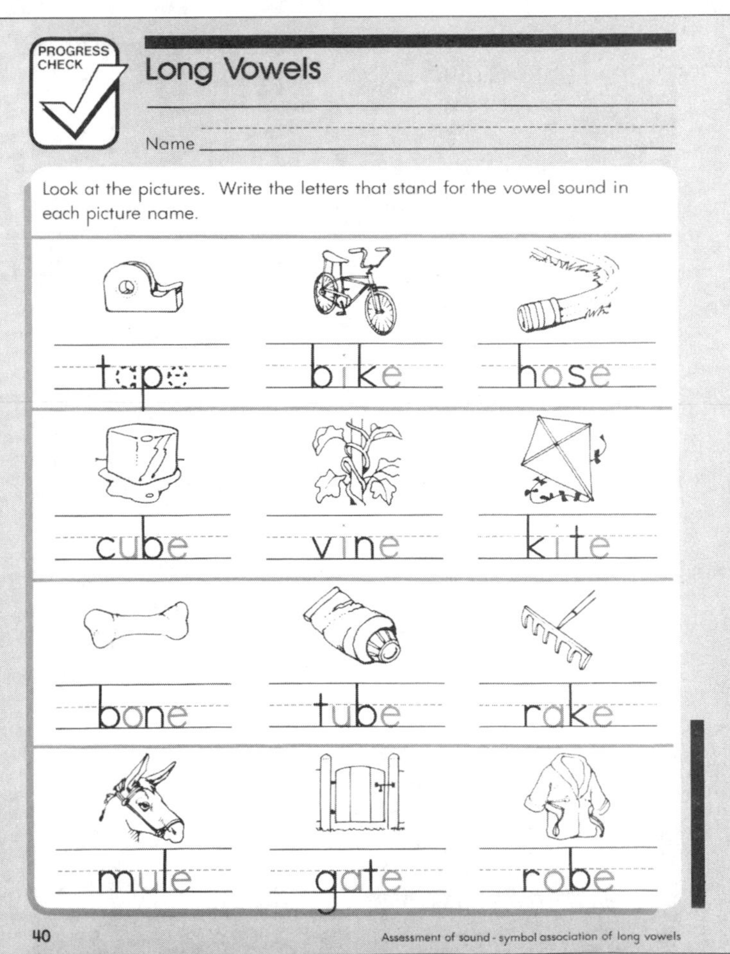

PROGRESS CHECK

Long Vowels

Name

Look at the pictures. Write the letters that stand for the vowel sound in each picture name.

tape	bike	hose
cube	vine	kite
bone	tube	rake
mule	gate	robe

40 Assessment of sound-symbol association of long vowels

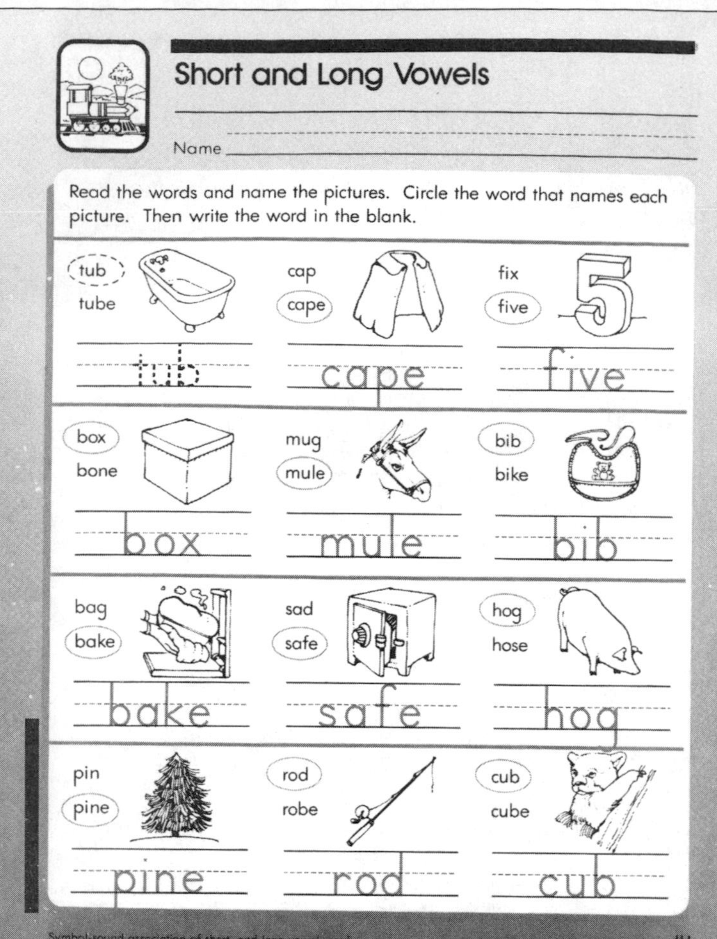

Short and Long Vowels

Name

Read the words and name the pictures. Circle the word that names each picture. Then write the word in the blank.

(tub) / tube — tub	cap / (cape) — cape	fix / (five) — five
(box) / bone — box	mug / (mule) — mule	(bib) / bike — bib
bag / (bake) — bake	sad / (safe) — safe	(hog) / hose — hog
pin / (pine) — pine	(rod) / robe — rod	(cub) / cube — cub

Symbol-sound association of short- and long-vowel words 41

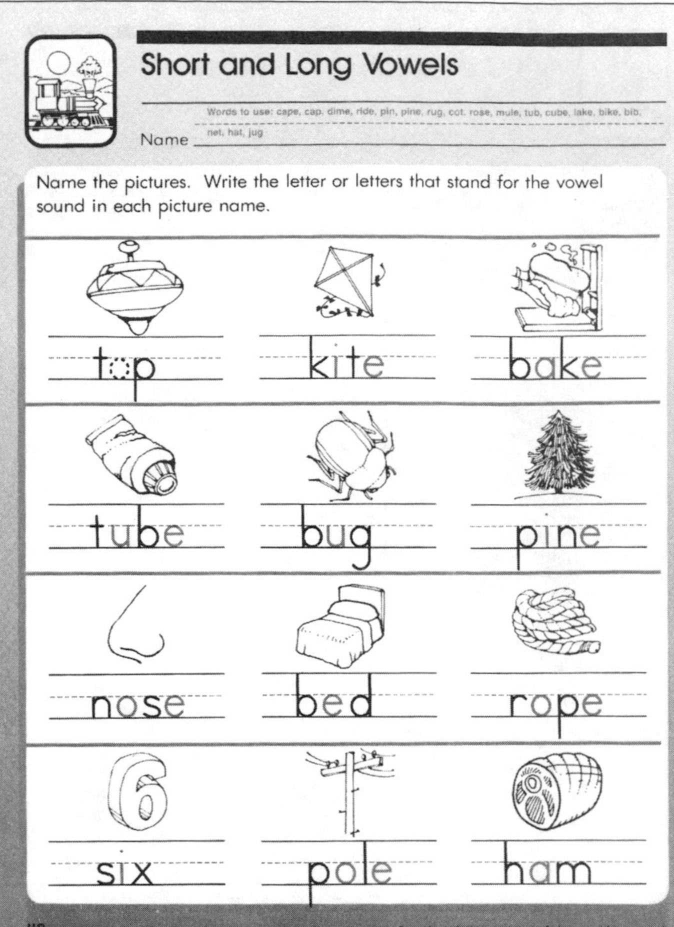

Short and Long Vowels

Words to use: cape, cap, dime, ride, pin, pine, rug, cot, rose, mule, tub, cube, lake, bike, bib, net, hat, jug

Name

Name the pictures. Write the letter or letters that stand for the vowel sound in each picture name.

top	kite	bake
tube	bug	pine
nose	bed	rope
six	pole	ham

42 Sound-symbol association of short and long vowels

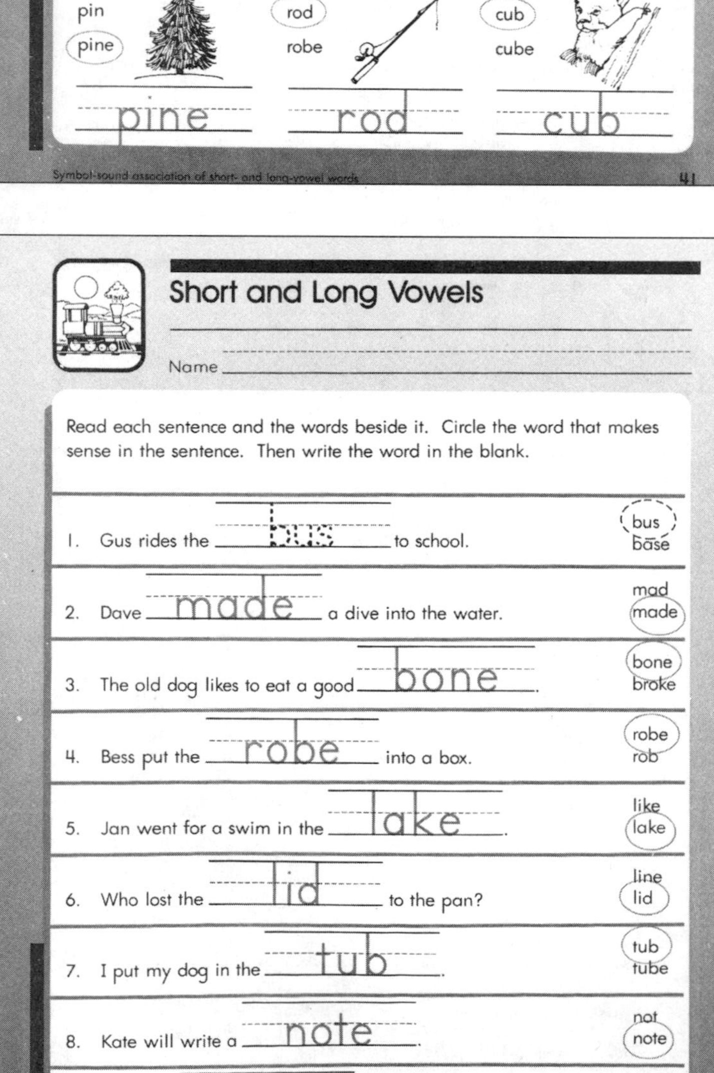

Short and Long Vowels

Name

Read each sentence and the words beside it. Circle the word that makes sense in the sentence. Then write the word in the blank.

1. Gus rides the bus to school. (bus) base
2. Dave made a dive into the water. mad (made)
3. The old dog likes to eat a good bone. (bone) broke
4. Bess put the robe into a box. (robe) rob
5. Jan went for a swim in the lake. like (lake)
6. Who lost the lid to the pan? line (lid)
7. I put my dog in the tub. (tub) tube
8. Kate will write a note. not (note)
9. Did Nate make his bed today? map (make)

Short- and long-vowel words in context 43

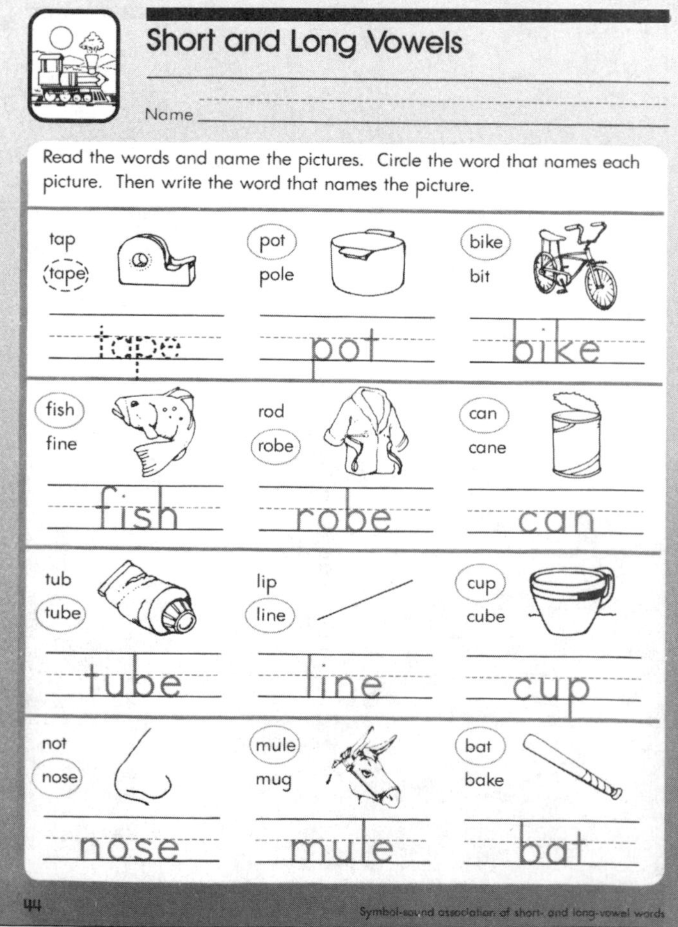

Short and Long Vowels

Name

Read the words and name the pictures. Circle the word that names each picture. Then write the word that names the picture.

tap / (tape) — tape	(pot) / pole — pot	(bike) / bit — bike
(fish) / fine — fish	rod / (robe) — robe	(can) / cane — can
tub / (tube) — tube	lip / (line) — line	(cup) / cube — cup
not / (nose) — nose	(mule) / mug — mule	(bat) / bake — bat

44 Symbol-sound association of short- and long-vowel words

Short and Long Vowels

Words to use: gate, bib, rope, jet, fun, vine, hat, tube, doll, bake, fish, poke, cot, sip, dime, late, jug, flute, sun, cane, net

Name

Read each sentence and the words beside it. Write the word that makes sense in the sentence.

1. Did Mom buy a new rug for my room?	rob, rug, rule
2. I like to swim.	line, lid, like
3. The fox ran into its cave.	fix, fox, five
4. My bike has a flat tire.	bib, bite, bike
5. Did you hear a tap on the window?	tape, tap, tan
6. I want to go home now.	home, hog, hose
7. Jimmy can play a pretty tune.	tub, tube, tune
8. The children ran down the hill.	hill, hide, hive
9. Rosa sleeps on a little cot.	cone, cot, cane

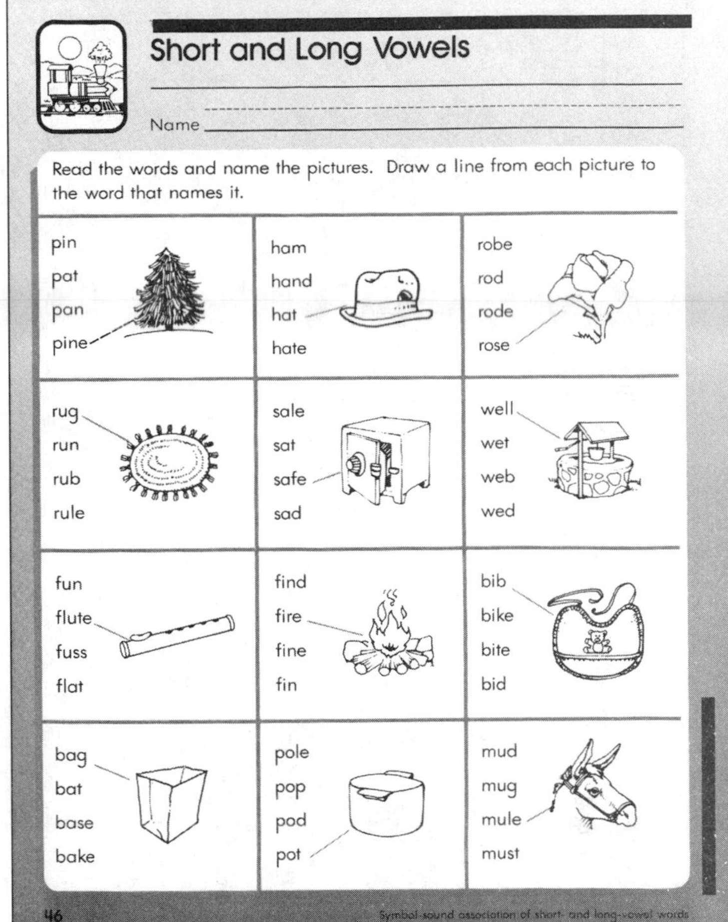

Short and Long Vowels

Name

Read the words and name the pictures. Draw a line from each picture to the word that names it.

pin, pat, pan, pine	ham, hand, hat, hate	robe, rod, rode, rose
rug, run, rub, rule	sale, sat, safe, sad	well, wet, web, wed
fun, flute, fuss, flat	find, fire, fine, fin	bib, bike, bite, bid
bag, bat, base, bake	pole, pop, pod, pot	mud, mug, mule, must

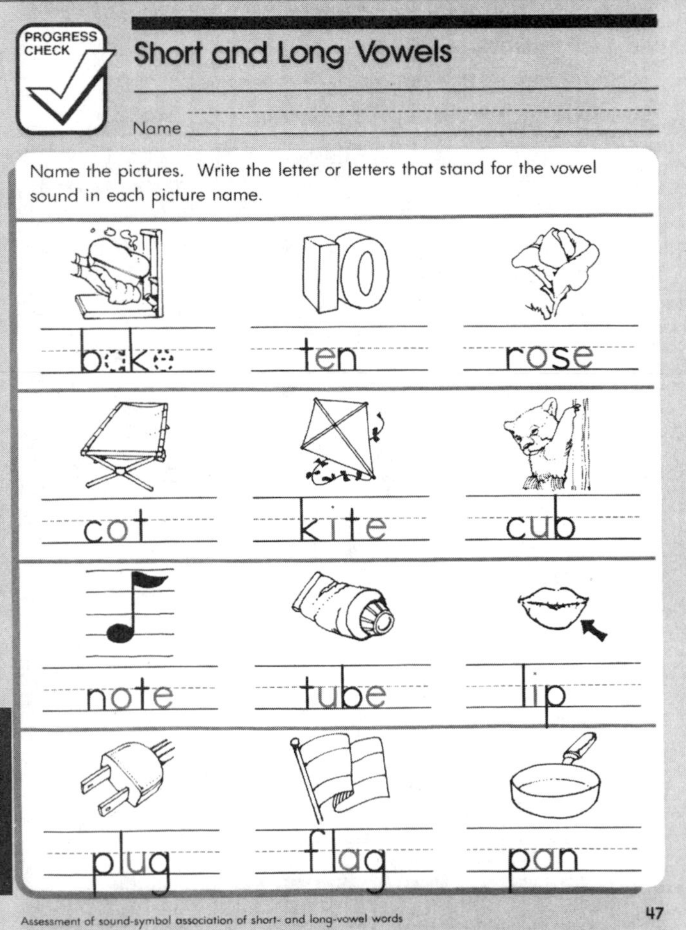

PROGRESS CHECK

Short and Long Vowels

Name

Name the pictures. Write the letter or letters that stand for the vowel sound in each picture name.

bake	ten	rose
cot	kite	cub
note	tube	lip
plug	flag	pan

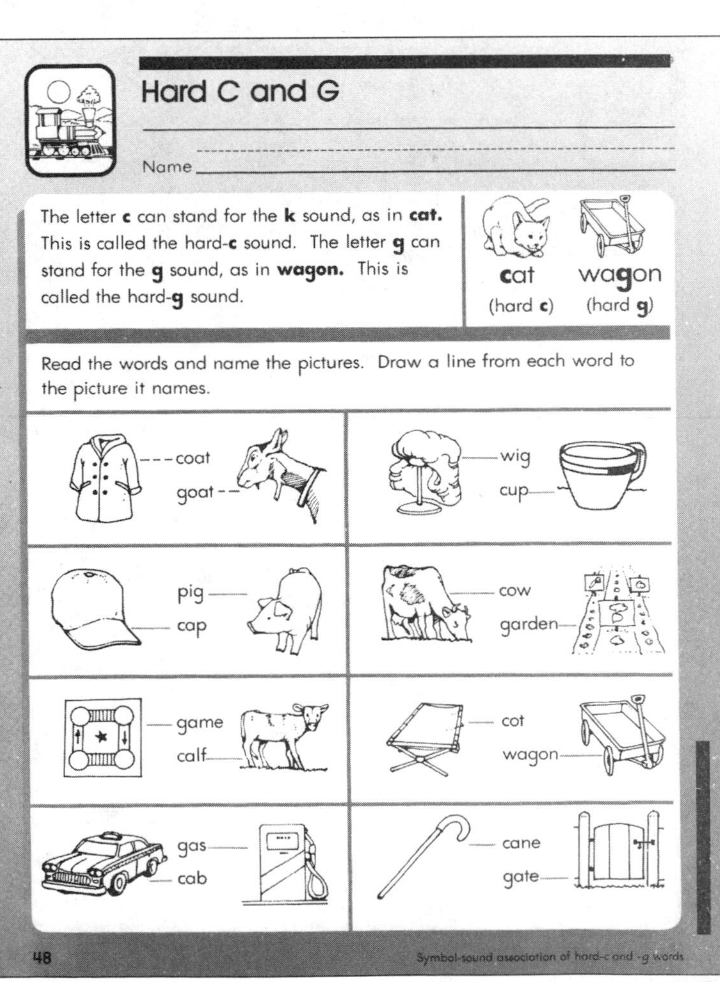

Hard C and G

Name

The letter **c** can stand for the **k** sound, as in **cat.** This is called the hard-**c** sound. The letter **g** can stand for the **g** sound, as in **wagon.** This is called the hard-**g** sound.

cat (hard **c**) wa**g**on (hard **g**)

Read the words and name the pictures. Draw a line from each word to the picture it names.

coat, goat	wig, cup
pig, cap	cow, garden
game, calf	cot, wagon
gas, cab	cane, gate

Hard C and G

Words to use: cape, car, cow, cane, calf, cave, cab, cap, can, coat, cook, cat, gate, go, bag, gave, garden, pig, game, goat, gas

Name

Read the words in the list below. Then name the pictures. Write the word from the list that names each picture.

cane car cup cat garden
gate gas cow goat

cat (hard **c**) wa**g**on (hard **g**)

cup goat car
garden cat gas
cane gate cow

Symbol-sound association of words containing hard *c* and *g* 49

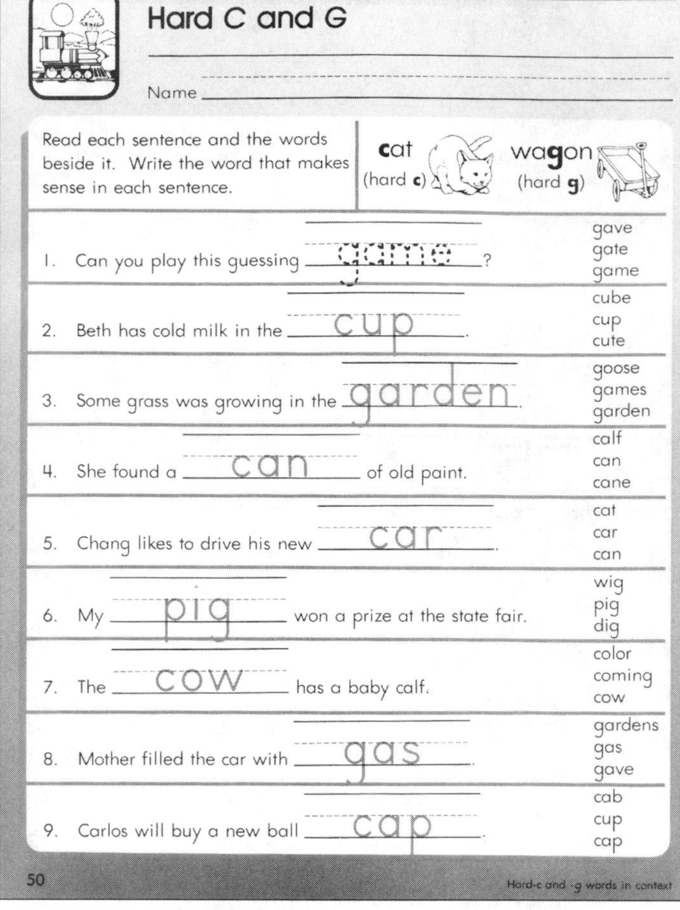

Hard C and G

Name

Read each sentence and the words beside it. Write the word that makes sense in each sentence.

cat (hard **c**) wa**g**on (hard **g**)

1. Can you play this guessing game? — gave, gate, game
2. Beth has cold milk in the cup. — cube, cup, cute
3. Some grass was growing in the garden. — goose, games, garden
4. She found a can of old paint. — calf, can, cane
5. Chang likes to drive his new car. — cat, car, can
6. My pig won a prize at the state fair. — wig, pig, dig
7. The cow has a baby calf. — color, coming, cow
8. Mother filled the car with gas. — gardens, gas, gave
9. Carlos will buy a new ball cap. — cab, cup, cap

50 Hard-*c* and -*g* words in context

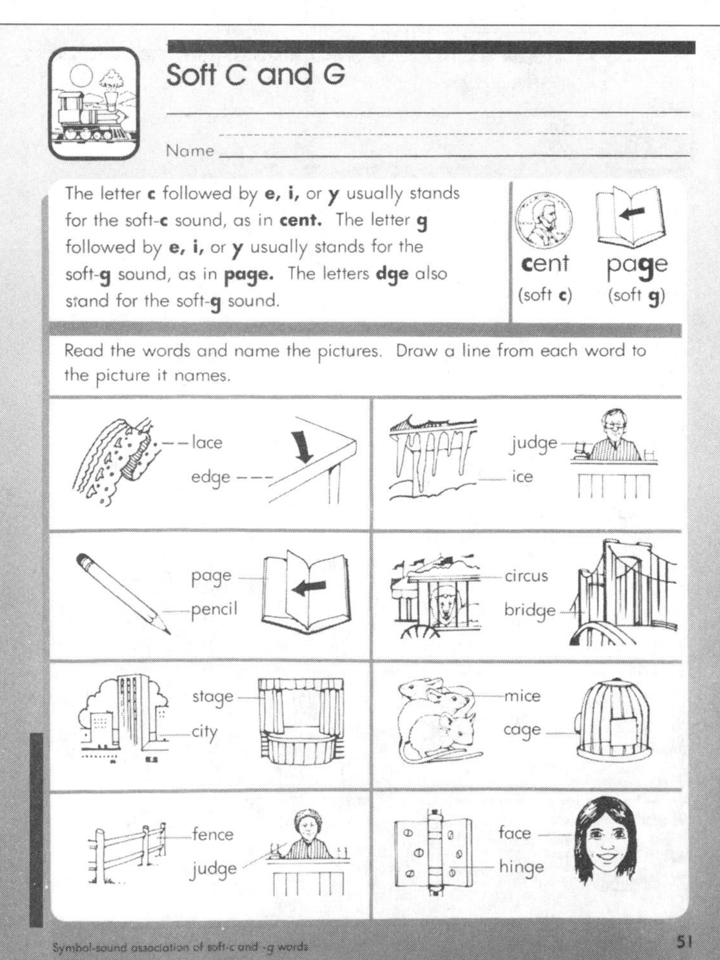

Soft C and G

Name

The letter **c** followed by **e, i,** or **y** usually stands for the soft-**c** sound, as in **cent.** The letter **g** followed by **e, i,** or **y** usually stands for the soft-**g** sound, as in **page.** The letters **dge** also stand for the soft-**g** sound.

cent (soft **c**) pa**g**e (soft **g**)

Read the words and name the pictures. Draw a line from each word to the picture it names.

lace, edge — judge, ice
page, pencil — circus, bridge
stage, city — mice, cage
fence, judge — face, hinge

Symbol-sound association of soft-*c* and -*g* words 51

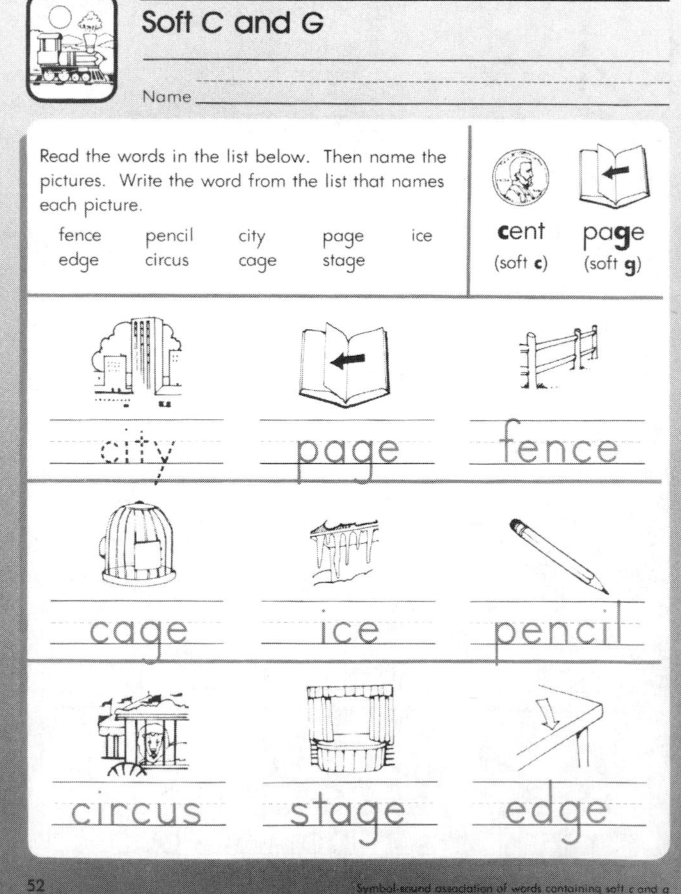

Soft C and G

Name

Read the words in the list below. Then name the pictures. Write the word from the list that names each picture.

fence pencil city page ice
edge circus cage stage

cent (soft **c**) pa**g**e (soft **g**)

city page fence
cage ice pencil
circus stage edge

52 Symbol-sound association of words containing soft *c* and *g*

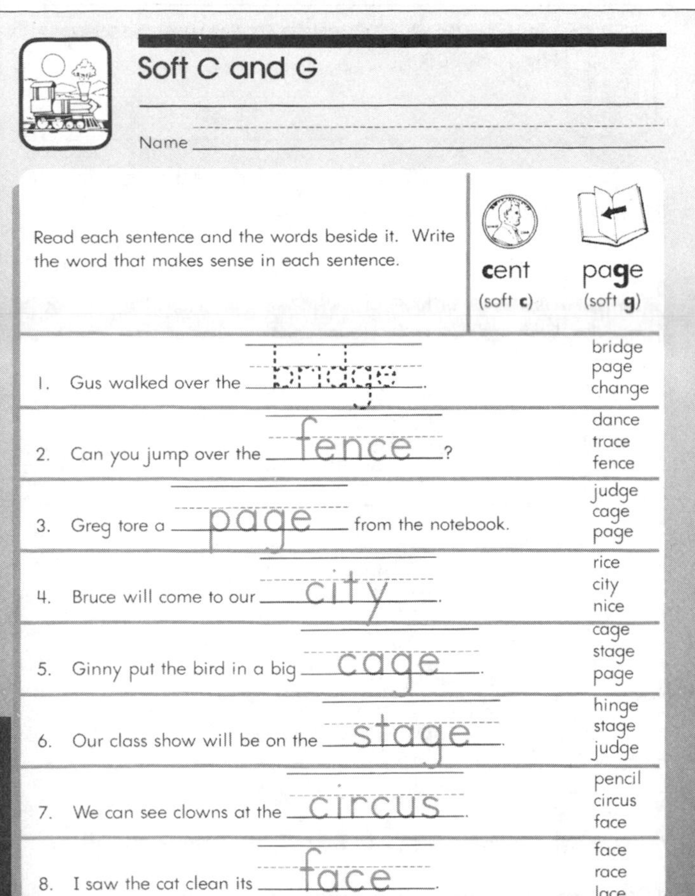

Soft C and G

Name ______________________

Read each sentence and the words beside it. Write the word that makes sense in each sentence.

cent (soft **c**) pa**g**e (soft **g**)

1. Gus walked over the bridge.	bridge, page, change
2. Can you jump over the fence?	dance, trace, fence
3. Greg tore a page from the notebook.	judge, cage, page
4. Bruce will come to our city.	rice, city, nice
5. Ginny put the bird in a big cage.	cage, stage, page
6. Our class show will be on the stage.	hinge, stage, judge
7. We can see clowns at the circus.	pencil, circus, face
8. I saw the cat clean its face.	face, race, lace

Soft-c and -g words in context 53

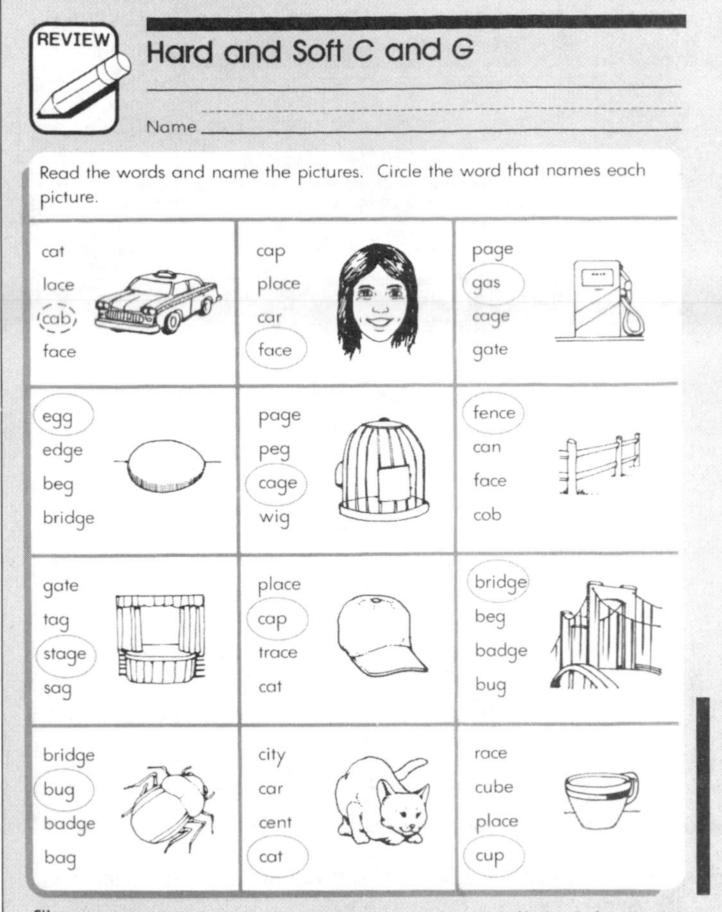

REVIEW

Hard and Soft C and G

Name ______________________

Read the words and name the pictures. Circle the word that names each picture.

cat, lace, (cab), face	cap, place, car, (face)	page, (gas), cage, gate
(egg), edge, beg, bridge	page, peg, (cage), wig	(fence), can, face, cob
gate, tag, (stage), sag	place, (cap), trace, cat	(bridge), beg, badge, bug
bridge, (bug), badge, bag	city, car, cent, (cat)	race, cube, place, (cup)

54 Review of symbol-sound association of hard- and soft-c and g words

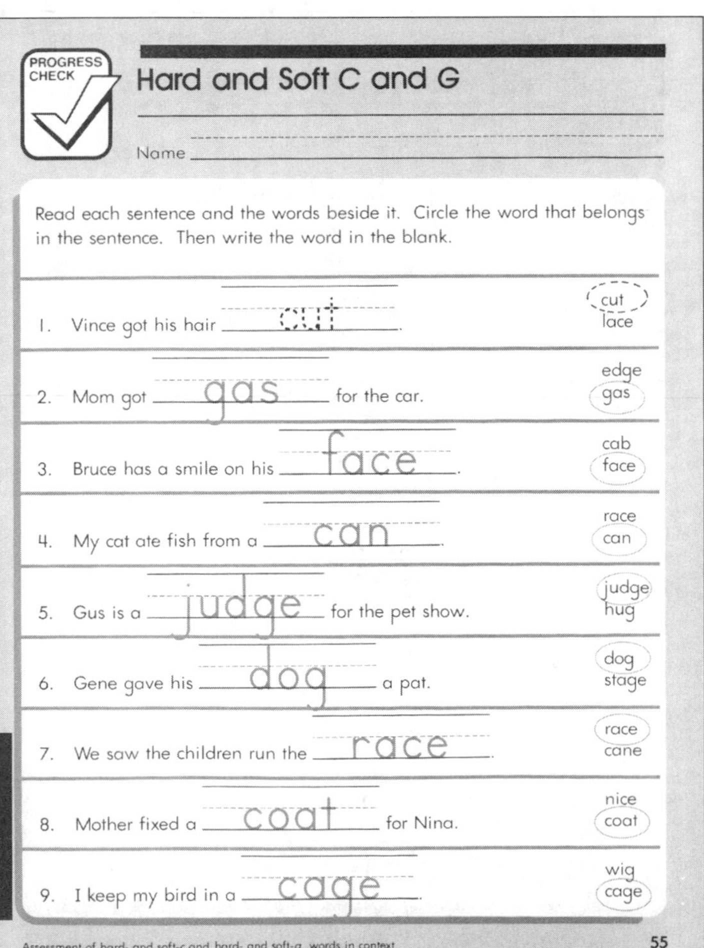

PROGRESS CHECK

Hard and Soft C and G

Name ______________________

Read each sentence and the words beside it. Circle the word that belongs in the sentence. Then write the word in the blank.

1. Vince got his hair cut.	(cut), lace
2. Mom got gas for the car.	edge, (gas)
3. Bruce has a smile on his face.	cab, (face)
4. My cat ate fish from a can.	race, (can)
5. Gus is a judge for the pet show.	(judge), hug
6. Gene gave his dog a pat.	(dog), stage
7. We saw the children run the race.	(race), cane
8. Mother fixed a coat for Nina.	nice, (coat)
9. I keep my bird in a cage.	wig, (cage)

Assessment of hard- and soft-c and hard- and soft-g words in context 55

Reading and Writing Wrap-Up

Name ______________________

Two Mice in a Cage

There once were two mice in a cage
Who wanted to go on the stage.
One could dance with a cane,
One could sing in the rain.
So they went on the stage in their cage.

A Goat in a Boat

There once was a funny brown goat
Who wanted to row in a boat.
So a boat she did make
And rowed out on a lake.
But the boat of the goat would not float.

1. Circle the words that tell about the mice.
   (They could dance and sing.)
   (They wanted to go on the stage.)
   They wanted new hats and coats.
2. Circle the words that tell about the goat.
   She wanted gas for her boat.
   (She was a funny brown goat.)
   She wanted to be a cow.

56 Application of reading and comprehension skills in a literature context

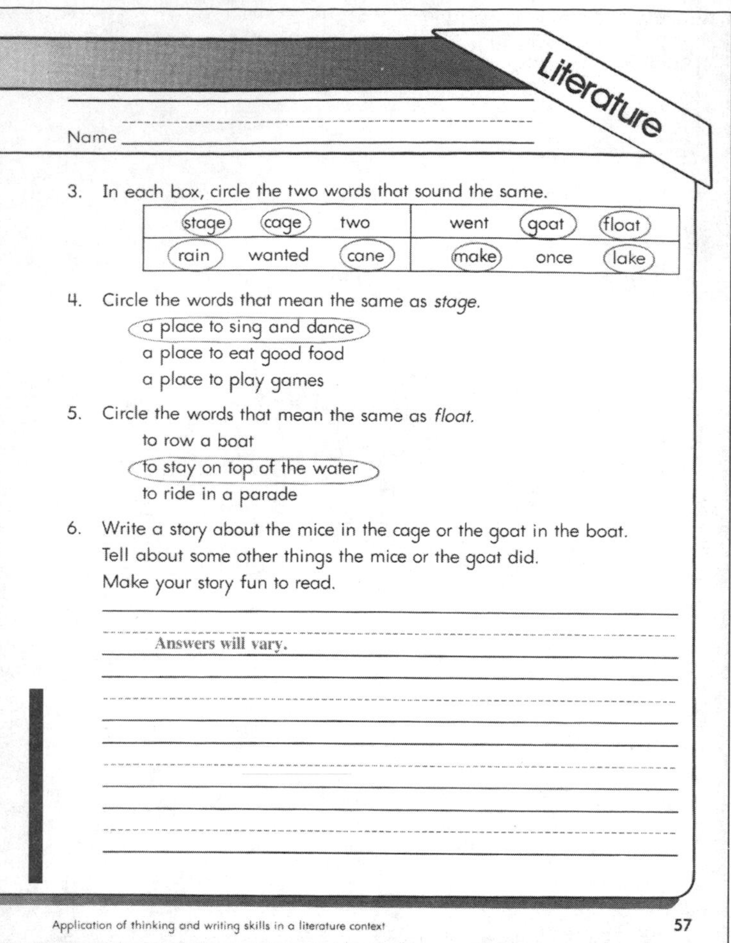

Literature

Name

3. In each box, circle the two words that sound the same.

(stage)	(cage)	two	went	(goat)	(float)
(rain)	wanted	(cane)	(make)	once	(lake)

4. Circle the words that mean the same as *stage.*
   (a place to sing and dance)
   a place to eat good food
   a place to play games

5. Circle the words that mean the same as *float.*
   to row a boat
   (to stay on top of the water)
   to ride in a parade

6. Write a story about the mice in the cage or the goat in the boat. Tell about some other things the mice or the goat did. Make your story fun to read.

Answers will vary.

Application of thinking and writing skills in a literature context 57

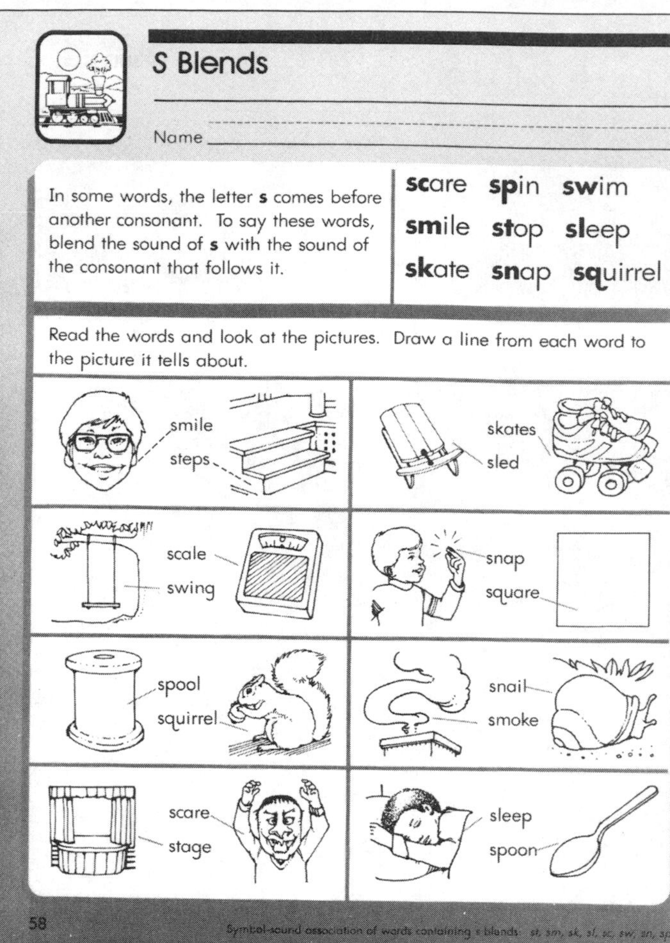

S Blends

Name

In some words, the letter **s** comes before another consonant. To say these words, blend the sound of **s** with the sound of the consonant that follows it.

scare **sp**in **sw**im
smile **st**op **sl**eep
skate **sn**ap **sq**uirrel

Read the words and look at the pictures. Draw a line from each word to the picture it tells about.

smile / steps
skates / sled
scale / swing
snap / square
spool / squirrel
snail / smoke
scare / stage
sleep / spoon

58 Symbol-sound association of words containing s blends: st, sm, sk, sl, sc, sw, sn, sp

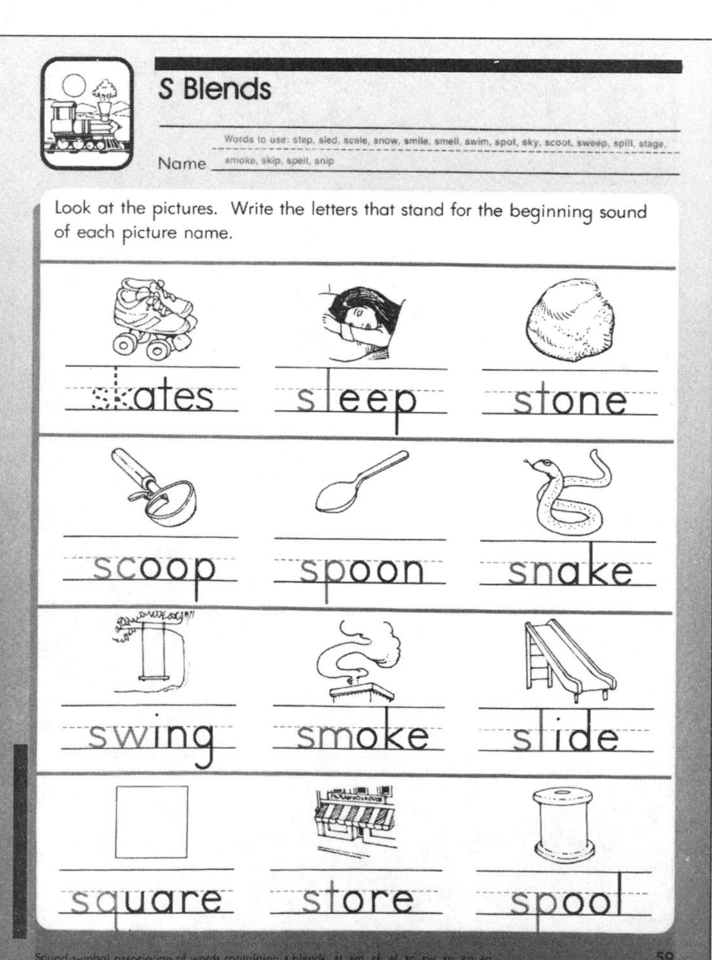

S Blends

Name

Words to use: step, sled, scale, snow, smile, smell, swim, spot, sky, scoot, sweep, spill, stage, smoke, skip, spell, snip

Look at the pictures. Write the letters that stand for the beginning sound of each picture name.

skates sleep stone
scoop spoon snake
swing smoke slide
square store spool

Sound-symbol association of words containing s blends: st, sm, sk, sl, sc, sw, sn, sp, sq 59

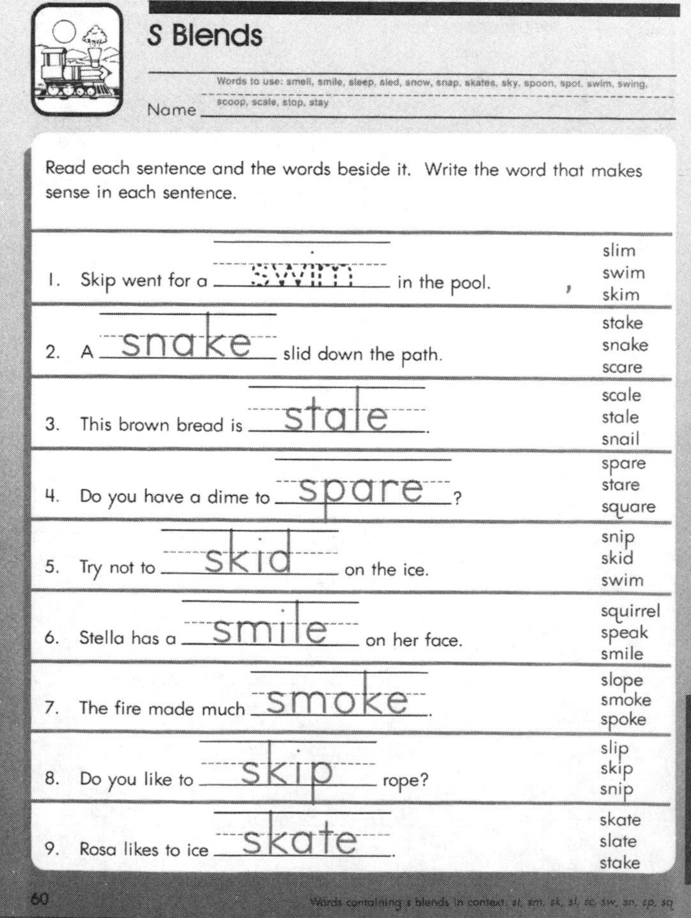

S Blends

Name

Words to use: smell, smile, sleep, sled, snow, snap, skates, sky, spoon, spot, swim, swing, scoop, scale, stop, stay

Read each sentence and the words beside it. Write the word that makes sense in each sentence.

1. Skip went for a swim in the pool.	slim swim skim
2. A snake slid down the path.	stake snake scare
3. This brown bread is stale.	scale stale snail
4. Do you have a dime to spare?	spare stare square
5. Try not to skid on the ice.	snip skid swim
6. Stella has a smile on her face.	squirrel speak smile
7. The fire made much smoke.	slope smoke spoke
8. Do you like to skip rope?	slip skip snip
9. Rosa likes to ice skate.	skate slate stake

60 Words containing s blends in context: st, sm, sk, sl, sc, sw, sn, sp, sq

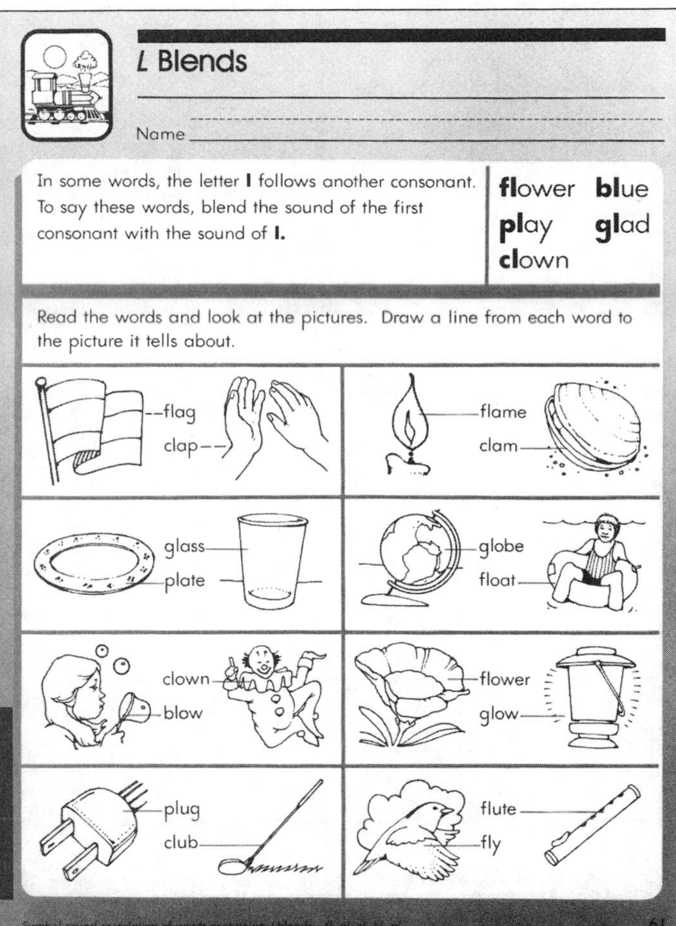

L Blends

Name

In some words, the letter **l** follows another consonant. To say these words, blend the sound of the first consonant with the sound of **l**.

flower **bl**ue **pl**ay **gl**ad **cl**own

Read the words and look at the pictures. Draw a line from each word to the picture it tells about.

flag, clap | flame, clam
glass, plate | globe, float
clown, blow | flower, glow
plug, club | flute, fly

Symbol-sound association of words containing *l* blends: *fl, pl, cl, bl, gl* 61

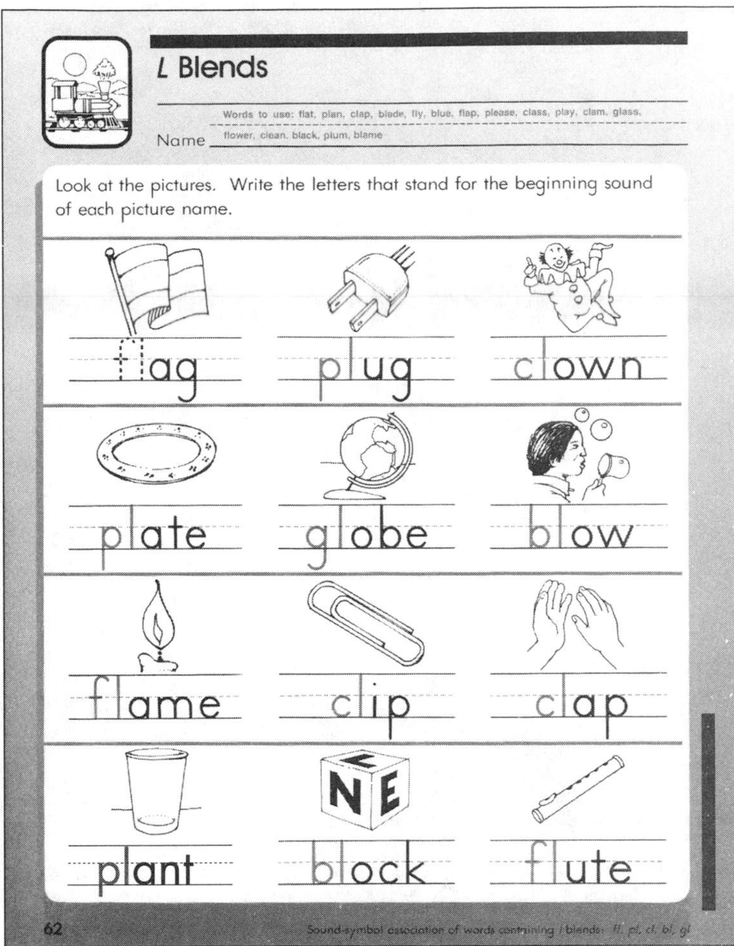

L Blends

Words to use: flat, plan, clap, blade, fly, blue, flap, please, class, play, clam, glass, flower, clean, black, plum, blame

Name

Look at the pictures. Write the letters that stand for the beginning sound of each picture name.

flag plug clown
plate globe blow
flame clip clap
plant block flute

62 Sound-symbol association of words containing *l* blends: *fl, pl, cl, bl, gl*

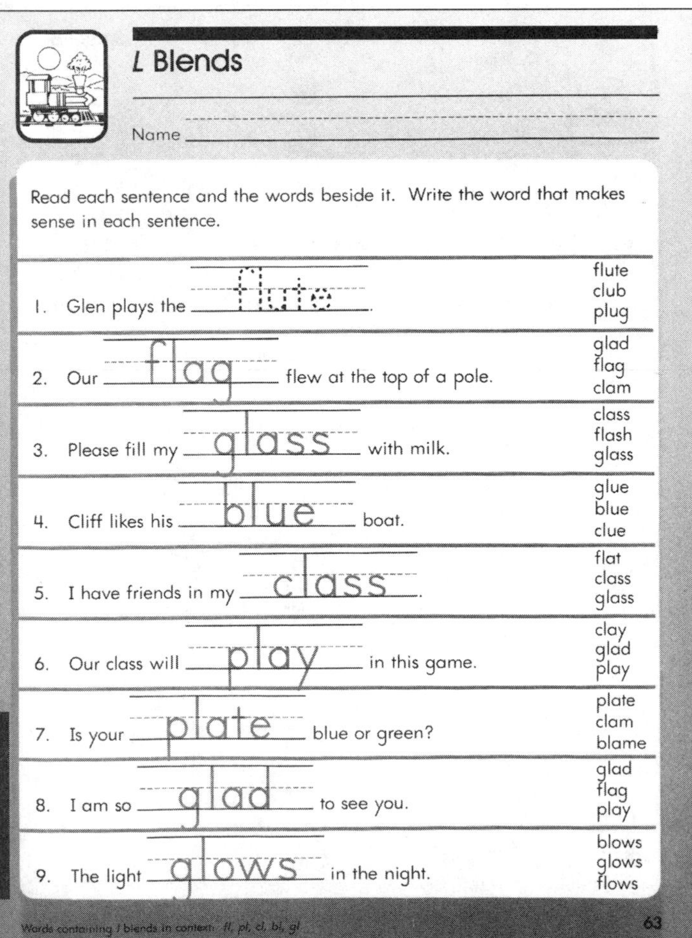

L Blends

Name

Read each sentence and the words beside it. Write the word that makes sense in each sentence.

1. Glen plays the flute.	flute club plug
2. Our flag flew at the top of a pole.	glad flag clam
3. Please fill my glass with milk.	class flash glass
4. Cliff likes his blue boat.	glue blue clue
5. I have friends in my class.	flat class glass
6. Our class will play in this game.	clay glad play
7. Is your plate blue or green?	plate clam blame
8. I am so glad to see you.	glad flag play
9. The light glows in the night.	blows glows flows

Words containing *l* blends in context: *fl, pl, cl, bl, gl* 63

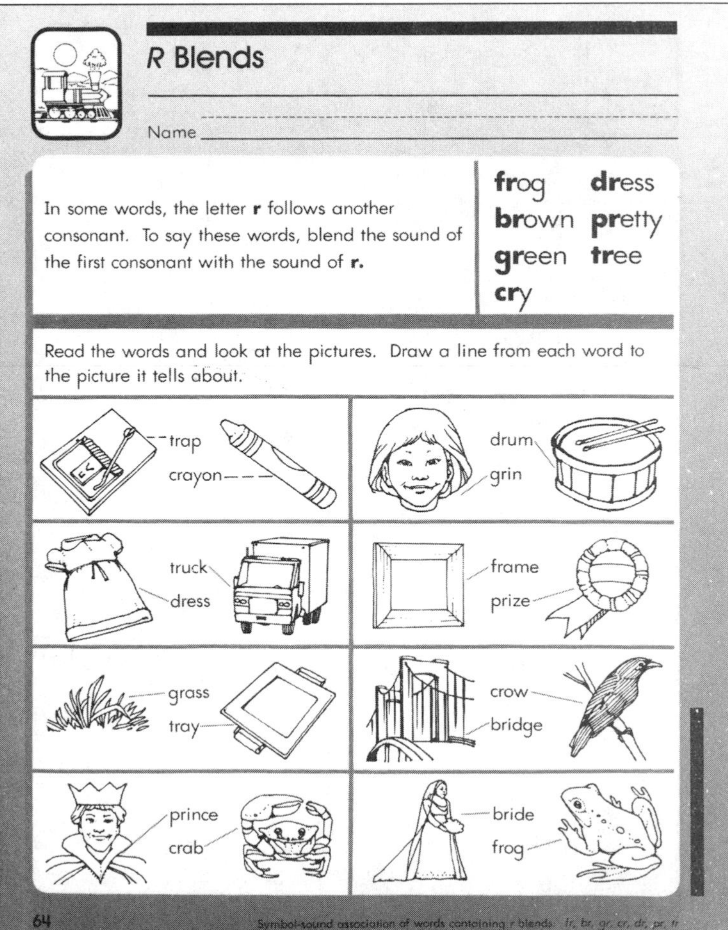

R Blends

Name

In some words, the letter **r** follows another consonant. To say these words, blend the sound of the first consonant with the sound of **r**.

frog **dr**ess **br**own **pr**etty **gr**een **tr**ee **cr**y

Read the words and look at the pictures. Draw a line from each word to the picture it tells about.

trap, crayon | drum, grin
truck, dress | frame, prize
grass, tray | crow, bridge
prince, crab | bride, frog

64 Symbol-sound association of words containing *r* blends: *fr, br, gr, cr, dr, pr, tr*

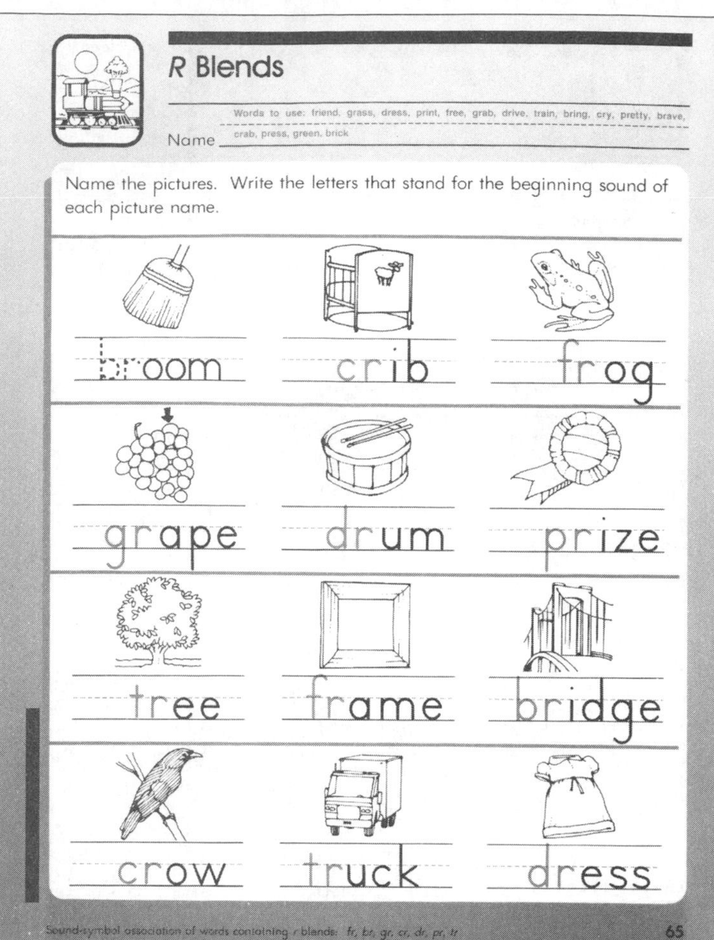

R Blends

Name ______ Words to use: friend, grass, dress, print, free, grab, drive, train, bring, cry, pretty, brave, crab, press, green, brick

Name the pictures. Write the letters that stand for the beginning sound of each picture name.

broom	crib	frog
grape	drum	prize
tree	frame	bridge
crow	truck	dress

Sound-symbol association of words containing r blends: fr, br, gr, cr, dr, pr, tr — 65

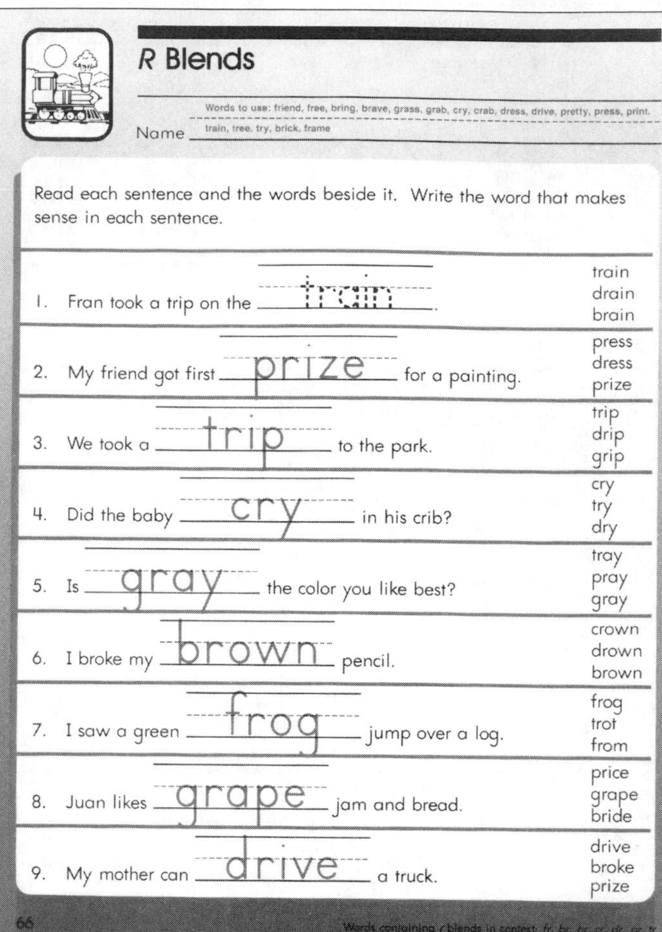

R Blends

Name ______ Words to use: friend, free, bring, brave, grass, grab, cry, crab, dress, drive, pretty, press, print, train, tree, try, brick, frame

Read each sentence and the words beside it. Write the word that makes sense in each sentence.

1. Fran took a trip on the train.	train drain brain
2. My friend got first prize for a painting.	press dress prize
3. We took a trip to the park.	trip drip grip
4. Did the baby cry in his crib?	cry try dry
5. Is gray the color you like best?	tray pray gray
6. I broke my brown pencil.	crown drown brown
7. I saw a green frog jump over a log.	frog trot from
8. Juan likes grape jam and bread.	price grape bride
9. My mother can drive a truck.	drive broke prize

66 — Words containing r blends in context: fr, br, gr, cr, dr, pr, tr

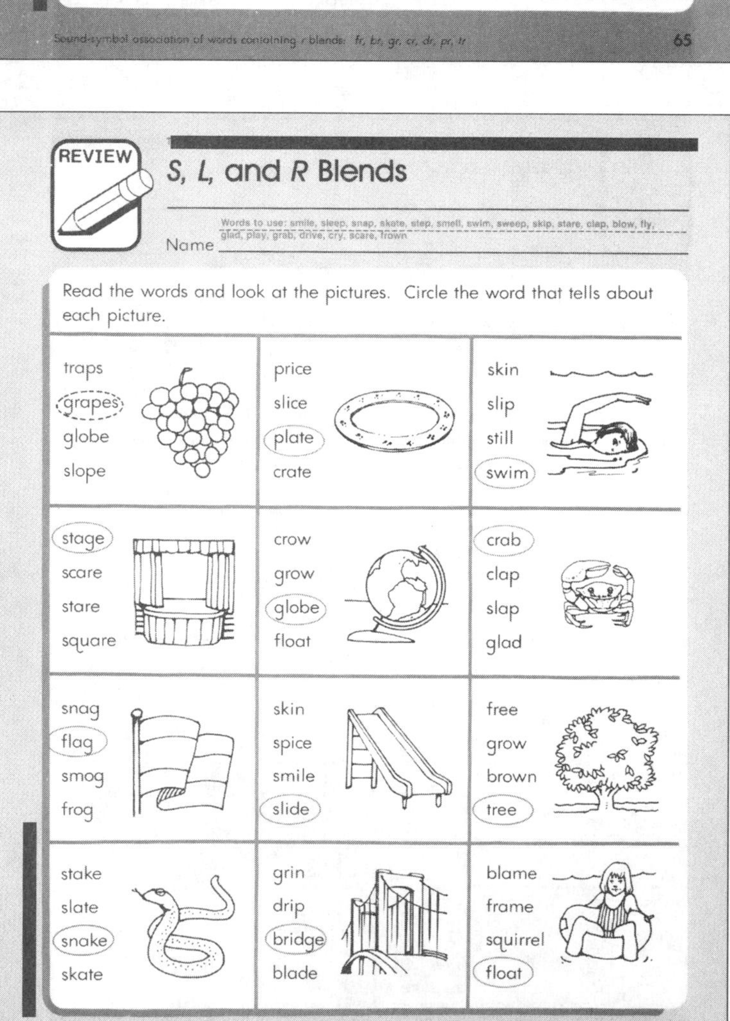

REVIEW

S, L, and R Blends

Name ______ Words to use: smile, sleep, snap, skate, step, smell, swim, sweep, skip, stare, clap, blow, fly, glad, play, grab, drive, cry, scare, frown

Read the words and look at the pictures. Circle the word that tells about each picture.

traps, grapes, globe, slope	price, slice, plate, crate	skin, slip, still, swim
stage, scare, stare, square	crow, grow, globe, float	crab, clap, slap, glad
snag, flag, smog, frog	skin, spice, smile, slide	free, grow, brown, tree
stake, slate, snake, skate	grin, drip, bridge, blade	blame, frame, squirrel, float

Review of symbol-sound association of words containing s, l, and r blends — 67

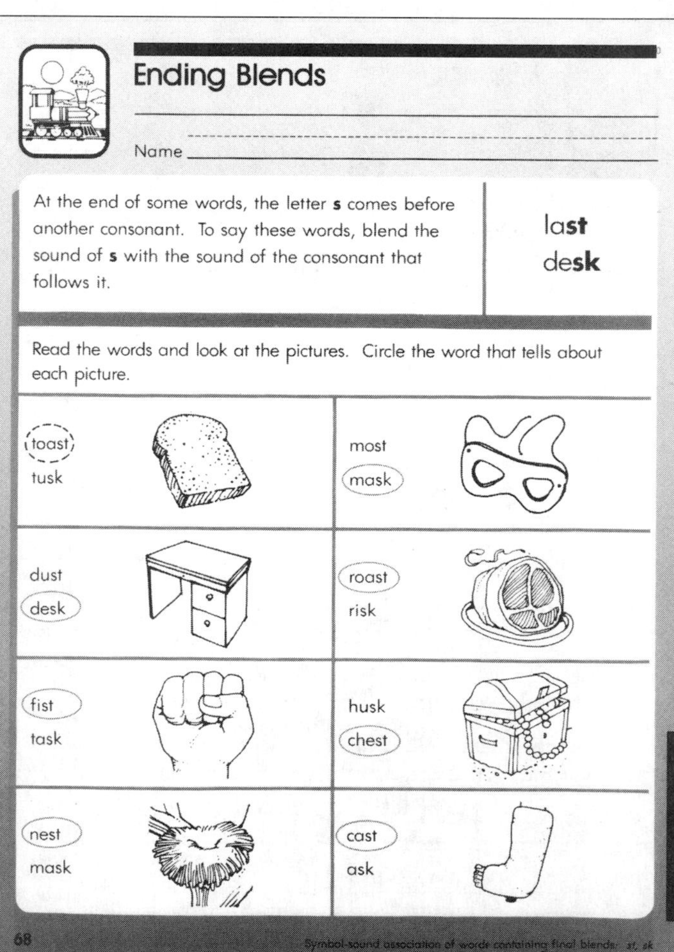

Ending Blends

Name ______

At the end of some words, the letter **s** comes before another consonant. To say these words, blend the sound of **s** with the sound of the consonant that follows it.

la**st**
de**sk**

Read the words and look at the pictures. Circle the word that tells about each picture.

toast, tusk	most, mask
dust, desk	roast, risk
fist, task	husk, chest
nest, mask	cast, ask

68 — Symbol-sound association of words containing final blends: st, sk

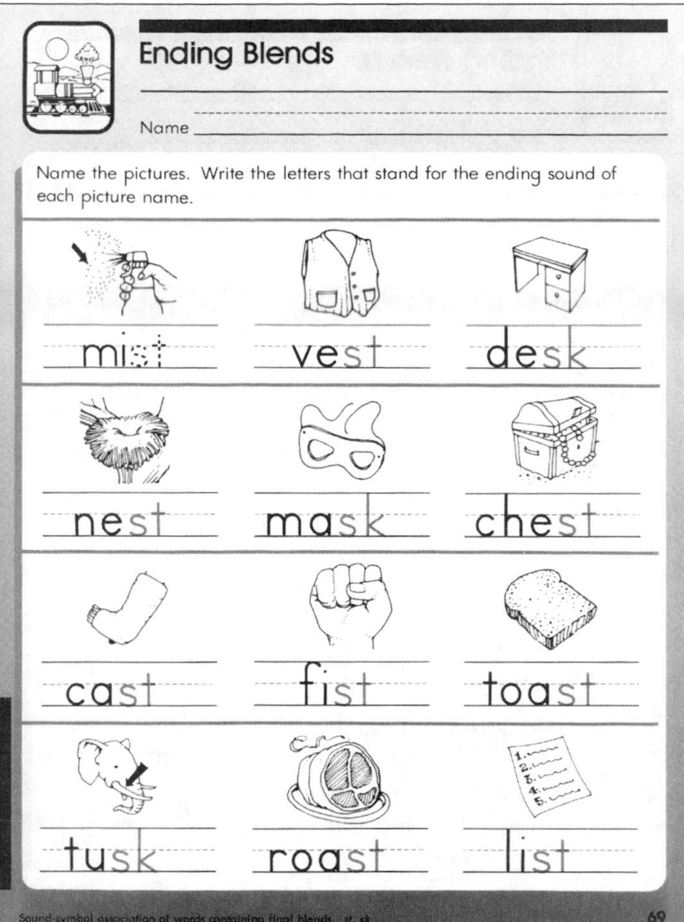

Ending Blends

Name

Name the pictures. Write the letters that stand for the ending sound of each picture name.

mist	vest	desk
nest	mask	chest
cast	fist	toast
tusk	roast	list

Sound-symbol association of words containing final blends: *st, sk* 69

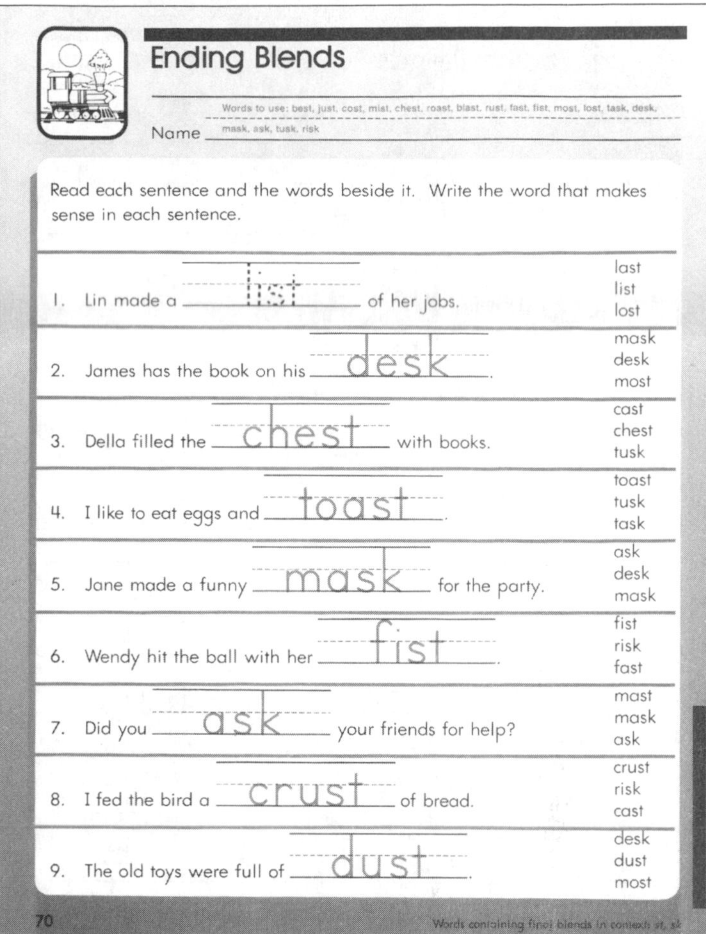

Ending Blends

Words to use: best, just, cost, mist, chest, roast, blast, rust, fast, fist, most, lost, task, desk, mask, ask, tusk, risk

Name

Read each sentence and the words beside it. Write the word that makes sense in each sentence.

1. Lin made a list of her jobs.	last list lost
2. James has the book on his desk.	mask desk most
3. Della filled the chest with books.	cast chest tusk
4. I like to eat eggs and toast.	toast tusk task
5. Jane made a funny mask for the party.	ask desk mask
6. Wendy hit the ball with her fist.	fist risk fast
7. Did you ask your friends for help?	mast mask ask
8. I fed the bird a crust of bread.	crust risk cast
9. The old toys were full of dust.	desk dust most

70 Words containing final blends in context: *st, sk*

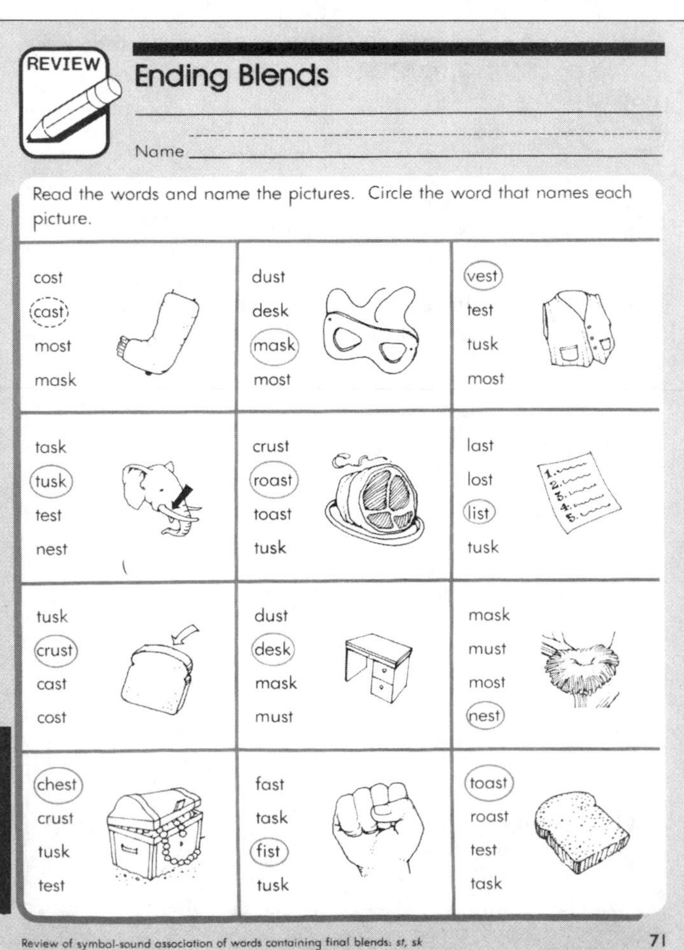

REVIEW

Ending Blends

Name

Read the words and name the pictures. Circle the word that names each picture.

cost (cast) most mask	dust desk (mask) most	(vest) test tusk most
task (tusk) test nest	crust (roast) toast tusk	last lost (list) tusk
tusk (crust) cast cost	dust (desk) mask must	mask must most (nest)
(chest) crust tusk test	fast task (fist) tusk	(toast) roast test task

Review of symbol-sound association of words containing final blends: *st, sk* 71

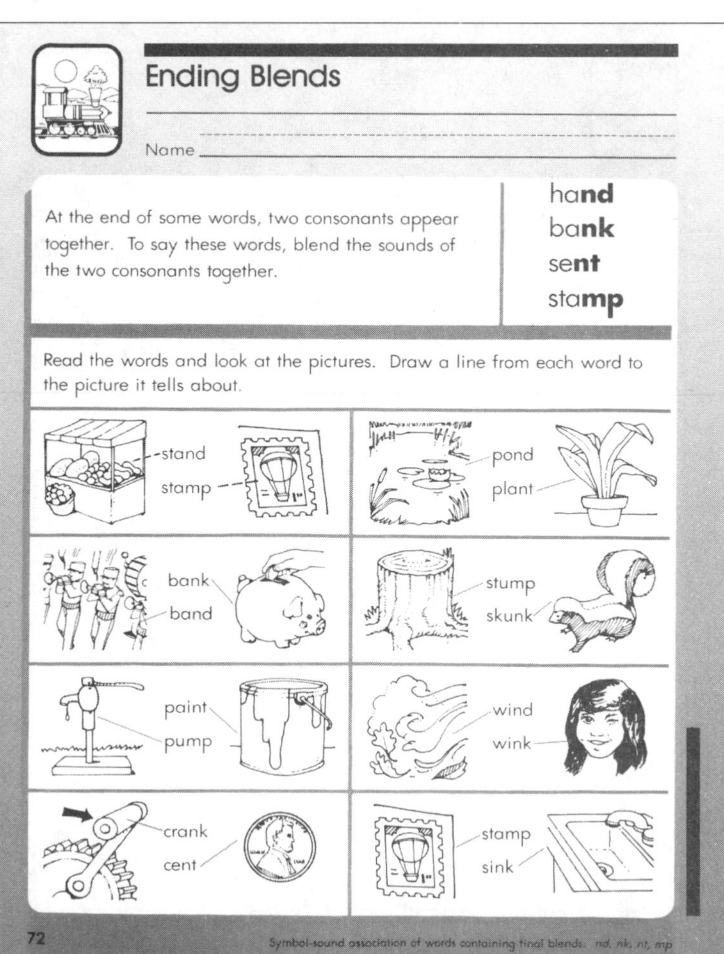

Ending Blends

Name

At the end of some words, two consonants appear together. To say these words, blend the sounds of the two consonants together.

ha**nd**
ba**nk**
se**nt**
sta**mp**

Read the words and look at the pictures. Draw a line from each word to the picture it tells about.

stand stamp	pond plant
bank band	stump skunk
paint pump	wind wink
crank cent	stamp sink

72 Symbol-sound association of words containing final blends: *nd, nk, nt, mp*

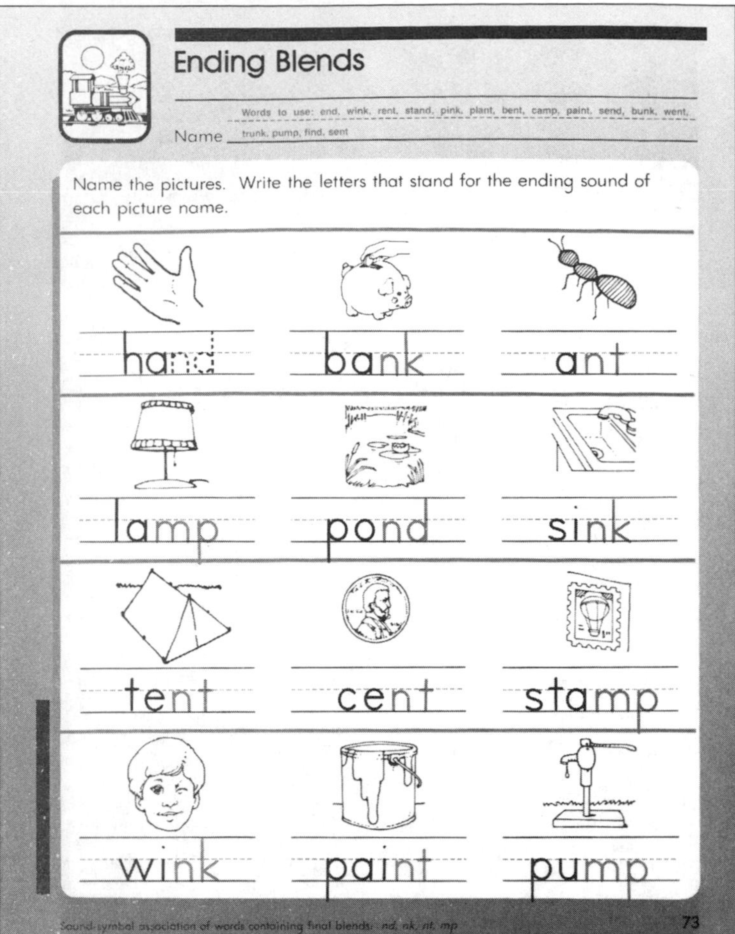

Ending Blends

Words to use: end, wink, rent, stand, pink, plant, bent, camp, paint, send, bunk, went, trunk, pump, find, sent

Name ______________________

Name the pictures. Write the letters that stand for the ending sound of each picture name.

hand	bank	ant
lamp	pond	sink
tent	cent	stamp
wink	paint	pump

Sound-symbol association of words containing final blends: *nd, nk, nt, mp* 73

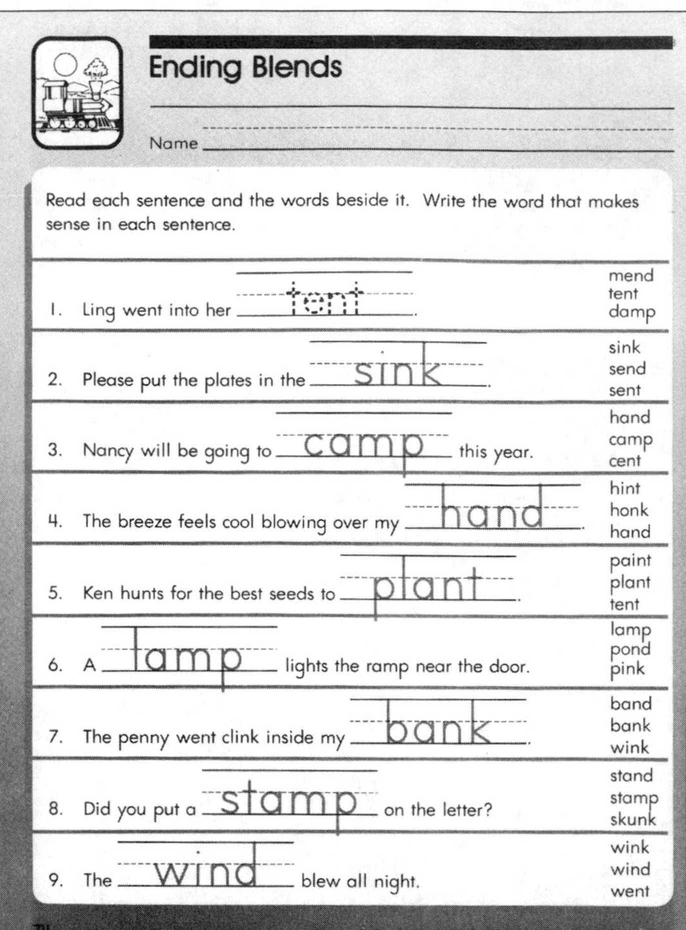

Ending Blends

Name ______________________

Read each sentence and the words beside it. Write the word that makes sense in each sentence.

1. Ling went into her ___tent___.	mend tent damp
2. Please put the plates in the ___sink___.	sink send sent
3. Nancy will be going to ___camp___ this year.	hand camp cent
4. The breeze feels cool blowing over my ___hand___.	hint honk hand
5. Ken hunts for the best seeds to ___plant___.	paint plant tent
6. A ___lamp___ lights the ramp near the door.	lamp pond pink
7. The penny went clink inside my ___bank___.	band bank wink
8. Did you put a ___stamp___ on the letter?	stand stamp skunk
9. The ___wind___ blew all night.	wink wind went

74 Words containing final blends in context: *nd, nk, nt, mp*

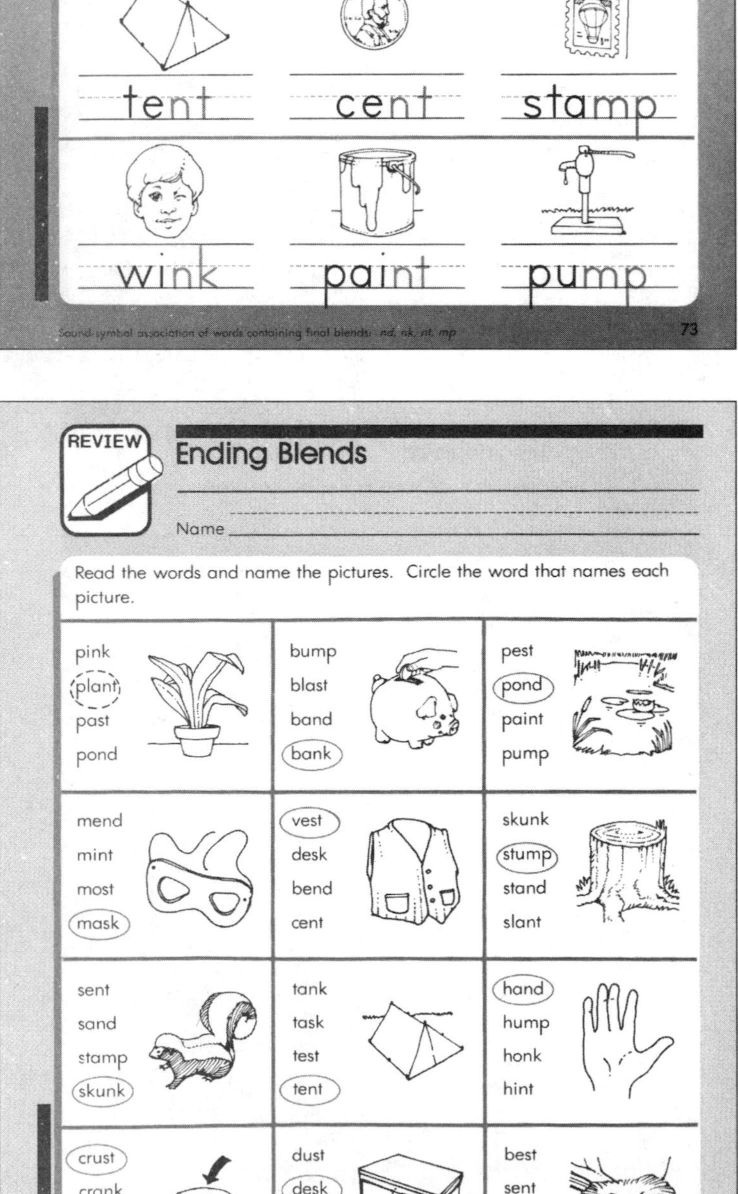

REVIEW

Ending Blends

Name ______________________

Read the words and name the pictures. Circle the word that names each picture.

pink (plant) past pond	bump blast band (bank)	pest (pond) paint pump
mend mint most (mask)	(vest) desk bend cent	skunk (stump) stand slant
sent sand stamp (skunk)	tank task test (tent)	(hand) hump honk hint
(crust) crank cramp cast	dust (desk) drink damp	best sent mend (nest)

Review of symbol-sound association of words containing final blends: *st, sk, nd, nk, nt, mp* 75

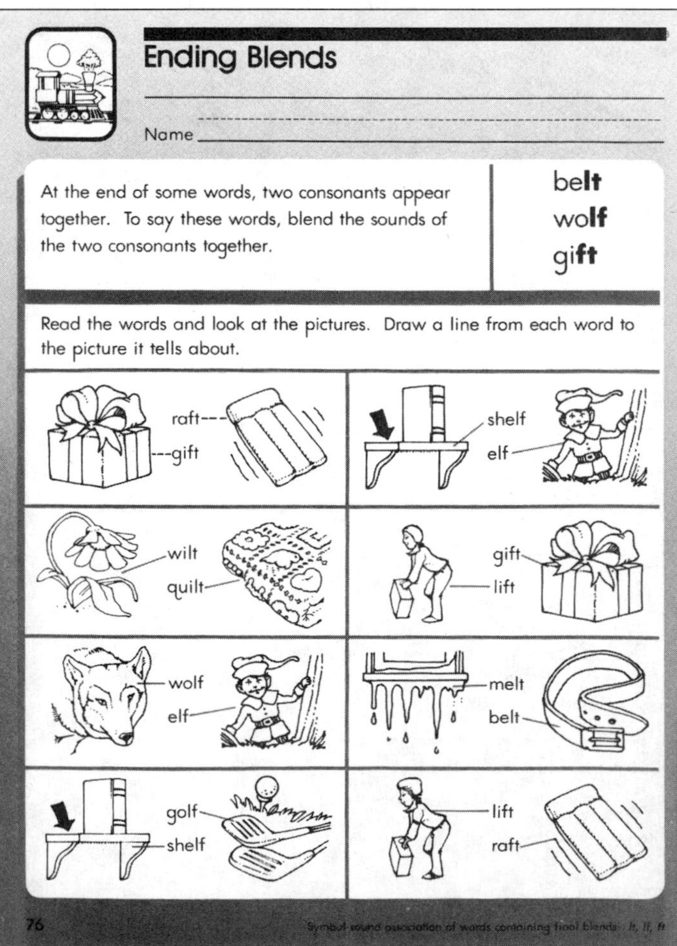

Ending Blends

Name ______________________

At the end of some words, two consonants appear together. To say these words, blend the sounds of the two consonants together.

be**lt**
wo**lf**
gi**ft**

Read the words and look at the pictures. Draw a line from each word to the picture it tells about.

raft gift	shelf elf
wilt quilt	gift lift
wolf elf	melt belt
golf shelf	lift raft

76 Symbol-sound association of words containing final blends: *lt, lf, ft*

Ending Blends

Name

Look at the pictures. Write the letters that stand for the ending sound of each picture name.

quilt	gift	shelf
elf	golf	belt
raft	melt	lift
wolf	wilt	left

Sound-symbol association of words containing final blends: *lt, lf, ft* 77

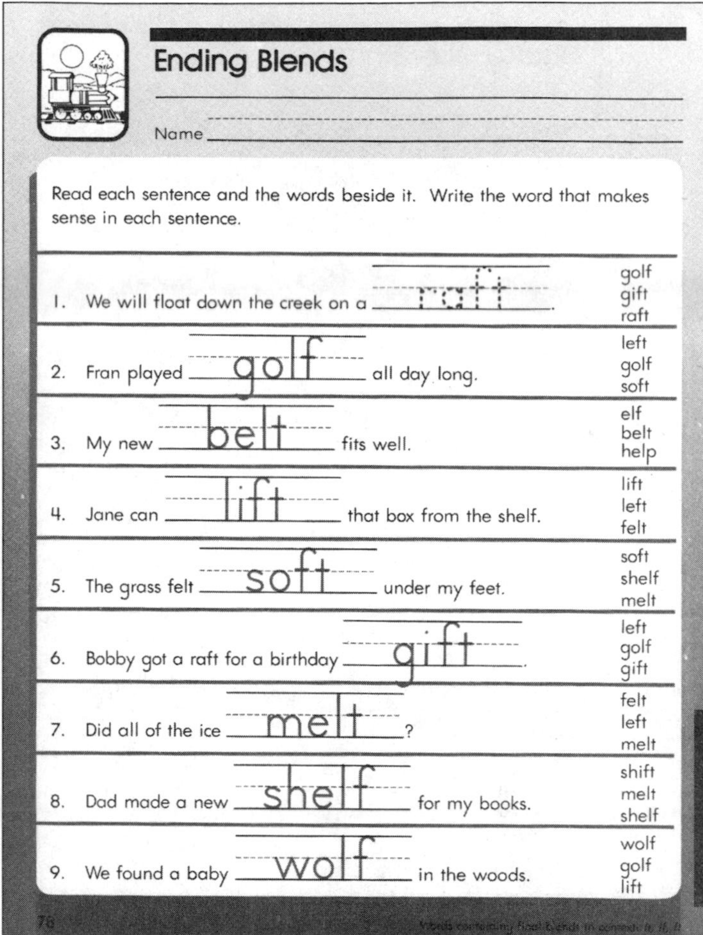

Ending Blends

Name

Read each sentence and the words beside it. Write the word that makes sense in each sentence.

1. We will float down the creek on a raft.	golf, gift, raft
2. Fran played golf all day long.	left, golf, soft
3. My new belt fits well.	elf, belt, help
4. Jane can lift that box from the shelf.	lift, left, felt
5. The grass felt soft under my feet.	soft, shelf, melt
6. Bobby got a raft for a birthday gift.	left, golf, gift
7. Did all of the ice melt?	felt, left, melt
8. Dad made a new shelf for my books.	shift, melt, shelf
9. We found a baby wolf in the woods.	wolf, golf, lift

78 Words containing final blends in context: *lt, lf, ft*

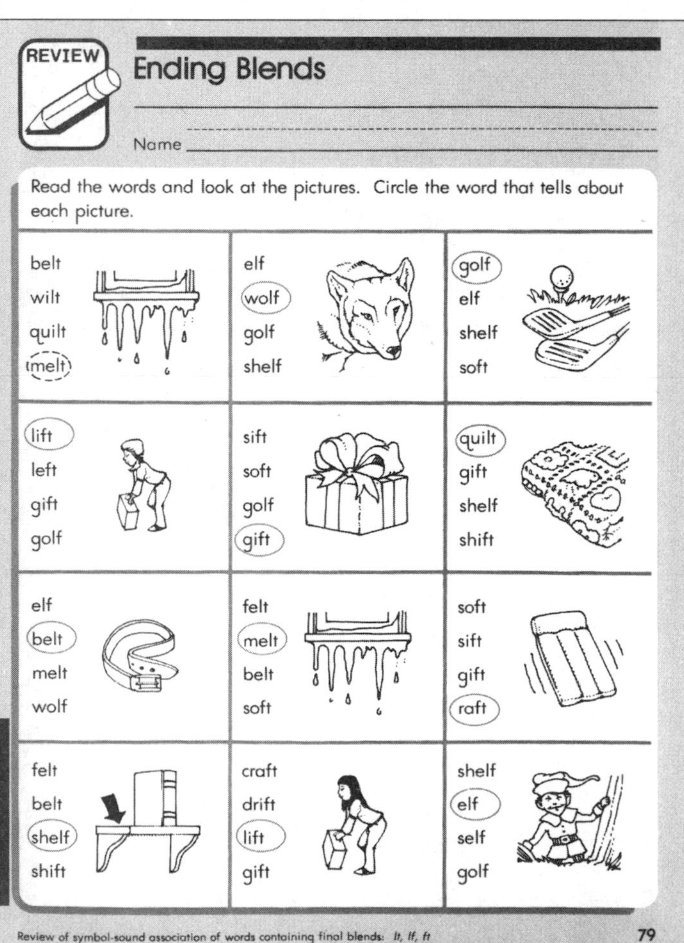

REVIEW

Ending Blends

Name

Read the words and look at the pictures. Circle the word that tells about each picture.

belt, wilt, quilt, (melt)	elf, (wolf), golf, shelf	(golf), elf, shelf, soft
(lift), left, gift, golf	sift, soft, golf, (gift)	(quilt), gift, shelf, shift
elf, (belt), melt, wolf	felt, (melt), belt, soft	soft, sift, gift, (raft)
felt, belt, (shelf), shift	craft, drift, (lift), gift	shelf, (elf), self, golf

Review of symbol-sound association of words containing final blends: *lt, lf, ft* 79

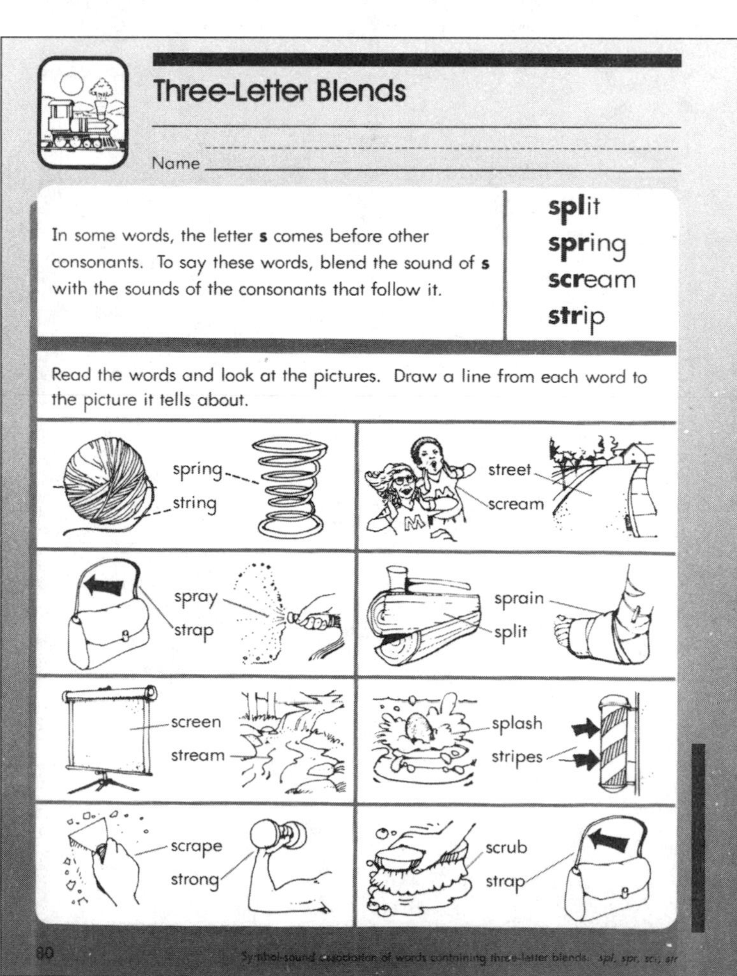

Three-Letter Blends

Name

In some words, the letter **s** comes before other consonants. To say these words, blend the sound of **s** with the sounds of the consonants that follow it.

split
spring
scream
strip

Read the words and look at the pictures. Draw a line from each word to the picture it tells about.

spring, string	street, scream
spray, strap	sprain, split
screen, stream	splash, stripes
scrape, strong	scrub, strap

80 Symbol-sound association of words containing three-letter blends: *spl, spr, scr, str*

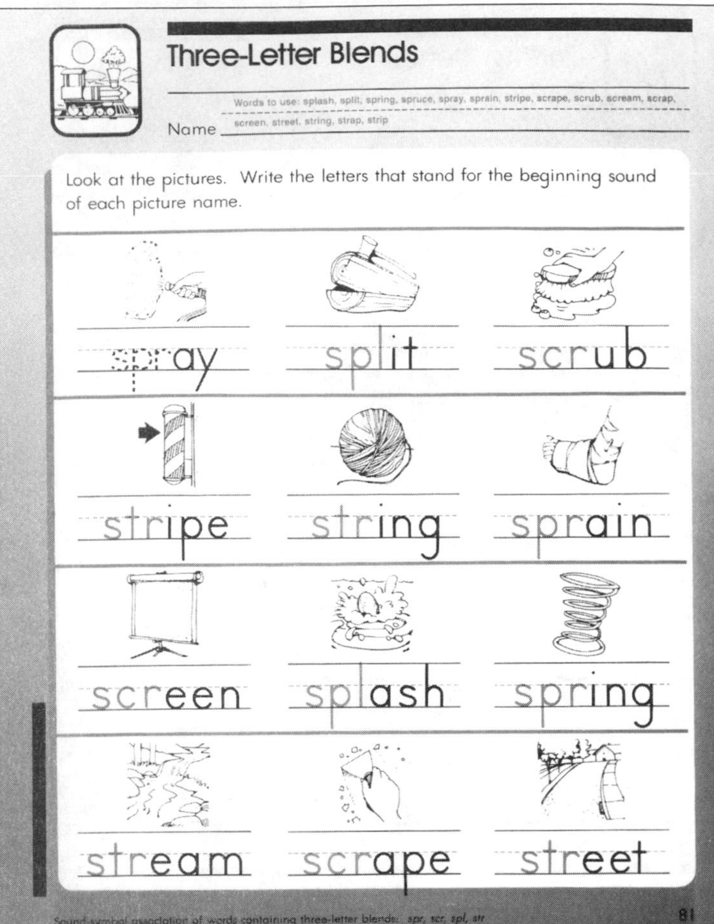

Three-Letter Blends

Words to use: splash, split, spring, spruce, spray, sprain, stripe, scrape, scrub, scream, scrap, screen, street, string, strap, strip

Name ______________________

Look at the pictures. Write the letters that stand for the beginning sound of each picture name.

spray	split	scrub
stripe	string	sprain
screen	splash	spring
stream	scrape	street

Sound-symbol association of words containing three-letter blends: *spr, scr, spl, str* 81

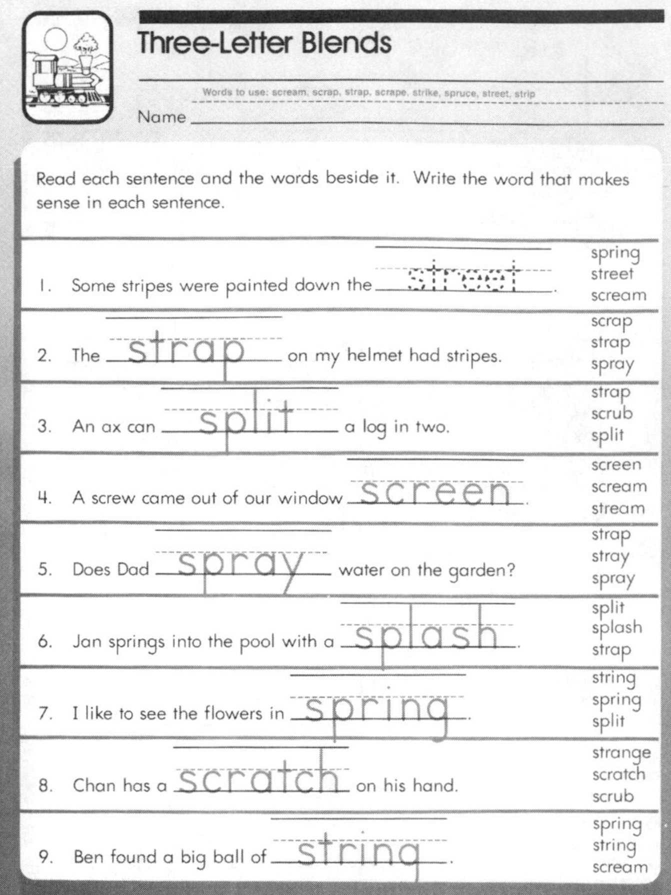

Three-Letter Blends

Words to use: scream, scrap, strap, scrape, strike, spruce, street, strip

Name ______________________

Read each sentence and the words beside it. Write the word that makes sense in each sentence.

1. Some stripes were painted down the street.	spring, street, scream
2. The strap on my helmet had stripes.	scrap, strap, spray
3. An ax can split a log in two.	strap, scrub, split
4. A screw came out of our window screen.	screen, scream, stream
5. Does Dad spray water on the garden?	strap, stray, spray
6. Jan springs into the pool with a splash.	split, splash, strap
7. I like to see the flowers in spring.	string, spring, split
8. Chan has a scratch on his hand.	strange, scratch, scrub
9. Ben found a big ball of string.	spring, string, scream

82 Words containing three-letter blends in context: *spl, spr, scr, str*

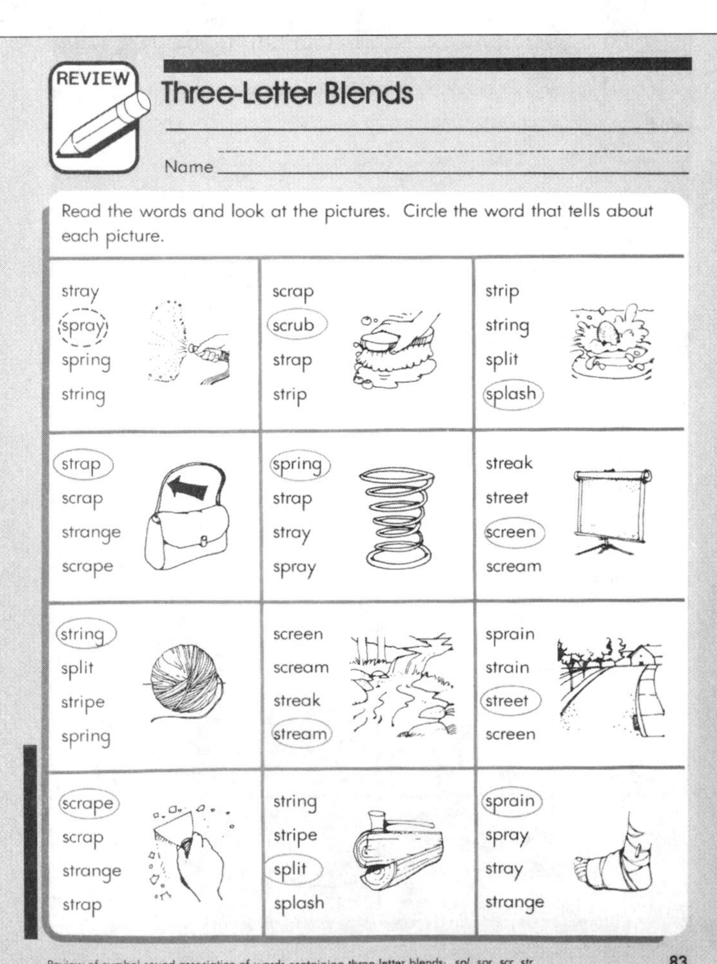

REVIEW

Three-Letter Blends

Name ______________________

Read the words and look at the pictures. Circle the word that tells about each picture.

stray, (spray), spring, string	scrap, (scrub), strap, strip	strip, string, split, (splash)
(strap), scrap, strange, scrape	(spring), strap, stray, spray	streak, street, (screen), scream
(string), split, stripe, spring	screen, scream, streak, (stream)	sprain, strain, (street), screen
(scrape), scrap, strange, strap	string, stripe, (split), splash	(sprain), spray, stray, strange

Review of symbol-sound association of words containing three-letter blends: *spl, spr, scr, str* 83

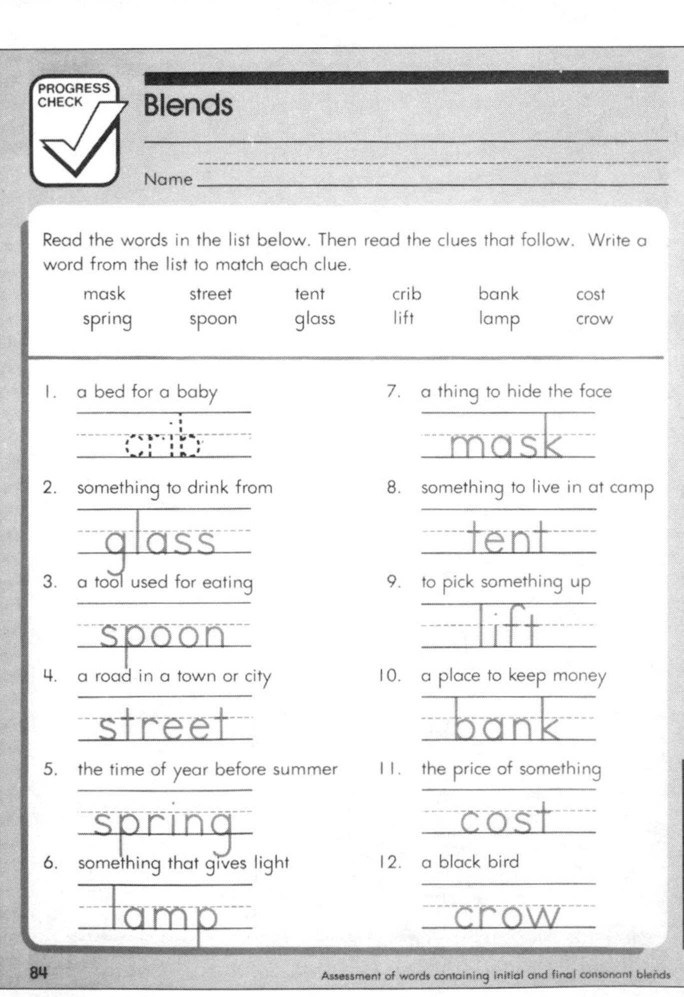

PROGRESS CHECK

Blends

Name ______________________

Read the words in the list below. Then read the clues that follow. Write a word from the list to match each clue.

mask	street	tent	crib	bank	cost
spring	spoon	glass	lift	lamp	crow

1. a bed for a baby — crib
2. something to drink from — glass
3. a tool used for eating — spoon
4. a road in a town or city — street
5. the time of year before summer — spring
6. something that gives light — lamp
7. a thing to hide the face — mask
8. something to live in at camp — tent
9. to pick something up — lift
10. a place to keep money — bank
11. the price of something — cost
12. a black bird — crow

84 Assessment of words containing initial and final consonant blends

Silent Consonants

Name ______________________

In some words, two consonants stand for one sound. The letters **kn** usually stand for the sound of **n**, as in **knot.** The letters **wr** usually stand for the sound of **r,** as in **write.**

knot **wr**ite

Look at the pictures. Circle the letter or letters that stand for the beginning sound in each picture name.

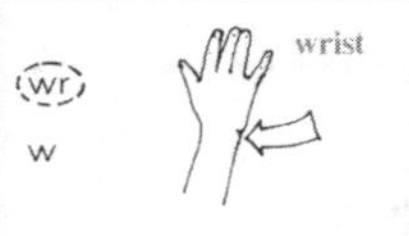
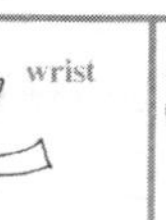

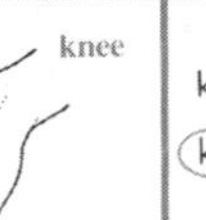

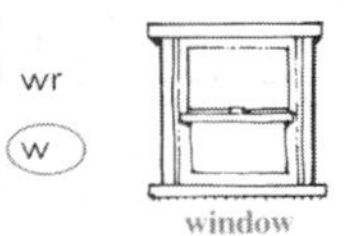
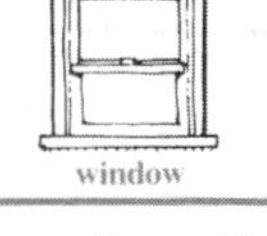

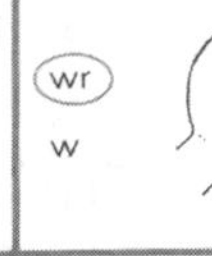

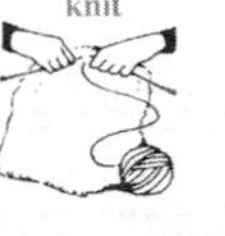

wr / w (wrist)	kn / k (knee)	kn / k (kitten)
wr / w (window)	wr / w (write)	kn / k (knife)
kn / k (kite)	kn / k (knot)	wr / w (wrench)
wr / w (wreath)	kn / k (knit)	kn / k (knock)

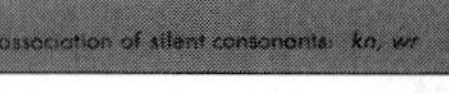

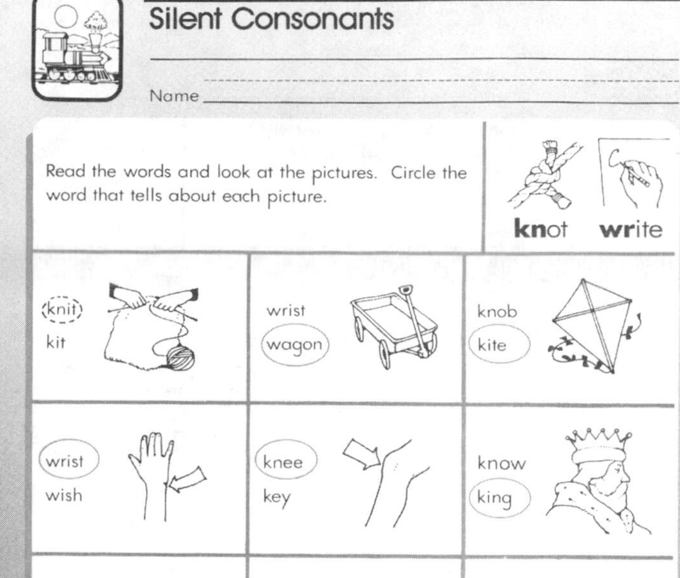

Silent Consonants

Name ______________________

Read the words and look at the pictures. Circle the word that tells about each picture.

knot **wr**ite

knit / kit	wrist / wagon	knob / kite
wrist / wish	knee / key	know / king
wrote / well	write / wing	kneel / keep
knot / kitten	wrap / wag	wrong / water

Silent Consonants

Words to use: wreath, know, knife, wrench, wrong, kneel, knot, knee, knew, wrap, write, wring, wrist, knock

Name ______________________

Read each sentence and the words beside it. Write the word that makes sense in each sentence.

knot **wr**ite

1. I fell and scraped my knee.	knee knot know
2. We drove down the wrong street.	wrap wrong wrist
3. The knob on that door is old.	knob knot knee
4. Did you find a knot in the rope?	knot knit knob
5. Kate will write a letter.	wrist wrote write
6. We need a knife to cut the apple.	knob knife knot
7. I hurt my left wrist.	write wrap wrist
8. We heard a knock on the door.	knock know knit
9. Will you help me wrap the gift?	wrap wrong wrote

Silent Consonants

Name ______________________

In some words, two consonants stand for one sound. The letters **ck** usually stand for the sound of **k,** as in **duck.**

du**ck**

Read the words and name the pictures. Circle the word that names each picture.

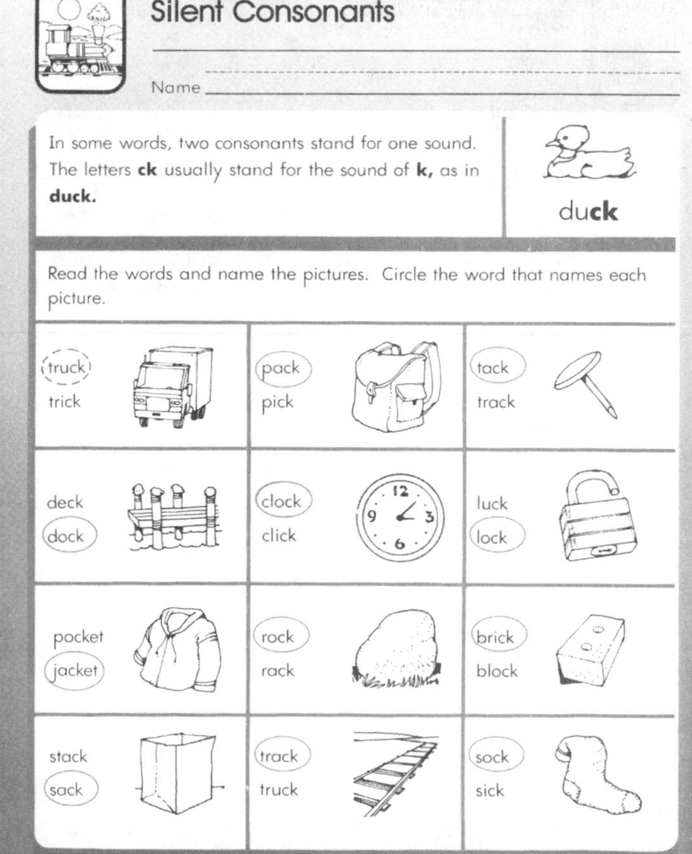

truck / trick	pack / pick	tack / track
deck / dock	clock / click	luck / lock
pocket / jacket	rock / rack	brick / block
stack / sack	track / truck	sock / sick

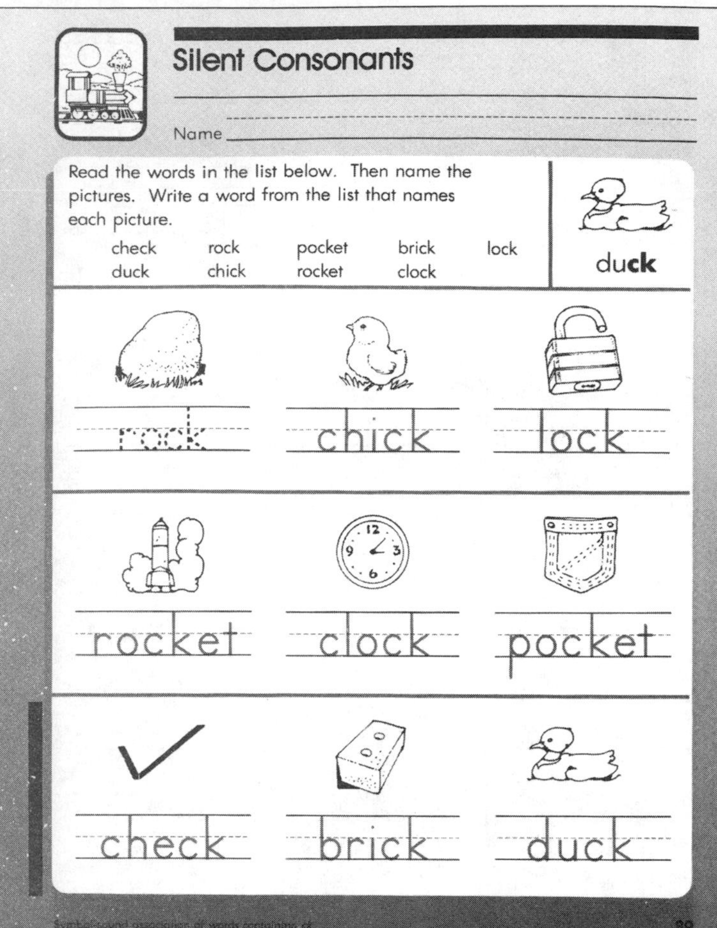

Silent Consonants

Name

Read the words in the list below. Then name the pictures. Write a word from the list that names each picture.

check rock pocket brick lock
duck chick rocket clock

du**ck**

rock chick lock

rocket clock pocket

check brick duck

Symbol-sound association of words containing ck 89

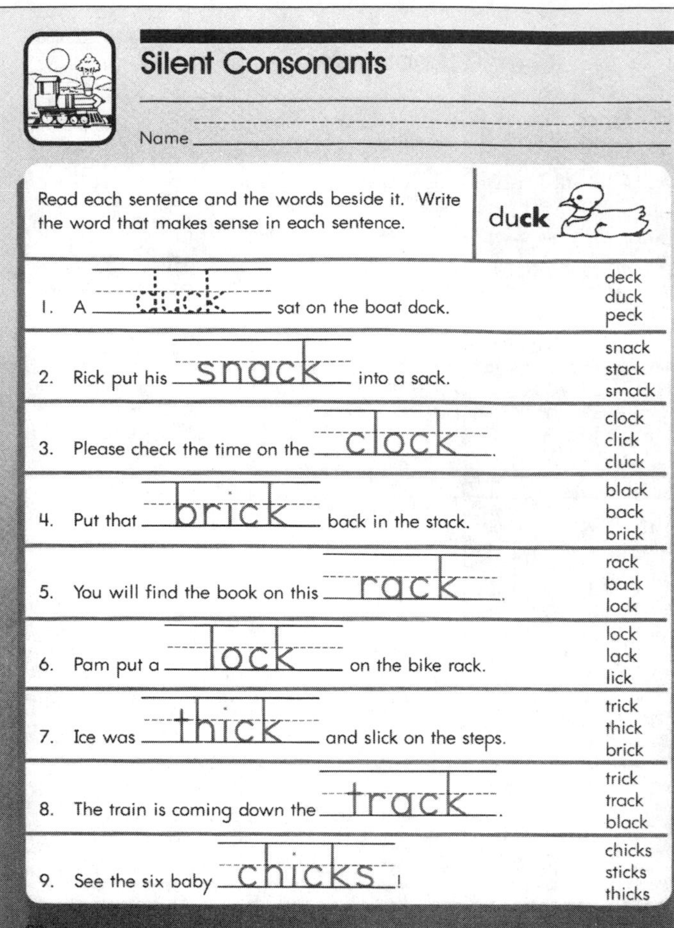

Silent Consonants

Name

Read each sentence and the words beside it. Write the word that makes sense in each sentence.

du**ck**

1.	A duck sat on the boat dock.	deck duck peck
2.	Rick put his snack into a sack.	snack stack smack
3.	Please check the time on the clock.	clock click cluck
4.	Put that brick back in the stack.	black back brick
5.	You will find the book on this rack.	rack back lock
6.	Pam put a lock on the bike rack.	lock lack lick
7.	Ice was thick and slick on the steps.	trick thick brick
8.	The train is coming down the track.	trick track black
9.	See the six baby chicks!	chicks sticks thicks

90 Words containing ck in context

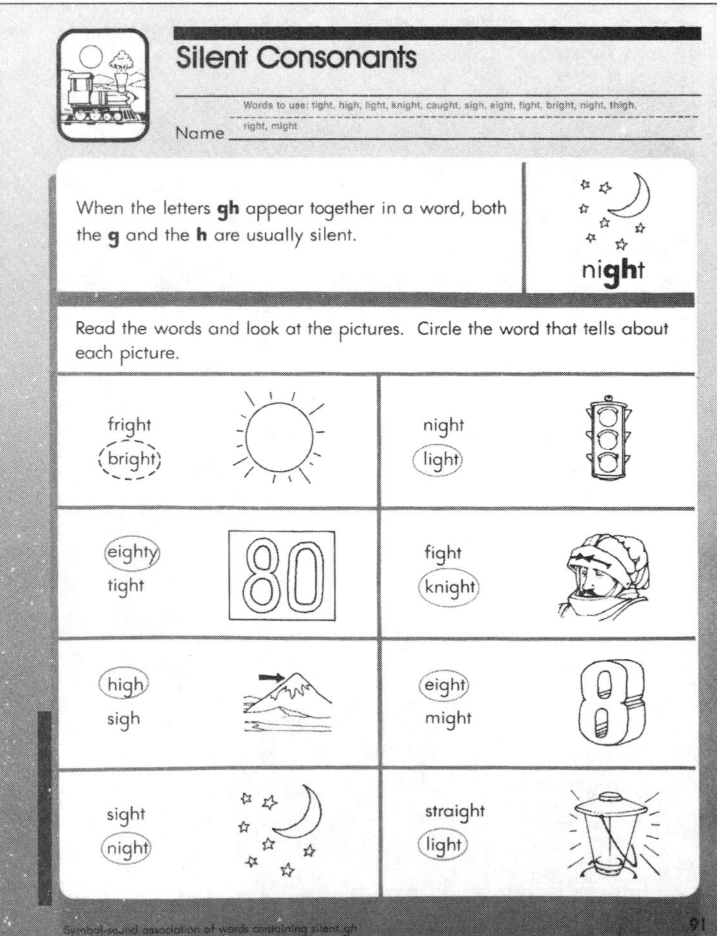

Silent Consonants

Words to use: tight, high, light, knight, caught, sigh, eight, fight, bright, night, thigh, right, might

Name

When the letters **gh** appear together in a word, both the **g** and the **h** are usually silent.

ni**gh**t

Read the words and look at the pictures. Circle the word that tells about each picture.

fright / bright	night / light
eighty / tight	fight / knight
high / sigh	eight / might
sight / night	straight / light

Symbol-sound association of words containing silent gh 91

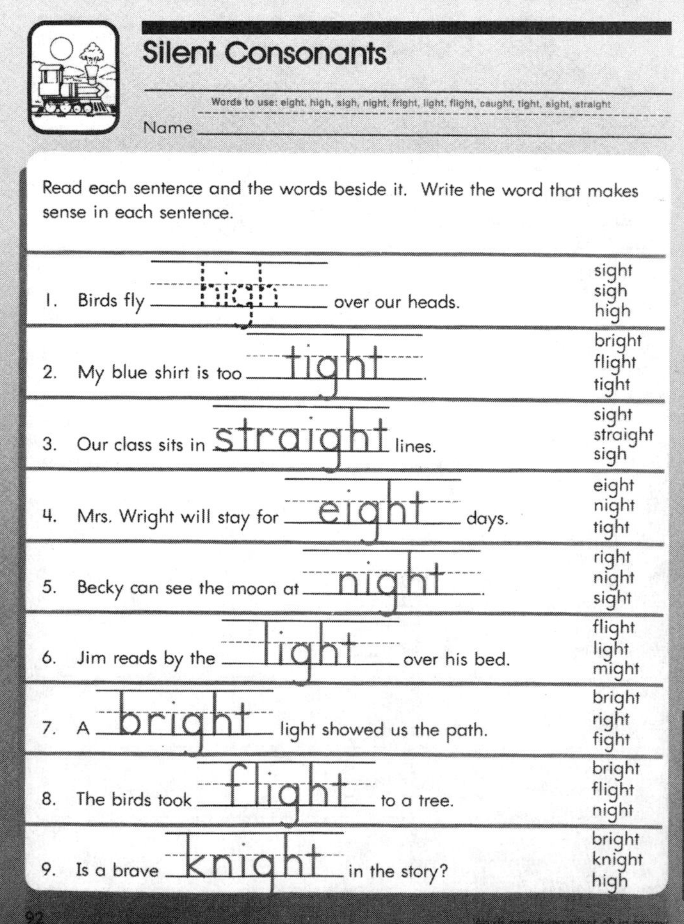

Silent Consonants

Words to use: eight, high, sigh, night, fright, light, flight, caught, tight, sight, straight

Name

Read each sentence and the words beside it. Write the word that makes sense in each sentence.

1.	Birds fly high over our heads.	sight sigh high
2.	My blue shirt is too tight.	bright flight tight
3.	Our class sits in straight lines.	sight straight sigh
4.	Mrs. Wright will stay for eight days.	eight night tight
5.	Becky can see the moon at night.	right night sight
6.	Jim reads by the light over his bed.	flight light might
7.	A bright light showed us the path.	bright right fight
8.	The birds took flight to a tree.	bright flight night
9.	Is a brave knight in the story?	bright knight high

92 Words containing silent gh in context

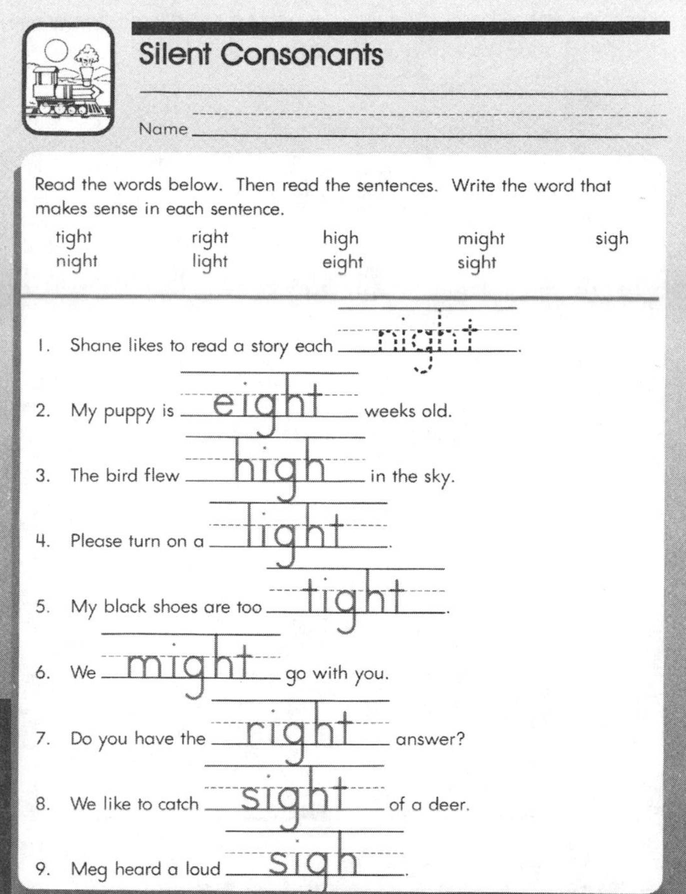

Silent Consonants

Name ______________________

Read the words below. Then read the sentences. Write the word that makes sense in each sentence.

tight	right	high	might	sigh
night	light	eight	sight	

1. Shane likes to read a story each night.
2. My puppy is eight weeks old.
3. The bird flew high in the sky.
4. Please turn on a light.
5. My black shoes are too tight.
6. We might go with you.
7. Do you have the right answer?
8. We like to catch sight of a deer.
9. Meg heard a loud sigh.

Words containing silent *gh* in context 93

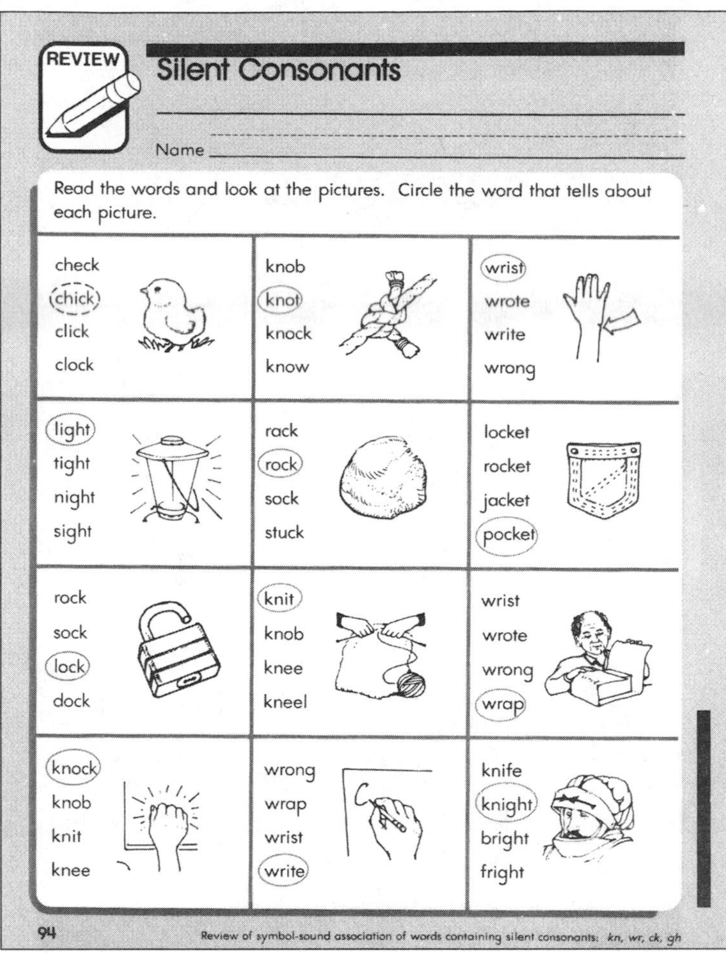

REVIEW

Silent Consonants

Name ______________________

Read the words and look at the pictures. Circle the word that tells about each picture.

check, (chick), click, clock	knob, (knot), knock, know	(wrist), wrote, write, wrong
(light), tight, night, sight	rack, (rock), sock, stuck	locket, rocket, jacket, (pocket)
rock, sock, (lock), dock	(knit), knob, knee, kneel	wrist, wrote, wrong, (wrap)
(knock), knob, knit, knee	wrong, wrap, wrist, (write)	knife, (knight), bright, fright

94 Review of symbol-sound association of words containing silent consonants: *kn, wr, ck, gh*

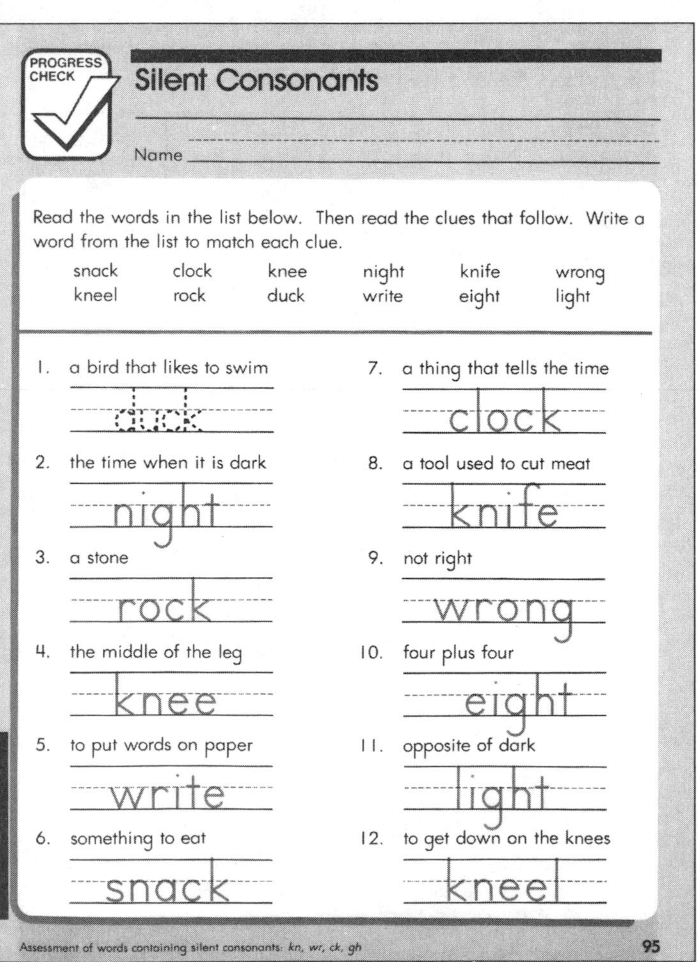

PROGRESS CHECK

Silent Consonants

Name ______________________

Read the words in the list below. Then read the clues that follow. Write a word from the list to match each clue.

snack	clock	knee	night	knife	wrong
kneel	rock	duck	write	eight	light

1. a bird that likes to swim — duck
2. the time when it is dark — night
3. a stone — rock
4. the middle of the leg — knee
5. to put words on paper — write
6. something to eat — snack
7. a thing that tells the time — clock
8. a tool used to cut meat — knife
9. not right — wrong
10. four plus four — eight
11. opposite of dark — light
12. to get down on the knees — kneel

Assessment of words containing silent consonants: *kn, wr, ck, gh* 95

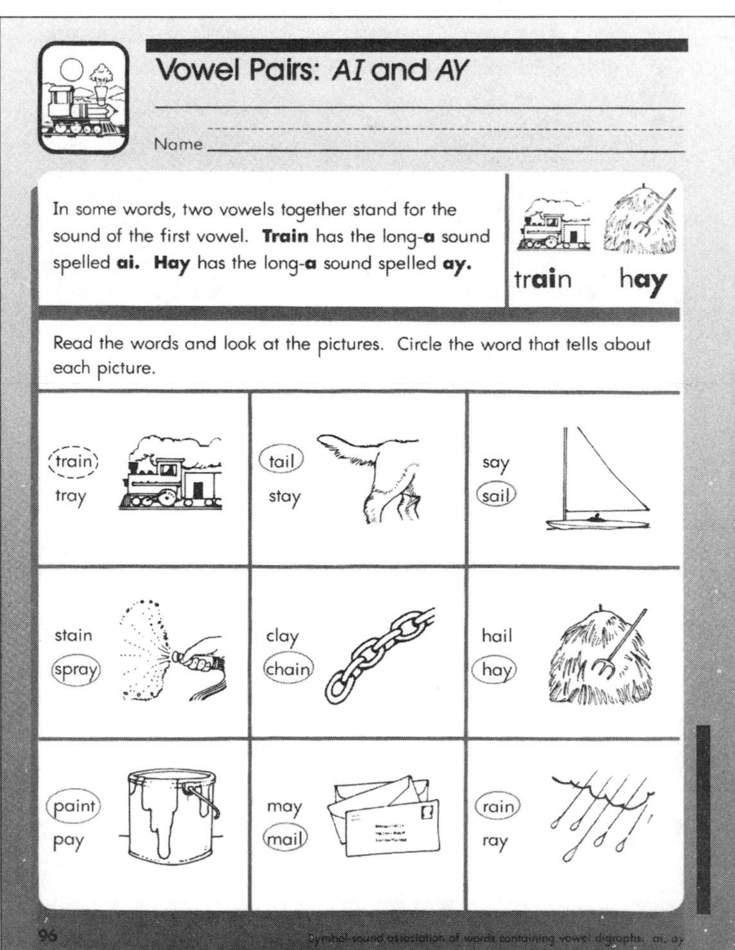

Vowel Pairs: *AI* and *AY*

Name ______________________

In some words, two vowels together stand for the sound of the first vowel. **Train** has the long-**a** sound spelled **ai.** **Hay** has the long-**a** sound spelled **ay.**

tr**ai**n h**ay**

Read the words and look at the pictures. Circle the word that tells about each picture.

(train), tray	(tail), stay	say, (sail)
stain, (spray)	clay, (chain)	hail, (hay)
(paint), pay	may, (mail)	(rain), ray

96 Symbol-sound association of words containing vowel digraphs: *ai, ay*

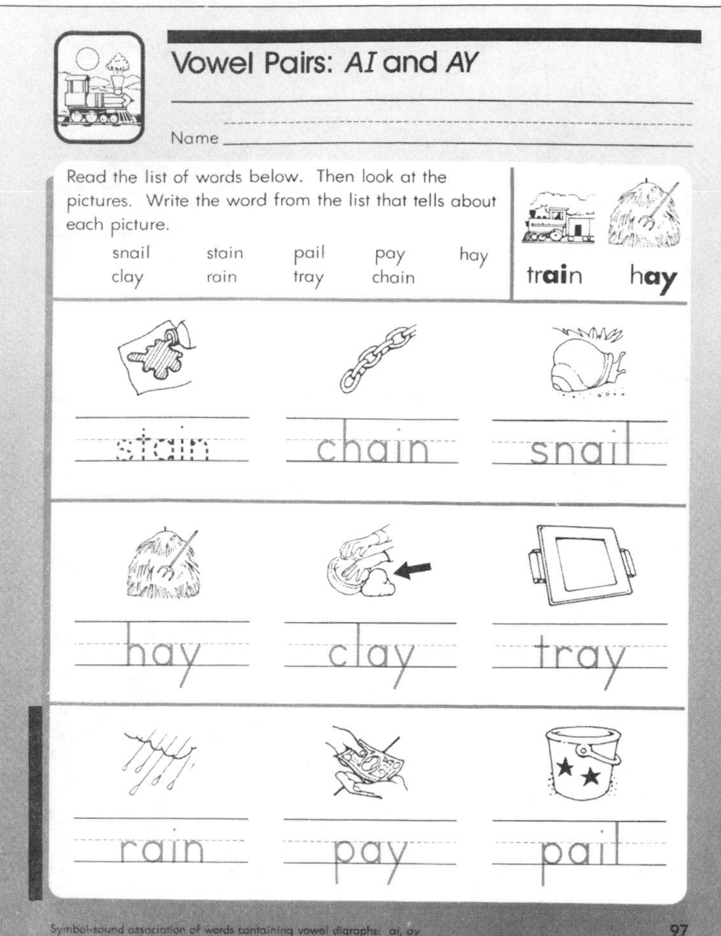

Vowel Pairs: *AI* and *AY*

Name ______________________

Read the list of words below. Then look at the pictures. Write the word from the list that tells about each picture.

snail	stain	pail	pay	hay
clay	rain	tray	chain	

train **hay**

stain	chain	snail
hay	clay	tray
rain	pay	pail

Symbol-sound association of words containing vowel digraphs: *ai, ay* 97

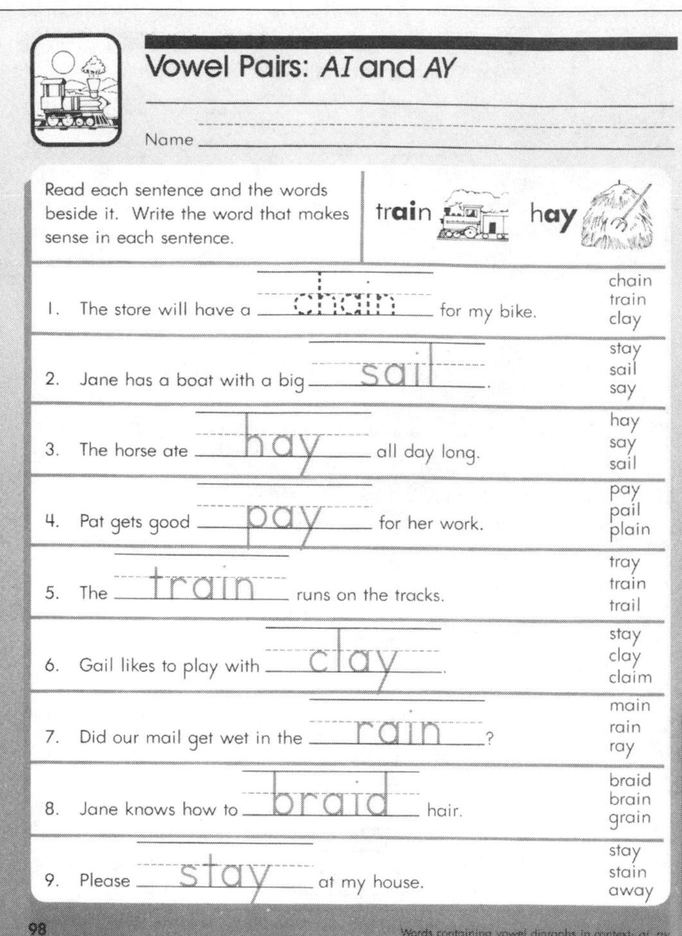

Vowel Pairs: *AI* and *AY*

Name ______________________

Read each sentence and the words beside it. Write the word that makes sense in each sentence.

train **hay**

1. The store will have a ___chain___ for my bike.	chain train clay
2. Jane has a boat with a big ___sail___.	stay sail say
3. The horse ate ___hay___ all day long.	hay say sail
4. Pat gets good ___pay___ for her work.	pay pail plain
5. The ___train___ runs on the tracks.	tray train trail
6. Gail likes to play with ___clay___.	stay clay claim
7. Did our mail get wet in the ___rain___?	main rain ray
8. Jane knows how to ___braid___ hair.	braid brain grain
9. Please ___stay___ at my house.	stay stain away

98 Words containing vowel digraphs in context: *ai, ay*

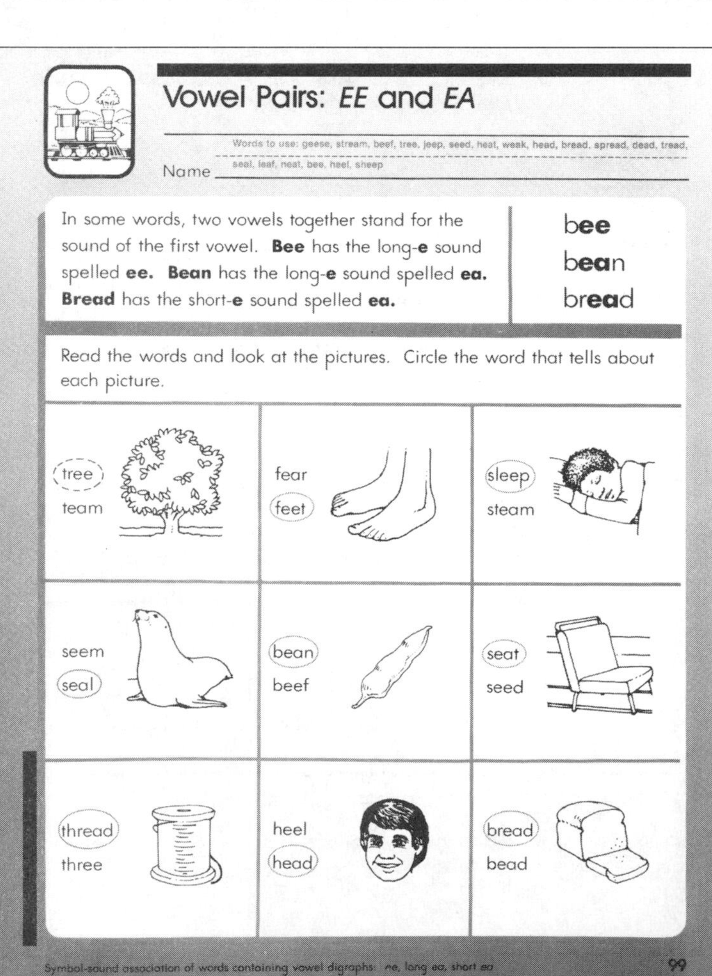

Vowel Pairs: *EE* and *EA*

Words to use: geese, stream, beef, tree, jeep, seed, heat, weak, head, bread, spread, dead, tread, seal, leaf, neat, bee, heel, sheep

Name ______________________

In some words, two vowels together stand for the sound of the first vowel. **Bee** has the long-**e** sound spelled **ee.** **Bean** has the long-**e** sound spelled **ea.** **Bread** has the short-**e** sound spelled **ea.**

bee
bean
bread

Read the words and look at the pictures. Circle the word that tells about each picture.

(tree) team	fear (feet)	(sleep) steam
seem (seal)	(bean) beef	(seat) seed
(thread) three	heel (head)	(bread) bead

Symbol-sound association of words containing vowel digraphs: *ee, long ea, short ea* 99

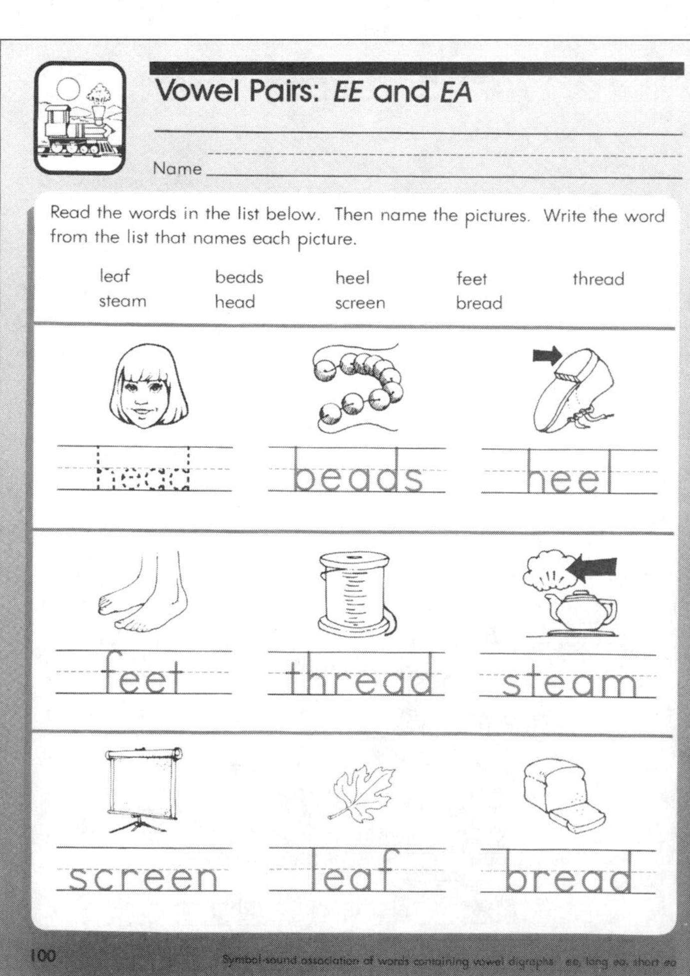

Vowel Pairs: *EE* and *EA*

Name ______________________

Read the words in the list below. Then name the pictures. Write the word from the list that names each picture.

leaf	beads	heel	feet	thread
steam	head	screen	bread	

head	beads	heel
feet	thread	steam
screen	leaf	bread

100 Symbol-sound association of words containing vowel digraphs: *ee, long ea, short ea*

Vowel Pairs: *EE* and *EA*

Name ______________________ Words to use: tree, seed, green, jeep, freeze, please, meal, leap, cream, beads, reach, clean, spread, bread, tread, dead

Read each sentence and the words beside it. Write the word that makes sense in each sentence.

1.	I need a new __heel__ on my boot.	heel heat heap
2.	There are ten __seats__ for each team.	seems seats seams
3.	Three cows were eating in the __meadow__.	meeting meatball meadow
4.	Dee put a bean __seed__ into the clay pot.	seal seed seek
5.	We need to sweep the __leaves__.	leap leaves leak
6.	Jean saw sixteen __sheep__ on the farm.	sleep cheap sheep
7.	Lee likes to eat wheat __bread__.	bread beads beach
8.	I like to swim at the __beach__.	been beach beak
9.	Do you like roast __beef__?	beef bead break

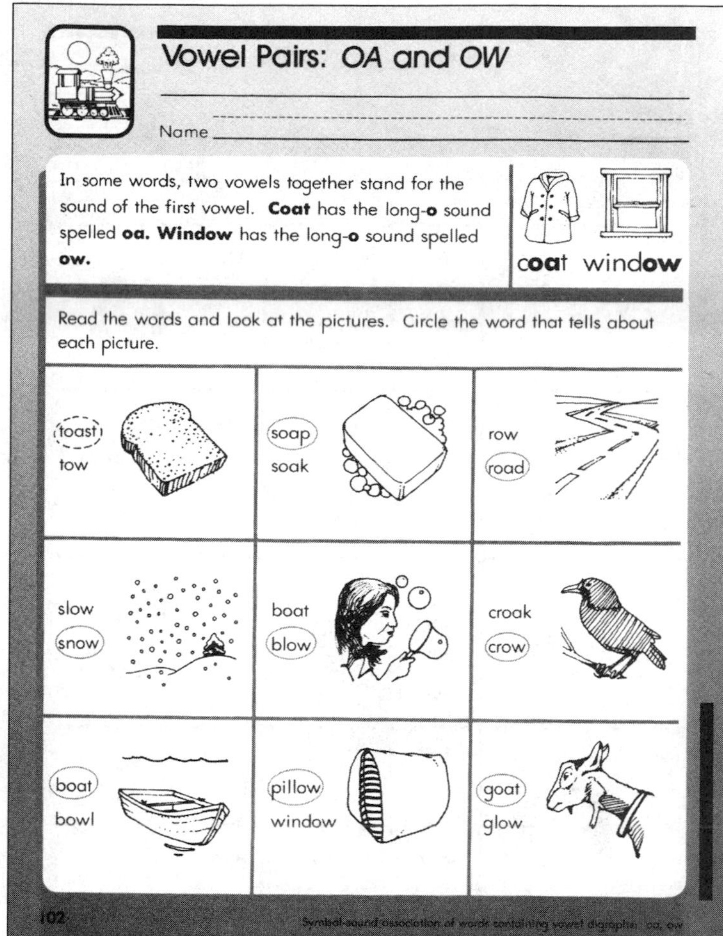

Vowel Pairs: *OA* and *OW*

Name ______________________

In some words, two vowels together stand for the sound of the first vowel. **Coat** has the long-**o** sound spelled **oa. Window** has the long-**o** sound spelled **ow.**

c**oa**t window

Read the words and look at the pictures. Circle the word that tells about each picture.

(toast) tow	(soap) soak	row (road)
slow (snow)	boat (blow)	croak (crow)
(boat) bowl	(pillow) window	(goat) glow

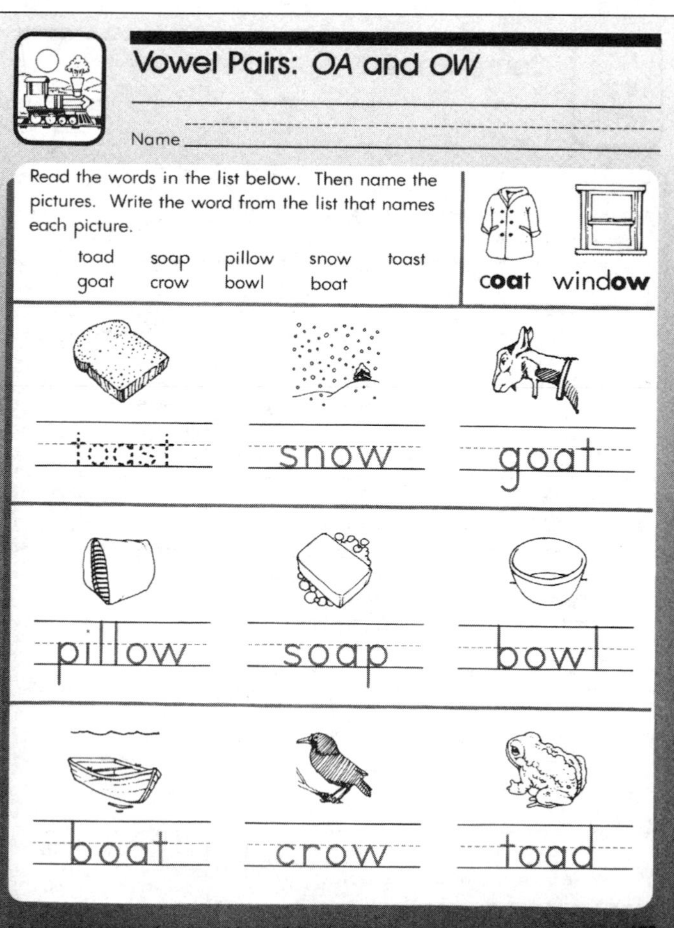

Vowel Pairs: *OA* and *OW*

Name ______________________

Read the words in the list below. Then name the pictures. Write the word from the list that names each picture.

toad soap pillow snow toast
goat crow bowl boat

c**oa**t window

toast	snow	goat
pillow	soap	bowl
boat	crow	toad

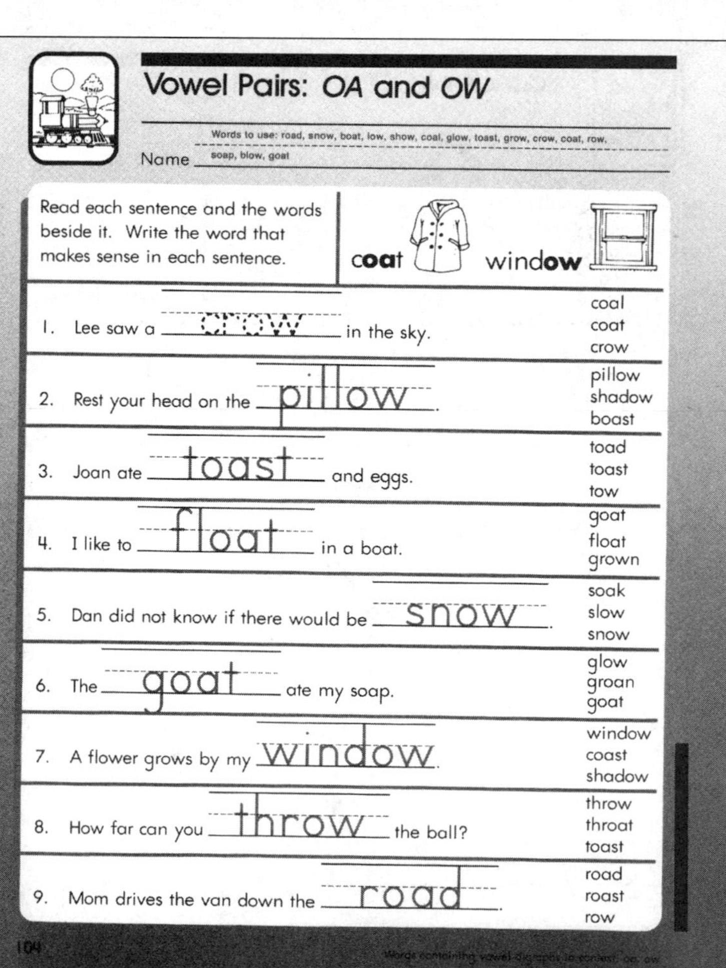

Vowel Pairs: *OA* and *OW*

Name ______________________ Words to use: road, snow, boat, low, show, coal, glow, toast, grow, crow, coat, row, soap, blow, goat

Read each sentence and the words beside it. Write the word that makes sense in each sentence.

c**oa**t window

1.	Lee saw a __crow__ in the sky.	coal coat crow
2.	Rest your head on the __pillow__.	pillow shadow boast
3.	Joan ate __toast__ and eggs.	toad toast tow
4.	I like to __float__ in a boat.	goat float grown
5.	Dan did not know if there would be __snow__.	soak slow snow
6.	The __goat__ ate my soap.	glow groan goat
7.	A flower grows by my __window__.	window coast shadow
8.	How far can you __throw__ the ball?	throw throat toast
9.	Mom drives the van down the __road__.	road roast row

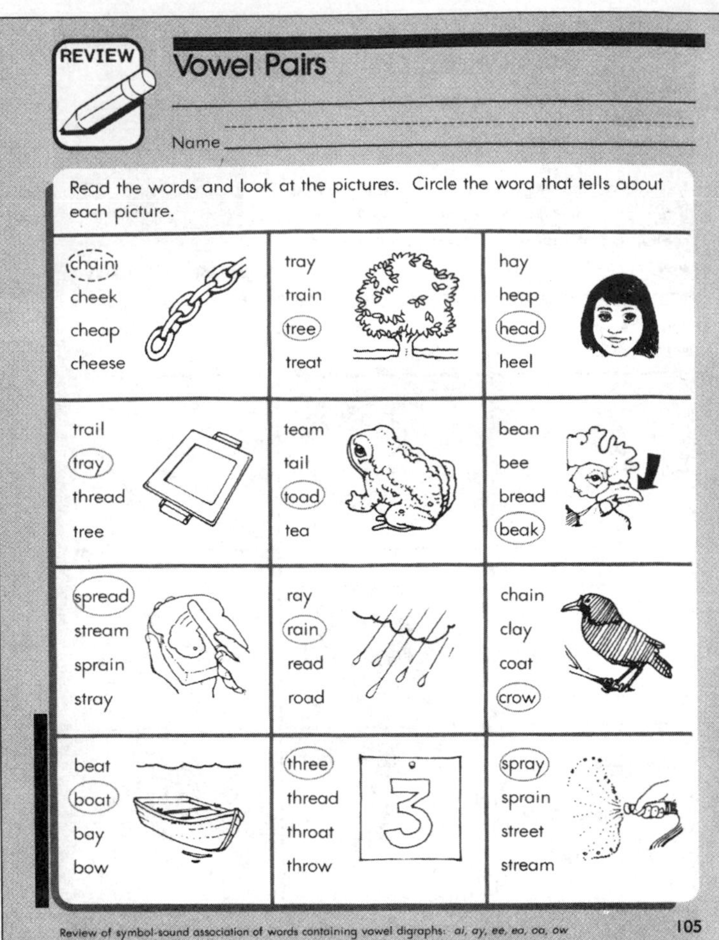

REVIEW

Vowel Pairs

Name

Read the words and look at the pictures. Circle the word that tells about each picture.

chain cheek cheap cheese	tray train tree treat	hay heap head heel
trail tray thread tree	team tail toad tea	bean bee bread beak
spread stream sprain stray	ray rain read road	chain clay coat crow
beat boat bay bow	three thread throat throw	spray sprain street stream

Review of symbol-sound association of words containing vowel digraphs: *ai, ay, ee, ea, oa, ow* 105

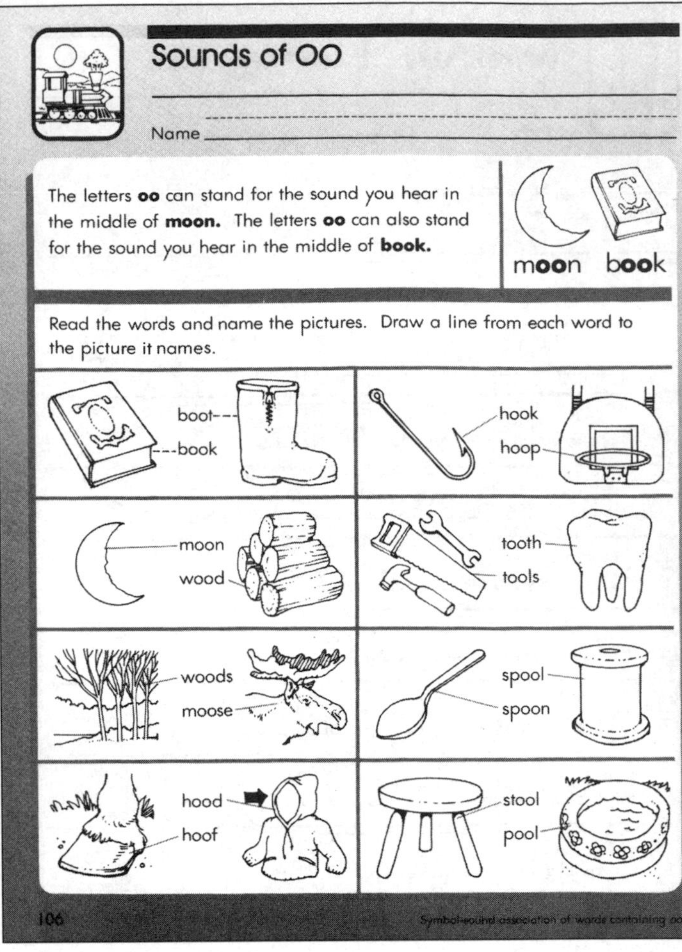

Sounds of OO

Name

The letters **oo** can stand for the sound you hear in the middle of **moon.** The letters **oo** can also stand for the sound you hear in the middle of **book.**

m**oo**n b**oo**k

Read the words and name the pictures. Draw a line from each word to the picture it names.

boot book	hook hoop
moon wood	tooth tools
woods moose	spool spoon
hood hoof	stool pool

106 Symbol-sound association of words containing oo

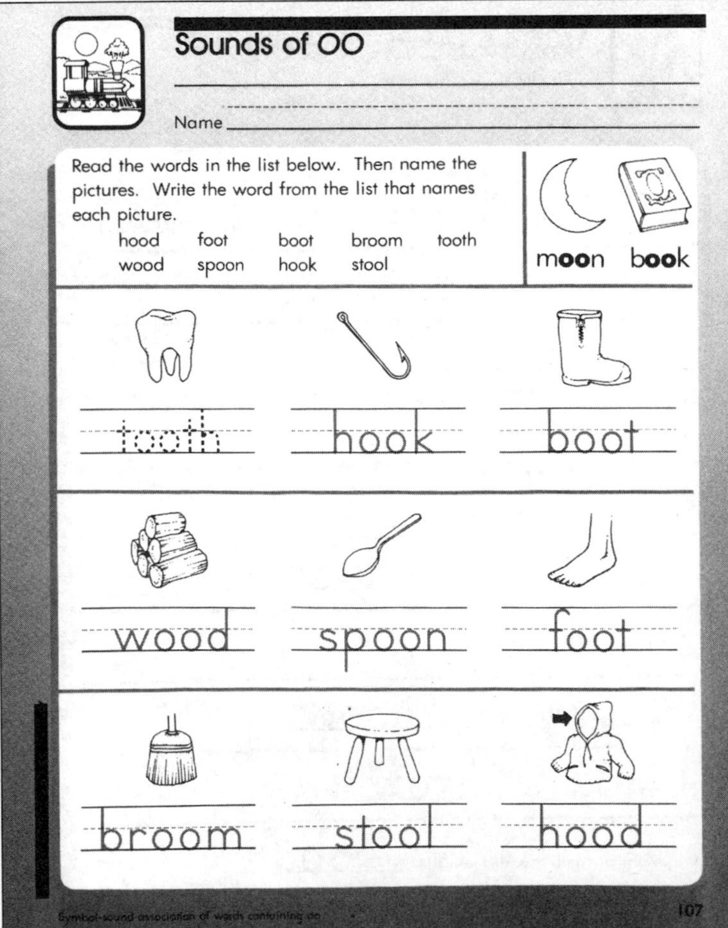

Sounds of OO

Name

Read the words in the list below. Then name the pictures. Write the word from the list that names each picture.

hood foot boot broom tooth
wood spoon hook stool

m**oo**n b**oo**k

tooth	hook	boot
wood	spoon	foot
broom	stool	hood

Symbol-sound association of words containing oo 107

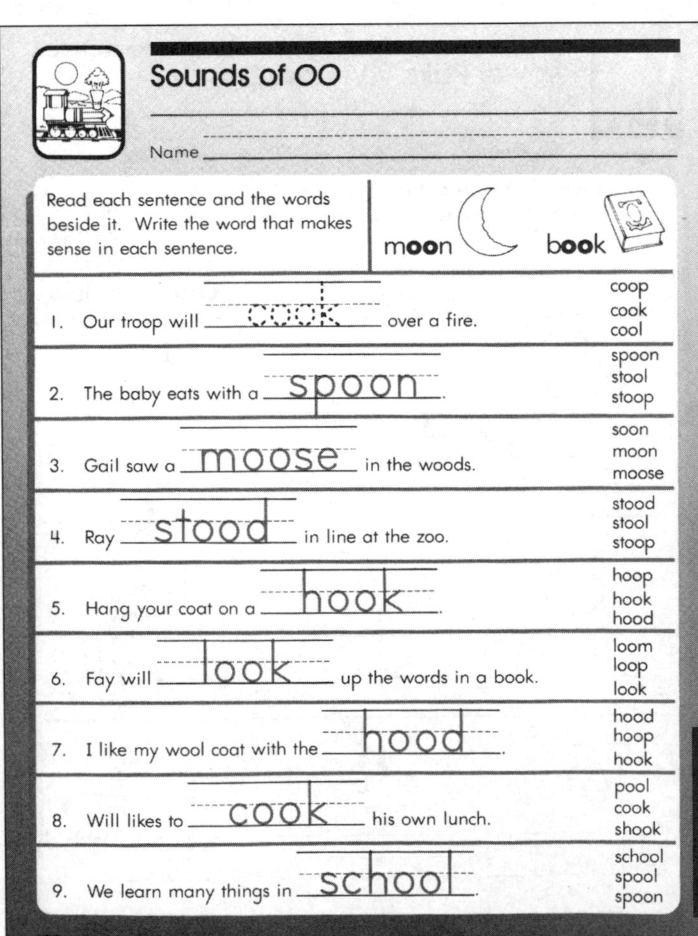

Sounds of OO

Name

Read each sentence and the words beside it. Write the word that makes sense in each sentence.

m**oo**n b**oo**k

1. Our troop will cook over a fire.	coop cook cool
2. The baby eats with a spoon.	spoon stool stoop
3. Gail saw a moose in the woods.	soon moon moose
4. Ray stood in line at the zoo.	stood stool stoop
5. Hang your coat on a hook.	hoop hook hood
6. Fay will look up the words in a book.	loom loop look
7. I like my wool coat with the hood.	hood hoop hook
8. Will likes to cook his own lunch.	pool cook shook
9. We learn many things in school.	school spool spoon

108 Words containing oo in context

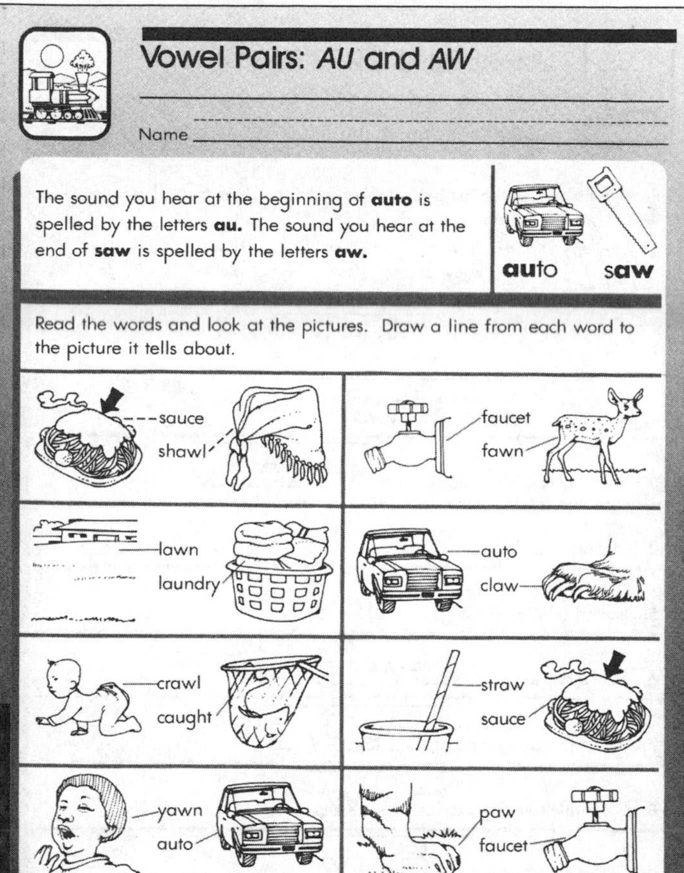

Vowel Pairs: *AU* and *AW*

Name ______________________

The sound you hear at the beginning of **auto** is spelled by the letters **au.** The sound you hear at the end of **saw** is spelled by the letters **aw.**

auto **saw**

Read the words and look at the pictures. Draw a line from each word to the picture it tells about.

sauce / shawl	faucet / fawn
lawn / laundry	auto / claw
crawl / caught	straw / sauce
yawn / auto	paw / faucet

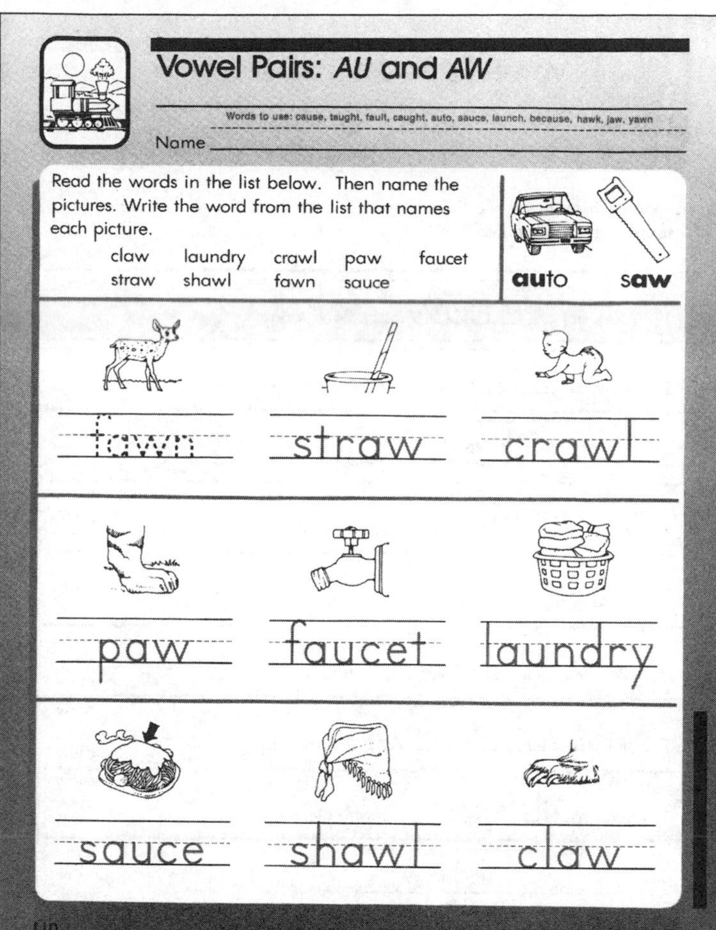

Vowel Pairs: *AU* and *AW*

Words to use: cause, taught, fault, caught, auto, sauce, launch, because, hawk, jaw, yawn

Name ______________________

Read the words in the list below. Then name the pictures. Write the word from the list that names each picture.

claw laundry crawl paw faucet
straw shawl fawn sauce

auto **saw**

fawn	straw	crawl
paw	faucet	laundry
sauce	shawl	claw

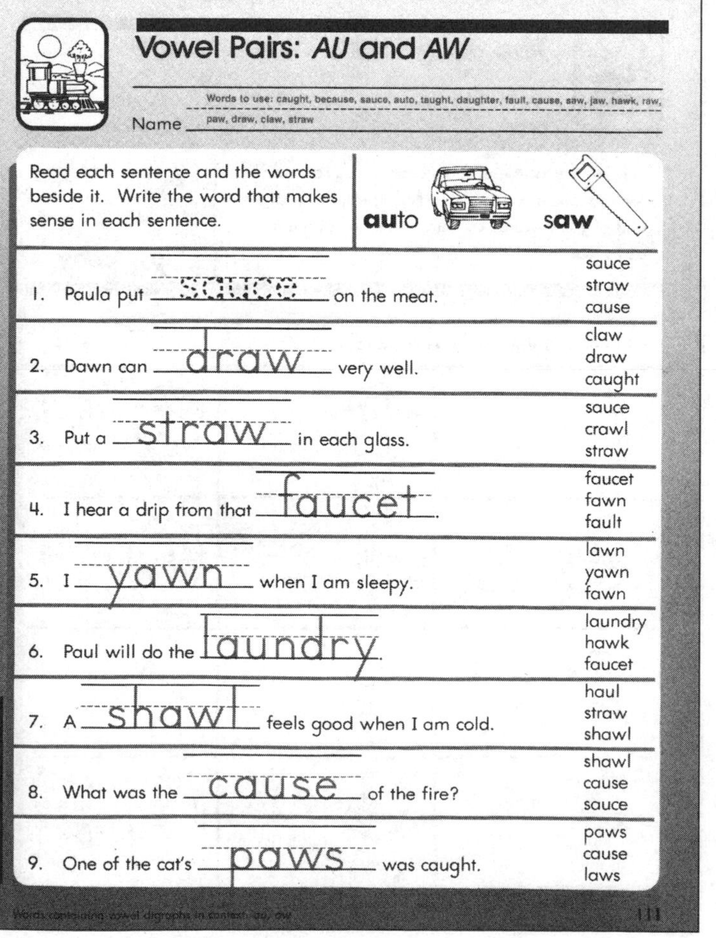

Vowel Pairs: *AU* and *AW*

Words to use: caught, because, sauce, auto, taught, daughter, fault, cause, saw, jaw, hawk, raw, paw, draw, claw, straw

Name ______________________

Read each sentence and the words beside it. Write the word that makes sense in each sentence.

auto **saw**

1. Paula put sauce on the meat.	sauce / straw / cause
2. Dawn can draw very well.	claw / draw / caught
3. Put a straw in each glass.	sauce / crawl / straw
4. I hear a drip from that faucet.	faucet / fawn / fault
5. I yawn when I am sleepy.	lawn / yawn / fawn
6. Paul will do the laundry.	laundry / hawk / faucet
7. A shawl feels good when I am cold.	haul / straw / shawl
8. What was the cause of the fire?	shawl / cause / sauce
9. One of the cat's paws was caught.	paws / cause / laws

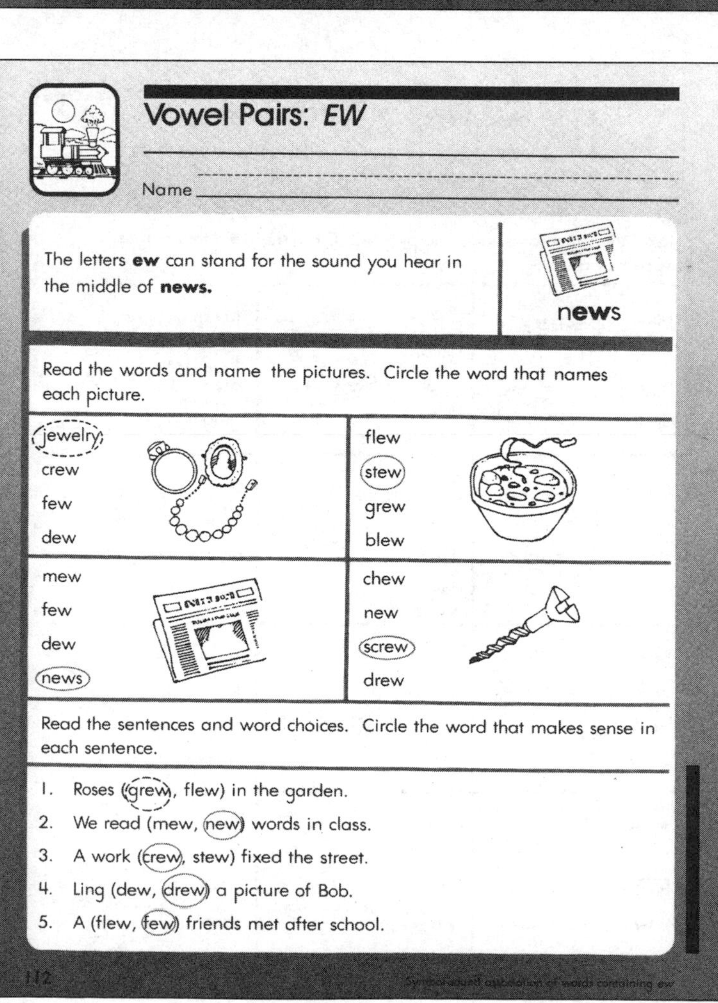

Vowel Pairs: *EW*

Name ______________________

The letters **ew** can stand for the sound you hear in the middle of **news.**

news

Read the words and name the pictures. Circle the word that names each picture.

jewelry / crew / few / dew	flew / **stew** / grew / blew
mew / few / dew / **news**	chew / new / **screw** / drew

Read the sentences and word choices. Circle the word that makes sense in each sentence.

1. Roses (**grew**, flew) in the garden.
2. We read (mew, **new**) words in class.
3. A work (**crew**, stew) fixed the street.
4. Ling (dew, **drew**) a picture of Bob.
5. A (flew, **few**) friends met after school.

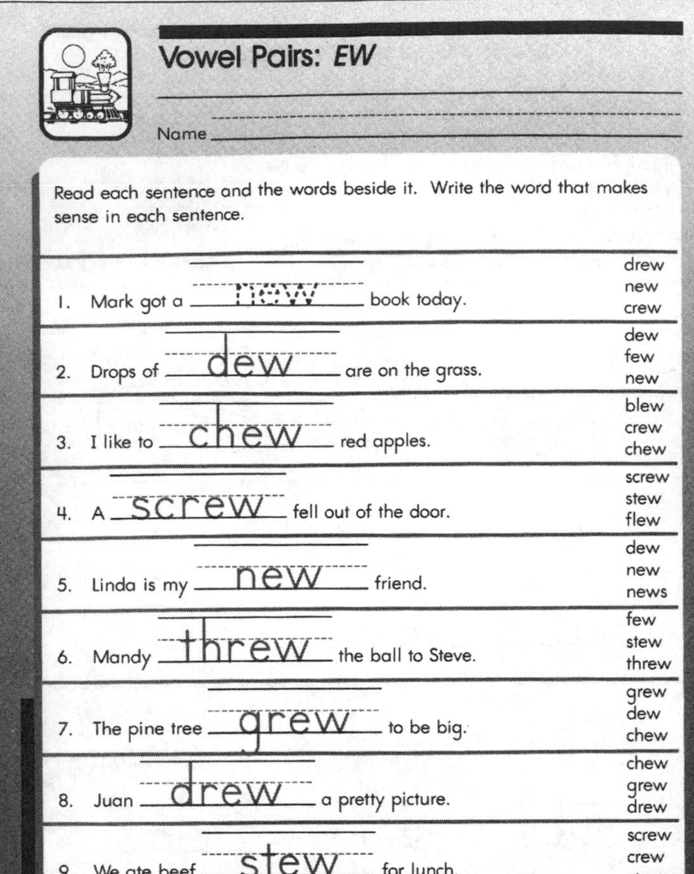

Vowel Pairs: *EW*

Name ____________________

Read each sentence and the words beside it. Write the word that makes sense in each sentence.

1. Mark got a __new__ book today.	drew, new, crew
2. Drops of __dew__ are on the grass.	dew, few, new
3. I like to __chew__ red apples.	blew, crew, chew
4. A __screw__ fell out of the door.	screw, stew, flew
5. Linda is my __new__ friend.	dew, new, news
6. Mandy __threw__ the ball to Steve.	few, stew, threw
7. The pine tree __grew__ to be big.	grew, dew, chew
8. Juan __drew__ a pretty picture.	chew, grew, drew
9. We ate beef __stew__ for lunch.	screw, crew, stew

Words containing ew in context 113

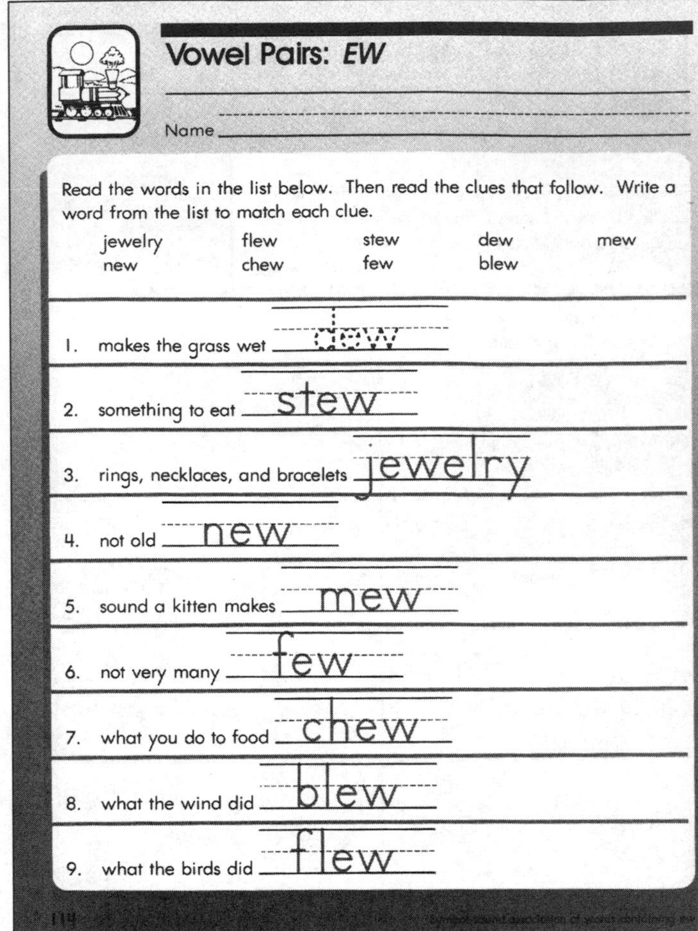

Vowel Pairs: *EW*

Name ____________________

Read the words in the list below. Then read the clues that follow. Write a word from the list to match each clue.

jewelry, flew, stew, dew, mew, new, chew, few, blew

1. makes the grass wet __dew__
2. something to eat __stew__
3. rings, necklaces, and bracelets __jewelry__
4. not old __new__
5. sound a kitten makes __mew__
6. not very many __few__
7. what you do to food __chew__
8. what the wind did __blew__
9. what the birds did __flew__

114 Symbol-sound association of words containing ew

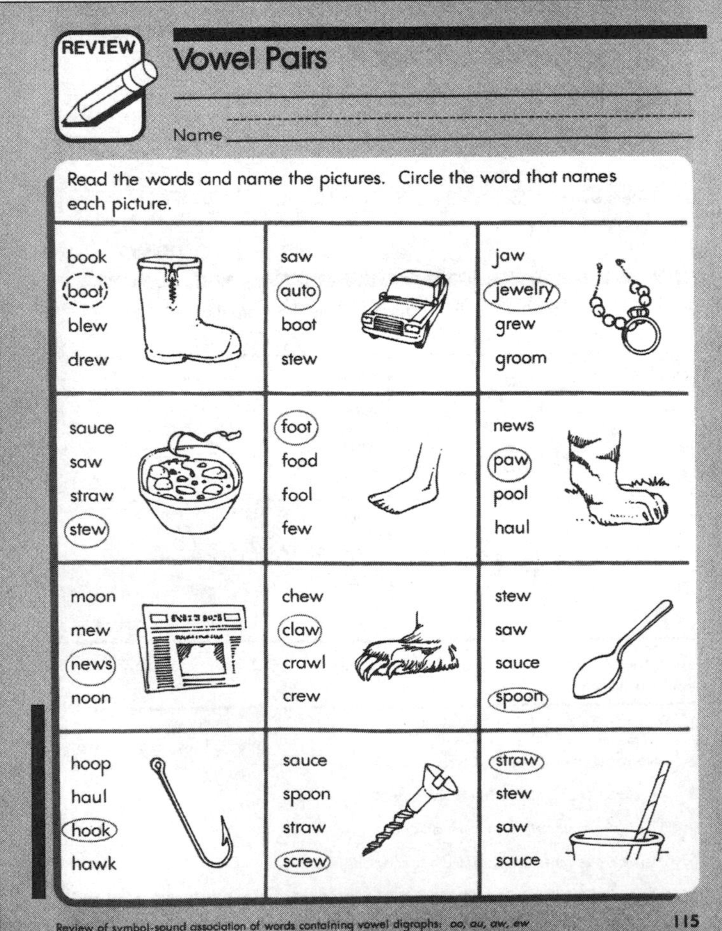

REVIEW

Vowel Pairs

Name ____________________

Read the words and name the pictures. Circle the word that names each picture.

book, (boot), blew, drew	saw, (auto), boot, stew	jaw, (jewelry), grew, groom
sauce, saw, straw, (stew)	(foot), food, fool, few	news, (paw), pool, haul
moon, mew, (news), noon	chew, (claw), crawl, crew	stew, saw, sauce, (spoon)
hoop, haul, (hook), hawk	sauce, spoon, straw, (screw)	(straw), stew, saw, sauce

Review of symbol-sound association of words containing vowel digraphs: oo, au, aw, ew 115

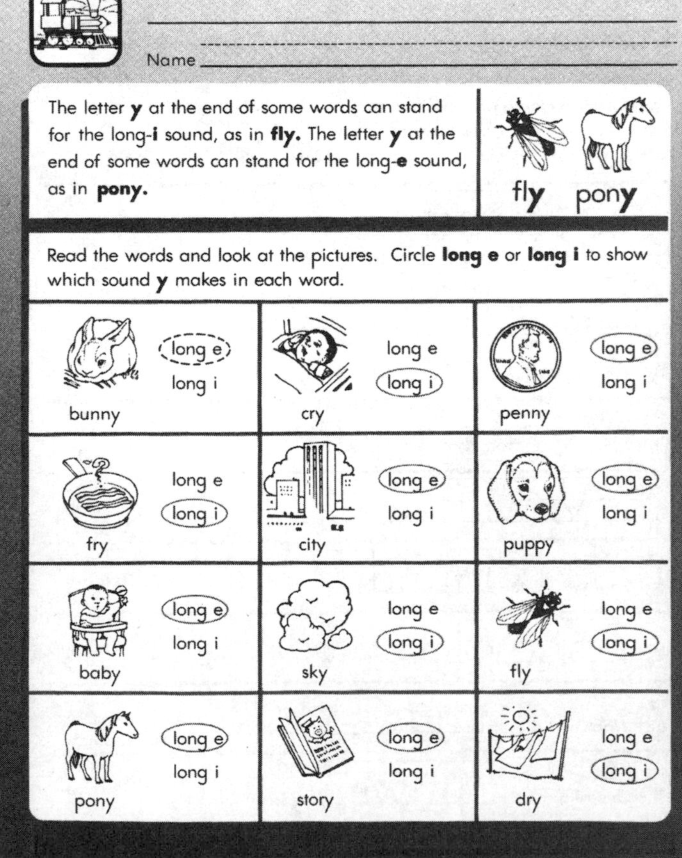

Two Sounds of *Y*

Name ____________________

The letter **y** at the end of some words can stand for the long-**i** sound, as in **fly.** The letter **y** at the end of some words can stand for the long-**e** sound, as in **pony.**

fl**y** pon**y**

Read the words and look at the pictures. Circle **long e** or **long i** to show which sound **y** makes in each word.

bunny: (long e) long i	cry: long e (long i)	penny: (long e) long i
fry: long e (long i)	city: (long e) long i	puppy: (long e) long i
baby: (long e) long i	sky: long e (long i)	fly: long e (long i)
pony: (long e) long i	story: (long e) long i	dry: long e (long i)

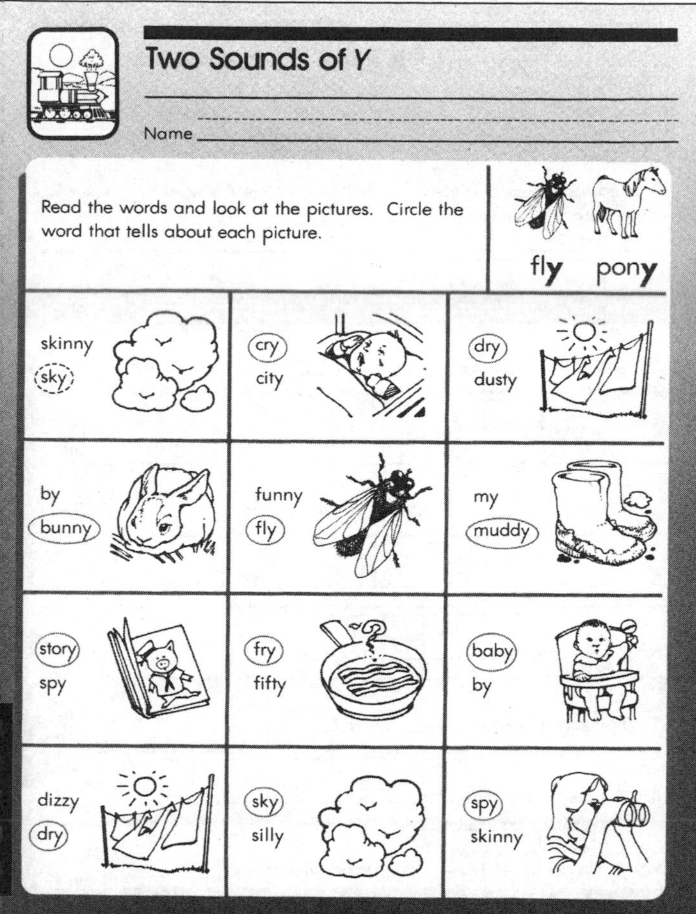

Two Sounds of *Y*

Name

Read the words and look at the pictures. Circle the word that tells about each picture.

fly pony

skinny / (sky)	(cry) / city	(dry) / dusty
by / (bunny)	funny / (fly)	my / (muddy)
(story) / spy	(fry) / fifty	(baby) / by
dizzy / (dry)	(sky) / silly	(spy) / skinny

117

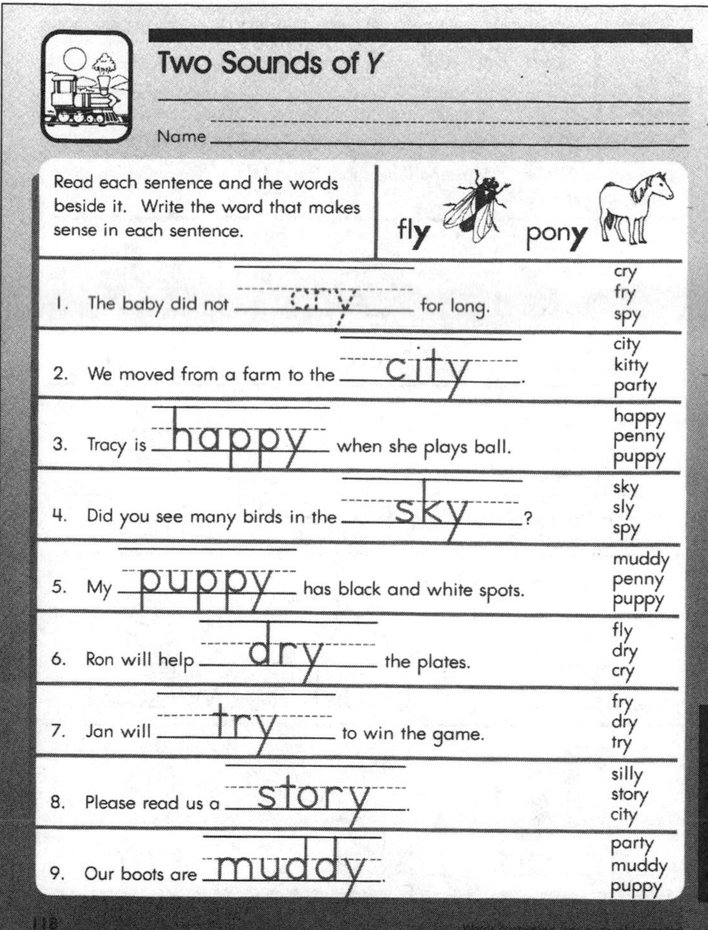

Two Sounds of *Y*

Name

Read each sentence and the words beside it. Write the word that makes sense in each sentence.

fly pony

1. The baby did not cry for long. — cry / fry / spy
2. We moved from a farm to the city. — city / kitty / party
3. Tracy is happy when she plays ball. — happy / penny / puppy
4. Did you see many birds in the sky? — sky / sly / spy
5. My puppy has black and white spots. — muddy / penny / puppy
6. Ron will help dry the plates. — fly / dry / cry
7. Jan will try to win the game. — fry / dry / try
8. Please read us a story. — silly / story / city
9. Our boots are muddy. — party / muddy / puppy

118

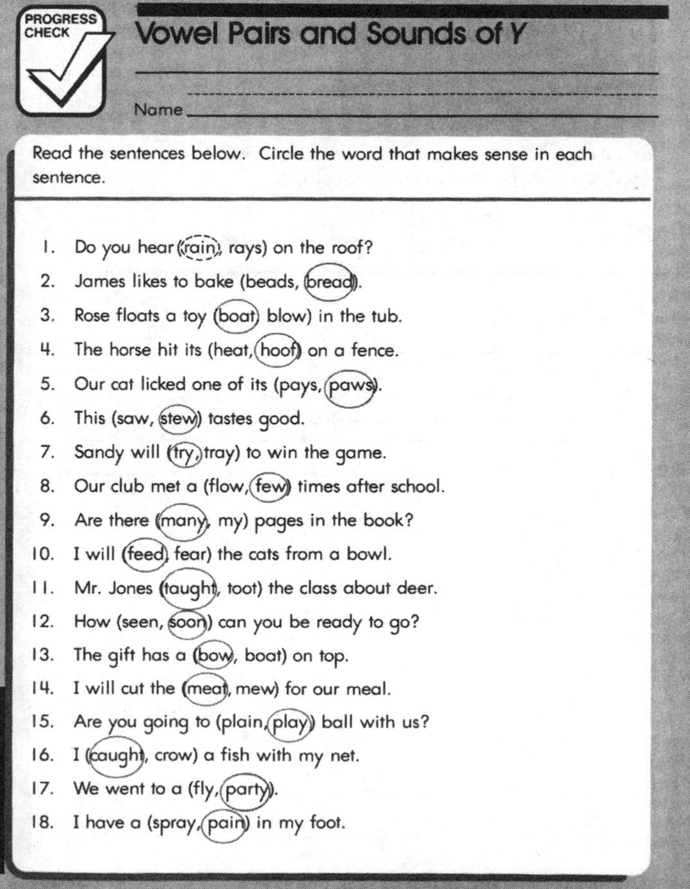

PROGRESS CHECK

Vowel Pairs and Sounds of *Y*

Name

Read the sentences below. Circle the word that makes sense in each sentence.

1. Do you hear (rain, rays) on the roof?
2. James likes to bake (beads, bread).
3. Rose floats a toy (boat, blow) in the tub.
4. The horse hit its (heat, hoof) on a fence.
5. Our cat licked one of its (pays, paws).
6. This (saw, stew) tastes good.
7. Sandy will (try, tray) to win the game.
8. Our club met a (flow, few) times after school.
9. Are there (many, my) pages in the book?
10. I will (feed, fear) the cats from a bowl.
11. Mr. Jones (taught, toot) the class about deer.
12. How (seen, soon) can you be ready to go?
13. The gift has a (bow, boat) on top.
14. I will cut the (meat, mew) for our meal.
15. Are you going to (plain, play) ball with us?
16. I (caught, crow) a fish with my net.
17. We went to a (fly, party).
18. I have a (spray, pain) in my foot.

Assessment of words containing vowel digraphs and *y* as a vowel in context 119

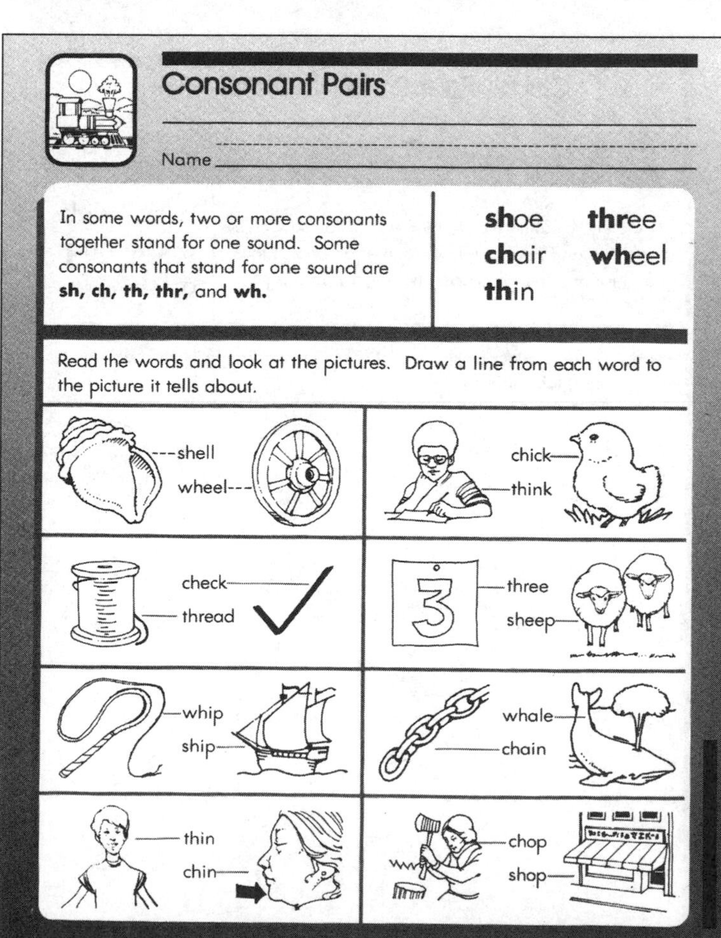

Consonant Pairs

Name

In some words, two or more consonants together stand for one sound. Some consonants that stand for one sound are **sh, ch, th, thr,** and **wh.**

shoe **thr**ee
chair **wh**eel
thin

Read the words and look at the pictures. Draw a line from each word to the picture it tells about.

120

Consonant Pairs

Name

Look at the pictures. Write the letters that stand for the beginning sound of each picture name.

thin	cheese	shelf
cheek	whale	chair
ship	think	wheel
thread	shoe	throat

121

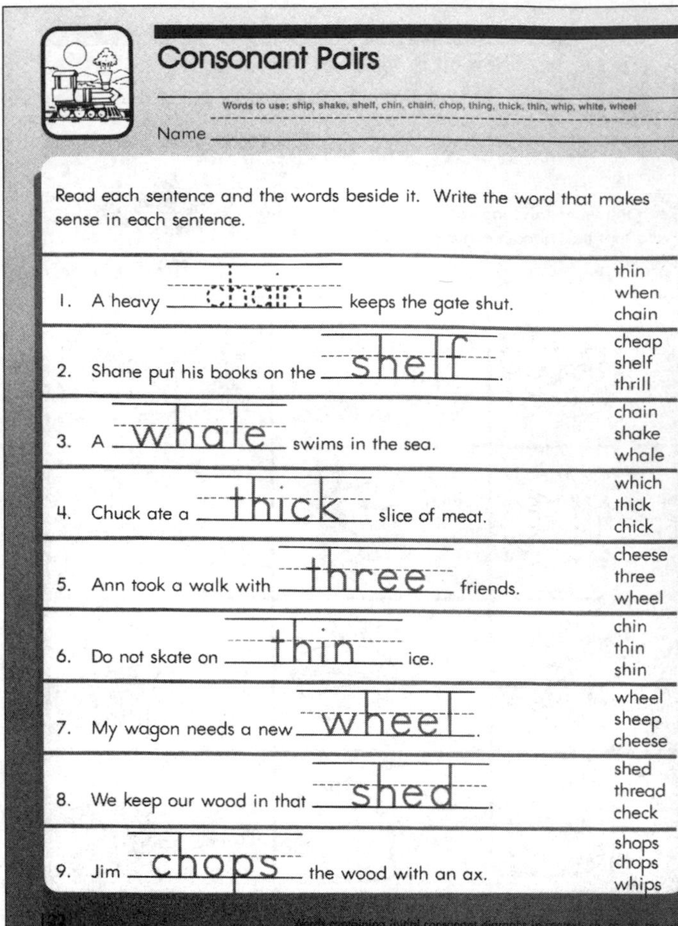
Consonant Pairs

Words to use: ship, shake, shelf, chin, chain, chop, thing, thick, thin, whip, white, wheel

Name

Read each sentence and the words beside it. Write the word that makes sense in each sentence.

1. A heavy chain keeps the gate shut.	thin when chain
2. Shane put his books on the shelf.	cheap shelf thrill
3. A whale swims in the sea.	chain shake whale
4. Chuck ate a thick slice of meat.	which thick chick
5. Ann took a walk with three friends.	cheese three wheel
6. Do not skate on thin ice.	chin thin shin
7. My wagon needs a new wheel.	wheel sheep cheese
8. We keep our wood in that shed.	shed thread check
9. Jim chops the wood with an ax.	shops chops whips

122

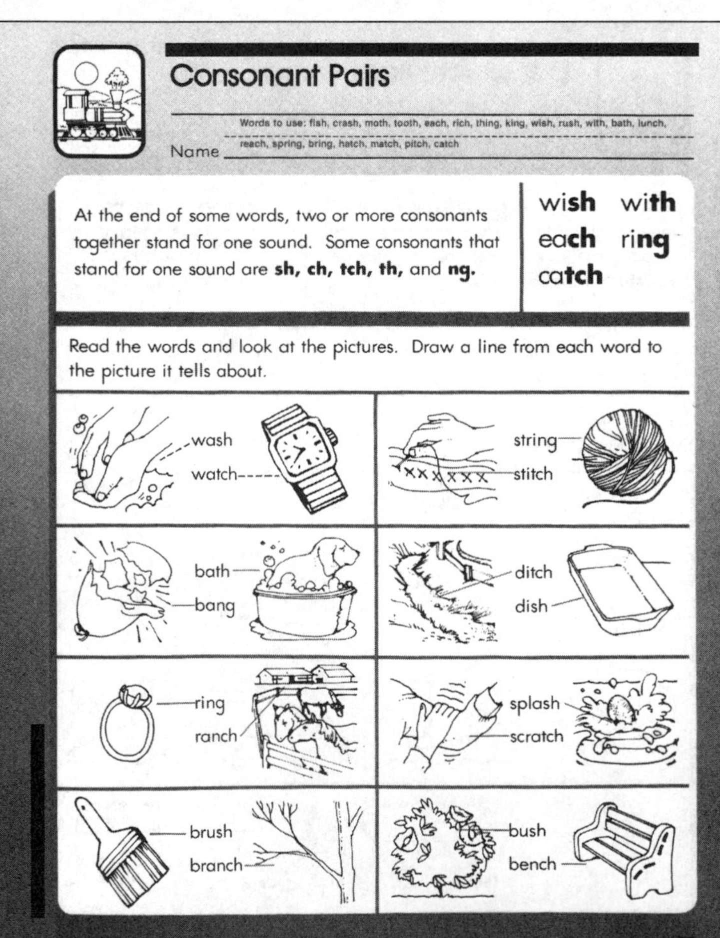
Consonant Pairs

Words to use: fish, crash, moth, tooth, each, rich, thing, king, wish, rush, with, bath, lunch, reach, spring, bring, hatch, match, pitch, catch

Name

At the end of some words, two or more consonants together stand for one sound. Some consonants that stand for one sound are **sh, ch, tch, th,** and **ng.**

wi**sh** wi**th**
ea**ch** ri**ng**
ca**tch**

Read the words and look at the pictures. Draw a line from each word to the picture it tells about.

wash watch	string stitch
bath bang	ditch dish
ring ranch	splash scratch
brush branch	bush bench

123

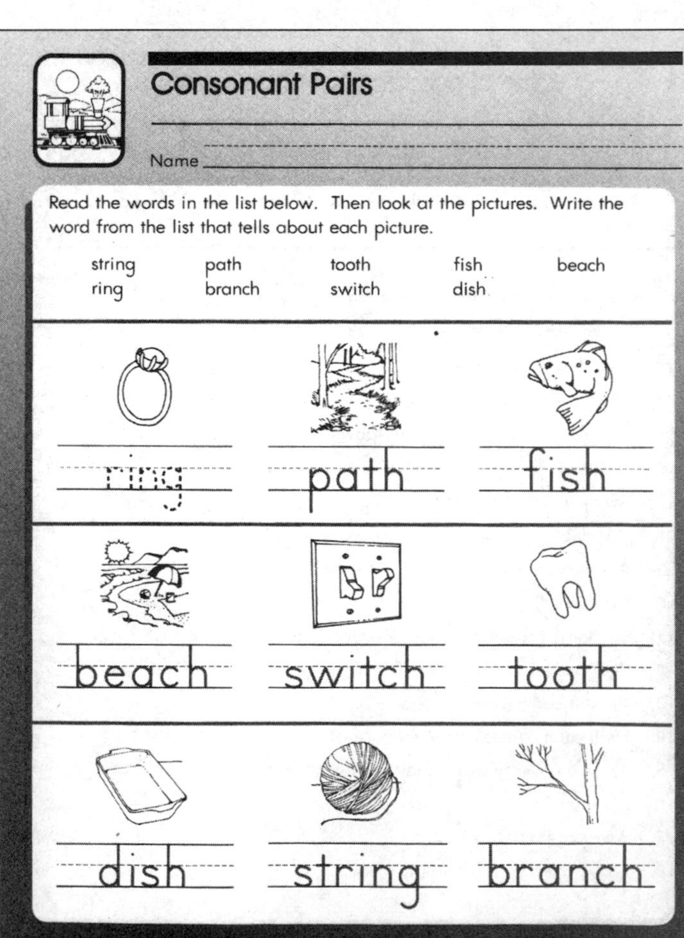
Consonant Pairs

Name

Read the words in the list below. Then look at the pictures. Write the word from the list that tells about each picture.

string path tooth fish beach
ring branch switch dish

ring	path	fish
beach	switch	tooth
dish	string	branch

Consonant Pairs

Name ______________________

Read each sentence and the words beside it. Write the word that makes sense in each sentence.

1. Ruth will give her dog a ___bath___.	batch, bush, bath
2. I looked at the time on my new ___watch___.	swing, watch, wash
3. My cat ate fish from a ___dish___.	watch, dish, with
4. Did you hear that bell ___ring___?	rich, ring, sting
5. We will sit and rest on this ___bench___.	bench, catch, bang
6. Brush your ___teeth___ after every meal.	teach, scratch, teeth
7. Jane needs a new ___brush___ for her paint set.	branch, brush, bush
8. The rope on my tree ___swing___ broke.	wish, switch, swing
9. We walked down a ___path___ in the woods.	peach, splash, path

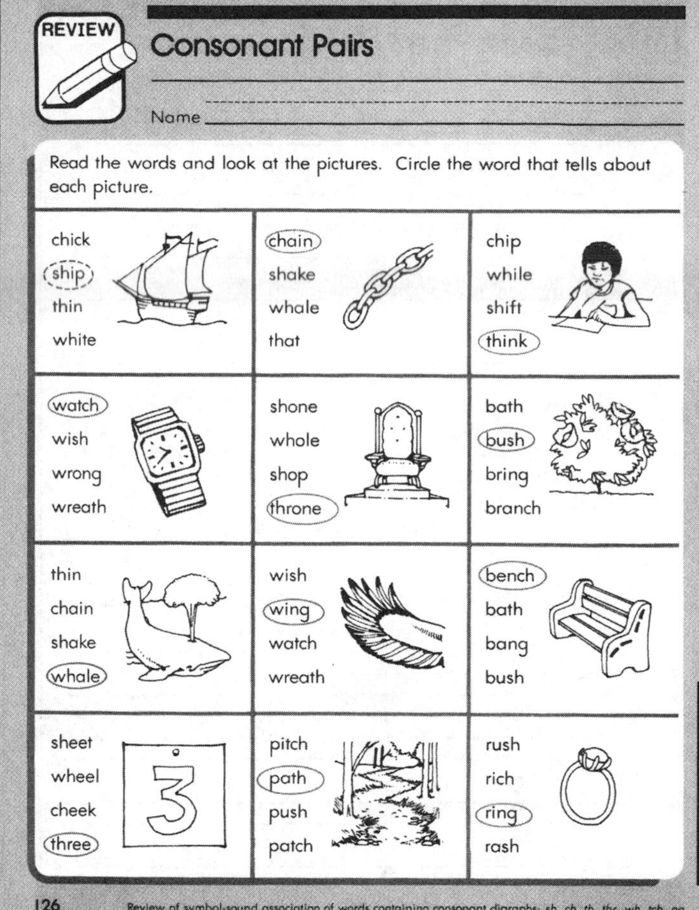

REVIEW

Consonant Pairs

Name ______________________

Read the words and look at the pictures. Circle the word that tells about each picture.

chick, ship, thin, white	chain, shake, whale, that	chip, while, shift, think
watch, wish, wrong, wreath	shone, whole, shop, throne	bath, bush, bring, branch
thin, chain, shake, whale	wish, wing, watch, wreath	bench, bath, bang, bush
sheet, wheel, cheek, three	pitch, path, push, patch	rush, rich, ring, rash

PROGRESS CHECK

Consonant Pairs

Name ______________________

Read the sentences below. Circle the word that makes sense in each sentence.

1. Chuck ate a (chunk, shut) of cheese with his lunch.
2. Shane put his new book on the (check, shelf).
3. The (branch, bring) of the tree will scratch the window.
4. I think this slice of meat is too (which, thick).
5. Who can fix the (wheel, cheek) on my bike?
6. Ling wants to (sing, such) for our class.
7. I wish our (bath, bush) would bloom soon.
8. A pinch made the pig (squeal, wheel).
9. We took a hike on that (patch, path).
10. I like to (watch, wash) the birds fly.
11. Ruth has (squeeze, three) new friends.
12. Sit down on the (bang, bench) and rest.
13. The clay is in the (shape, chase) of a ball.
14. Please go (with, witch) me to a show.
15. I had to (chase, shade) my dog last night.
16. Did you (bring, brush) your new books?
17. I (wish, with) we could go out to play.
18. The (squirrel, wheel) ran up a tree.

Reading and Writing Wrap-Up

Name ______________________

Growing Up

When you were a baby, there were many things you could not do. You could not walk or talk. You could not dress without help, and you could not eat without help. Your family dressed you. They gave you good things to eat. They played with you and made you laugh. Your family was there to help you when you were a baby.

Now you are older. Your family is not around to help you all the time. You can do many things you could not do when you were a baby. You are growing up.

A. Tell two things a baby can not do that you can do.

1. **Answers may vary. Possible answers: walk, talk, dress without help,**
2. **eat without help.**

B. Tell two things the family does to help a baby.

1. **Answers may vary. Possible answers: dress the baby, feed the baby,**
2. **play with the baby, make the baby laugh.**

C. What can a baby do? What can you do? Circle the things a baby can do. Draw a box around the things you can do that a baby can not do.

cry | ride a bike | read | sleep | go to school
make a bed | smile | see | write | add two and two

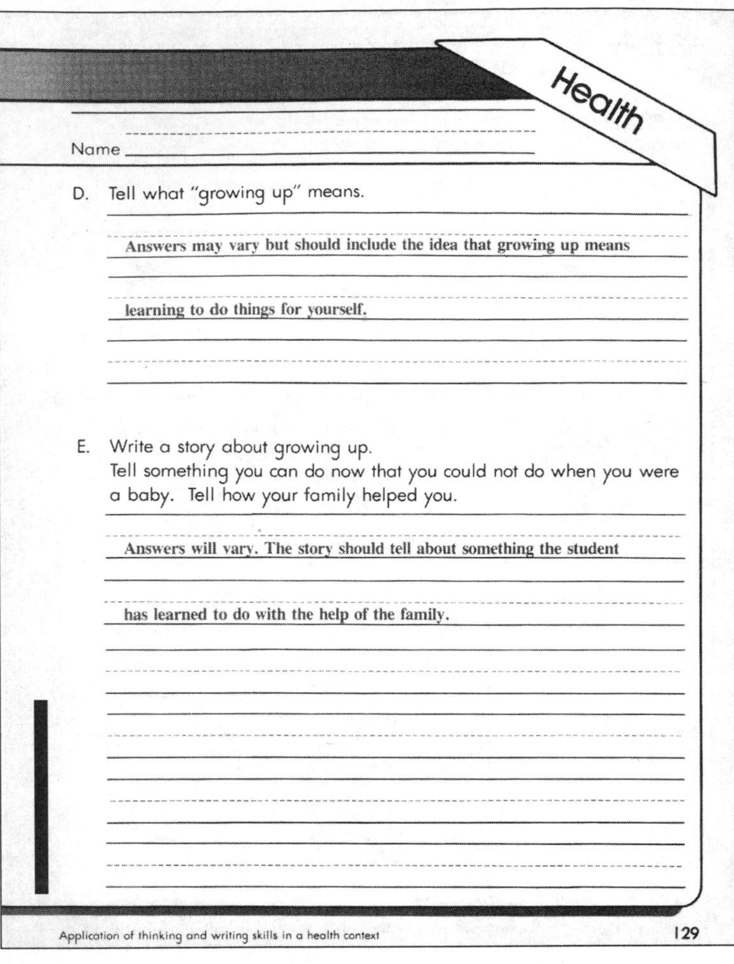

Health

Name

D. Tell what "growing up" means.

Answers may vary but should include the idea that growing up means learning to do things for yourself.

E. Write a story about growing up.
Tell something you can do now that you could not do when you were a baby. Tell how your family helped you.

Answers will vary. The story should tell about something the student has learned to do with the help of the family.

Application of thinking and writing skills in a health context 129

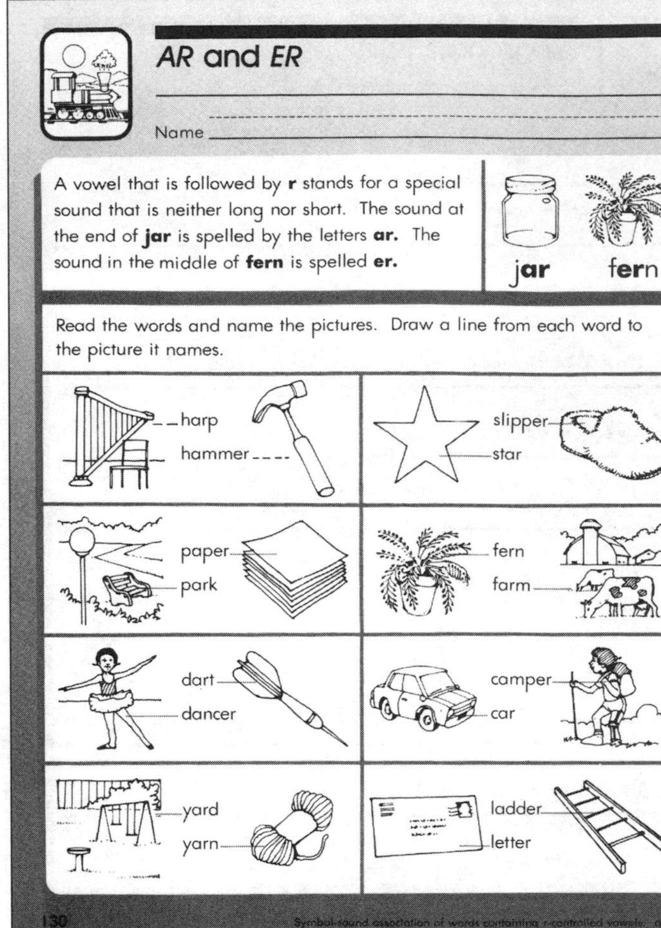

AR and ER

Name

A vowel that is followed by **r** stands for a special sound that is neither long nor short. The sound at the end of **jar** is spelled by the letters **ar.** The sound in the middle of **fern** is spelled **er.**

j**ar** f**er**n

Read the words and name the pictures. Draw a line from each word to the picture it names.

harp, hammer, slipper, star, paper, park, fern, farm, dart, dancer, camper, car, yard, yarn, ladder, letter

130 Symbol-sound association of words containing r-controlled vowels: ar, er

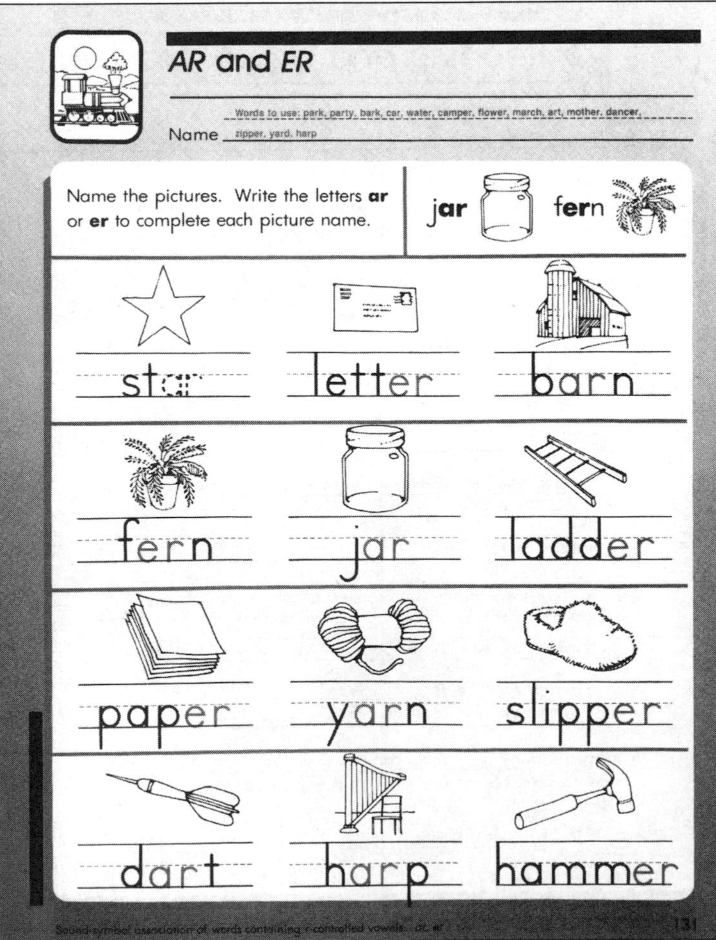

AR and ER

Words to use: park, party, bark, car, water, camper, flower, march, art, mother, dancer, zipper, yard, harp

Name

Name the pictures. Write the letters **ar** or **er** to complete each picture name.

j**ar** f**er**n

star	letter	barn
fern	jar	ladder
paper	yarn	slipper
dart	harp	hammer

Sound-symbol association of words containing r-controlled vowels: ar, er 131

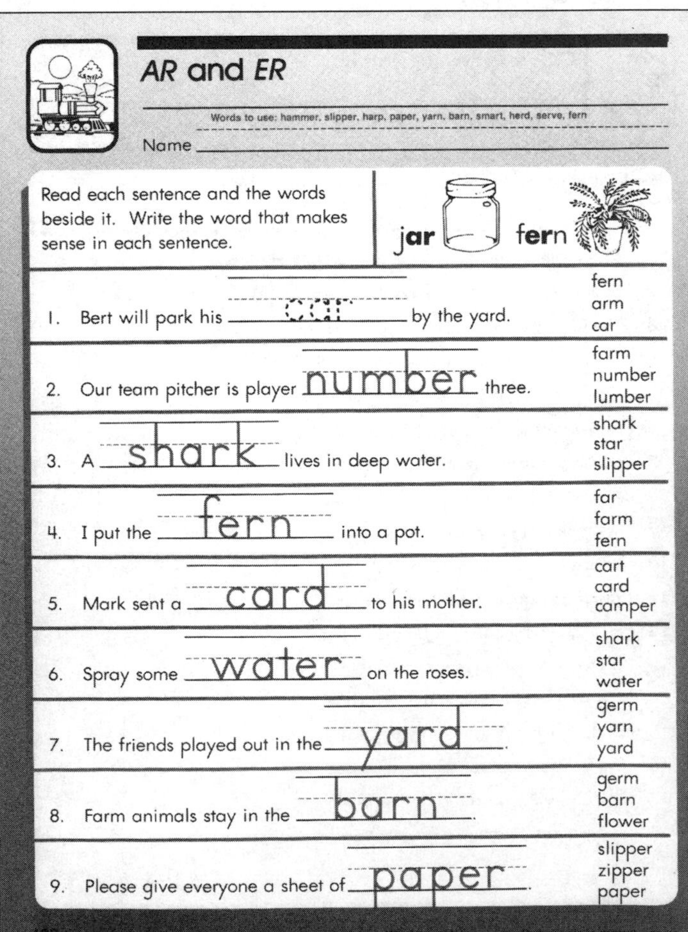

AR and ER

Words to use: hammer, slipper, harp, paper, yarn, barn, smart, herd, serve, fern

Name

Read each sentence and the words beside it. Write the word that makes sense in each sentence.

j**ar** f**er**n

1. Bert will park his car by the yard. — fern, arm, car
2. Our team pitcher is player number three. — farm, number, lumber
3. A shark lives in deep water. — shark, star, slipper
4. I put the fern into a pot. — far, farm, fern
5. Mark sent a card to his mother. — cart, card, camper
6. Spray some water on the roses. — shark, star, water
7. The friends played out in the yard. — germ, yarn, yard
8. Farm animals stay in the barn. — germ, barn, flower
9. Please give everyone a sheet of paper. — slipper, zipper, paper

132 Words containing r-controlled vowels in context: ar, er

IR and OR

Name

A vowel that is followed by **r** stands for a special sound that is neither long nor short. The sound in the middle of **bird** is spelled by the letters **ir.** The sound in the middle of **horn** is spelled by the letters **or.**

bi**r**d ho**r**n

Read the words and look at the pictures. Draw a line from each word to the picture it tells about.

133

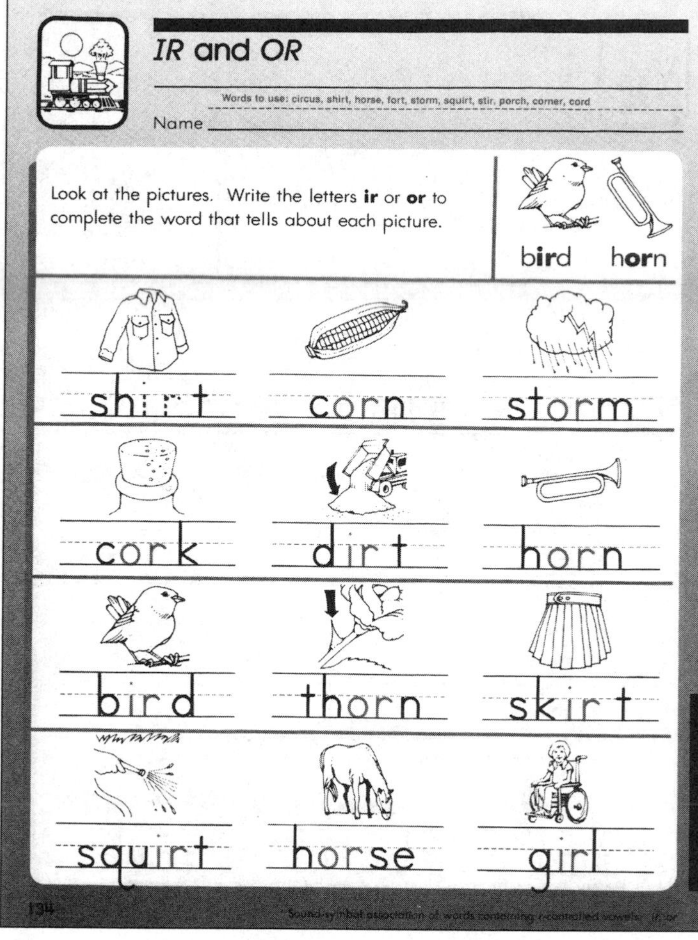

IR and OR

Words to use: circus, shirt, horse, fort, storm, squirt, stir, porch, corner, cord

Name

Look at the pictures. Write the letters **ir** or **or** to complete the word that tells about each picture.

bi**r**d ho**r**n

134 Sound/symbol association of words containing r-controlled vowels: ir, or

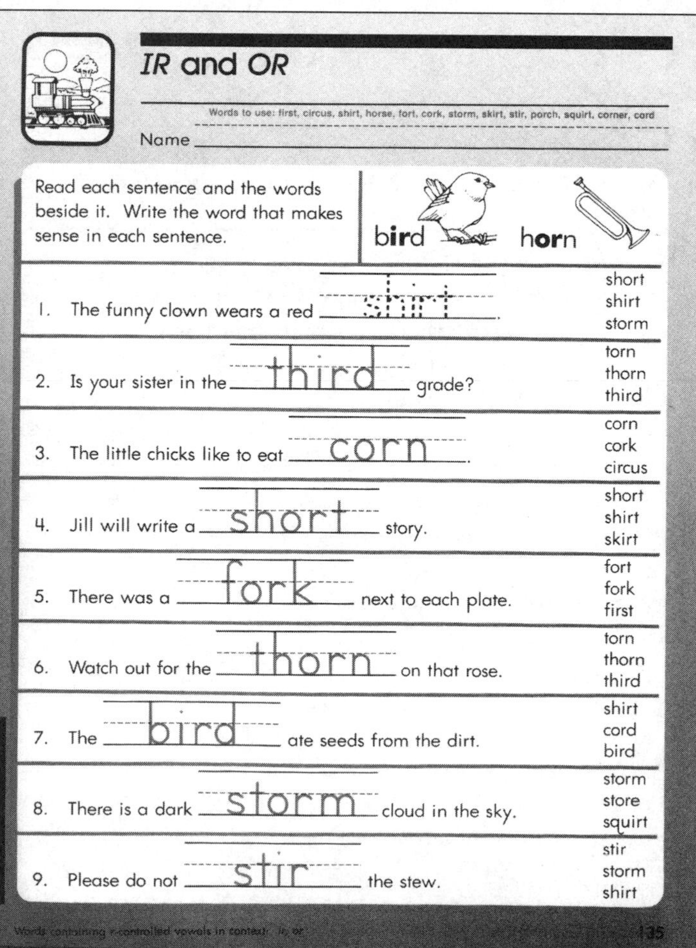

IR and OR

Words to use: first, circus, shirt, horse, fort, cork, storm, skirt, stir, porch, squirt, corner, cord

Name

Read each sentence and the words beside it. Write the word that makes sense in each sentence.

bi**r**d ho**r**n

1. The funny clown wears a red shirt. — short / shirt / storm
2. Is your sister in the third grade? — torn / thorn / third
3. The little chicks like to eat corn. — corn / cork / circus
4. Jill will write a short story. — short / shirt / skirt
5. There was a fork next to each plate. — fort / fork / first
6. Watch out for the thorn on that rose. — torn / thorn / third
7. The bird ate seeds from the dirt. — shirt / cord / bird
8. There is a dark storm cloud in the sky. — storm / store / squirt
9. Please do not stir the stew. — stir / storm / shirt

Words containing r-controlled vowels in context: ir, or 135

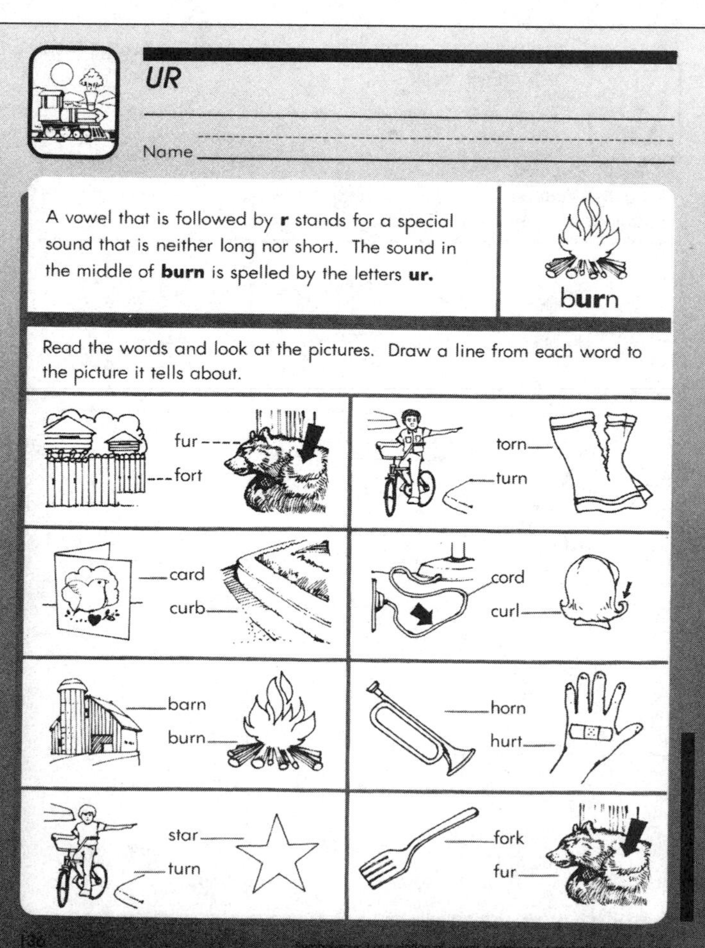

UR

Name

A vowel that is followed by **r** stands for a special sound that is neither long nor short. The sound in the middle of **burn** is spelled by the letters **ur.**

bu**r**n

Read the words and look at the pictures. Draw a line from each word to the picture it tells about.

136

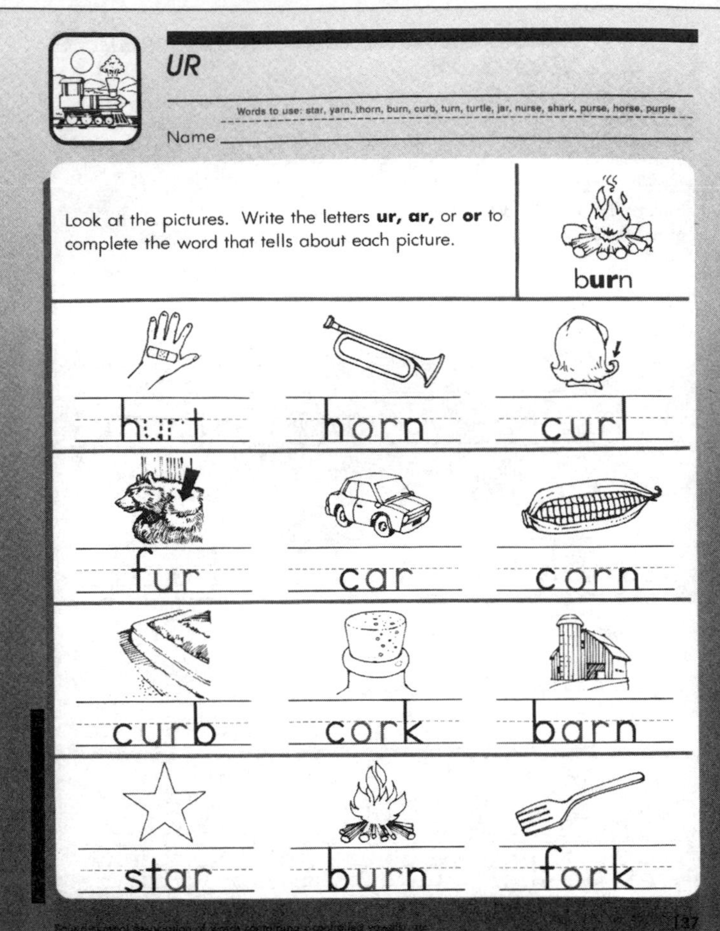

UR

Words to use: star, yarn, thorn, burn, curb, turn, turtle, jar, nurse, shark, purse, horse, purple

Name ______

Look at the pictures. Write the letters **ur, ar,** or **or** to complete the word that tells about each picture.

b**ur**n

hurt	horn	curl
fur	car	corn
curb	cork	barn
star	burn	fork

Sound-symbol association of words containing r-controlled vowels: ur 137

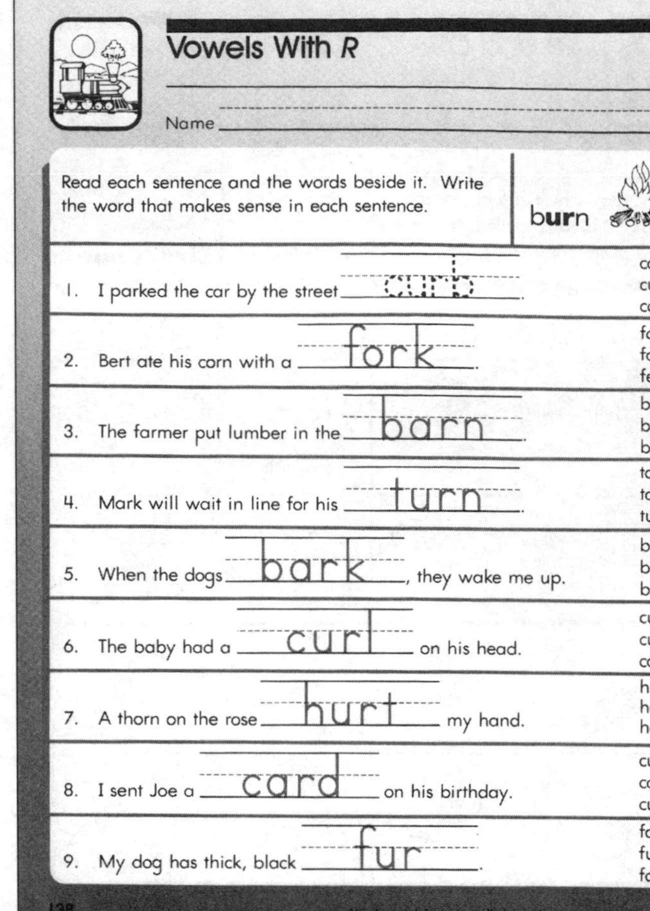

Vowels With *R*

Name ______

Read each sentence and the words beside it. Write the word that makes sense in each sentence.

b**ur**n

1. I parked the car by the street curb.	card, curb, corn
2. Bert ate his corn with a fork.	fort, fork, fern
3. The farmer put lumber in the barn.	bird, born, barn
4. Mark will wait in line for his turn.	torn, tar, turn
5. When the dogs bark, they wake me up.	barn, bark, bird
6. The baby had a curl on his head.	curb, curl, cart
7. A thorn on the rose hurt my hand.	hurt, horn, harp
8. I sent Joe a card on his birthday.	curb, card, curl
9. My dog has thick, black fur.	for, fur, far

138 Words containing r-controlled vowels in context: ar, er, ir, or, ur

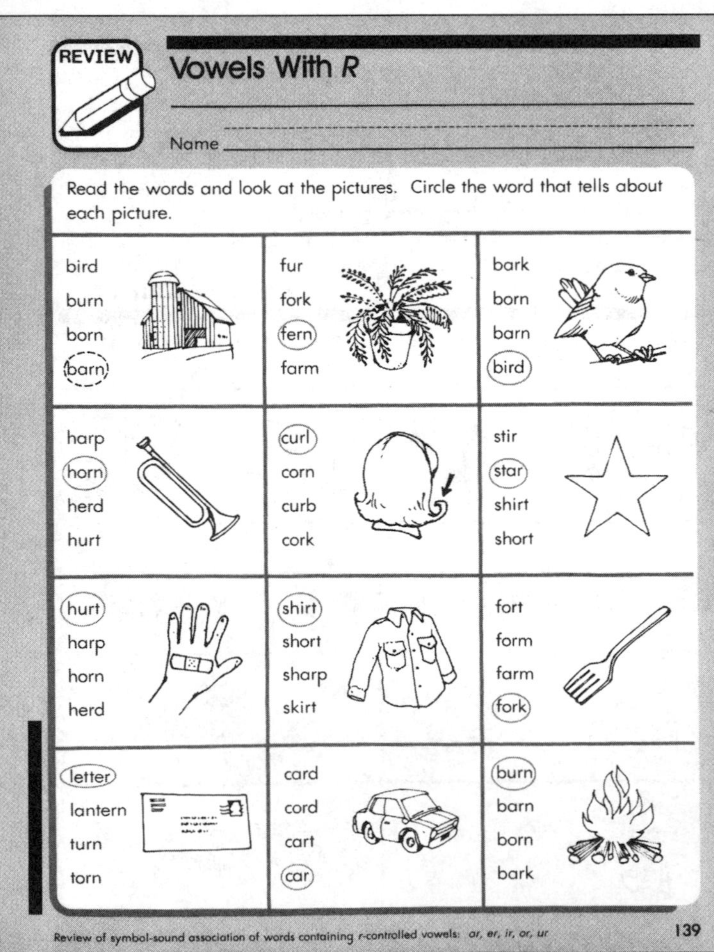

REVIEW

Vowels With *R*

Name ______

Read the words and look at the pictures. Circle the word that tells about each picture.

bird, burn, born, (barn)	fur, fork, (fern), farm	bark, born, barn, (bird)
harp, (horn), herd, hurt	(curl), corn, curb, cork	stir, (star), shirt, short
(hurt), harp, horn, herd	(shirt), short, sharp, skirt	fort, form, farm, (fork)
(letter), lantern, turn, torn	card, cord, cart, (car)	(burn), barn, born, bark

Review of symbol-sound association of words containing r-controlled vowels: ar, er, ir, or, ur 139

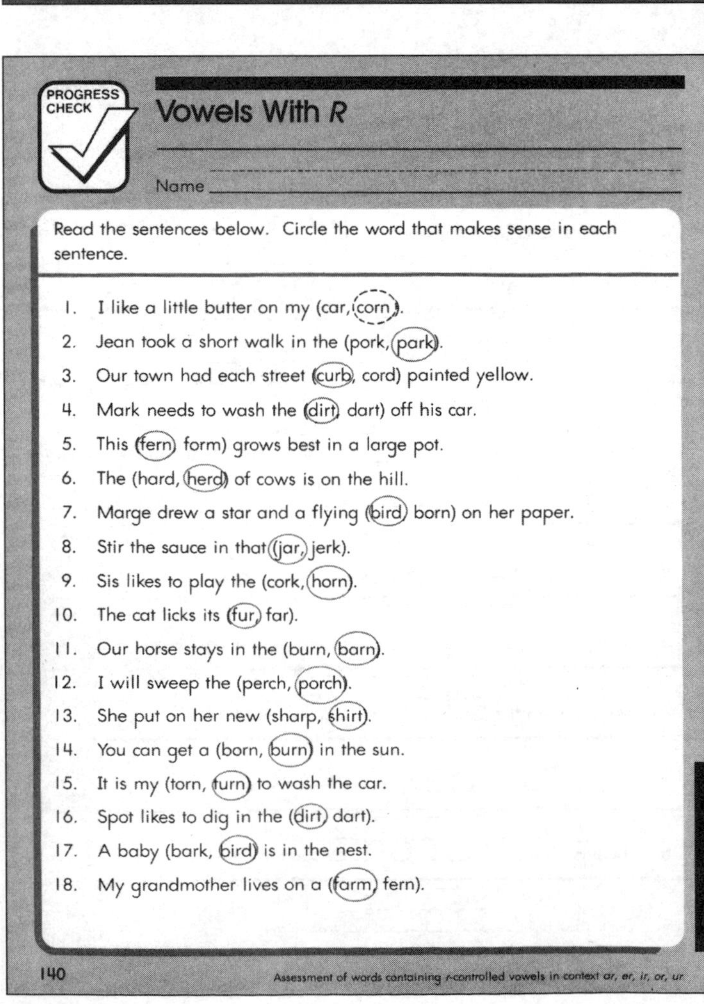

PROGRESS CHECK

Vowels With *R*

Name ______

Read the sentences below. Circle the word that makes sense in each sentence.

1. I like a little butter on my (car, (corn)).
2. Jean took a short walk in the (pork, (park)).
3. Our town had each street ((curb), cord) painted yellow.
4. Mark needs to wash the ((dirt), dart) off his car.
5. This ((fern), form) grows best in a large pot.
6. The (hard, (herd)) of cows is on the hill.
7. Marge drew a star and a flying ((bird), born) on her paper.
8. Stir the sauce in that ((jar), jerk).
9. Sis likes to play the (cork, (horn)).
10. The cat licks its ((fur), far).
11. Our horse stays in the (burn, (barn)).
12. I will sweep the (perch, (porch)).
13. She put on her new (sharp, (shirt)).
14. You can get a (born, (burn)) in the sun.
15. It is my (torn, (turn)) to wash the car.
16. Spot likes to dig in the ((dirt), dart).
17. A baby (bark, (bird)) is in the nest.
18. My grandmother lives on a ((farm), fern).

140 Assessment of words containing r-controlled vowels in context ar, er, ir, or, ur

OI and OY

Name ____________________

The sound in the middle of **coin** is spelled by the letters **oi.** The sound in the middle of **toys** is spelled by the letters **oy.**

coin toys

Read the words and look at the pictures. Circle the word that tells about each picture.

oyster / noise	toys / foil	choice / coins
soil / spoil	boil / boy	boil / coil
coin / coil	oil / oyster	joy / toy
boil / point	join / boys	foil / voice

Symbol-sound association of words containing diphthongs: oi, oy 141

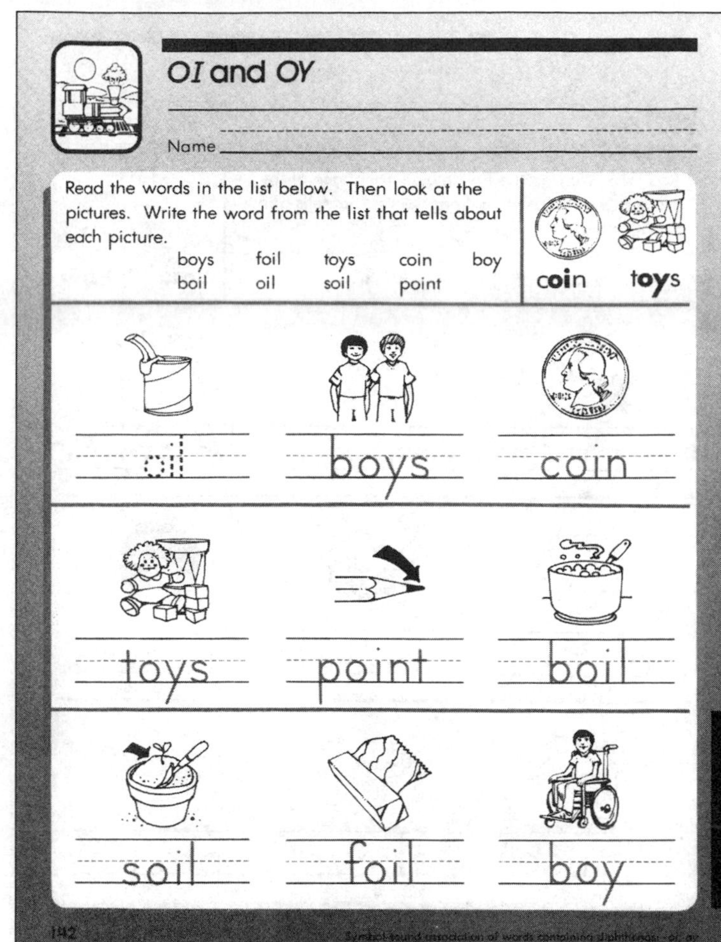

OI and OY

Name ____________________

Read the words in the list below. Then look at the pictures. Write the word from the list that tells about each picture.

boys foil toys coin boy
boil oil soil point

coin toys

oil	boys	coin
toys	point	boil
soil	foil	boy

142 Symbol-sound association of words containing diphthongs: oi, oy

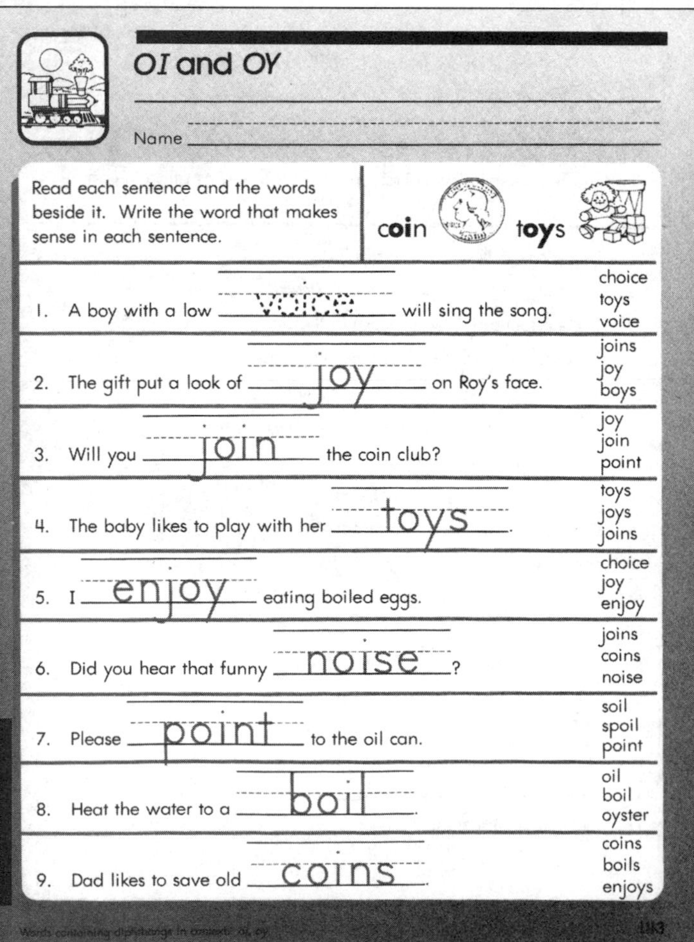

OI and OY

Name ____________________

Read each sentence and the words beside it. Write the word that makes sense in each sentence.

coin toys

1. A boy with a low voice will sing the song.	choice / toys / voice
2. The gift put a look of joy on Roy's face.	joins / joy / boys
3. Will you join the coin club?	joy / join / point
4. The baby likes to play with her toys.	toys / joys / joins
5. I enjoy eating boiled eggs.	choice / joy / enjoy
6. Did you hear that funny noise?	joins / coins / noise
7. Please point to the oil can.	soil / spoil / point
8. Heat the water to a boil.	oil / boil / oyster
9. Dad likes to save old coins.	coins / boils / enjoys

Words containing diphthongs in context: oi, oy 143

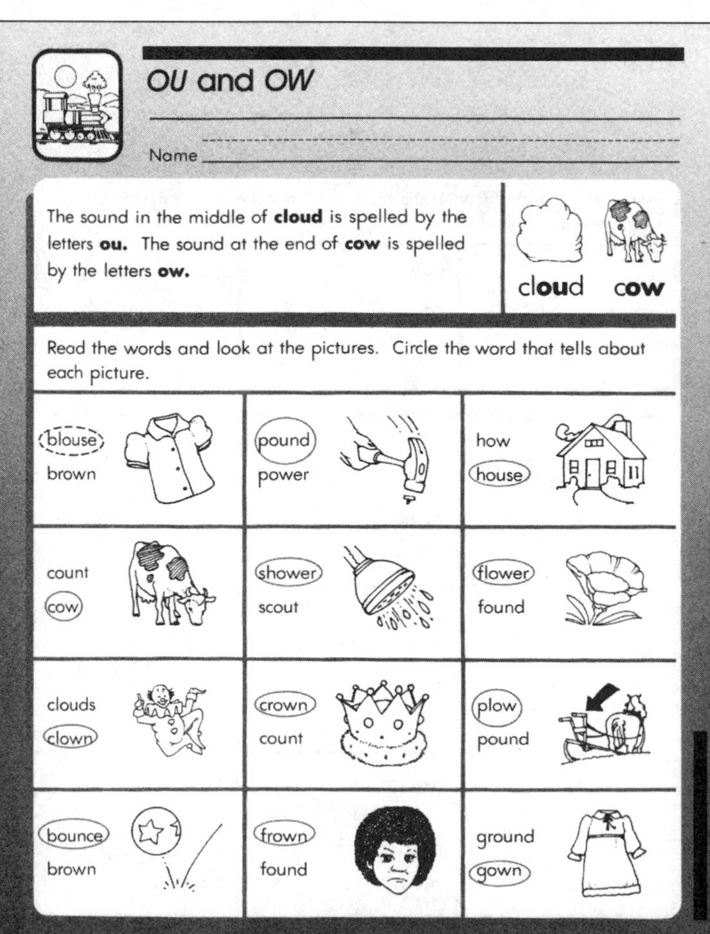

OU and OW

Name ____________________

The sound in the middle of **cloud** is spelled by the letters **ou.** The sound at the end of **cow** is spelled by the letters **ow.**

cloud cow

Read the words and look at the pictures. Circle the word that tells about each picture.

blouse / brown	pound / power	how / house
count / cow	shower / scout	flower / found
clouds / clown	crown / count	plow / pound
bounce / brown	frown / found	ground / gown

144 Symbol-sound association of words containing diphthongs: ou, ow

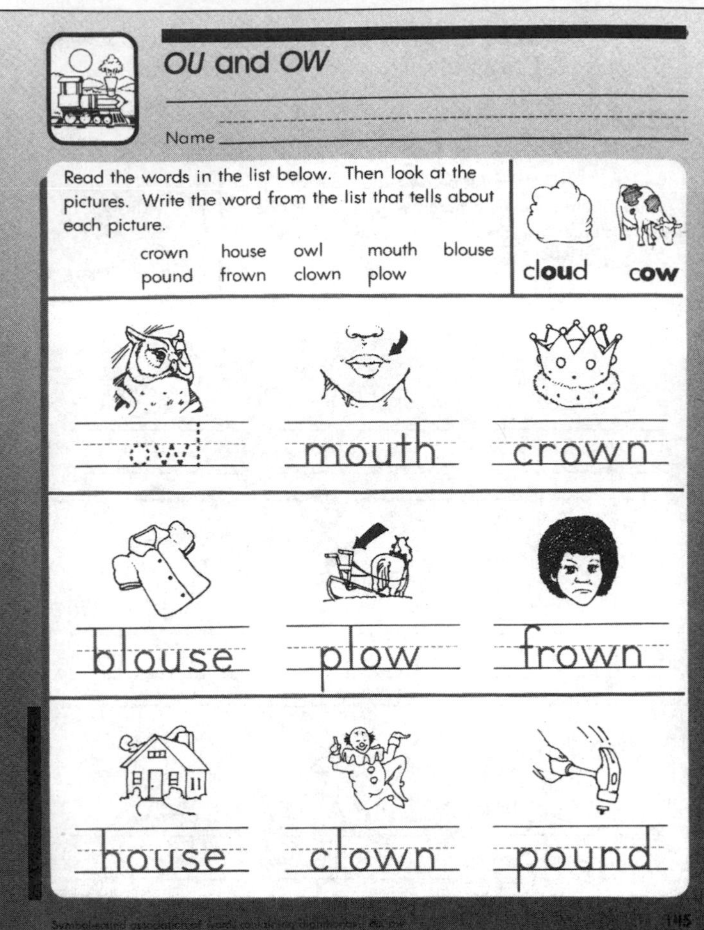

OU and OW

Name

Read the words in the list below. Then look at the pictures. Write the word from the list that tells about each picture.

crown house owl mouth blouse
pound frown clown plow

cloud cow

owl mouth crown

blouse plow frown

house clown pound

Symbol-sound association of words containing diphthongs: ou, ow 145

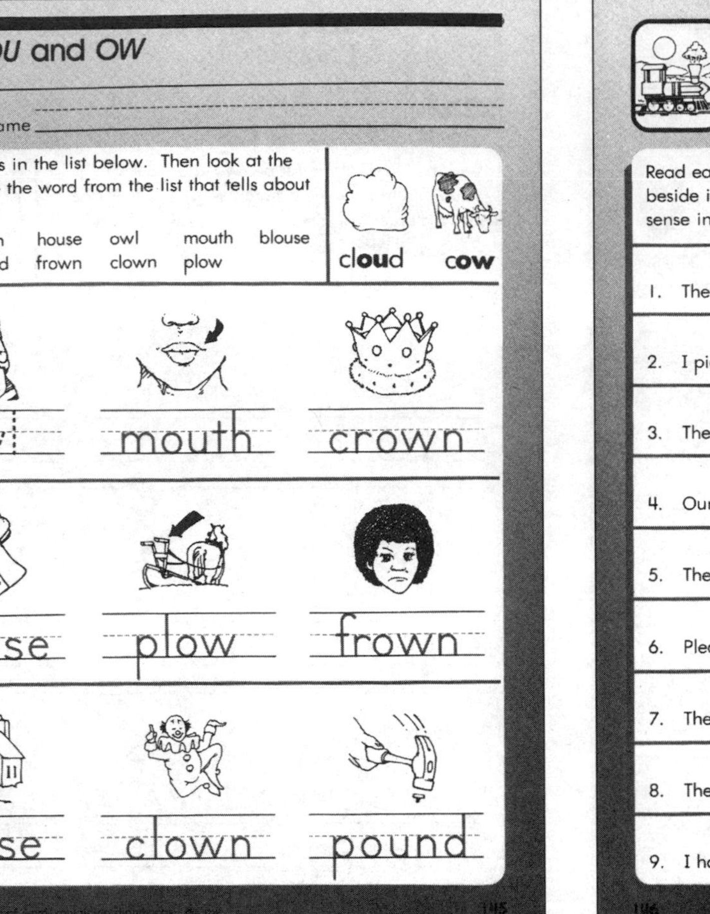

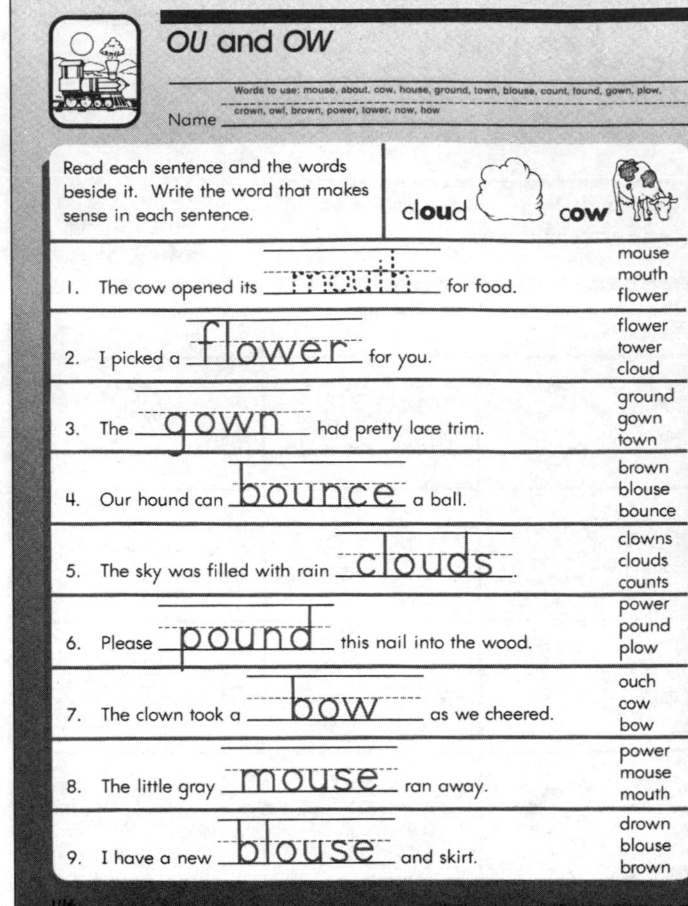

OU and OW

Words to use: mouse, about, cow, house, ground, town, blouse, count, found, gown, plow, crown, owl, brown, power, tower, now, how

Name

Read each sentence and the words beside it. Write the word that makes sense in each sentence.

cloud cow

1.	The cow opened its mouth for food.	mouse, mouth, flower
2.	I picked a flower for you.	flower, tower, cloud
3.	The gown had pretty lace trim.	ground, gown, town
4.	Our hound can bounce a ball.	brown, blouse, bounce
5.	The sky was filled with rain clouds.	clowns, clouds, counts
6.	Please pound this nail into the wood.	power, pound, plow
7.	The clown took a bow as we cheered.	ouch, cow, bow
8.	The little gray mouse ran away.	power, mouse, mouth
9.	I have a new blouse and skirt.	drown, blouse, brown

146 Words containing diphthongs in context: ou, ow

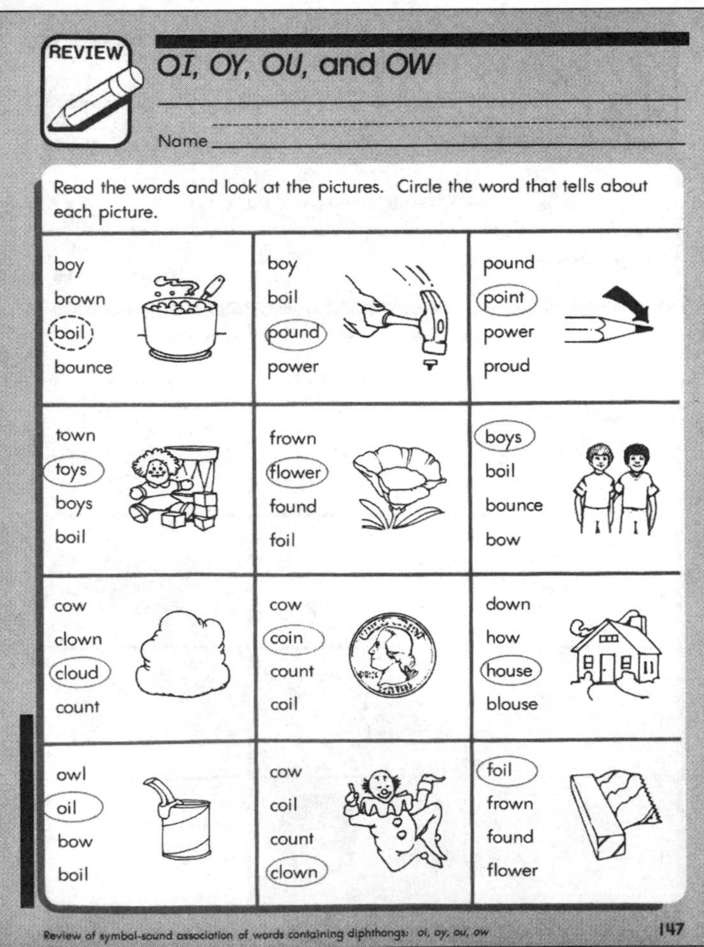

REVIEW

OI, OY, OU, and OW

Name

Read the words and look at the pictures. Circle the word that tells about each picture.

boy, brown, boil, bounce	boy, boil, pound, power	pound, point, power, proud
town, toys, boys, boil	frown, flower, found, foil	boys, boil, bounce, bow
cow, clown, cloud, count	cow, coin, count, coil	down, how, house, blouse
owl, oil, bow, boil	cow, coil, count, clown	foil, frown, found, flower

Review of symbol-sound association of words containing diphthongs: oi, oy, ou, ow 147

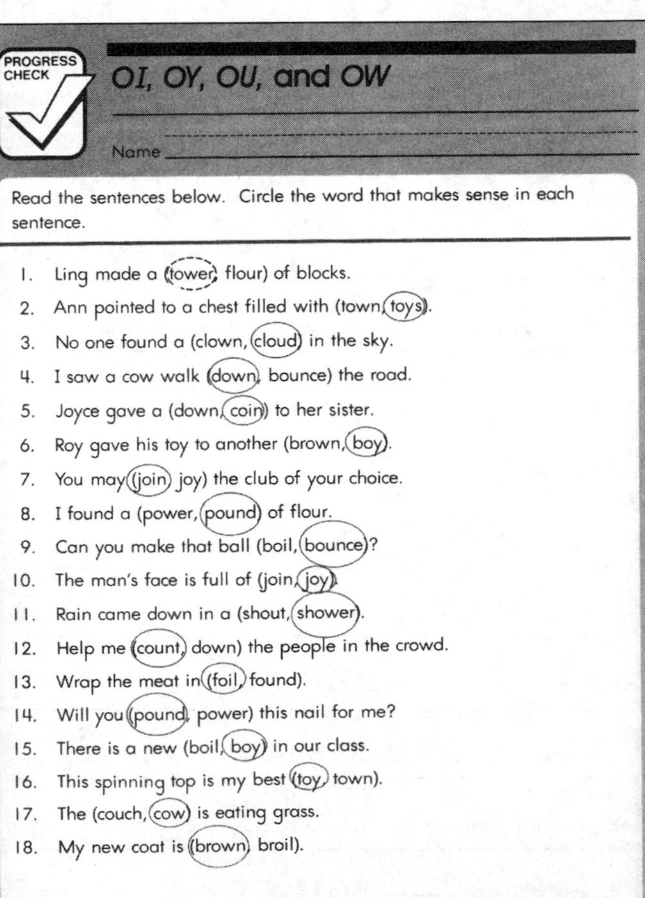

PROGRESS CHECK

OI, OY, OU, and OW

Name

Read the sentences below. Circle the word that makes sense in each sentence.

1. Ling made a (tower, flour) of blocks.
2. Ann pointed to a chest filled with (town, toys).
3. No one found a (clown, cloud) in the sky.
4. I saw a cow walk (down, bounce) the road.
5. Joyce gave a (down, coin) to her sister.
6. Roy gave his toy to another (brown, boy).
7. You may (join, joy) the club of your choice.
8. I found a (power, pound) of flour.
9. Can you make that ball (boil, bounce)?
10. The man's face is full of (join, joy).
11. Rain came down in a (shout, shower).
12. Help me (count, down) the people in the crowd.
13. Wrap the meat in (foil, found).
14. Will you (pound, power) this nail for me?
15. There is a new (boil, boy) in our class.
16. This spinning top is my best (toy, town).
17. The (couch, cow) is eating grass.
18. My new coat is (brown, broil).

148 Assessment of words containing diphthongs in context: oi, oy, ou, ow

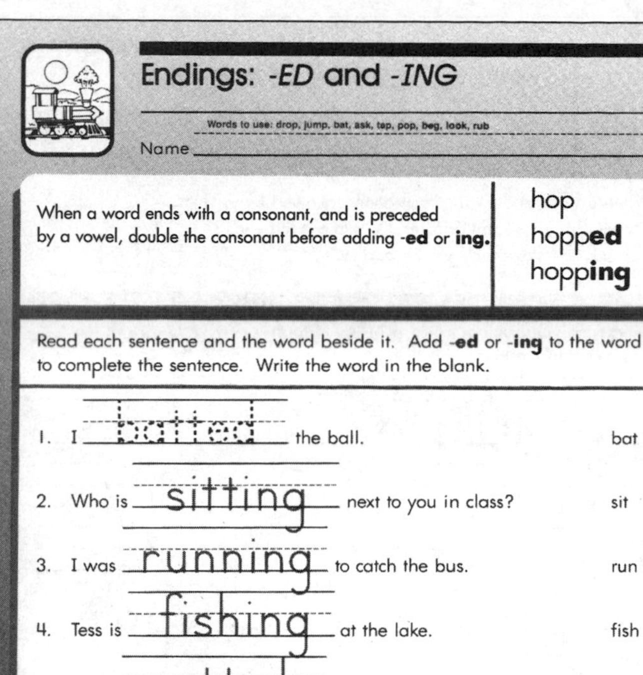

Endings: *-ED* and *-ING*

Words to use: drop, jump, bat, ask, tap, pop, beg, look, rub

Name ______

When a word ends with a consonant, and is preceded by a vowel, double the consonant before adding **-ed** or **ing.**

hop
hopp**ed**
hopp**ing**

Read each sentence and the word beside it. Add **-ed** or **-ing** to the word to complete the sentence. Write the word in the blank.

1. I __batted__ the ball. — bat
2. Who is __sitting__ next to you in class? — sit
3. I was __running__ to catch the bus. — run
4. Tess is __fishing__ at the lake. — fish
5. Andy __patted__ the cat on its head. — pat
6. Jean __painted__ the fence at our school. — paint
7. Pablo is __helping__ Father. — help
8. Mother __dropped__ a blue glass. — drop

149

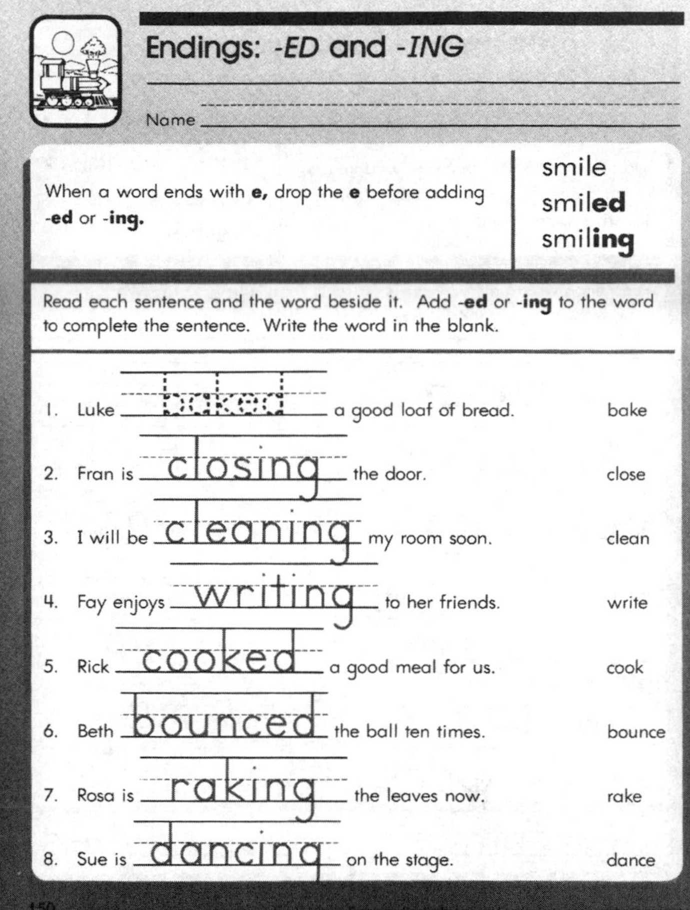

Endings: *-ED* and *-ING*

Name ______

When a word ends with **e,** drop the **e** before adding **-ed** or **-ing.**

smile
smil**ed**
smil**ing**

Read each sentence and the word beside it. Add **-ed** or **-ing** to the word to complete the sentence. Write the word in the blank.

1. Luke __baked__ a good loaf of bread. — bake
2. Fran is __closing__ the door. — close
3. I will be __cleaning__ my room soon. — clean
4. Fay enjoys __writing__ to her friends. — write
5. Rick __cooked__ a good meal for us. — cook
6. Beth __bounced__ the ball ten times. — bounce
7. Rosa is __raking__ the leaves now. — rake
8. Sue is __dancing__ on the stage. — dance

150

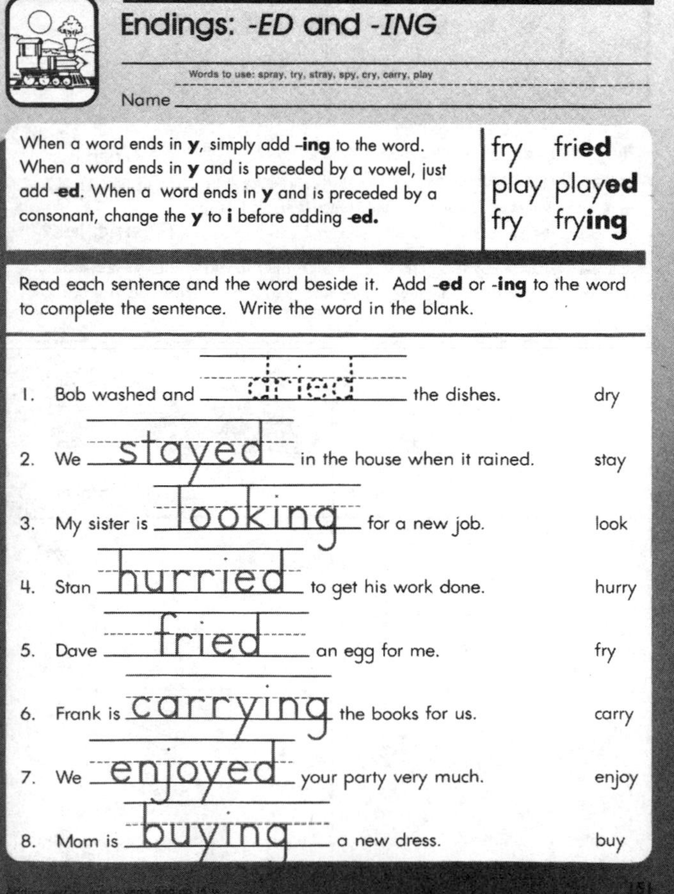

Endings: *-ED* and *-ING*

Words to use: spray, try, stray, spy, cry, carry, play

Name ______

When a word ends in **y**, simply add **–ing** to the word. When a word ends in **y** and is preceded by a vowel, just add **-ed**. When a word ends in **y** and is preceded by a consonant, change the **y** to **i** before adding **-ed.**

fry fri**ed**
play play**ed**
fry fry**ing**

Read each sentence and the word beside it. Add **-ed** or **-ing** to the word to complete the sentence. Write the word in the blank.

1. Bob washed and __dried__ the dishes. — dry
2. We __stayed__ in the house when it rained. — stay
3. My sister is __looking__ for a new job. — look
4. Stan __hurried__ to get his work done. — hurry
5. Dave __fried__ an egg for me. — fry
6. Frank is __carrying__ the books for us. — carry
7. We __enjoyed__ your party very much. — enjoy
8. Mom is __buying__ a new dress. — buy

151

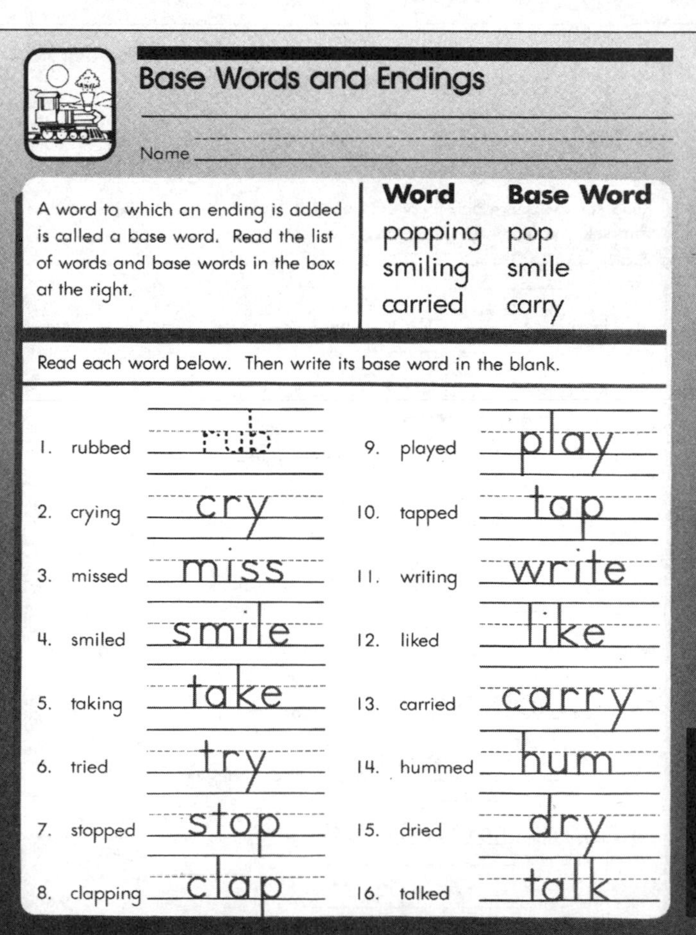

Base Words and Endings

Name ______

A word to which an ending is added is called a base word. Read the list of words and base words in the box at the right.

Word	Base Word
popping	pop
smiling	smile
carried	carry

Read each word below. Then write its base word in the blank.

1. rubbed __rub__
2. crying __cry__
3. missed __miss__
4. smiled __smile__
5. taking __take__
6. tried __try__
7. stopped __stop__
8. clapping __clap__
9. played __play__
10. tapped __tap__
11. writing __write__
12. liked __like__
13. carried __carry__
14. hummed __hum__
15. dried __dry__
16. talked __talk__

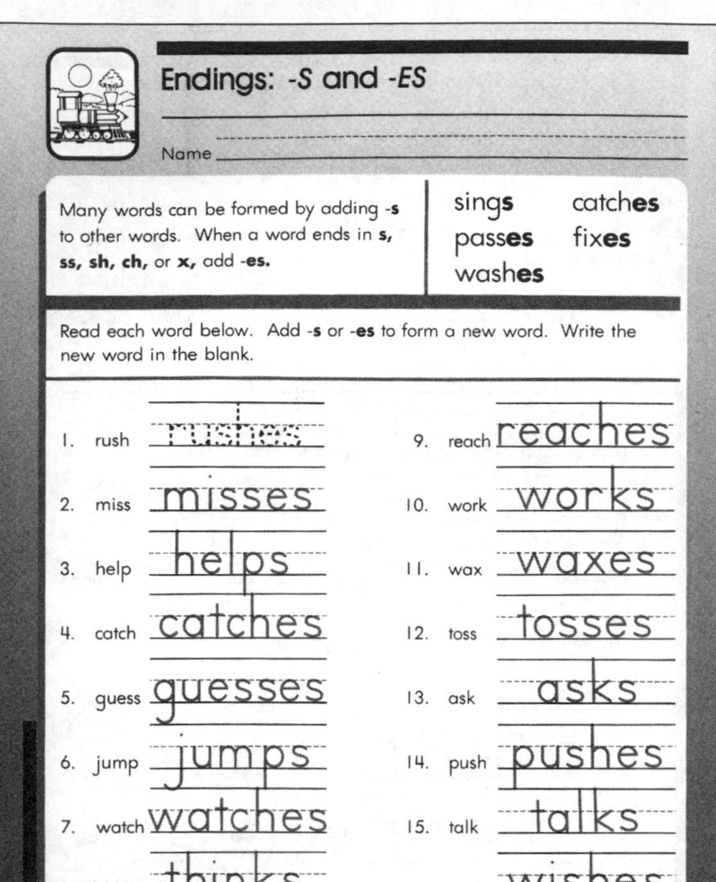

Endings: -S and -ES

Name

Many words can be formed by adding **-s** to other words. When a word ends in **s, ss, sh, ch,** or **x,** add **-es.**

sing**s** catch**es** pass**es** fix**es** wash**es**

Read each word below. Add **-s** or **-es** to form a new word. Write the new word in the blank.

1. rush rushes
2. miss misses
3. help helps
4. catch catches
5. guess guesses
6. jump jumps
7. watch watches
8. think thinks
9. reach reaches
10. work works
11. wax waxes
12. toss tosses
13. ask asks
14. push pushes
15. talk talks
16. wish wishes

153

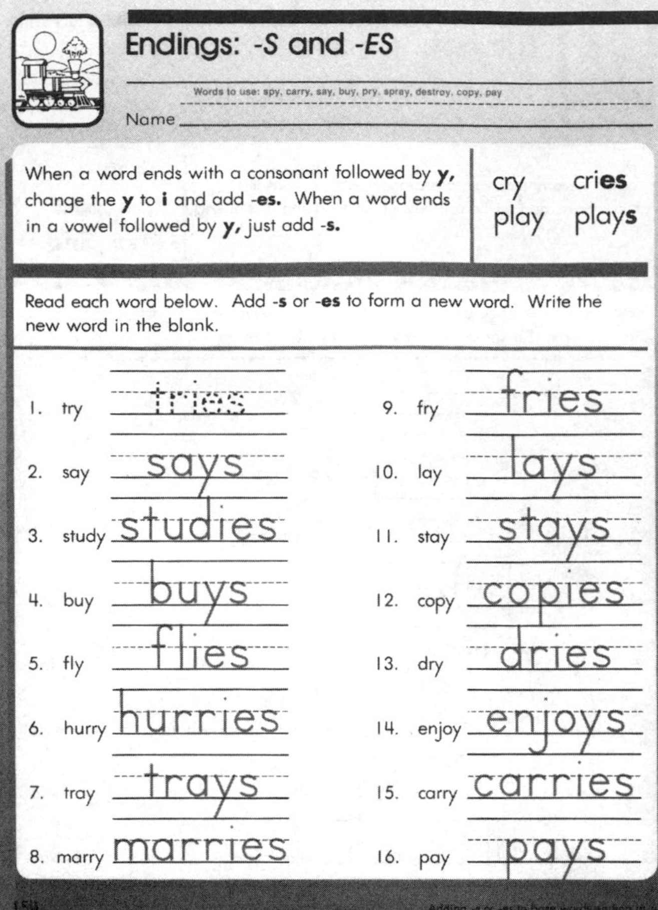

Endings: -S and -ES

Words to use: spy, carry, say, buy, pry, spray, destroy, copy, pay

Name

When a word ends with a consonant followed by **y,** change the **y** to **i** and add **-es.** When a word ends in a vowel followed by **y,** just add **-s.**

cry cr**ies** play play**s**

Read each word below. Add **-s** or **-es** to form a new word. Write the new word in the blank.

1. try tries
2. say says
3. study studies
4. buy buys
5. fly flies
6. hurry hurries
7. tray trays
8. marry marries
9. fry fries
10. lay lays
11. stay stays
12. copy copies
13. dry dries
14. enjoy enjoys
15. carry carries
16. pay pays

154 Adding -s or -es to base words ending in y

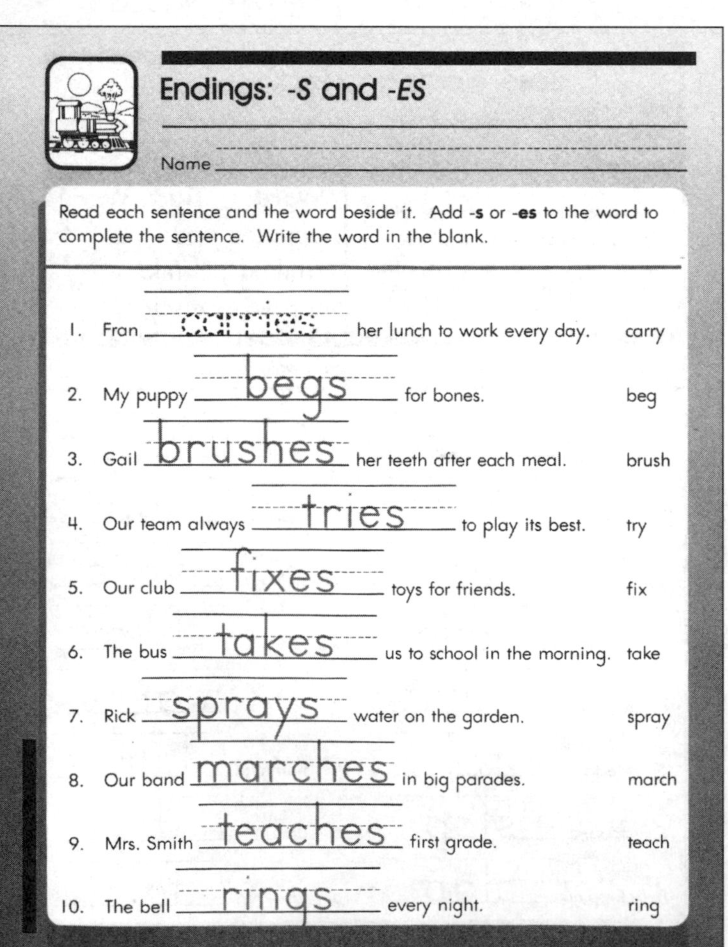

Endings: -S and -ES

Name

Read each sentence and the word beside it. Add **-s** or **-es** to the word to complete the sentence. Write the word in the blank.

1. Fran carries her lunch to work every day. carry
2. My puppy begs for bones. beg
3. Gail brushes her teeth after each meal. brush
4. Our team always tries to play its best. try
5. Our club fixes toys for friends. fix
6. The bus takes us to school in the morning. take
7. Rick sprays water on the garden. spray
8. Our band marches in big parades. march
9. Mrs. Smith teaches first grade. teach
10. The bell rings every night. ring

Adding -s or -es to base words in context 155

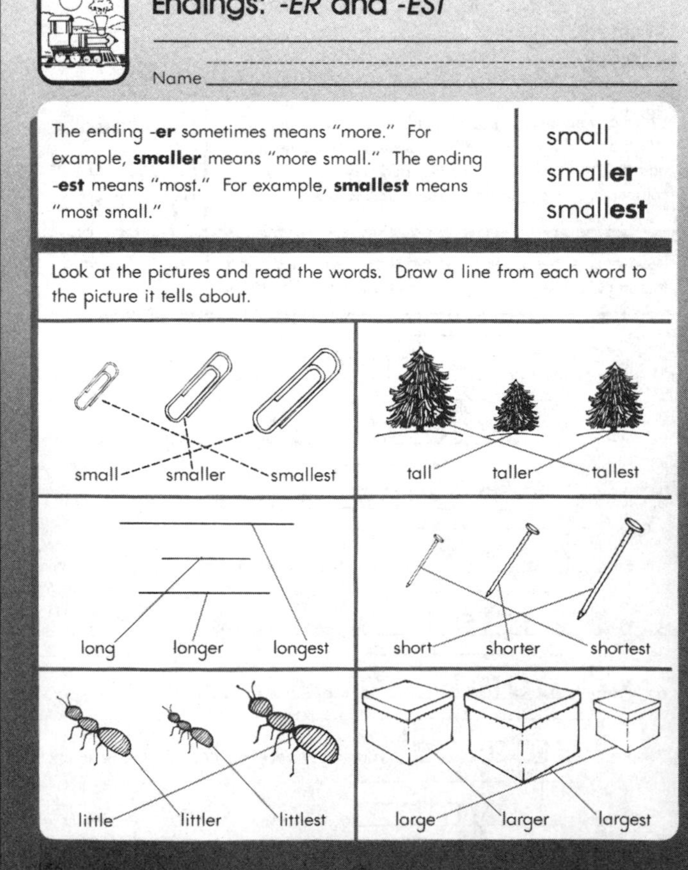

Endings: -ER and -EST

Name

The ending **-er** sometimes means "more." For example, **smaller** means "more small." The ending **-est** means "most." For example, **smallest** means "most small."

small small**er** small**est**

Look at the pictures and read the words. Draw a line from each word to the picture it tells about.

156

Endings: *-ER* and *-EST*

Name ______________________

The ending **-er** can be used to compare two things. The ending **-est** can be used to compare more than two things.

Read each sentence and the words beside it. Write the word that makes sense in each sentence.

1.	The tree is taller than a house.	tall taller
2.	My cat is a lighter color than my dog.	light lighter
3.	That is the oldest tree in these woods.	older oldest
4.	My hair is darker than yours.	dark darker
5.	The blue car is the smallest of all.	smaller smallest
6.	Tom's turtle was slower than mine.	slow slower
7.	Sam is the fastest boy in the class.	faster fastest
8.	The lake is deeper than the pond.	deeper deepest

Endings: *-ER* and *-EST*

Name ______________________

Read each sentence and the word beside it. Add **-er** or **-est** to the word to complete the sentence. Write the word in the blank.

1.	Our team was the slower of the two.	slow
2.	The lake is nearer than the pond.	near
3.	This plant is the tallest in my garden.	tall
4.	I will take longer walks than before.	long
5.	Ted's pillow is softer than mine.	soft
6.	Play the highest note in this song.	high
7.	This test is the hardest one of all.	hard
8.	I read the shortest story in my book.	short
9.	Chad's shirt looks cleaner than mine.	clean
10.	The river is wider than the stream.	wide

REVIEW

Endings

Name ______________________

Read each word below. Add the ending shown beside the word to form a new word. Write the new word in the blank.

1.	wash + s or es =	washes
2.	carry + s =	carries
3.	dark + er =	darker
4.	smile + ing =	smiling
5.	come + ing =	coming
6.	near + est =	nearest
7.	stop + ing =	stopping
8.	match + s or es =	matches
9.	close + ed =	closed
10.	smart + est =	smartest

Endings

Name ______________________

Read each sentence and the word beside it. Add an ending from the list below to the word. Write the word in the blank. You may use an ending more than once. **-ed** **-ing** **-s** **-es** **-er** **-est**

1.	Mom hurried to work this morning.	hurry
2.	The puppy dropped the ball.	drop
3.	This is the steepest hill in our town.	steep
4.	A free pencil comes with the paper.	come
5.	Jim catches the ball for our team.	catch
6.	Mandy is smiling at me.	smile
7.	Is your pen newer than mine?	new
8.	Marsha will be carrying her flute to school.	carry
9.	Ben dried the dishes after dinner.	dry
10.	Anna will be taking her nap soon.	take

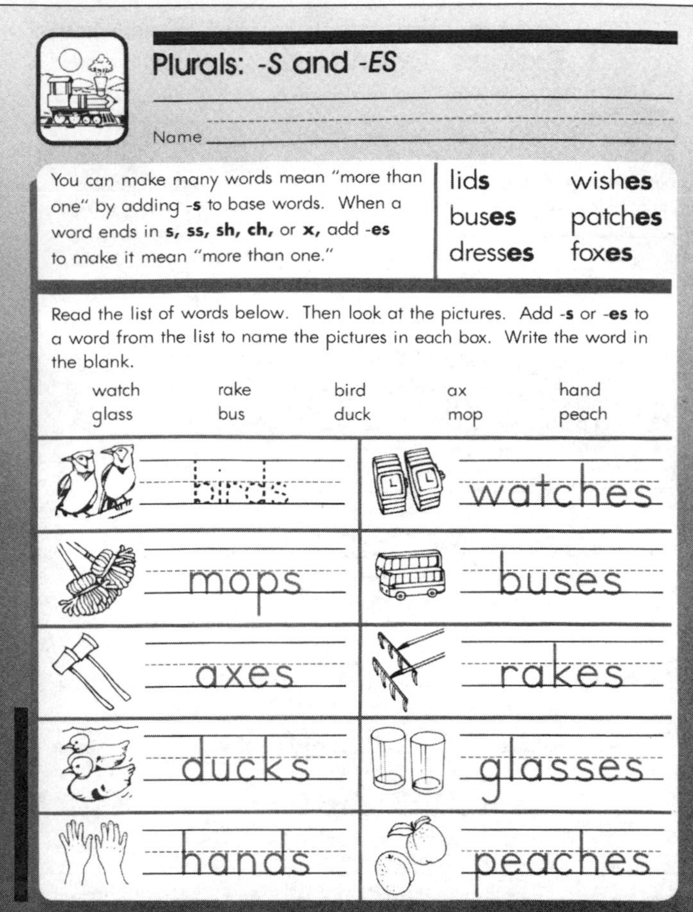

Plurals: -*S* and -*ES*

Name ______________________

You can make many words mean "more than one" by adding **-s** to base words. When a word ends in **s, ss, sh, ch,** or **x,** add **-es** to make it mean "more than one."

lid**s**	wish**es**
bus**es**	patch**es**
dress**es**	fox**es**

Read the list of words below. Then look at the pictures. Add **-s** or **-es** to a word from the list to name the pictures in each box. Write the word in the blank.

watch	rake	bird	ax	hand
glass	bus	duck	mop	peach

birds	watches
mops	buses
axes	rakes
ducks	glasses
hands	peaches

Adding -s or -es to nouns to form plurals 161

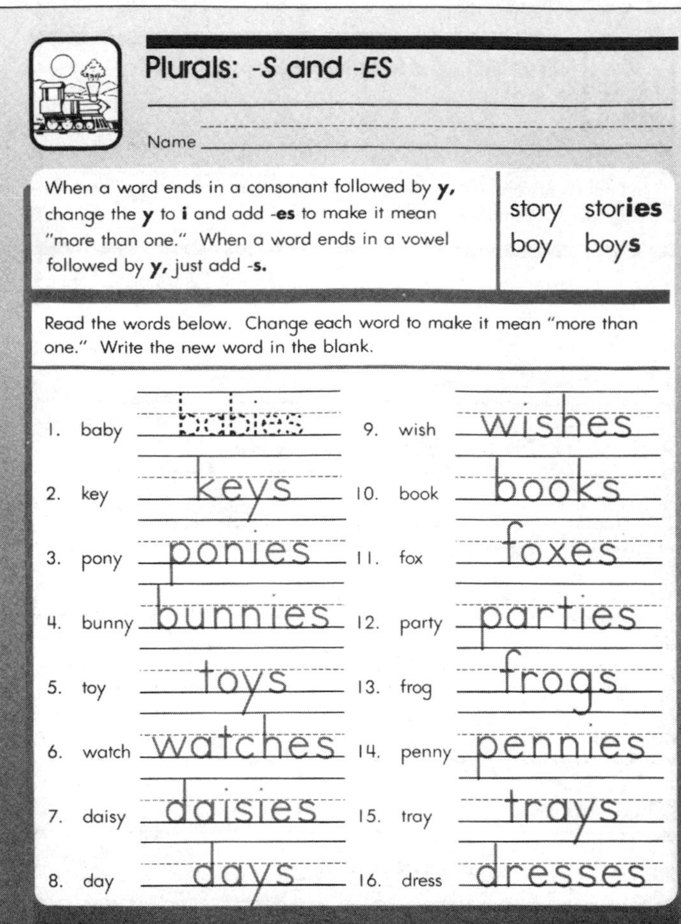

Plurals: -*S* and -*ES*

Name ______________________

When a word ends in a consonant followed by **y,** change the **y** to **i** and add **-es** to make it mean "more than one." When a word ends in a vowel followed by **y,** just add **-s.**

story	stor**ies**
boy	boy**s**

Read the words below. Change each word to make it mean "more than one." Write the new word in the blank.

1.	baby	babies	9.	wish	wishes
2.	key	keys	10.	book	books
3.	pony	ponies	11.	fox	foxes
4.	bunny	bunnies	12.	party	parties
5.	toy	toys	13.	frog	frogs
6.	watch	watches	14.	penny	pennies
7.	daisy	daisies	15.	tray	trays
8.	day	days	16.	dress	dresses

162 Adding -s or -es to nouns to form plurals

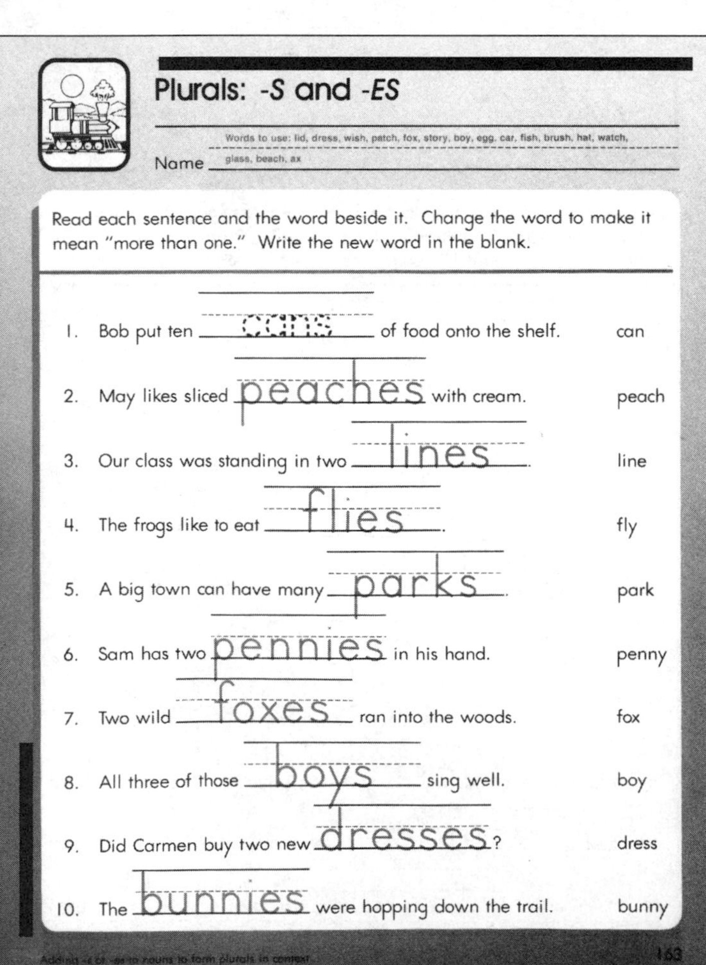

Plurals: -*S* and -*ES*

Words to use: lid, dress, wish, patch, fox, story, boy, egg, car, fish, brush, hat, watch, glass, beach, ax

Name ______________________

Read each sentence and the word beside it. Change the word to make it mean "more than one." Write the new word in the blank.

1.	Bob put ten cans of food onto the shelf.	can
2.	May likes sliced peaches with cream.	peach
3.	Our class was standing in two lines.	line
4.	The frogs like to eat flies.	fly
5.	A big town can have many parks.	park
6.	Sam has two pennies in his hand.	penny
7.	Two wild foxes ran into the woods.	fox
8.	All three of those boys sing well.	boy
9.	Did Carmen buy two new dresses?	dress
10.	The bunnies were hopping down the trail.	bunny

Adding -s or -es to nouns to form plurals in context 163

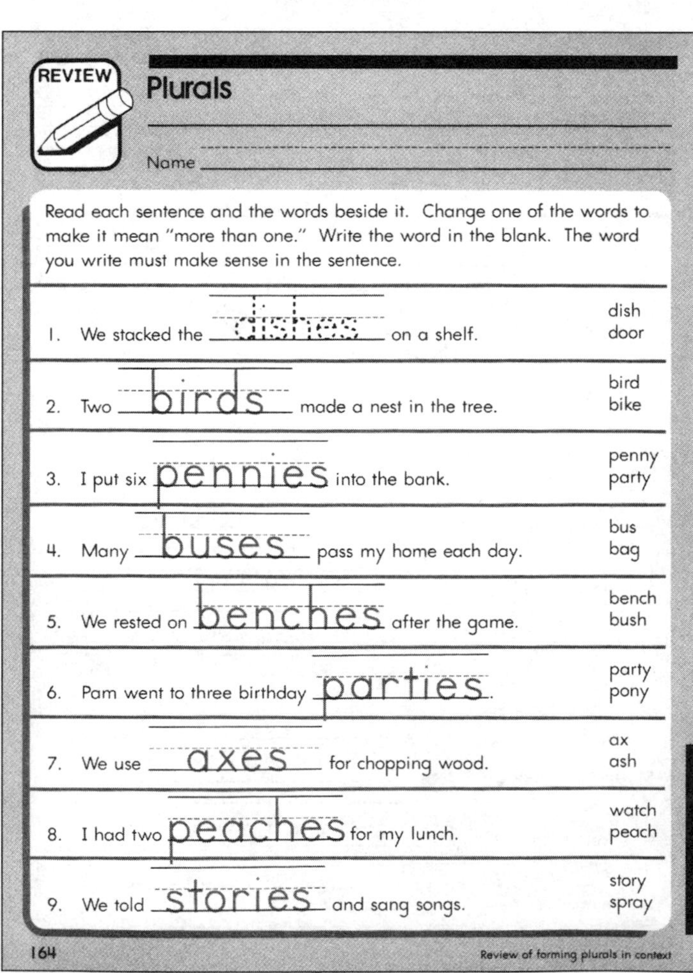

REVIEW

Plurals

Name ______________________

Read each sentence and the words beside it. Change one of the words to make it mean "more than one." Write the word in the blank. The word you write must make sense in the sentence.

1.	We stacked the dishes on a shelf.	dish door
2.	Two birds made a nest in the tree.	bird bike
3.	I put six pennies into the bank.	penny party
4.	Many buses pass my home each day.	bus bag
5.	We rested on benches after the game.	bench bush
6.	Pam went to three birthday parties.	party pony
7.	We use axes for chopping wood.	ax ash
8.	I had two peaches for my lunch.	watch peach
9.	We told stories and sang songs.	story spray

164 Review of forming plurals in context

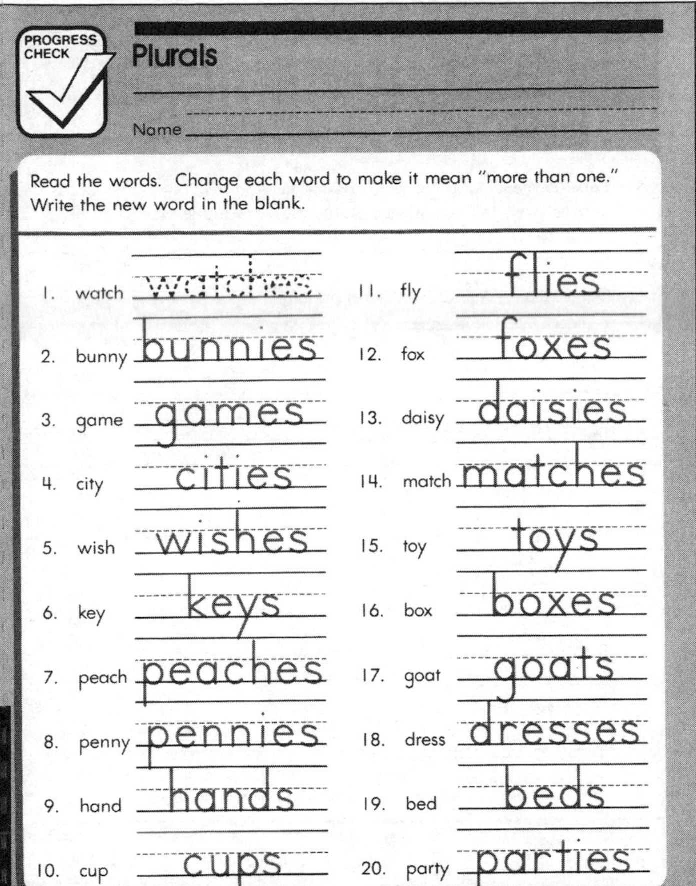

PROGRESS CHECK

Plurals

Name ______________________

Read the words. Change each word to make it mean "more than one." Write the new word in the blank.

1. watch	watches	11. fly	flies
2. bunny	bunnies	12. fox	foxes
3. game	games	13. daisy	daisies
4. city	cities	14. match	matches
5. wish	wishes	15. toy	toys
6. key	keys	16. box	boxes
7. peach	peaches	17. goat	goats
8. penny	pennies	18. dress	dresses
9. hand	hands	19. bed	beds
10. cup	cups	20. party	parties

Assessment of forming plurals 165

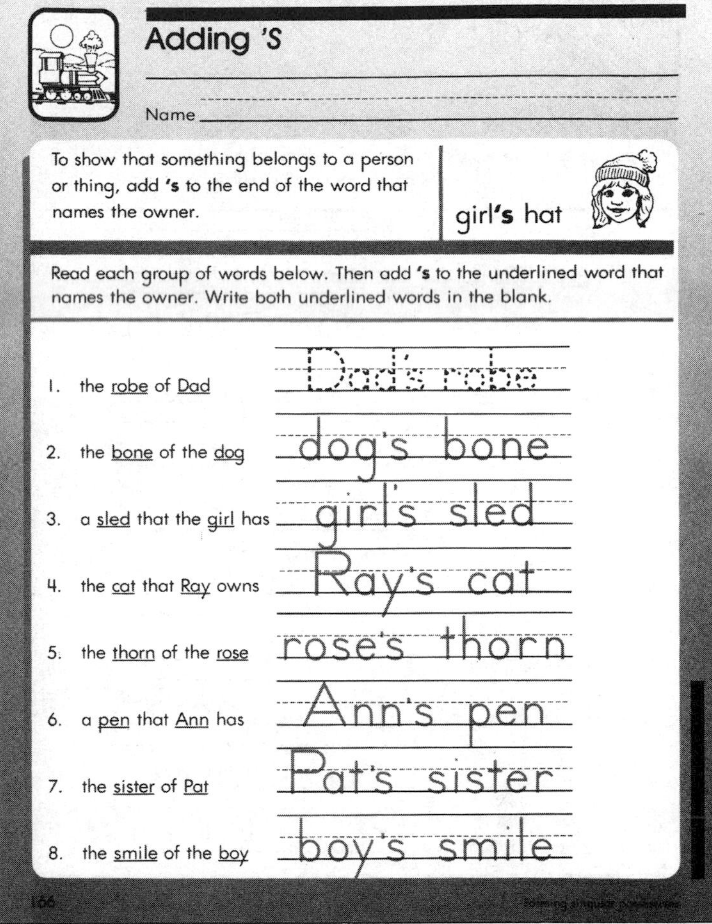

Adding 'S

Name ______________________

To show that something belongs to a person or thing, add **'s** to the end of the word that names the owner.

girl**'s** hat

Read each group of words below. Then add **'s** to the underlined word that names the owner. Write both underlined words in the blank.

1. the robe of Dad — Dad's robe
2. the bone of the dog — dog's bone
3. a sled that the girl has — girl's sled
4. the cat that Ray owns — Ray's cat
5. the thorn of the rose — rose's thorn
6. a pen that Ann has — Ann's pen
7. the sister of Pat — Pat's sister
8. the smile of the boy — boy's smile

166 Forming singular possessives

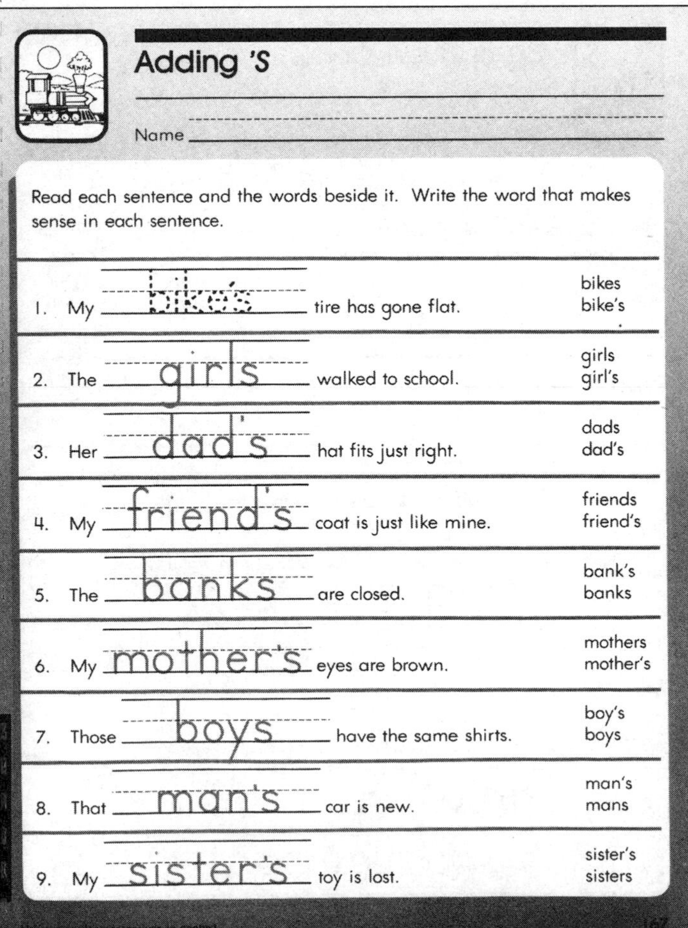

Adding 'S

Name ______________________

Read each sentence and the words beside it. Write the word that makes sense in each sentence.

1. My bike's tire has gone flat. — bikes / bike's
2. The girls walked to school. — girls / girl's
3. Her dad's hat fits just right. — dads / dad's
4. My friend's coat is just like mine. — friends / friend's
5. The banks are closed. — bank's / banks
6. My mother's eyes are brown. — mothers / mother's
7. Those boys have the same shirts. — boy's / boys
8. That man's car is new. — man's / mans
9. My sister's toy is lost. — sister's / sisters

Using singular possessives in context 167

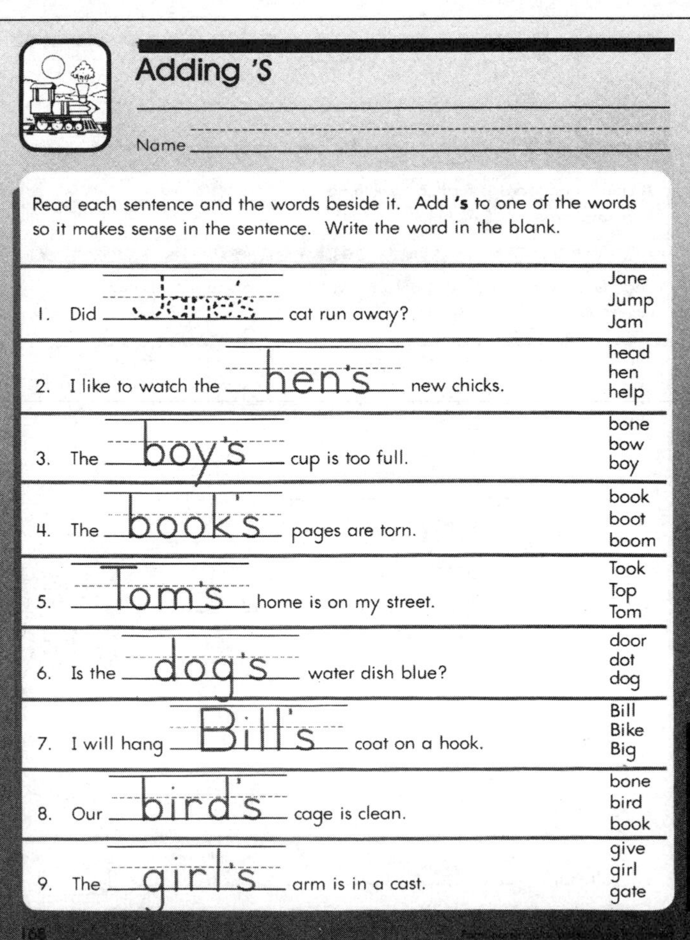

Adding 'S

Name ______________________

Read each sentence and the words beside it. Add **'s** to one of the words so it makes sense in the sentence. Write the word in the blank.

1. Did Jane's cat run away? — Jane / Jump / Jam
2. I like to watch the hen's new chicks. — head / hen / help
3. The boy's cup is too full. — bone / bow / boy
4. The book's pages are torn. — book / boot / boom
5. Tom's home is on my street. — Took / Top / Tom
6. Is the dog's water dish blue? — door / dot / dog
7. I will hang Bill's coat on a hook. — Bill / Bike / Big
8. Our bird's cage is clean. — bone / bird / book
9. The girl's arm is in a cast. — give / girl / gate

168

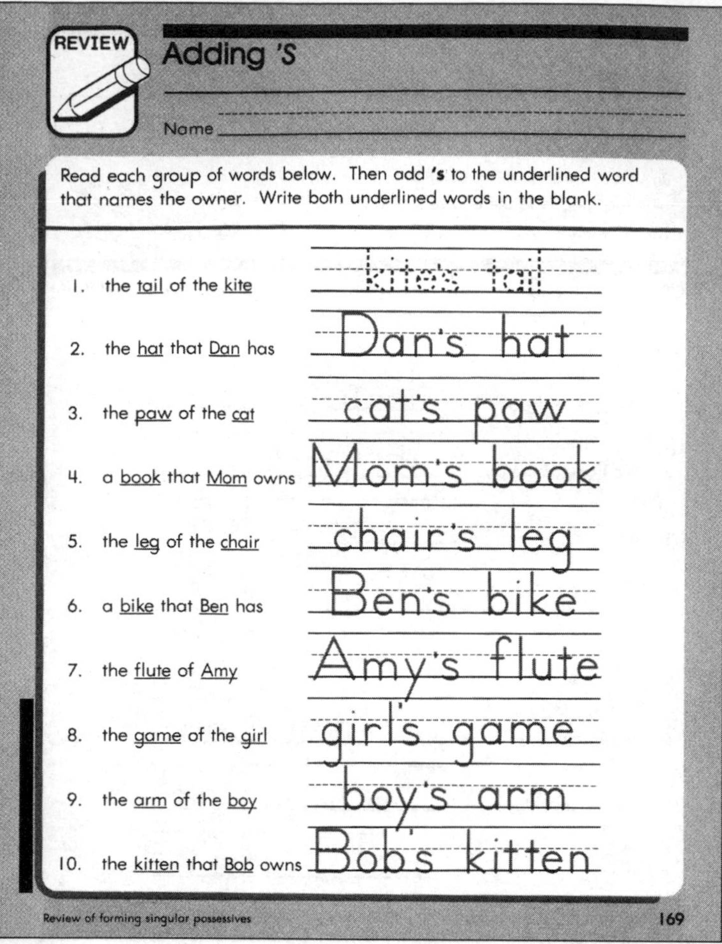
REVIEW

Adding 'S

Name

Read each group of words below. Then add **'s** to the underlined word that names the owner. Write both underlined words in the blank.

1. the tail of the kite kite's tail
2. the hat that Dan has Dan's hat
3. the paw of the cat cat's paw
4. a book that Mom owns Mom's book
5. the leg of the chair chair's leg
6. a bike that Ben has Ben's bike
7. the flute of Amy Amy's flute
8. the game of the girl girl's game
9. the arm of the boy boy's arm
10. the kitten that Bob owns Bob's kitten

Review of forming singular possessives 169

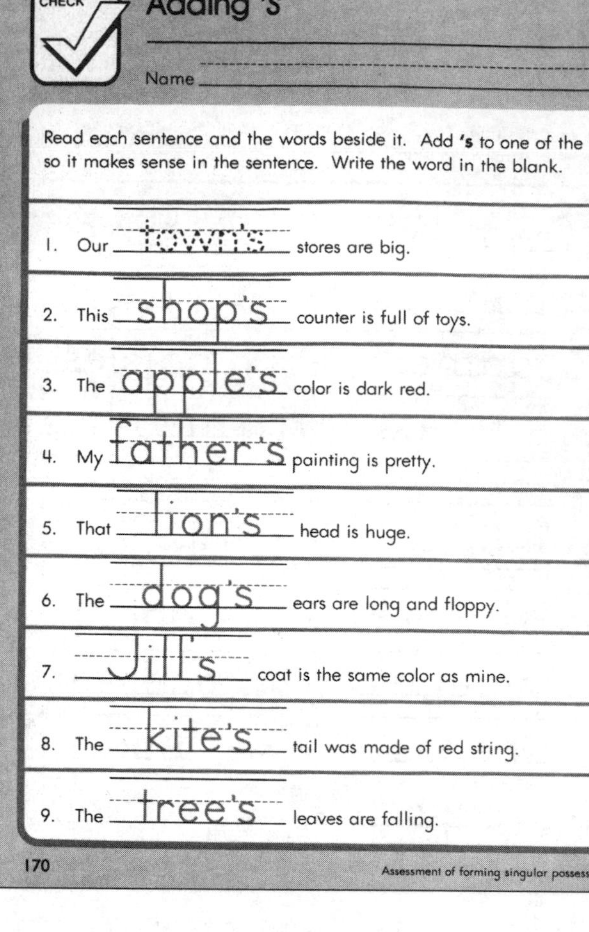
PROGRESS CHECK

Adding 'S

Name

Read each sentence and the words beside it. Add **'s** to one of the words so it makes sense in the sentence. Write the word in the blank.

1. Our town's stores are big. (too, tune, town)
2. This shop's counter is full of toys. (stop, shop, spot)
3. The apple's color is dark red. (ash, apple, at)
4. My father's painting is pretty. (fatter, father, feather)
5. That lion's head is huge. (lion, lean, leaf)
6. The dog's ears are long and floppy. (dot, dog, dig)
7. Jill's coat is the same color as mine. (Jump, Jill, Jeep)
8. The kite's tail was made of red string. (kit, kite, kick)
9. The tree's leaves are falling. (trap, tree, trot)

170 Assessment of forming singular possessives in context

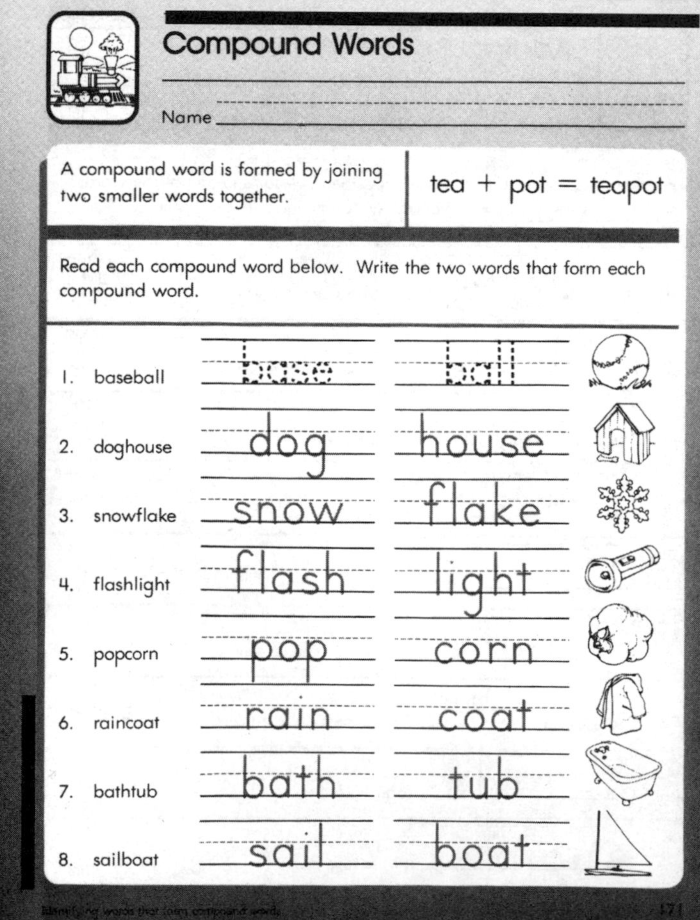

Compound Words

Name

A compound word is formed by joining two smaller words together.	tea + pot = teapot

Read each compound word below. Write the two words that form each compound word.

1. baseball base ball
2. doghouse dog house
3. snowflake snow flake
4. flashlight flash light
5. popcorn pop corn
6. raincoat rain coat
7. bathtub bath tub
8. sailboat sail boat

Identifying words that form compound words 171

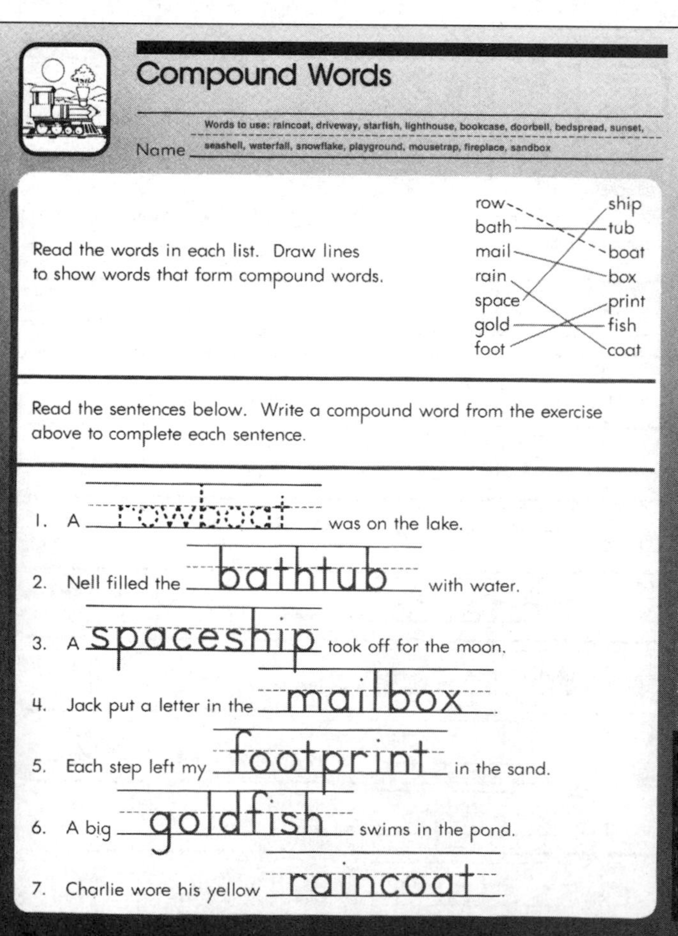

Compound Words

Name Words to use: raincoat, driveway, starfish, lighthouse, bookcase, doorbell, bedspread, sunset, seashell, waterfall, snowflake, playground, mousetrap, fireplace, sandbox

Read the words in each list. Draw lines to show words that form compound words.

row	ship
bath	tub
mail	boat
rain	box
space	print
gold	fish
foot	coat

Read the sentences below. Write a compound word from the exercise above to complete each sentence.

1. A rowboat was on the lake.
2. Nell filled the bathtub with water.
3. A spaceship took off for the moon.
4. Jack put a letter in the mailbox.
5. Each step left my footprint in the sand.
6. A big goldfish swims in the pond.
7. Charlie wore his yellow raincoat.

172

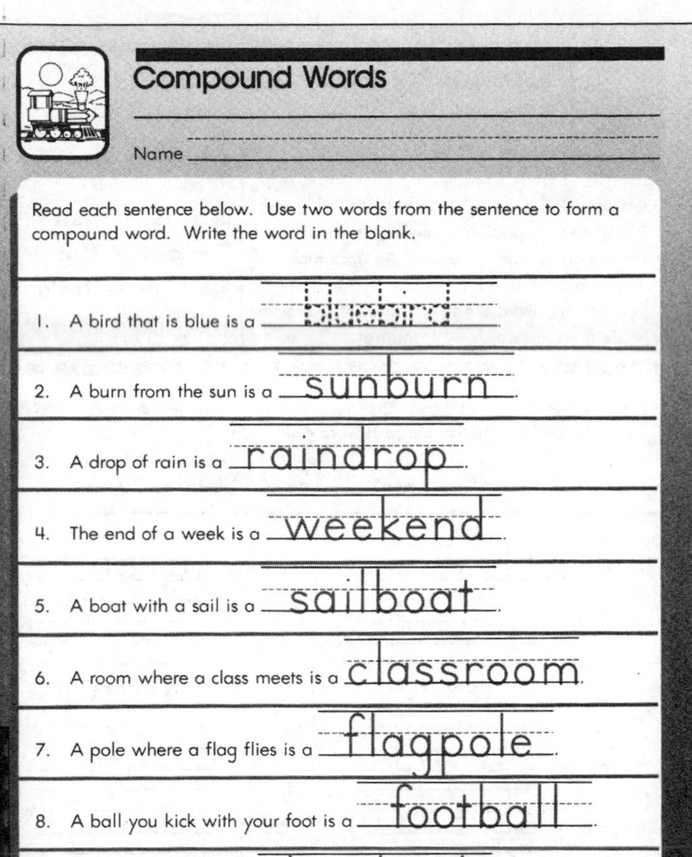

Compound Words

Name ______________________

Read each sentence below. Use two words from the sentence to form a compound word. Write the word in the blank.

1. A bird that is blue is a bluebird.
2. A burn from the sun is a sunburn.
3. A drop of rain is a raindrop.
4. The end of a week is a weekend.
5. A boat with a sail is a sailboat.
6. A room where a class meets is a classroom.
7. A pole where a flag flies is a flagpole.
8. A ball you kick with your foot is a football.
9. A knob on a door is a doorknob.

173

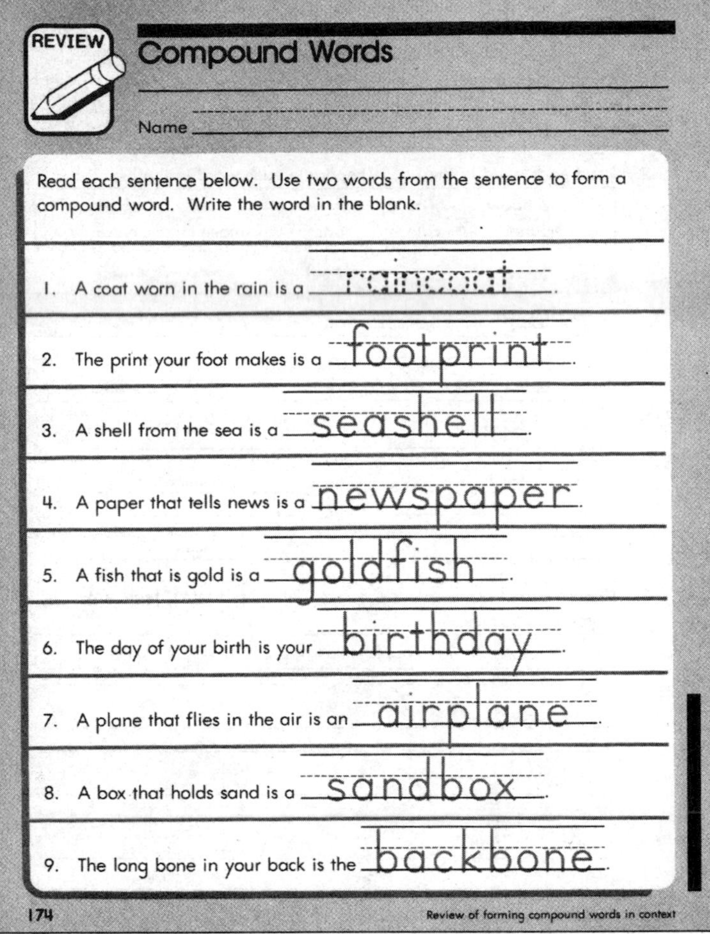

REVIEW

Compound Words

Name ______________________

Read each sentence below. Use two words from the sentence to form a compound word. Write the word in the blank.

1. A coat worn in the rain is a raincoat.
2. The print your foot makes is a footprint.
3. A shell from the sea is a seashell.
4. A paper that tells news is a newspaper.
5. A fish that is gold is a goldfish.
6. The day of your birth is your birthday.
7. A plane that flies in the air is an airplane.
8. A box that holds sand is a sandbox.
9. The long bone in your back is the backbone.

174 Review of forming compound words in context

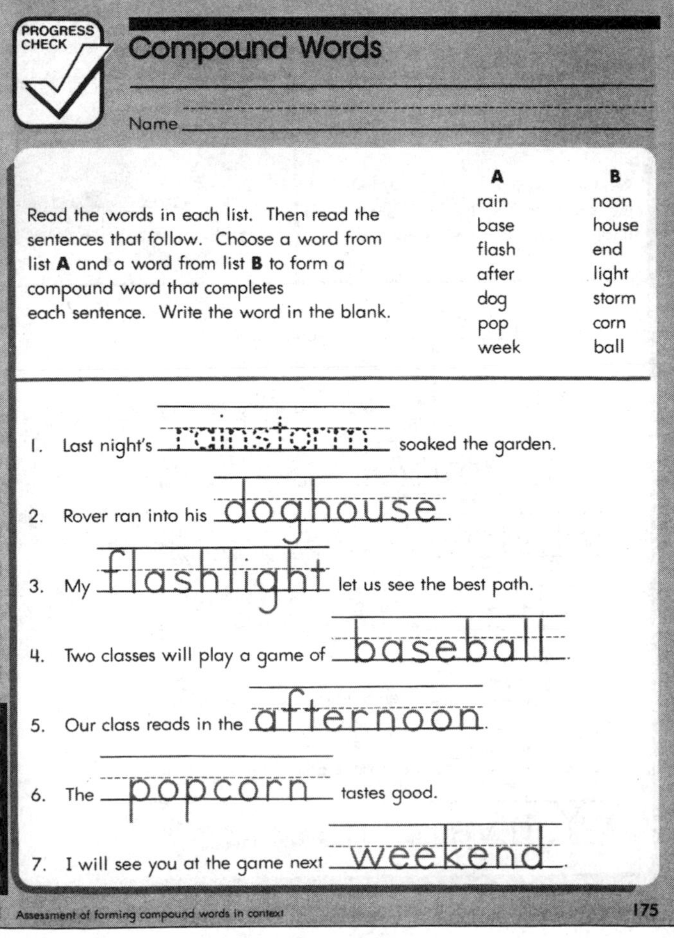

PROGRESS CHECK

Compound Words

Name ______________________

Read the words in each list. Then read the sentences that follow. Choose a word from list **A** and a word from list **B** to form a compound word that completes each sentence. Write the word in the blank.

A	B
rain	noon
base	house
flash	end
after	light
dog	storm
pop	corn
week	ball

1. Last night's rainstorm soaked the garden.
2. Rover ran into his doghouse.
3. My flashlight let us see the best path.
4. Two classes will play a game of baseball.
5. Our class reads in the afternoon.
6. The popcorn tastes good.
7. I will see you at the game next weekend.

Assessment of forming compound words in context 175

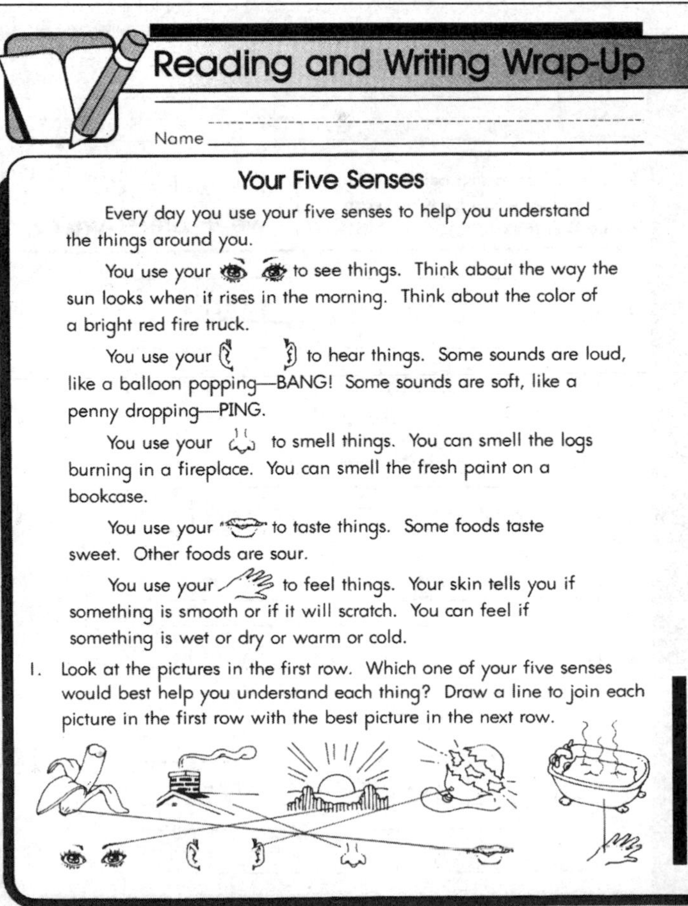

Reading and Writing Wrap-Up

Name ______________________

Your Five Senses

Every day you use your five senses to help you understand the things around you.

You use your (eyes) to see things. Think about the way the sun looks when it rises in the morning. Think about the color of a bright red fire truck.

You use your (ears) to hear things. Some sounds are loud, like a balloon popping—BANG! Some sounds are soft, like a penny dropping—PING.

You use your (nose) to smell things. You can smell the logs burning in a fireplace. You can smell the fresh paint on a bookcase.

You use your (mouth) to taste things. Some foods taste sweet. Other foods are sour.

You use your (hand) to feel things. Your skin tells you if something is smooth or if it will scratch. You can feel if something is wet or dry or warm or cold.

1. Look at the pictures in the first row. Which one of your five senses would best help you understand each thing? Draw a line to join each picture in the first row with the best picture in the next row.

176 Application of reading and comprehension skills in a science context

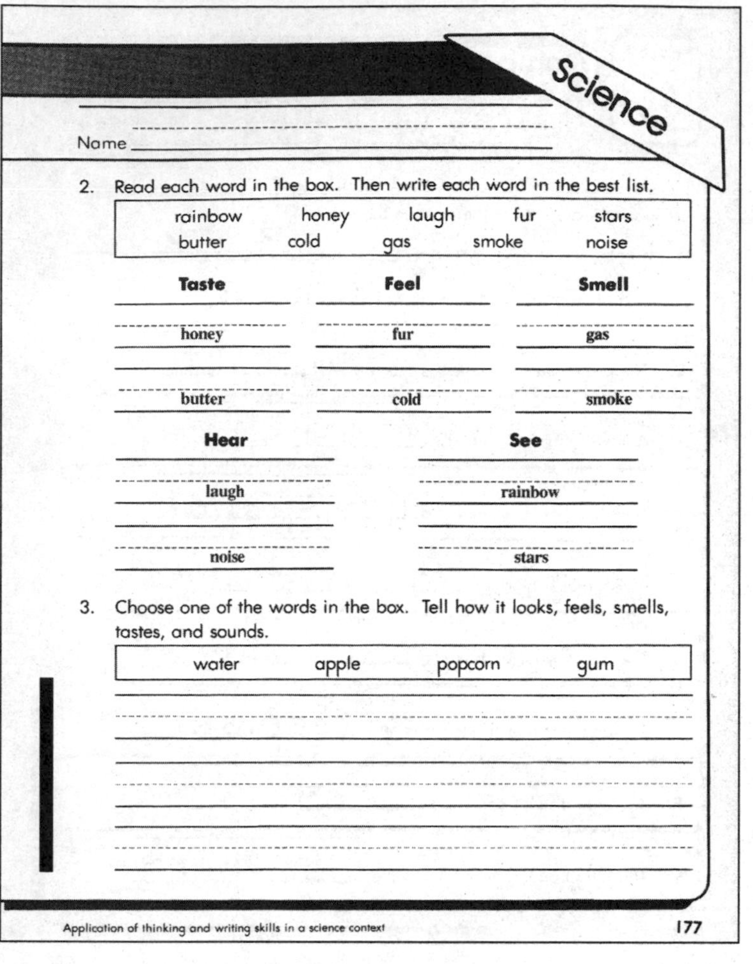

Science

Name

2. Read each word in the box. Then write each word in the best list.

rainbow	honey	laugh	fur	stars
butter	cold	gas	smoke	noise

Taste	Feel	Smell
honey	fur	gas
butter	cold	smoke

Hear	See
laugh	rainbow
noise	stars

3. Choose one of the words in the box. Tell how it looks, feels, smells, tastes, and sounds.

water	apple	popcorn	gum

Application of thinking and writing skills in a science context 177

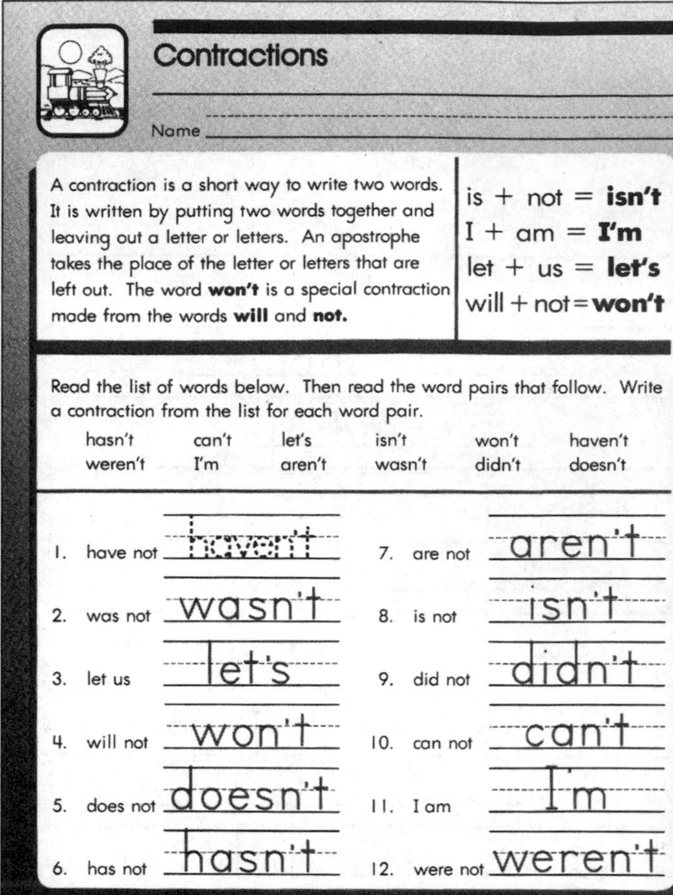

Contractions

Name

A contraction is a short way to write two words. It is written by putting two words together and leaving out a letter or letters. An apostrophe takes the place of the letter or letters that are left out. The word **won't** is a special contraction made from the words **will** and **not.**

is + not = **isn't**
I + am = **I'm**
let + us = **let's**
will + not = **won't**

Read the list of words below. Then read the word pairs that follow. Write a contraction from the list for each word pair.

hasn't	can't	let's	isn't	won't	haven't
weren't	I'm	aren't	wasn't	didn't	doesn't

1. have not haven't
2. was not wasn't
3. let us let's
4. will not won't
5. does not doesn't
6. has not hasn't
7. are not aren't
8. is not isn't
9. did not didn't
10. can not can't
11. I am I'm
12. were not weren't

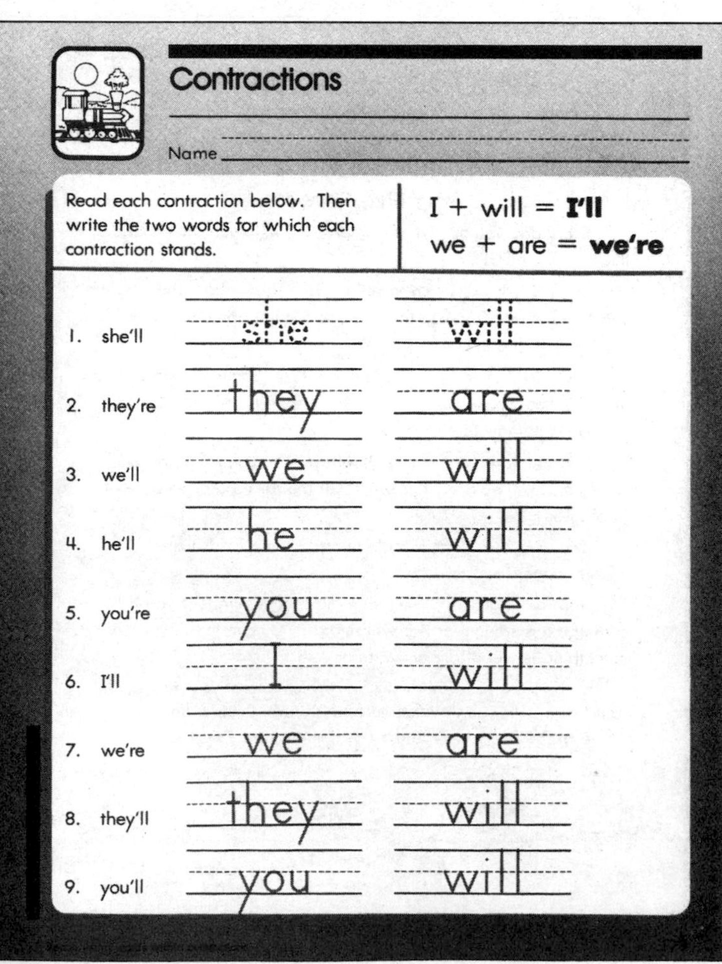

Contractions

Name

Read each contraction below. Then write the two words for which each contraction stands.

I + will = **I'll**
we + are = **we're**

1. she'll — she will
2. they're — they are
3. we'll — we will
4. he'll — he will
5. you're — you are
6. I'll — I will
7. we're — we are
8. they'll — they will
9. you'll — you will

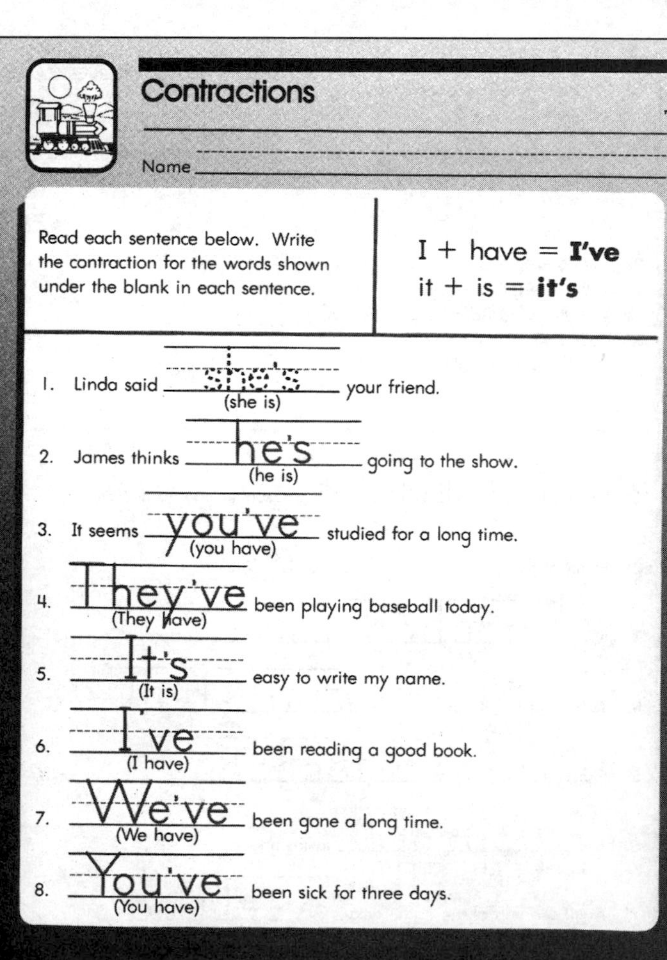

Contractions

Name

Read each sentence below. Write the contraction for the words shown under the blank in each sentence.

I + have = **I've**
it + is = **it's**

1. Linda said she's (she is) your friend.
2. James thinks he's (he is) going to the show.
3. It seems you've (you have) studied for a long time.
4. They've (They have) been playing baseball today.
5. It's (It is) easy to write my name.
6. I've (I have) been reading a good book.
7. We've (We have) been gone a long time.
8. You've (You have) been sick for three days.

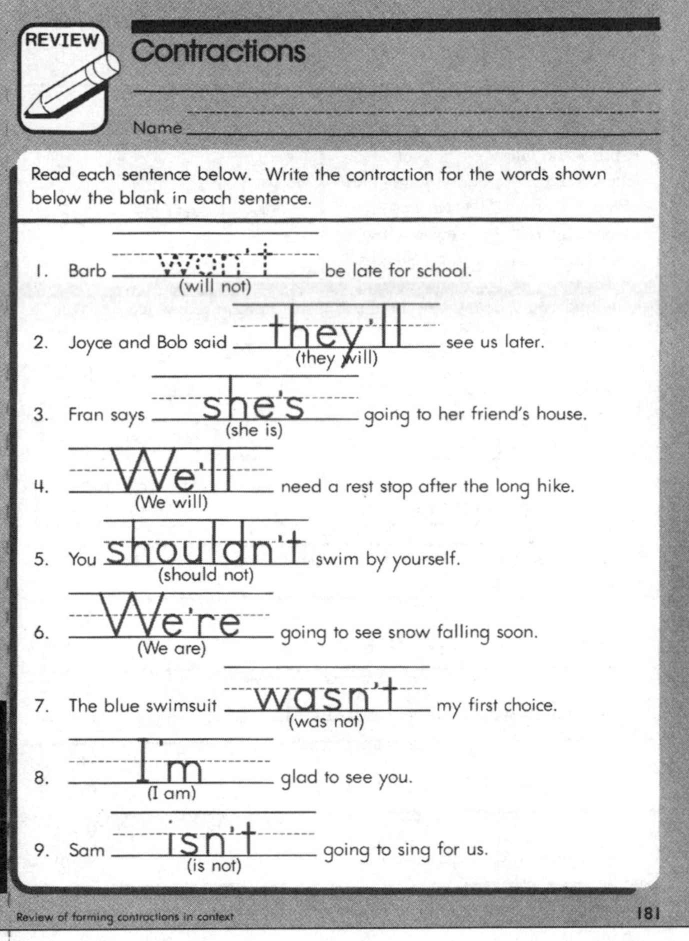

REVIEW

Contractions

Name

Read each sentence below. Write the contraction for the words shown below the blank in each sentence.

1. Barb won't (will not) be late for school.
2. Joyce and Bob said they'll (they will) see us later.
3. Fran says she's (she is) going to her friend's house.
4. We'll (We will) need a rest stop after the long hike.
5. You shouldn't (should not) swim by yourself.
6. We're (We are) going to see snow falling soon.
7. The blue swimsuit wasn't (was not) my first choice.
8. I'm (I am) glad to see you.
9. Sam isn't (is not) going to sing for us.

Review of forming contractions in context 181

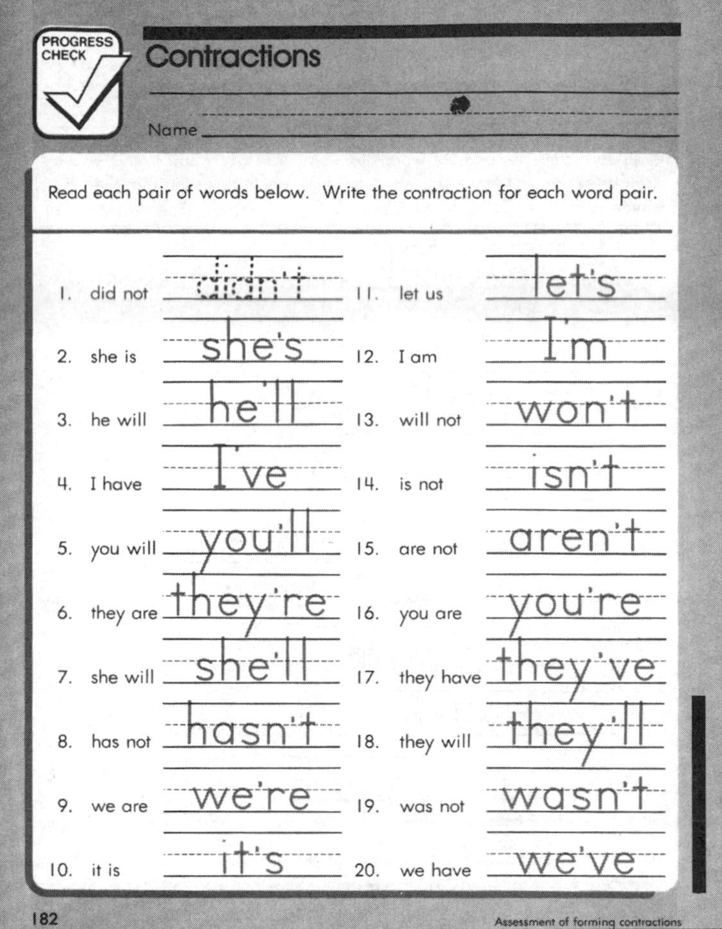

PROGRESS CHECK

Contractions

Name

Read each pair of words below. Write the contraction for each word pair.

1. did not	didn't	11. let us	let's
2. she is	she's	12. I am	I'm
3. he will	he'll	13. will not	won't
4. I have	I've	14. is not	isn't
5. you will	you'll	15. are not	aren't
6. they are	they're	16. you are	you're
7. she will	she'll	17. they have	they've
8. has not	hasn't	18. they will	they'll
9. we are	we're	19. was not	wasn't
10. it is	it's	20. we have	we've

182 Assessment of forming contractions

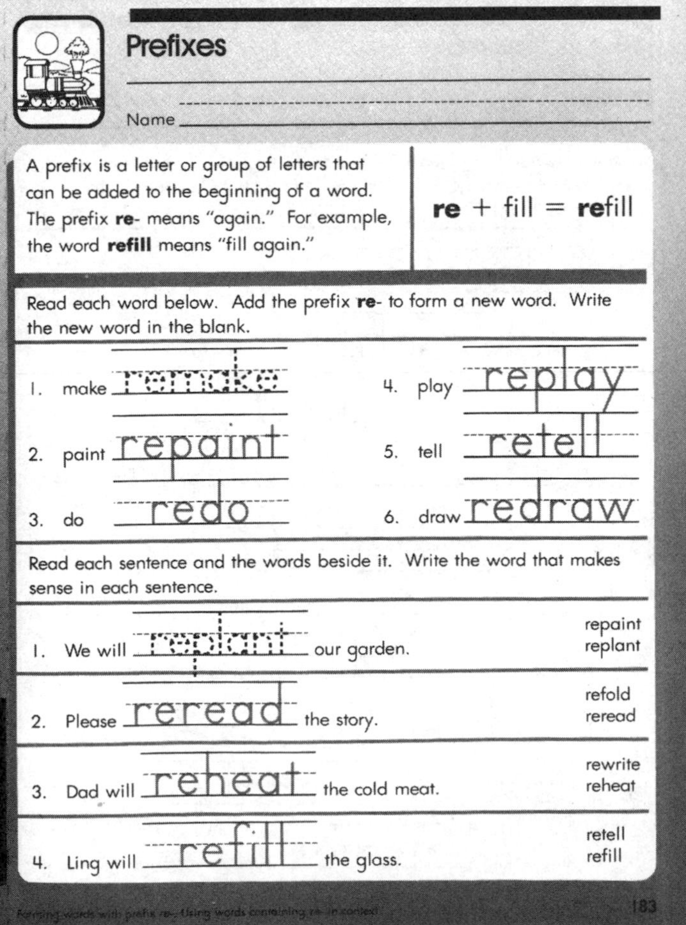

Prefixes

Name

A prefix is a letter or group of letters that can be added to the beginning of a word. The prefix **re**- means "again." For example, the word **refill** means "fill again."

re + fill = **re**fill

Read each word below. Add the prefix **re**- to form a new word. Write the new word in the blank.

1. make	remake	4. play	replay
2. paint	repaint	5. tell	retell
3. do	redo	6. draw	redraw

Read each sentence and the words beside it. Write the word that makes sense in each sentence.

1. We will replant our garden. (repaint, replant)
2. Please reread the story. (refold, reread)
3. Dad will reheat the cold meat. (rewrite, reheat)
4. Ling will refill the glass. (retell, refill)

Forming words with prefix re-; Using words containing re- in context 183

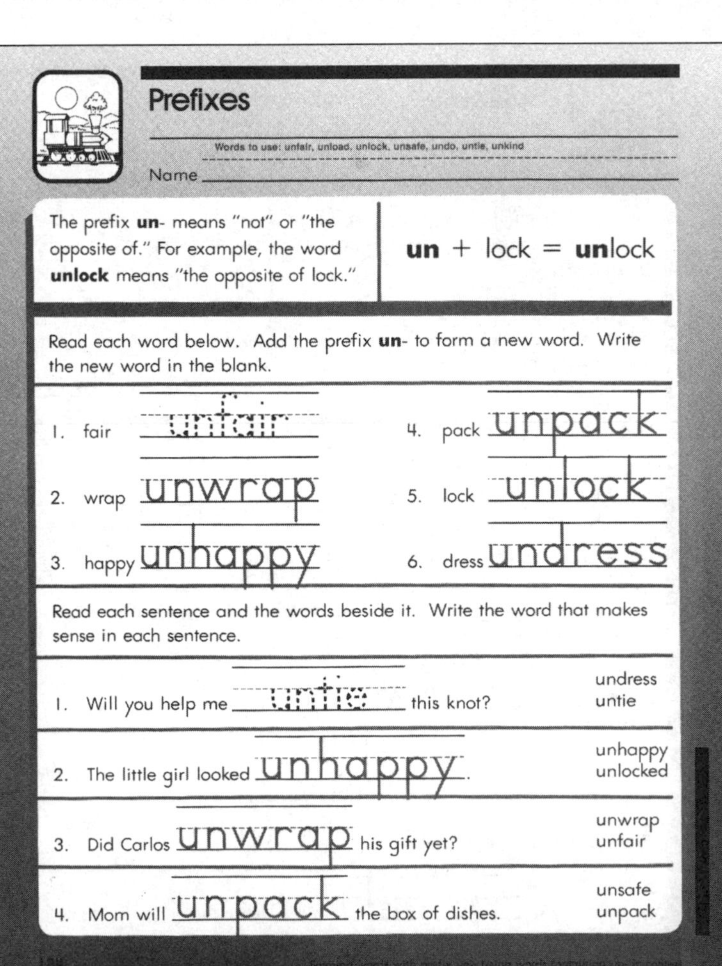

Prefixes

Words to use: unfair, unload, unlock, unsafe, undo, untie, unkind

Name

The prefix **un**- means "not" or "the opposite of." For example, the word **unlock** means "the opposite of lock."

un + lock = **un**lock

Read each word below. Add the prefix **un**- to form a new word. Write the new word in the blank.

1. fair	unfair	4. pack	unpack
2. wrap	unwrap	5. lock	unlock
3. happy	unhappy	6. dress	undress

Read each sentence and the words beside it. Write the word that makes sense in each sentence.

1. Will you help me untie this knot? (undress, untie)
2. The little girl looked unhappy. (unhappy, unlocked)
3. Did Carlos unwrap his gift yet? (unwrap, unfair)
4. Mom will unpack the box of dishes. (unsafe, unpack)

184 Forming words with prefix un-; Using words containing un- in context

Prefixes

Words to use: unpack, refill, redo, unlock, undress, unwrap, replay, unhappy, reuse

Name ____________________

Read each sentence and the word beside it. Add **re-** or **un-** to the word to complete each sentence. The word you form must make sense in the sentence.

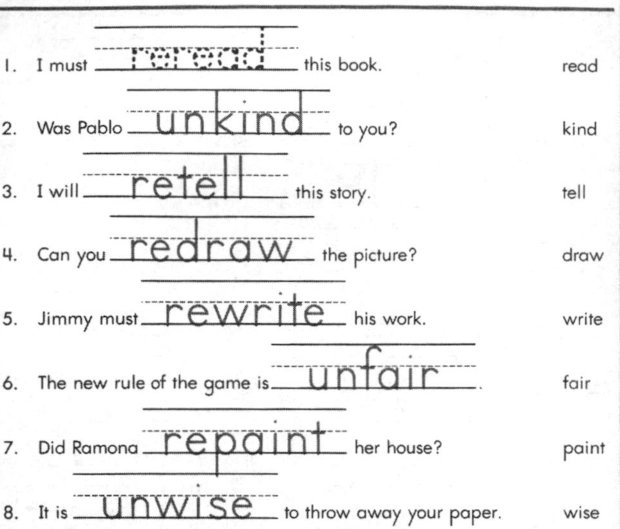

1. I must reread this book. read
2. Was Pablo unkind to you? kind
3. I will retell this story. tell
4. Can you redraw the picture? draw
5. Jimmy must rewrite his work. write
6. The new rule of the game is unfair. fair
7. Did Ramona repaint her house? paint
8. It is unwise to throw away your paper. wise
9. Driving too fast is unsafe. safe
10. The unpaid bill is a week late. paid

Suffixes

Name ____________________

A suffix is a letter or group of letters that can be added to the end of a word. The suffix **-ful** usually means "full of." For example, the word helpful means "full of help."

help + **ful** = help**ful**

Read each word below. Add the suffix **-ful** to form a new word. Write the new word in the blank.

1. color colorful
2. care careful
3. use useful
4. pain painful
5. hope hopeful
6. thank thankful

Read each sentence and the words beside it. Write the word that makes sense in each sentence.

1. I was thankful to get home. useful / thankful
2. The falling leaves are very colorful. colorful / careful
3. My cut hand is painful. playful / painful
4. I have a joyful smile on my face. joyful / useful

Suffixes

Words to use: gladly, safely, neatly, fairly, loudly, badly, lightly

Name ____________________

The suffix **-ly** can be added to some words. For example, something done in a **nice** way is done **nicely.**

nice + **ly** = nice**ly**

Read each word below. Add the suffix **-ly** to form a new word. Write the new word in the blank.

1. soft softly
2. friend friendly
3. slow slowly
4. brave bravely
5. tight tightly
6. quick quickly

Read each sentence and the words beside it. Write the word that makes sense in each sentence.

1. Dress warmly when it is cold. warmly / badly
2. The gloves fit too tightly. tightly / slowly
3. The little girl pet the kitten softly. softly / nearly
4. Chang ran quickly down the street. quickly / fairly

Suffixes

Words to use: colorful, slowly, thankful, bravely, helpful, painful, tightly, useful, quickly, warmly

Name ____________________

Read each sentence and the word beside it. Add **-ful** or **-ly** to the word to complete each sentence. The word you form must make sense in the sentence.

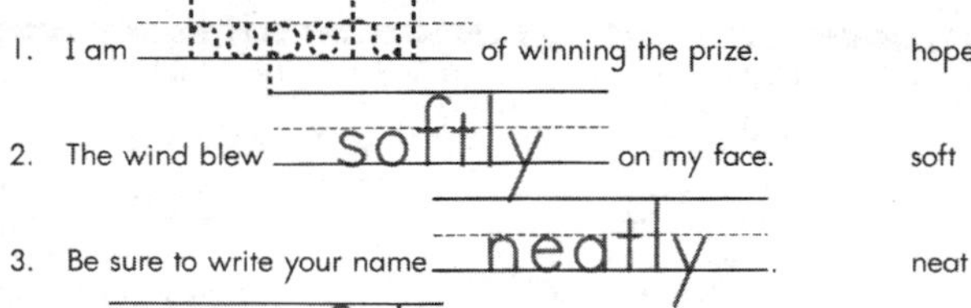

1. I am hopeful of winning the prize. hope
2. The wind blew softly on my face. soft
3. Be sure to write your name neatly. neat
4. Be careful when you cross the street. care
5. Stan plays the horn loudly. loud
6. Jose gladly gave up his turn. glad
7. Our new puppy is very playful. play
8. I like your friendly smile. friend
9. Alma wants to go home very badly. bad
10. We study many useful things in school. use

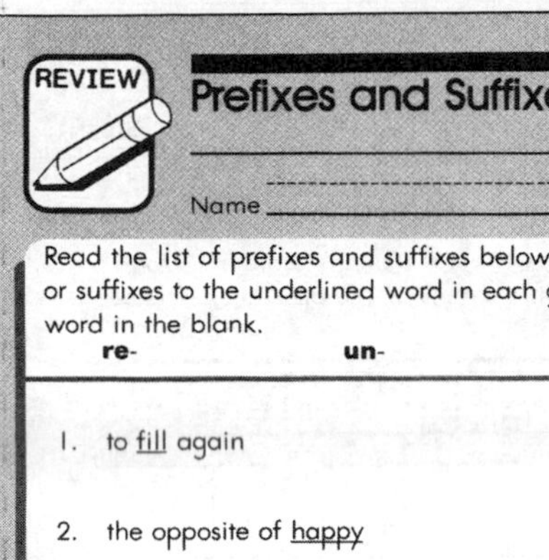

Prefixes and Suffixes

Name ______________________

Read the list of prefixes and suffixes below. Then add one of the prefixes or suffixes to the underlined word in each group of words. Write the new word in the blank.

re- **un-** **-ful** **-ly**

1. to fill again — refill
2. the opposite of happy — unhappy
3. in a quick way — quickly
4. full of hope — hopeful
5. the opposite of pack — unpack
6. full of pain — painful
7. in a safe way — safely
8. the opposite of fair — unfair
9. full of cheer — cheerful
10. to read again — reread

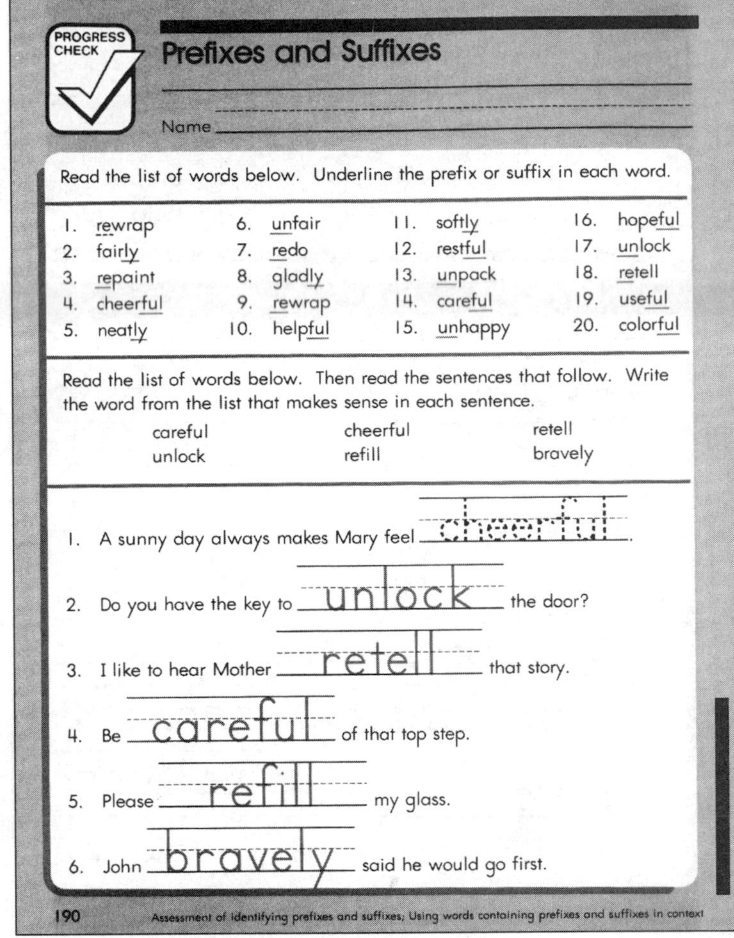

Prefixes and Suffixes

Name ______________________

Read the list of words below. Underline the prefix or suffix in each word.

1. rewrap	6. unfair	11. softly	16. hopeful
2. fairly	7. redo	12. restful	17. unlock
3. repaint	8. gladly	13. unpack	18. retell
4. cheerful	9. rewrap	14. careful	19. useful
5. neatly	10. helpful	15. unhappy	20. colorful

Read the list of words below. Then read the sentences that follow. Write the word from the list that makes sense in each sentence.

careful cheerful retell
unlock refill bravely

1. A sunny day always makes Mary feel cheerful.
2. Do you have the key to unlock the door?
3. I like to hear Mother retell that story.
4. Be careful of that top step.
5. Please refill my glass.
6. John bravely said he would go first.

Syllables

Name ______________________

Many words are made of small parts called syllables. Because each syllable has one vowel sound, a word has as many syllables as it has vowel sounds. The word **stone** has one vowel sound, so it has one syllable. The word **raincoat** has two vowel sounds, so it has two syllables.

Name the pictures. Write the number of syllables you hear in each picture name.

bathtub 2	umbrella 3	slipper 2
chick 1	fork 1	pocket 2
bird 1	garden 2	butterfly 3
valentine 3	frog 1	wagon 2

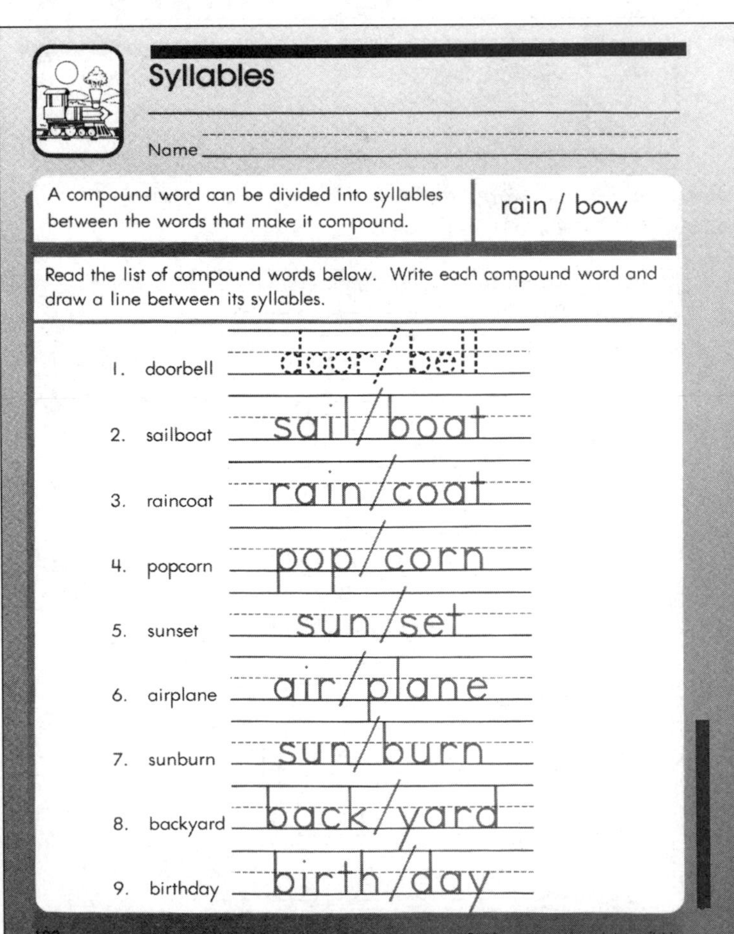

Syllables

Name ______________________

A compound word can be divided into syllables between the words that make it compound. — rain / bow

Read the list of compound words below. Write each compound word and draw a line between its syllables.

1. doorbell — door/bell
2. sailboat — sail/boat
3. raincoat — rain/coat
4. popcorn — pop/corn
5. sunset — sun/set
6. airplane — air/plane
7. sunburn — sun/burn
8. backyard — back/yard
9. birthday — birth/day

Syllables

Words to use: careful, unwrap, thankful, bravely, helpful, painful, tightly, useful, quickly, warmly reuse, slowly, useful, redo

Name ____________________

A word that has a prefix or suffix can be divided into syllables between the prefix or suffix and the base word.

un / tie
help / ful

Read the list of words. Write each word and draw a line between its syllables.

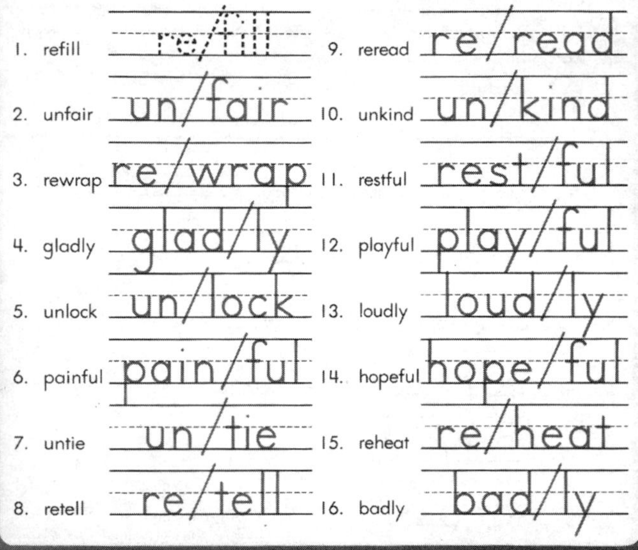

1. refill	re/fill		9. reread	re/read
2. unfair	un/fair		10. unkind	un/kind
3. rewrap	re/wrap		11. restful	rest/ful
4. gladly	glad/ly		12. playful	play/ful
5. unlock	un/lock		13. loudly	loud/ly
6. painful	pain/ful		14. hopeful	hope/ful
7. untie	un/tie		15. reheat	re/heat
8. retell	re/tell		16. badly	bad/ly

Dividing words containing prefixes and suffixes into syllables 193

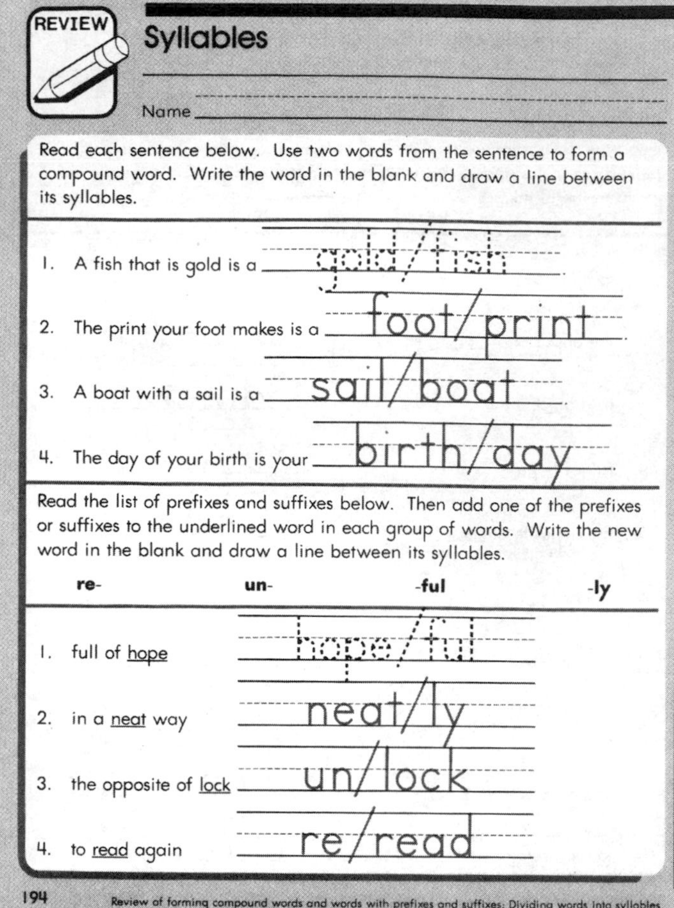

REVIEW

Syllables

Name ____________________

Read each sentence below. Use two words from the sentence to form a compound word. Write the word in the blank and draw a line between its syllables.

1. A fish that is gold is a gold/fish.
2. The print your foot makes is a foot/print.
3. A boat with a sail is a sail/boat.
4. The day of your birth is your birth/day.

Read the list of prefixes and suffixes below. Then add one of the prefixes or suffixes to the underlined word in each group of words. Write the new word in the blank and draw a line between its syllables.

re- **un-** **-ful** **-ly**

1. full of hope — hope/ful
2. in a neat way — neat/ly
3. the opposite of lock — un/lock
4. to read again — re/read

194 Review of forming compound words and words with prefixes and suffixes; Dividing words into syllables

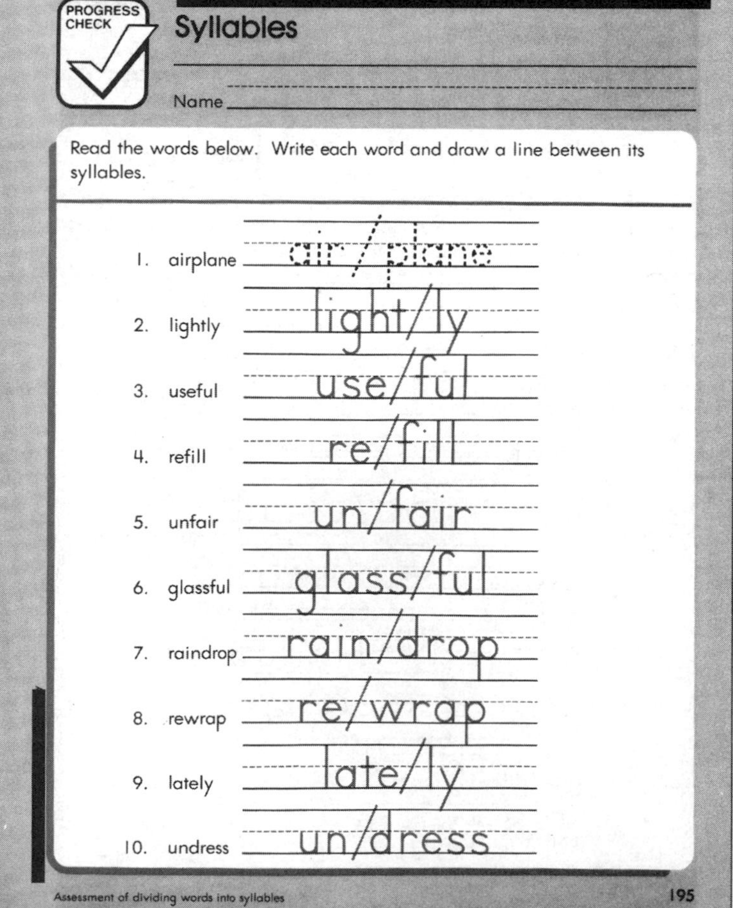

PROGRESS CHECK

Syllables

Name ____________________

Read the words below. Write each word and draw a line between its syllables.

1. airplane — air/plane
2. lightly — light/ly
3. useful — use/ful
4. refill — re/fill
5. unfair — un/fair
6. glassful — glass/ful
7. raindrop — rain/drop
8. rewrap — re/wrap
9. lately — late/ly
10. undress — un/dress

Assessment of dividing words into syllables 195

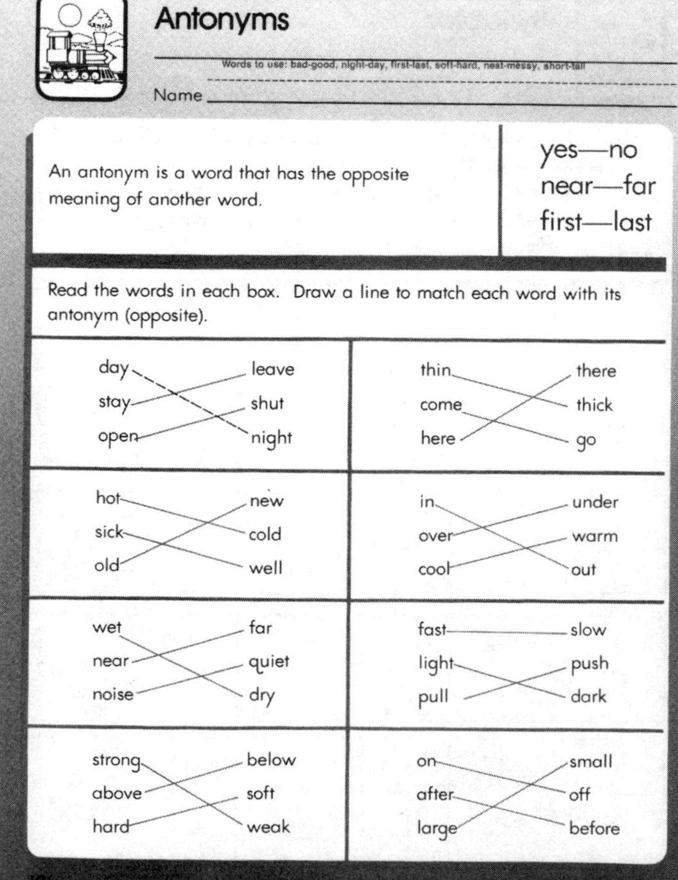

Antonyms

Words to use: bad-good, night-day, first-last, soft-hard, neat-messy, short-tall

Name ____________________

An antonym is a word that has the opposite meaning of another word.

yes—no
near—far
first—last

Read the words in each box. Draw a line to match each word with its antonym (opposite).

day	leave	thin	there
stay	shut	come	thick
open	night	here	go
hot	new	in	under
sick	cold	over	warm
old	well	cool	out
wet	far	fast	slow
near	quiet	light	push
noise	dry	pull	dark
strong	below	on	small
above	soft	after	off
hard	weak	large	before

196

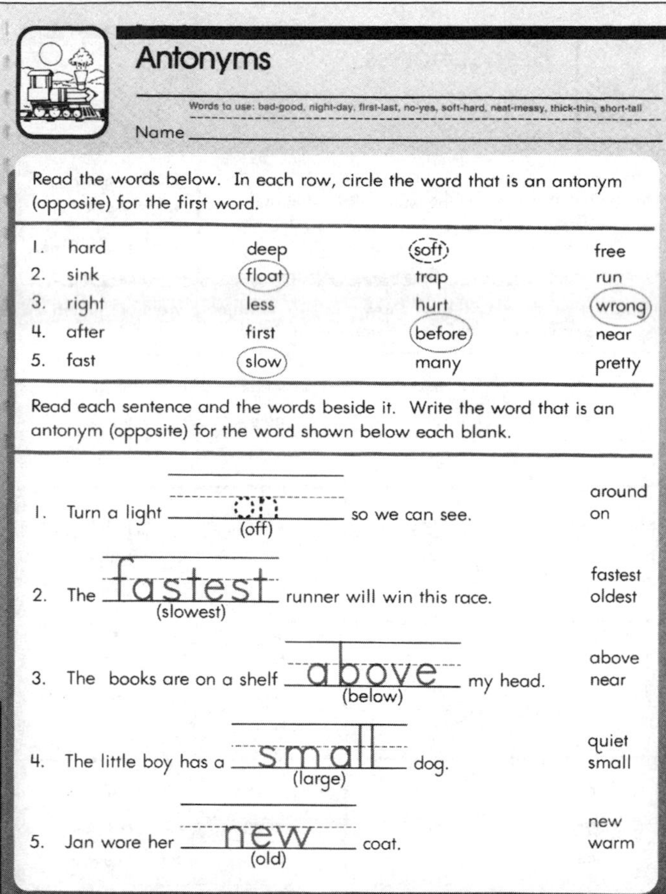

Antonyms

Words to use: bad-good, night-day, first-last, no-yes, soft-hard, neat-messy, thick-thin, short-tall

Name ____________________

Read the words below. In each row, circle the word that is an antonym (opposite) for the first word.

1.	hard	deep	(soft)	free
2.	sink	(float)	trap	run
3.	right	less	hurt	(wrong)
4.	after	first	(before)	near
5.	fast	(slow)	many	pretty

Read each sentence and the words beside it. Write the word that is an antonym (opposite) for the word shown below each blank.

1. Turn a light __on__ (off) so we can see. — around / on
2. The __fastest__ (slowest) runner will win this race. — fastest / oldest
3. The books are on a shelf __above__ (below) my head. — above / near
4. The little boy has a __small__ (large) dog. — quiet / small
5. Jan wore her __new__ (old) coat. — new / warm

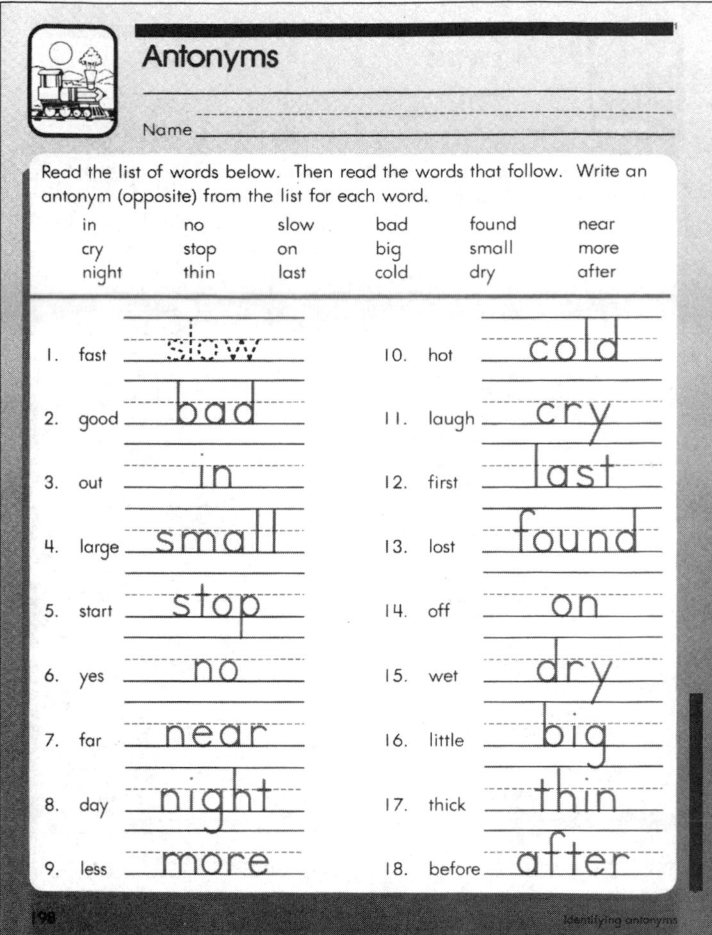

Antonyms

Name ____________________

Read the list of words below. Then read the words that follow. Write an antonym (opposite) from the list for each word.

in	no	slow	bad	found	near
cry	stop	on	big	small	more
night	thin	last	cold	dry	after

1. fast __slow__
2. good __bad__
3. out __in__
4. large __small__
5. start __stop__
6. yes __no__
7. far __near__
8. day __night__
9. less __more__
10. hot __cold__
11. laugh __cry__
12. first __last__
13. lost __found__
14. off __on__
15. wet __dry__
16. little __big__
17. thick __thin__
18. before __after__

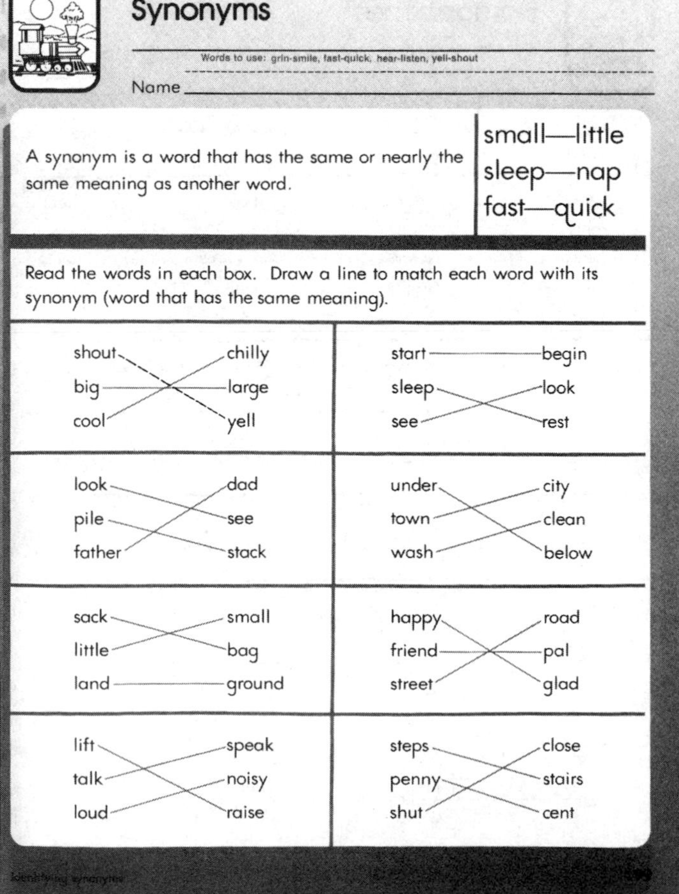

Synonyms

Words to use: grin-smile, fast-quick, hear-listen, yell-shout

Name ____________________

A synonym is a word that has the same or nearly the same meaning as another word.

small—little
sleep—nap
fast—quick

Read the words in each box. Draw a line to match each word with its synonym (word that has the same meaning).

shout — yell big — large cool — chilly	start — begin sleep — rest see — look
look — see pile — stack father — dad	under — below town — city wash — clean
sack — bag little — small land — ground	happy — glad friend — pal street — road
lift — raise talk — speak loud — noisy	steps — stairs penny — cent shut — close

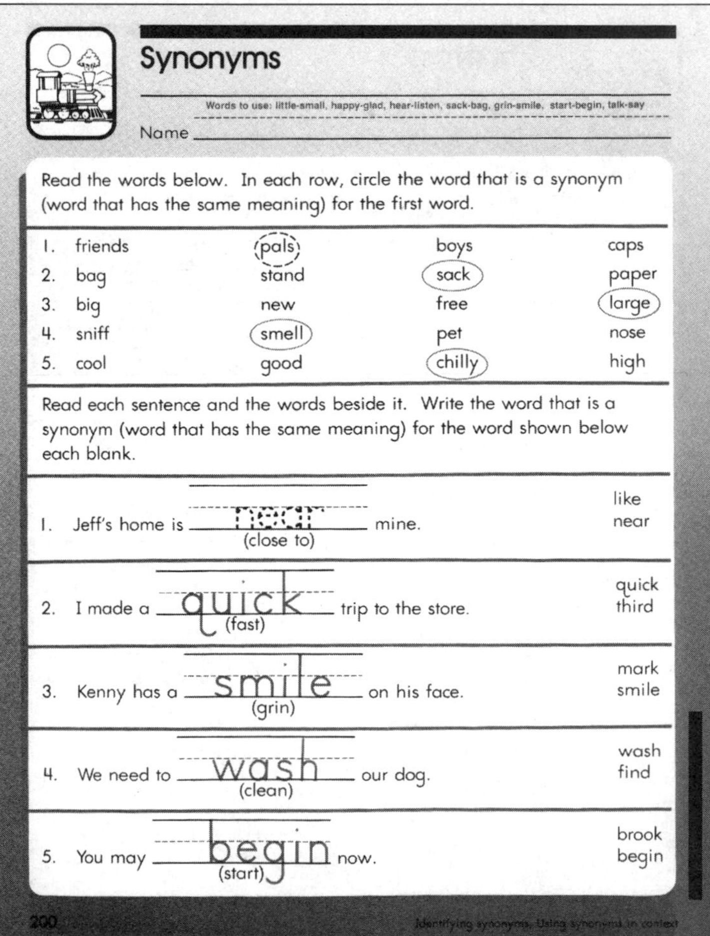

Synonyms

Words to use: little-small, happy-glad, hear-listen, sack-bag, grin-smile, start-begin, talk-say

Name ____________________

Read the words below. In each row, circle the word that is a synonym (word that has the same meaning) for the first word.

1.	friends	(pals)	boys	caps
2.	bag	stand	(sack)	paper
3.	big	new	free	(large)
4.	sniff	(smell)	pet	nose
5.	cool	good	(chilly)	high

Read each sentence and the words beside it. Write the word that is a synonym (word that has the same meaning) for the word shown below each blank.

1. Jeff's home is __near__ (close to) mine. — like / near
2. I made a __quick__ (fast) trip to the store. — quick / third
3. Kenny has a __smile__ (grin) on his face. — mark / smile
4. We need to __wash__ (clean) our dog. — wash / find
5. You may __begin__ (start) now. — brook / begin

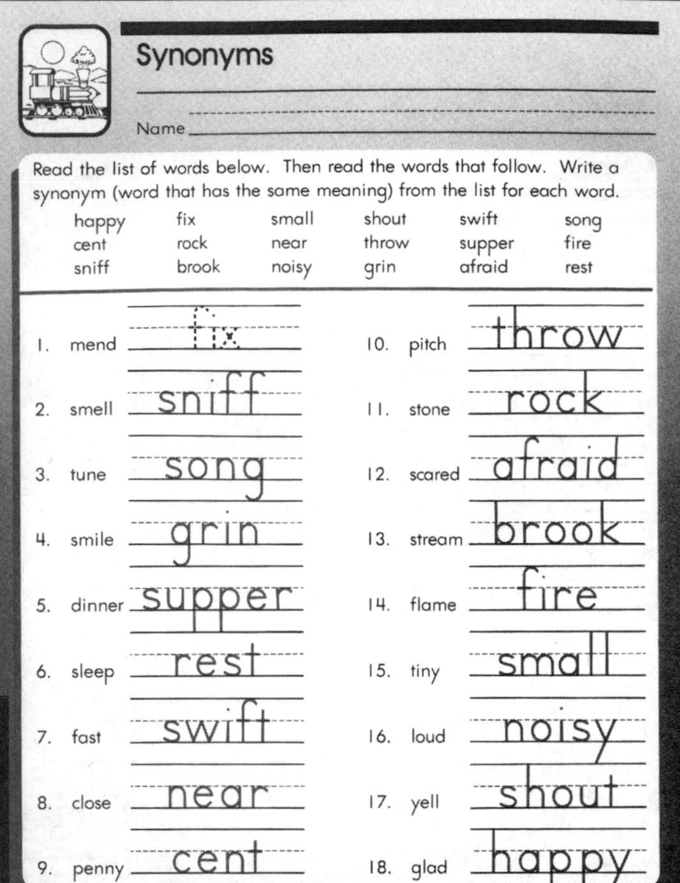

Synonyms

Name ____________

Read the list of words below. Then read the words that follow. Write a synonym (word that has the same meaning) from the list for each word.

happy	fix	small	shout	swift	song
cent	rock	near	throw	supper	fire
sniff	brook	noisy	grin	afraid	rest

1. mend fix
2. smell sniff
3. tune song
4. smile grin
5. dinner supper
6. sleep rest
7. fast swift
8. close near
9. penny cent
10. pitch throw
11. stone rock
12. scared afraid
13. stream brook
14. flame fire
15. tiny small
16. loud noisy
17. yell shout
18. glad happy

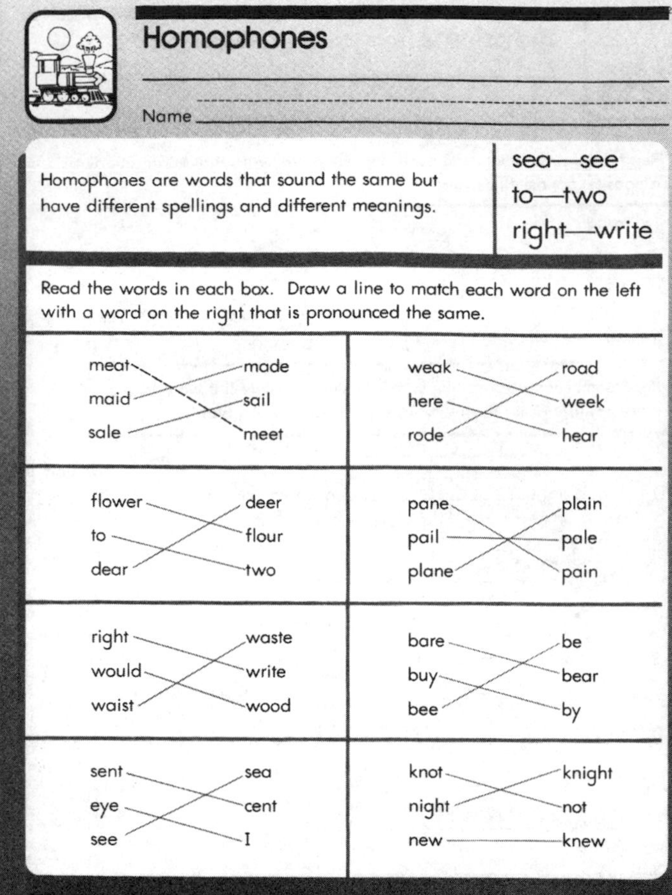

Homophones

Name ____________

Homophones are words that sound the same but have different spellings and different meanings.

sea—see
to—two
right—write

Read the words in each box. Draw a line to match each word on the left with a word on the right that is pronounced the same.

meat	made	weak	road
maid	sail	here	week
sale	meet	rode	hear
flower	deer	pane	plain
to	flour	pail	pale
dear	two	plane	pain
right	waste	bare	be
would	write	buy	bear
waist	wood	bee	by
sent	sea	knot	knight
eye	cent	night	not
see	I	new	knew

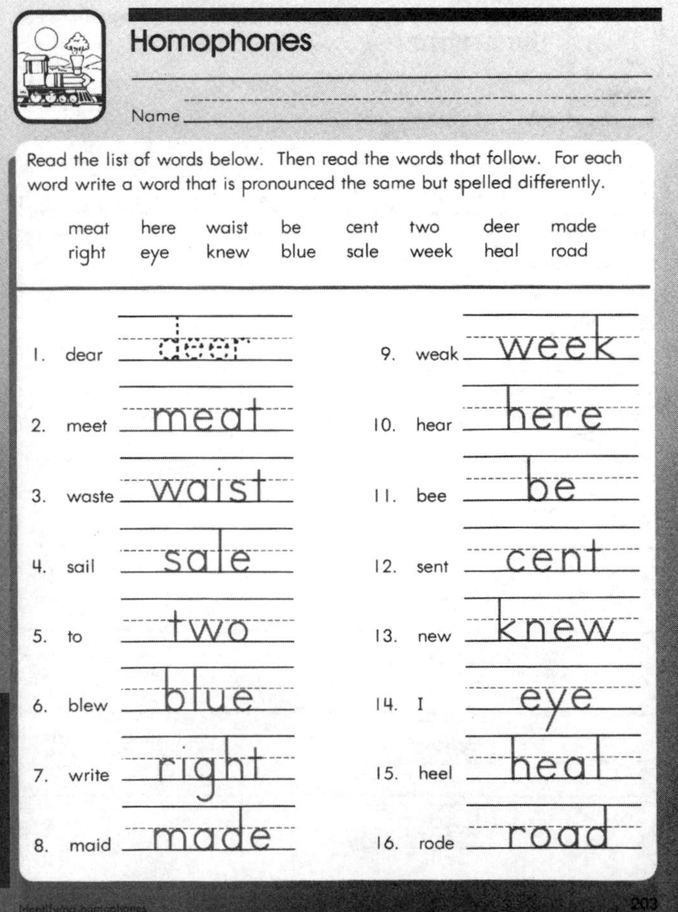

Homophones

Name ____________

Read the list of words below. Then read the words that follow. For each word write a word that is pronounced the same but spelled differently.

meat	here	waist	be	cent	two	deer	made
right	eye	knew	blue	sale	week	heal	road

1. dear deer
2. meet meat
3. waste waist
4. sail sale
5. to two
6. blew blue
7. write right
8. maid made
9. weak week
10. hear here
11. bee be
12. sent cent
13. new knew
14. I eye
15. heel heal
16. rode road

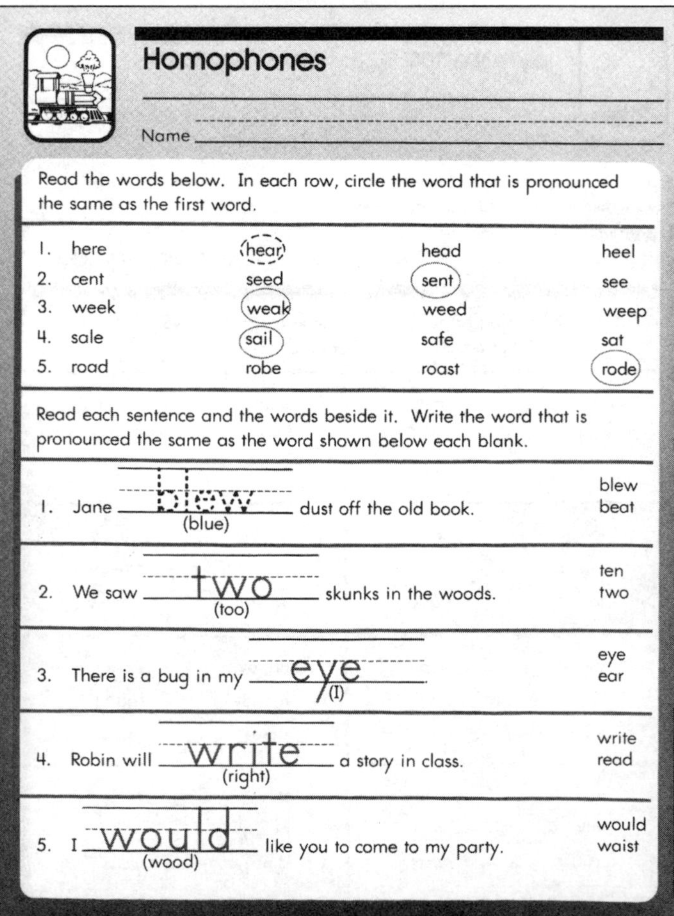

Homophones

Name ____________

Read the words below. In each row, circle the word that is pronounced the same as the first word.

1. here	(hear)	head	heel
2. cent	seed	(sent)	see
3. week	(weak)	weed	weep
4. sale	(sail)	safe	sat
5. road	robe	roast	(rode)

Read each sentence and the words beside it. Write the word that is pronounced the same as the word shown below each blank.

1. Jane blew (blue) dust off the old book. — blew / beat
2. We saw two (too) skunks in the woods. — ten / two
3. There is a bug in my eye (I). — eye / ear
4. Robin will write (right) a story in class. — write / read
5. I would (wood) like you to come to my party. — would / waist

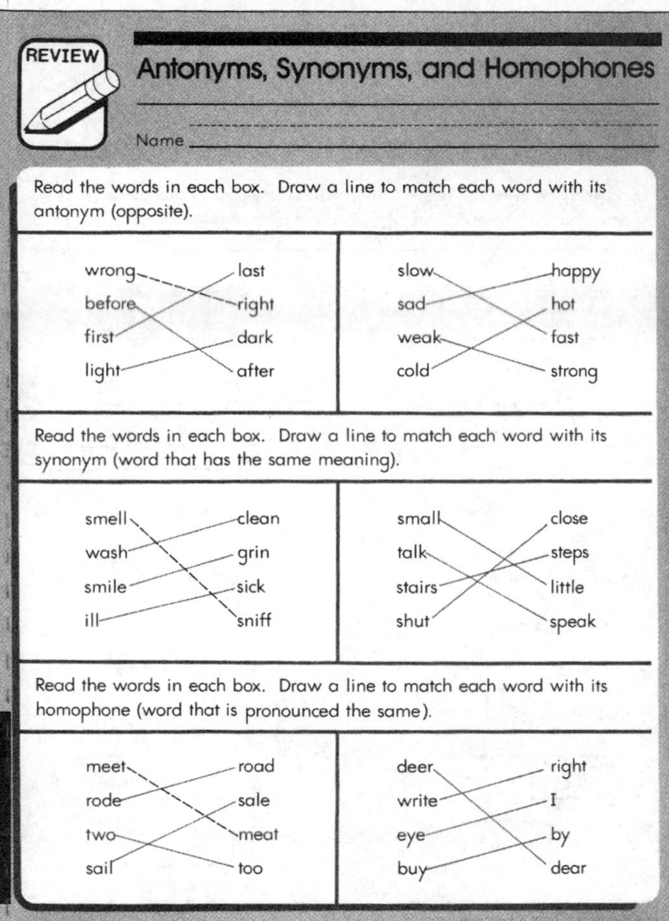
REVIEW

Antonyms, Synonyms, and Homophones

Name ______________________

Read the words in each box. Draw a line to match each word with its antonym (opposite).

wrong	last	slow	happy
before	right	sad	hot
first	dark	weak	fast
light	after	cold	strong

Read the words in each box. Draw a line to match each word with its synonym (word that has the same meaning).

smell	clean	small	close
wash	grin	talk	steps
smile	sick	stairs	little
ill	sniff	shut	speak

Read the words in each box. Draw a line to match each word with its homophone (word that is pronounced the same).

meet	road	deer	right
rode	sale	write	I
two	meat	eye	by
sail	too	buy	dear

Review of identification of antonyms, synonyms, and homophones 205

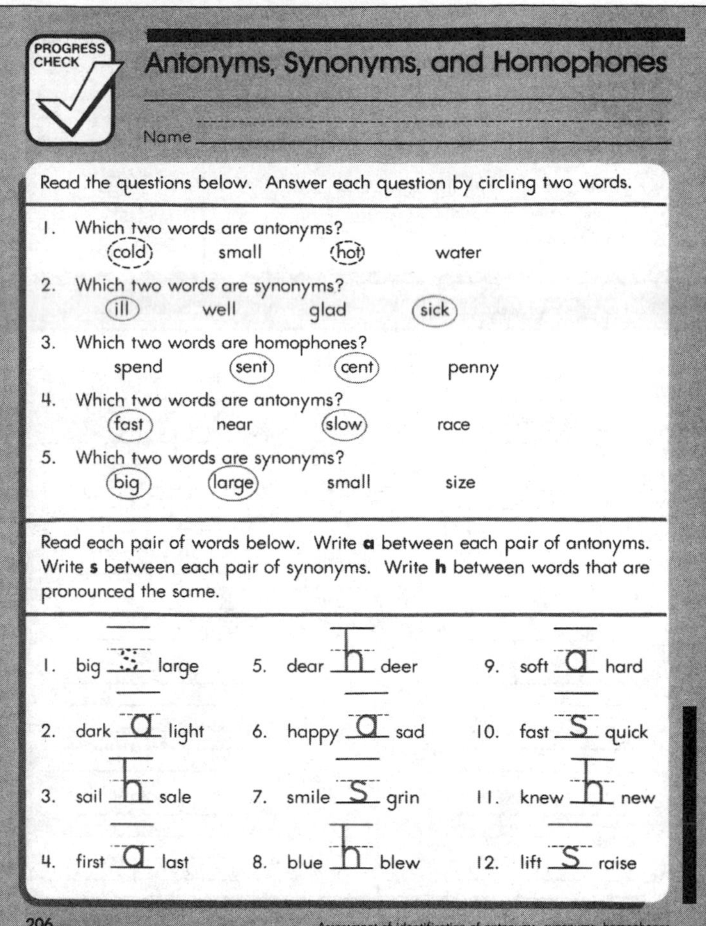
PROGRESS CHECK

Antonyms, Synonyms, and Homophones

Name ______________________

Read the questions below. Answer each question by circling two words.

1. Which two words are antonyms?
   (cold) small (hot) water
2. Which two words are synonyms?
   (ill) well glad (sick)
3. Which two words are homophones?
   spend (sent) (cent) penny
4. Which two words are antonyms?
   (fast) near (slow) race
5. Which two words are synonyms?
   (big) (large) small size

Read each pair of words below. Write **a** between each pair of antonyms. Write **s** between each pair of synonyms. Write **h** between words that are pronounced the same.

1. big s large	5. dear h deer	9. soft a hard
2. dark a light	6. happy a sad	10. fast s quick
3. sail h sale	7. smile s grin	11. knew h new
4. first a last	8. blue h blew	12. lift s raise

206 Assessment of identification of antonyms, synonyms, homophones

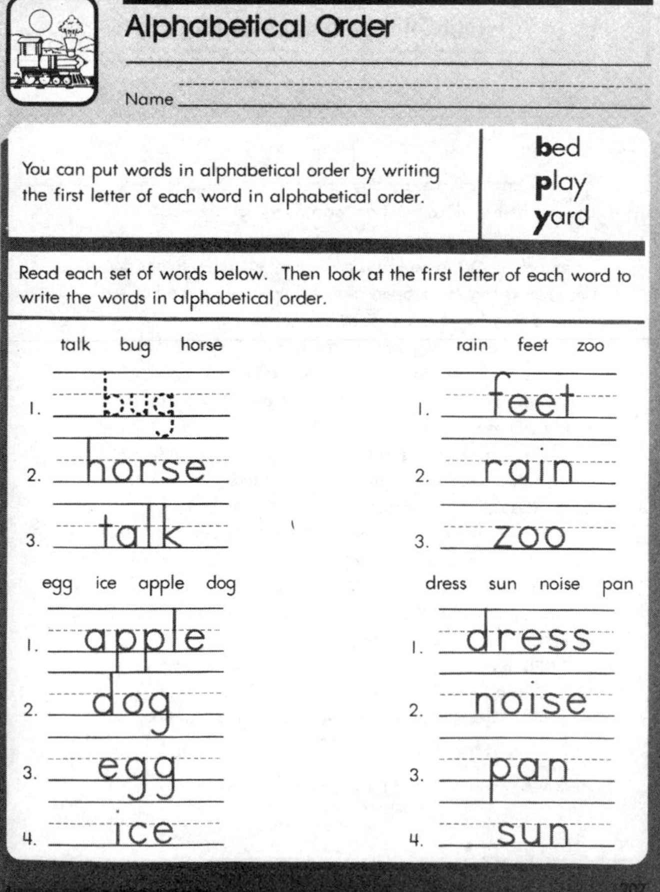

Alphabetical Order

Name ______________________

You can put words in alphabetical order by writing the first letter of each word in alphabetical order.

bed
play
yard

Read each set of words below. Then look at the first letter of each word to write the words in alphabetical order.

talk bug horse
1. bug
2. horse
3. talk

rain feet zoo
1. feet
2. rain
3. zoo

egg ice apple dog
1. apple
2. dog
3. egg
4. ice

dress sun noise pan
1. dress
2. noise
3. pan
4. sun

207

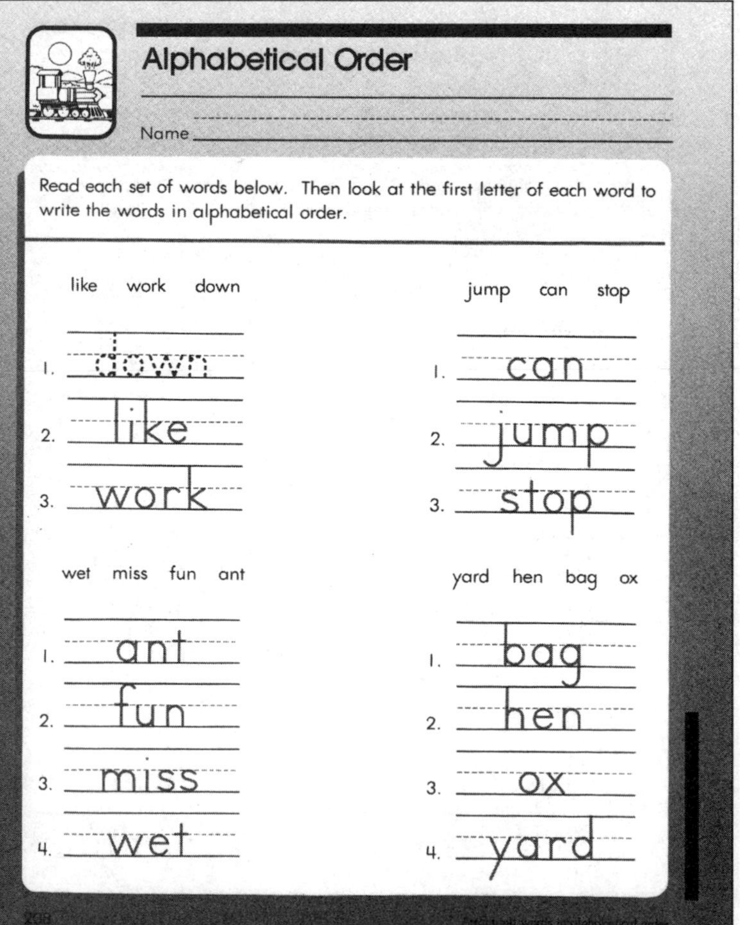

Alphabetical Order

Name ______________________

Read each set of words below. Then look at the first letter of each word to write the words in alphabetical order.

like work down
1. down
2. like
3. work

jump can stop
1. can
2. jump
3. stop

wet miss fun ant
1. ant
2. fun
3. miss
4. wet

yard hen bag ox
1. bag
2. hen
3. ox
4. yard

208

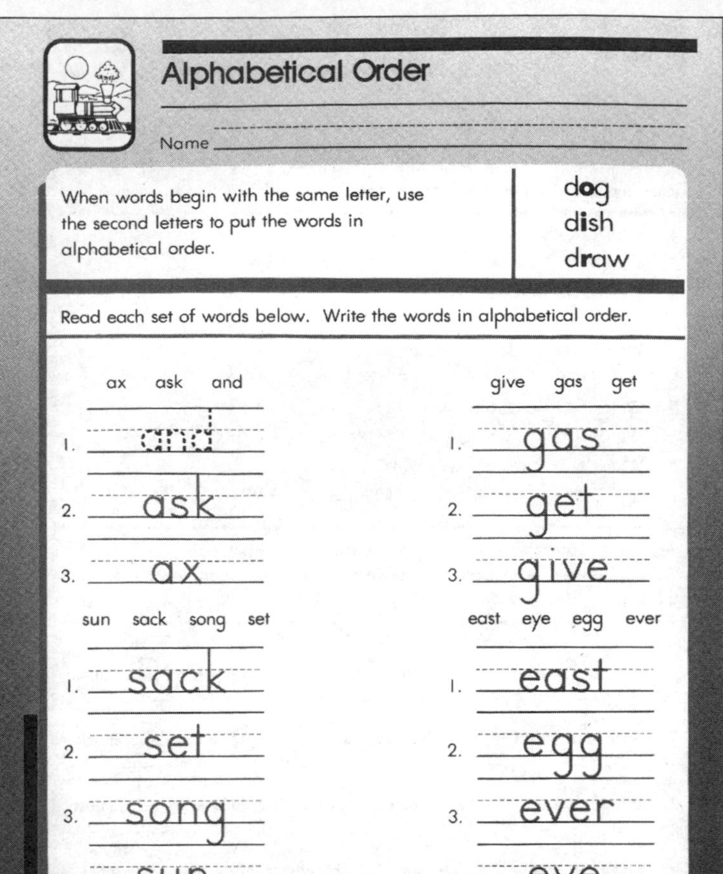

Alphabetical Order

Name

When words begin with the same letter, use the second letters to put the words in alphabetical order.

dog
dish
draw

Read each set of words below. Write the words in alphabetical order.

ax ask and

1. and
2. ask
3. ax

give gas get

1. gas
2. get
3. give

sun sack song set

1. sack
2. set
3. song
4. sun

east eye egg ever

1. east
2. egg
3. ever
4. eye

Arranging words in alphabetical order 209

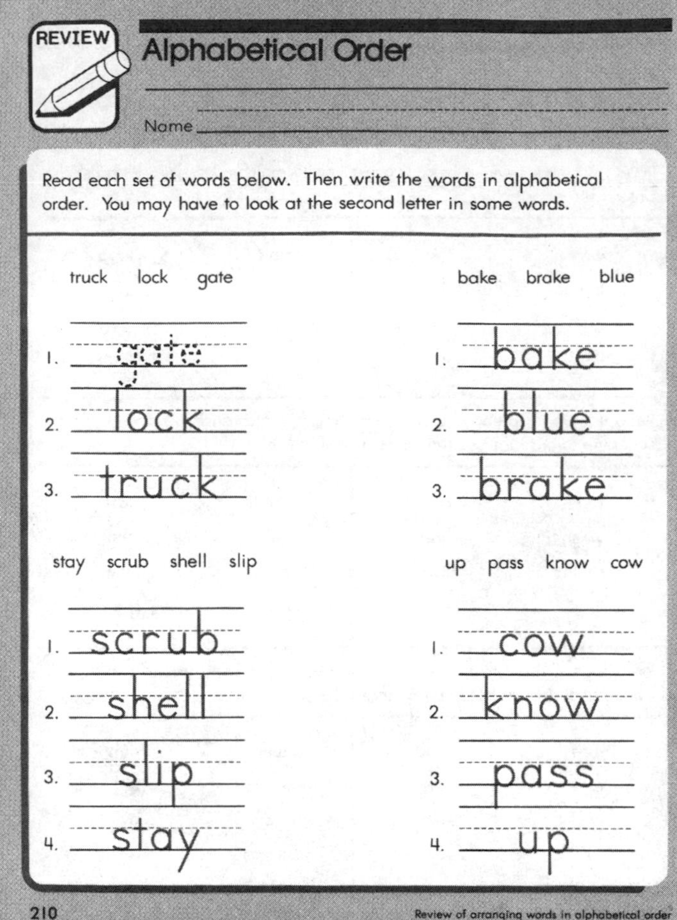

REVIEW

Alphabetical Order

Name

Read each set of words below. Then write the words in alphabetical order. You may have to look at the second letter in some words.

truck lock gate

1. gate
2. lock
3. truck

bake brake blue

1. bake
2. blue
3. brake

stay scrub shell slip

1. scrub
2. shell
3. slip
4. stay

up pass know cow

1. cow
2. know
3. pass
4. up

210 Review of arranging words in alphabetical order

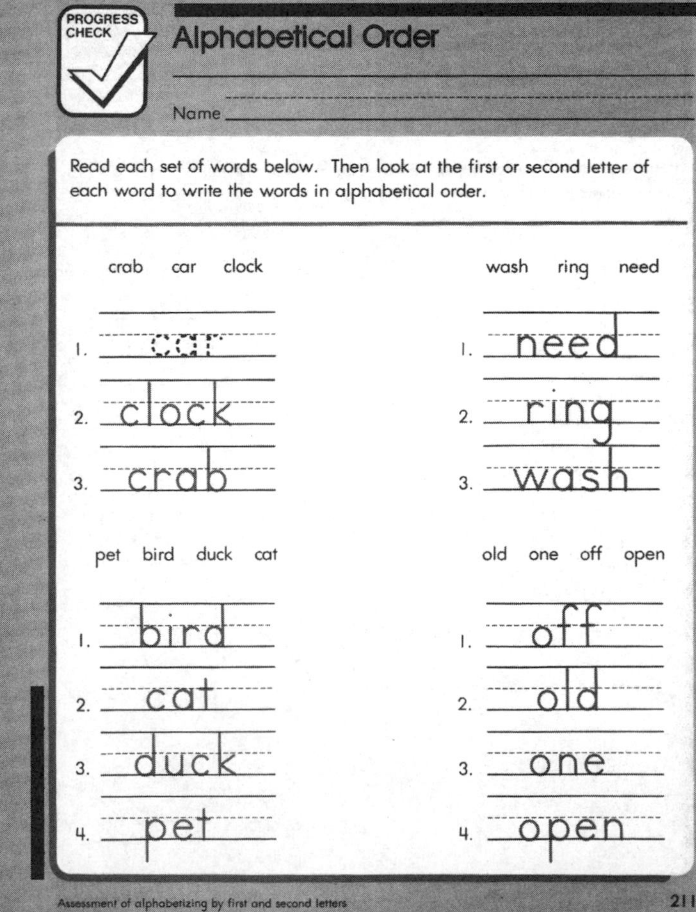

PROGRESS CHECK

Alphabetical Order

Name

Read each set of words below. Then look at the first or second letter of each word to write the words in alphabetical order.

crab car clock

1. car
2. clock
3. crab

wash ring need

1. need
2. ring
3. wash

pet bird duck cat

1. bird
2. cat
3. duck
4. pet

old one off open

1. off
2. old
3. one
4. open

Assessment of alphabetizing by first and second letters 211

Reading and Writing Wrap-Up

Name

Milk

You drink milk every day. Have you stopped to think about where milk comes from and how it gets to you?

The milk you drink comes from cows. The cows feed on green grass. On some farms cows may eat other things, too. Corn plants that have been chopped up may be used as feed. Farmers may buy grain to feed their cows, too.

At night the cows come to the barn, where the farmer milks them. In the morning the cows are milked again. The milk goes into a steel tank that is kept very clean. Then the milk is checked to be sure it is good.

A milk truck comes to the farm to pick up the milk. The tank on the milk truck is just as clean as the milk tank on the farm. The milk truck takes the milk to the milk plant.

In the milk plant, the milk is heated. This makes it safe to drink. Then the milk is put into boxes and cases and the lids are sealed. The boxed milk is put onto another truck.

This truck takes the milk to the store where your family will buy it and bring it home for you to drink.

Milk has many uses. First of all, milk is a good food. Milk is used to make cheese and ice cream. But you may be surprised to know that milk is used in making paint and some kinds of dishes, too.

1. Check the two words that mean feed.

✓ grain ✓ eat ___ buy

212 Application of reading and comprehension skills in a social studies context

Social Studies

Name ________________

2. Write two things that are made from milk that are not foods.

paint   dishes

3. Write 1, 2, 3, and 4 to show what comes first, next, and so on.

3 The milk is heated at the milk plant to make it safe to drink.

2 The farmer milks the cows in the morning and at night.

4 People buy the milk in stores.

1 The cows eat grass, chopped corn, and other kinds of feed.

4. Find out something about another kind of food. Tell where it comes from and how it gets to you. Choose one of these foods or think of another one you would like to know more about.

apple drink   ground beef   bread   oatmeal

Answers will vary.